"Thrilling . . . *Forgotten* manages to weave the intricate complexities of history into a clear, convincing text that is accessible to both the layperson and the history buff. Here is a stunning achievement that will add much to the historical scholarship of our country." —*The Root*

"Compelling . . . a welcome addition to our understanding of the war and the American military." —*Washington Post*

"*Forgotten* by Linda Hervieux is the riveting story of an all-black battalion's heroism at D-Day—partly military history, and partly a portrait of the tension between race relations in the Jim Crow South and national service in wartime America." —*Harlem World* pick

"Hervieux, in her first monograph, powerfully gives voice to the African Americans who were also on those beaches in northern France on that fateful day in June 1944. The author uncovers the story of the 320th Barrage Balloon Battalion, an African American unit, whose mission was to set up balloons as a defense perimeter, carefully piecing together the story of these soldiers and how the balloons were used in warfare. She also effectively depicts how these soldiers encountered Jim Crow stateside and within the army. . . . This highly readable account will sit well alongside Nat Brandt's *Harlem at War* and Graham Smith's *When Jim Crow Met John Bull*." —*Library Journal* (starred review)

"This is a story about war heroes, certainly, but it's also a story about racism and bigotry in American history, a story about brave soldiers who were denied recognition for their heroic acts. Based on interviews with some surviving members of the 320th . . . the book is carefully documented and, in places, quite moving. An important story that has remained untold for far too long." —*Booklist* Online

"A long-overdue, sympathetic treatment of the barrage balloon operators who fought valiantly on the beaches of France." —*Kirkus Reviews*

"*Forgotten* is an utterly compelling account of the African Americans who played a crucial and dangerous role in the invasion of Europe. The story of their heroic duty is long overdue."
—Tom Brokaw, author of *The Greatest Generation*

"Hard to believe this story hasn't been written before. Linda Hervieux's *Forgotten* is essential, fiercely dramatic, and ultimately inspiring. All Americans should read this World War II history, which doubles as a civil rights primer, to learn the true cost of freedom."
—Douglas Brinkley, author of *Cronkite*

"Linda Hervieux's *Forgotten* is a magnificent achievement, an inspiring story . . . long overdue. . . . Mesmerizing. . . . *Forgotten* will surely appeal to both general readers and those with an abiding interest in World War II history."   —Joseph Balkoski, author of
Omaha Beach: D-Day, June 6, 1944

"Linda Hervieux's passionate excavation of the saga of the segregated 320th Barrage Balloon Battalion reaps huge rewards, not the least of which brave men have finally gotten their rightful due."
—Wil Haygood, bestselling author of *Showdown:
Thurgood Marshall and the Supreme Court
Nomination That Changed America*

FORGOTTEN

THE UNTOLD STORY OF D-DAY'S BLACK HEROES, AT HOME AND AT WAR

LINDA HERVIEUX

HARPER

NEW YORK • LONDON • TORONTO • SYDNEY

HARPER

A hardcover edition of this book was published in 2015 by Harper, an imprint of HarperCollins Publishers.

HarperCollins books may be purchased for educational, business, or sales promotional use. For information, please e-mail the Special Markets Department at SPsales@harpercollins.com.

FIRST HARPER PAPERBACKS EDITION PUBLISHED 2016.

Designed by Renato Stanisic

Library of Congress Cataloging-in-Publication Data

Hervieux, Linda.

Forgotten : the untold story of D-Day's Black heroes, at home and at war / Linda Hervieux.

pages cm

Includes bibliographical references and index.

ISBN 978-0-06-231380-5 (pbk.)

1. United States. Army. Anti-Aircraft Barrage Balloon Battalion, 320th—History. 2. World War, 1939–1945—Campaigns—France—Normandy. 3. World War, 1939–1945—Balloons—United States. 4. African American soldiers—Biography. 5. World War, 1939–1945—Participation, African American. 6. World War, 1939–1945—Regimental histories—United States. I. Title. II. Title: Untold story of D-Day's Black heroes, at home and at war.

D769.343320th .H467 2015
940.54'1273—dc23   2015017941

16 17 18 19   ov/rrd   10 9 8 7 6 5 4 3 2 1

For my parents,
Rosette Hervieux and her sailor, the late Paul Hervieux,
petty officer 2nd class, U.S. Navy (1942–1951)

You may write me down in history
With your bitter, twisted lies,
You may trod me in the very dirt
But still, like dust, I'll rise.

—Maya Angelou, from "Still I Rise"

Contents

PART II

PART III

Author's Note

've been waiting for someone to call me for fifty years," Wilson Caldwell Monk told me on the phone on a warm spring day in 2010. A year of reporting and digging had brought me to Monk, a master sergeant during World War II in charge of the bullet-shaped balloons floating over the Normandy beaches after the Allied invasion on June 6, 1944. The balloons formed a defensive line in the sky, shielding the men and matériel from German planes. They had been set up there by the men of the 320th Barrage Balloon Battalion, the only African American combat unit to land on D-Day. I was calling Monk because I had committed myself to telling the story of the 320th, a story largely lost to history, even amid the thousands of books, films, and oral histories of what some consider the most important day of the twentieth century.

I first heard about America's barrage balloon flyers in June 2009 while reporting on the sixty-fifth anniversary of D-Day for the New York *Daily News*. William Garfield Dabney, a veteran from Virginia, had traveled to France to receive the Legion of Honor, that country's highest award. Organizers said Dabney was likely the only member of the 320th still alive. It turns out nobody had checked.

I knew nothing about barrage balloons, beyond seeing iconic images of them floating over the Normandy coast after the Allied invasion. I had thought little of the presence of African Americans on those blood-soaked beaches. Even many military historians believed that the only black soldiers to land on D-Day had lent their muscle to labor units and other support work. Not that the contributions of these men were unimportant—on the contrary. Of the nearly two thousand African Americans who participated in the greatest military operation the world had ever seen, the majority were service troops who performed heroically as stevedores and truck drivers, unloading and transporting crucial supplies. On the beaches, they carried the wounded to safety and buried the dead.

Yet only one highly trained black combat force landed on Omaha and Utah Beaches. They would struggle to stay alive and get their balloons aloft, under withering German fire. The 320th medics would see glory, credited with saving scores of men wounded in the early hours of the invasion. One of them, a college student twice hit by shrapnel named Waverly Woodson, was recommended for the Medal of Honor, the United States' highest decoration for valor. It was an award he would never receive, and I wanted to know why.

Soon after the invasion, the story of the balloon troops extended far beyond their berths on the beaches. They made headlines in the crusading black newspapers of the day, in the white press, and in the military newspaper *Stars and Stripes*. Under pressure to give black soldiers more meaningful roles, the army sent out glowing reports praising the 320th. "It seems the whole front knows the story of the Negro barrage balloon battalion outfit which was one of the first ashore on D-Day," wrote a war correspondent in July 1944. "They have gotten the reputation of hard workers and good soldiers." That dispatch was sent to Gen. Dwight D. Eisenhower, who later that month issued a commendation praising the battalion for carrying out its mission "with courage and determination." Ike said the unit "proved an important element of the air defense team."

Yet time had stripped away traces of the men and their balloons.

When I expressed interest in their story, I was warned off. "You won't find enough to write a book about them," one military historian told me. Other experts agreed. Another suggested I write about "that black tank unit instead," a reference to the 761st Tank Battalion, the hard-fighting Black Panthers, who helped Gen. George S. Patton roll to victory across Europe.

Like the 761st, other black units have been chronicled in print and film, among them the inspiring Tuskegee Airmen, whose exploits were ignored for decades. Even the Red Ball Express, the group of indefatigable truckers who supplied the Allied front in France, has its place in history. But so little had been written about the men of the 320th, even in the military history books in which they *should* appear. And what about those balloons? I was intrigued.

To be sure, I was an unlikely candidate to write a book about the army's balloon flyers. I began this project with little knowledge of war—any war. And if I had ever learned about it to begin with, I had long forgotten that the U.S. military was segregated in World War II. It was a Jim Crow system of extraordinary breadth underpinned by virulent racism that mirrored life in many parts of my own country. As a white woman from Massachusetts, I was angry that the history classes I'd taken from grade school through college had downplayed, or even ignored, this shameful reality. I was also aware of my own failure to educate myself about the African American experience. So, bringing that baggage with me, and hoping I was qualified to tell their story, I set out to find veterans of the 320th. These men would be in their nineties, and time was running out.

In the end, I would interview twelve men from the battalion, and the families of several others. Some of the men had never spoken of their wartime adventures until I showed up at their doors. Some of their children had no idea that their fathers had been at D-Day. Over the next four years, I repeatedly visited Monk; Dabney, the man honored in France; and a third veteran, named Henry Parham. Their wives and children became my friends. These men are the main subjects of this book, but they are not alone. I was fortunate to find other memorable

320th men who shared their stories with me, including Samuel Matti-son, a charming raconteur from Columbus, Ohio; soft-spoken Willie Howard from Olivia, North Carolina; and the future preacher Arthur Guest from Bonneau, South Carolina. Thanks to interviews Waverly Woodson gave before his death in 2005, we have a glimpse of the hero medic from West Philadelphia.

Finding the men of the 320th wasn't easy, but unearthing records about their mission was even more difficult. There was little beyond a bare-bones history of the unit in army archives. I spent months trolling for more at archives around the United States and, later, in Britain. The information I found traced the broad strokes, but the details were exceedingly tough to nail down. I couldn't complain; I'd been warned. In the story of the 320th men was another story to be told, that of the lives of African Americans during the heyday of Jim Crow. The men I spoke to recounted how their lives had profoundly changed when they entered the army, leaving home for the Deep South (training at Camp Tyson, Tennessee), where they were subjected to levels of racism more venomous than many had ever experienced.

Their subsequent journey to Europe took them to New York City, where they boarded a converted passenger liner and set off on a har-rowing trip across the North Atlantic, during which German U-boats hunted for ships just like theirs. Finally, they landed in Britain, where, to their delight, they were welcomed by people who had never heard of segregation. The freedoms they experienced there were life-changing. In villages in Wales and Oxfordshire, they lifted pints in pubs alongside white men for the first time and danced with white girls. This warm welcome infuriated many white American soldiers, particularly southern ones, who tried, and failed, to poison the Brit-ons against the "Negroes."

Over time, a portrait of this battalion began to emerge. Yet many questions remained, and still do. Important records have been de-stroyed or lost. Age has taken its toll on the men and their memories.

Few kept their wartime letters, with the notable exception of Wilson Monk, who handed me a bag of faded, yellowed envelopes and said, smiling, "Here you go."

The men of the 320th unwittingly contributed to their own obscurity. Most of them told me that during the war, and after, they didn't consider their service to be particularly noteworthy. After all, it was their duty and, they wondered, who cared about the deeds of black men anyway? After Japan surrendered and they returned home, there were no parades. They slipped back into the lives they had left behind, which meant Jim Crow and all that it entailed: separate restrooms and restaurants, seats at the back of the bus. No matter if the restaurant patron or passenger was wearing a crisp army uniform decorated with a medal or two. If America was grateful to these men for their service, they weren't aware of it.

Over five years, I was able to assemble the story of these men visit by visit, phone call by phone call, fact by fact. Before my eyes, the story of America's black barrage balloon flyers came into focus. Yet some of the pieces of this elusive puzzle would never fall into place. Any omissions are unintentional; any mistakes or misrepresentations are entirely my own. All quoted dialogue is taken from my interviews or as recorded in documents, memoirs, letters, or other sources such as newspaper articles. I prefer to use the terms *African American* and *black*, but in sections spotlighting Jim Crow, I use the language of the period, *Negro* and *colored*.

With *Forgotten*, I have attempted to recount the story of ordinary men called upon to undertake an unusual and extraordinary mission, which they accomplished with self-assurance and bravery. I hope to carve a place in history for the 320th Barrage Balloon Battalion.

Linda Hervieux
Paris, France
February 2015

PART I

CHAPTER 1

War Brewing

———

Every night was our party, and we invited the world.

—Atlantic City musician Sid Trusty
Atlantic City, New Jersey
June 1941

T he windows of Heilig's Restaurant are big—big like the portions of
fresh Atlantic lobster and stewed snapper that Joe Heilig serves up
seven days a week. From the windows, diners are treated to a never-
ending parade along the Boardwalk: ladies in colorful dresses cinched at
the waist, with T-strap pumps and white cotton gloves light enough for a
fine spring day. They stroll, arm in arm, with fellows turned out in linen
suit jackets and straw hats the color of their trousers. It's not unusual
to see a silver-tipped walking stick tap-tap-tapping along the wooden
planks, or a gold watch chain glinting in the sun. Wicker rolling chairs
keep pace, on hire for those who prefer a cushioned ride under the shade
of a white parasol. From the carousel come the squeals of children. The
air is filled with music. There are buskers and showmen, hucksters and
carnival barkers calling out the latest wonderments to be seen: *Ladies
and Gentlemen, right here, right now, in Atlaaaaantic City.*

Wilson Caldwell Monk juggles plates piled high with Heilig's spe-
cialties, careful not to spill a drop on the crisp white tablecloths. He
sneaks glances out the huge glass windows at the show playing out

before him. America's first boardwalk is a homegrown version of a European promenade, a wide wood-planked expanse where flâneurs sporting the latest fashions come to see and be seen. *Excess* is the watchword in America's pioneer resort community, the first city dedicated solely to leisure. Hotel marquees announce the biggest headliners of the day, among them Bing Crosby, Artie Shaw, and Tommy Dorsey. There is seemingly no end to the good times.

If the Boardwalk's attractions aren't enough, jutting far into the sea are a half dozen grand piers lined with carnival rides, shows, and other diversions. The king of them all, the self-styled "Showplace of the Nation," is the Steel Pier, every inch crammed with amusements such as the Hawaiian Village, with real hula dancers, and the giant Ferris wheel. Resounding cheers echo as the Diving Horse and its attractive lady rider, clad in a smart bathing costume and cap, surface in a pool after plunging from a forty-foot-high platform.

Wilson never tires of the Boardwalk, never grows weary of the crackle and hum. This four-mile-long walkway is the center of his world, just as it is the pulsing heart that sustains "the Season," the three crucial months when Atlantic City is open for business. The summer's grand finale, the Miss America Pageant, is followed hard by Labor Day, when the closing bell sounds and the curtain drops. Heilig's and most of the other Boardwalk haunts will close up tight, their thousands of workers, the vast majority of them African Americans, left to struggle through another long, bone-chilling winter with little chance of finding an off-season job.

The Boardwalk was built in the early 1850s, by leveling natural dunes that protected the wild barrier island known as Absecon from the off-season fury that the Atlantic Ocean unleashed from time to time. A powerful hurricane could break this famed promenade to bits, though nobody is thinking about that. Atlantic City is already in its declining years, though nobody knows it. The war raging across the ocean is destined to engulf a generation of young Americans like Wilson, though few believe it. Looking at the summertime spectacle playing out before the windows of Heilig's, the future Private Monk, twenty-one years old, sees only opportunity.

Yet opportunity was fickle in Atlantic City. Though in-season jobs were ample for everyone, on a social level, advancement was divided strictly by race. Heilig's Restaurant wasn't a place where Negroes like Wilson Monk could enjoy a lobster or a plate of stewed snapper, even if they could afford it. One time, Wilson watched as a colored nurse came to lunch at Heilig's with the old woman in her care and the rest of the woman's large white family. With a Negro caretaker in tow, the family could hardly hope for a prime window seat with a view of the famous Steel Pier. Their table was in the back, which was *far* back, since Heilig's cavernous dining room seated six hundred. Atlantic City's Negroes knew their place, and it wasn't at Heilig's or at any other Boardwalk restaurant, or hotel. Even the carousel and other rides along the Boardwalk, which had once been open to all, were deemed "Whites Only" in 1904. Two years later, a color line was drawn in the sand, literally, when hoteliers, worried about offending the new waves of southern tourists, asked their black employees and their families not to "bathe or lounge" in front of hotel properties. Eventually, the slice of sand relegated to Negroes between Missouri and Mississippi Avenues came to be known as "Chicken Bone Beach." Even though it evolved into the most happening spot along the entire expanse of the Atlantic City shore, it was still separate. Even if Sammy Davis Jr. and other visiting black celebrities kept the sunbathers in stitches with improvised skits and general fooling, it was still separate. And separate was not equal.

Atlantic City wasn't the South, where so-called Jim Crow laws kept the races officially apart with whites-only drinking fountains, waiting rooms, hospitals, and just about everything else you would find in a civil society. The name Jim Crow came from a white minstrel show performer who copied a silly dance called Jump Jim Crow from a black man in the 1820s. The New Jersey seaside town preferred a quieter approach. As the black population grew, the city's whites decided to separate from their black neighbors, many of whom were descendants of African Americans whose backbreaking work had transformed those twelve square miles on the northern end of barren Absecon Island into a leisure destination that attracted, from the earliest days, vacationers of both races.

The workforce that built Atlantic City from little more than sand and hope in the mid-1800s included freedmen and likely runaway slaves terrified of discovery, with no laws to protect them if they were found out. Although New Jersey had repealed slavery in 1804—it was the last northern state to do so—a clause requiring "apprenticeships for life" to former masters kept many Negroes and their children in indentured servitude for decades longer. It is likely, then, that black men still in bondage toiled alongside white European immigrants to turn sand dunes into hotels and salt marshes into hard-packed ground that brought the first trains to the island in July 1854.

The newly incorporated Atlantic City didn't begin its history with a proud record where African Americans were concerned. Yet by the 1880s, black workers from southern states were flocking to the island, intent on escaping the venomous race hatred that blossomed across the South like a poisonous weed in the decades following Emancipation. Black migrants were lured by the possibility of expanding their employment opportunities, which had hardly been improved since the days of slavery, with sharecropping and domestic work the only real options. Each multistory hotel that rose along the Boardwalk brought with it the promise of jobs that paid wages and tips, which meant that the emerging black working class could save money and envision the possibility of a better future for their children.

By 1900, Atlantic City's year-round population of thirty thousand included about seven thousand African Americans, with perhaps double that number coming to work during the Season. About 95 percent of workers in the city's twelve hundred hotels were black, which white vacationers found either charming or upsetting. America's new vacation class included working-class blacks with factory jobs in rapidly expanding cities such as Philadelphia. They could pay the $1.50 round-trip train ticket for a day at the shore and twenty-five cents to rent a bathing suit and a locker. As the numbers of dark-skinned vacationers grew, white Atlantic City became concerned. The annual "Excursion Day" set aside for Negro vacationers attracted thousands of day-trippers in 1900, and drew a snide broadside in the *Atlantic City Daily Press*, which mocked the "great long line of Sambos and Liza Janes" enjoying themselves along the waterfront. "Considering the event and the low price of razors," the newspaper sniped, "it is wonderful that so few disturbances occurred during the day."

At the turn of the twentieth century, Atlantic City was a racially and ethnically diverse stew that was unusual in America, where hatred toward migrating blacks was creeping north like a quiet infection and where segregation was no longer a southern preserve. Forty years after the slaves were freed, their children and grandchildren knew that the South never truly intended to free them. From Florida to Virginia, many were living as sharecroppers in conditions barely distinguishable from the bondage their parents and grandparents had endured as slaves before the Civil War. In the supposedly emancipated South, the price for insubordination under Jim Crow was a fine, a hammer to the head, or a hangman's noose. America's blacks were whispering about the great northern cities, with jobs and strange apartment houses, and they began to plot their escape, in secret, to avoid retribution from their white employers.

The Great Migration began as a trickle and grew into a torrent that would see six million southern blacks resettled in the North over the next seven decades, shattering for good the feudal southern order. It was "the first big step the nation's servant class ever took without asking," writes journalist and historian Isabel Wilkerson. These migrants found work as servants in the northern cities. If they were lucky, they were allowed to share in the wealth of booming industries: the textile mills of Philadelphia, steel factories of Chicago, and assembly lines of Detroit. Yet they also found, as their numbers grew and pushed beyond the borders of the segregated enclaves in which they lived, that the larger white community pushed back, sometimes with violence. These white people, many of them European newcomers, were not keen to cede the gains they had made. And unfortunately for the black arrivals, many of these white immigrants had bought into the southern creed that their race was naturally superior and that the descendants of Africans who had preceded them to American shores by four hundred years were not worthy of the better places in society that they were seeking. Across the North, segregation evolved into a state as natural as air.

In Atlantic City, the races had lived together in relative peace until one too many southern blacks arrived. They were joined by immigrants from the West Indies, attracted by the city's prosperity and unaccustomed to American racism. As the black population grew, their presence stirred resentment. The areas where Negroes were not welcome expanded. Landlords refused to rent to them. There is no simple answer as to why the city's dominant population, which held all the power, turned on the black community with whom they shared—and to whom they owed—so much. The rapidly increasing black presence alone doesn't explain it. The sort of toxic hatred that plagued the South, where fear of lynching and other violence was a part of black life, did not exist in Atlantic City. Still, black Atlantic City got the message: their labor was wanted, but little else.

Over time, African Americans clustered a few blocks north of the gleaming hotels of the Boardwalk. What had been a largely integrated city in 1880 was now divided along racial lines. The black section, dubbed the Northside, evolved into a mini-city so vibrant and complete that few seemed to mind that they weren't welcome to live elsewhere. As the Northside thrived, its working class was joined by an emerging upper class of business owners and professionals. By day, the streets around Arctic Avenue, the main drag, buzzed with shoppers who had their choice of scores of homegrown businesses, from butchers to bakers to beauty makers. There was a drugstore that delivered, even to whites. There were a dozen doctors and churches that helped foster black ingenuity and talent. The schools were good and the teachers, white and black women, made a deep impression on their students.

In 1927, six-year-old Vernon Hollingsworth was so proud the day she walked into the newly opened New Jersey Avenue Elementary School. To the little girl's eye, the teachers were beautiful in their long skirts, their hair pulled into tight buns. School was a refuge from home, which was happy but poor. Vernon's father earned twenty-four dollars a week as an elevator man, a job he had taken after his asthma no longer allowed him to work as a baker. Her mother cleaned the homes of white folks and took in laundry on the side. Vernon sparkled onstage in school plays, interpreting Sojourner Truth and other important historical black personalities, all the while encouraged by her beloved teachers. Those experiences had a profound effect on young Vernon, who would carry them in her heart as life got tough later on, when her opportunities were limited by her very dark skin. Though she was beautiful and statuesque, with a smart pageboy cut that set off her deep brown eyes, she was dark. Being dark meant no summer job at the local ice-cream stand or, years later, at the phone company. But Vernon would always have the stage and those moments when she could pretend to be somebody else. "That school was the best thing that ever happened to me," she would recall nine decades later.

A few blocks away, at Westside Elementary School, seven-year-old Mertina Madison revered her white principal, Miss Woodward, and the white secretary, Miss Stevens, who clicked along the corridors in strappy pumps that hugged her slim ankles. To Mertina, they looked like Mary Janes for grown-ups, and the little girl dreamed of one day wearing shoes like that. She would work in a school, just like those fine ladies. It was an ambition fostered by Northside teachers, even some white ones, who could have directed the black girls in their care to the lower-class work that white society expected of them. At the time, Mertina didn't know that the colored children didn't have it as good as it seemed. She would learn years later that she and her classmates were given the castoffs from the white schools. The textbooks came used, and the crayons already broken. She would learn the truth when she found herself in Miss Stevens's old job as secretary of Westside Elementary.

AFTER SCHOOL, THE STREETS of the Northside morphed into a giant playing field, where there was never any trouble finding a game of baseball, football, or Kick the Can. "We were poor, but we had everything," Vernon said. If life got boring, there was always the Boardwalk and the piers just a few blocks away, a never-ending show. For Vernon, it was enough to watch the rich white ladies strolling the Boardwalk in their furs and jewels. Mertina would gaze in the windows of Heilig's, dazzled by the patrons "with their white napkins and sparkling crystal stem wineglasses," and imagine "how rich they were." It was only later that the slights of segregation would grate and offend.

As tranquil and stable as the Northside was by day, it was hopping and unpredictable by night. Outside of Harlem, there was no better place if you liked to be in the middle of the action. By the spring of 1941, the Northside brimmed with revelers dancing and drinking in nightclubs that rivaled the white hotel clubs. You never knew whom you might see. The biggest names played the Northside, stars like Count Basie and his sixteen-piece orchestra, Duke Ellington, Sarah Vaughn, and the bawdy comedian Jackie "Moms" Mabley. The Paradise Club on North Illinois Avenue was said to be one of the world's first nightclubs, followed by many others, including the Wonder Gardens and Grace's Little Belmont, which the ladies liked for its comfy booths. The grand-daddy of them all was Club Harlem, which packed them in with three shows on Saturday night.

Outside, the streets crackled and pulsed with crowds that swarmed on weekend nights, with the epicenter along Kentucky Avenue, which was a show in itself: Ladies turned out in satin cocktail dresses trimmed with fur, their hair curled just so; their dates impeccable in dark suits and ties and leather shoes polished until they shimmered. Trying to drive a car down Kentucky Avenue on a Saturday night was like trying to thread a needle with a saxophone.

The scents were sweet and smoky, with restaurants serving up short ribs, baked pork chops, and big pots of greens—the sort of home cooking their patrons preferred any day to the fancy fare on the Boardwalk. If there were customers to serve, Wash's Restaurant stayed open, shifting to bacon and eggs when Club Harlem, across the street, let out in the not-so-early morning. Everybody knew that Club Harlem's six o'clock "breakfast show" was the one to catch, often featuring headliners who had performed hours earlier at the Boardwalk hotels, even white stars such as Frank Sinatra and Dean Martin. "Every night was our party, and we invited the world," said musician Sid Trusty.

The longest queue snaked from below the neon marquee above Club Harlem down along Kentucky Avenue. Sometimes whites outnumbered blacks, who scrambled to get a place in line lest the white folks take all the best seats. "There were so many whites slumming to see black entertainers, they just didn't leave any room for us," said musician Chris Columbo. Unlike in the whites-only clubs on the Boardwalk, on the Northside everyone was welcome—even whites who behaved badly. During one set at Club Harlem, a belligerent white man yelled in the direction of the band, "Why do you niggers play so loud?" In response, Columbo, a local sensation, shushed the band and grabbed the mike. "So that your wife won't hear you asking the broads how much it costs. That's why we play so loud."

Vice wasn't the only attribute the two Atlantic Cities shared, but it was an important one. The "World's Playground," as the city billed itself, chalked up its enormous success to an unholy trinity of "booze, broads, and gambling." Since Absecon Island's transformation, so-called bishops' laws banning liquor sales on Sunday were roundly ignored. But it was Prohibition that made Atlantic City the nation's most popular resort. In practice, Prohibition never really happened in Atlantic City, giving the vacation spot a tremendous advantage over its rivals for the thirteen long years during which making, buying, and drinking alcohol were banned in America.

Official corruption went hand in hand with the city's flouting of the Eighteenth Amendment, with establishments making regular payoffs to the local Republican political bosses to keep the liquor flowing. A pair of West Indians were said to have introduced the so-called numbers game, a lucrative under-the-table lottery run out of the Northside and beyond. It was eventually taken over by the city's political bosses, who knew a good racket when they saw one.

It was this renegade spirit that gave Atlantic City—and the Northside—an unparalleled mystique. It was no surprise when Philadelphia salesman Charles Darrow chose the city by the sea as the setting for his board game Monopoly. When the game debuted in 1935, the Northside was represented on Darrow's board, along with the ritzier white enclaves. Nobody seemed to mind that Arctic and Mediterranean Avenues were the low-rent squares, with swanky Park Place and Boardwalk far across the board.

As Atlantic City's fortunes rose, so did those of the Northside. African Americans were proud to call home a city that attracted not just legions of black workers and vacationers but also the top white names in show business, industry, and even politics. The Ambassador Hotel counted Bing Crosby and the tenor Enrico Caruso among its guests; President Franklin Delano Roosevelt lodged at the Chelsea. As the city's business base expanded, the resulting jobs offered Northsiders the chance to move up and send their kids to college, something that was nearly unthinkable in, say, rural Virginia, to which many Northsiders traced their roots. "Atlantic City was the place to be, better than

Philadelphia or New York City even," writes local historian Turiya S. A. Raheem. "There was room for advancement in every field, especially if you were educated."

That's not to say that life was easy. Everyone had a "hustle." Two jobs weren't enough. If you had a few hours free, you found a third. Fathers, mothers, kids—everyone worked seven days a week during the Season. You pooled your money with your family; with cousins, uncles, and godparents. If you were lucky, you had enough to buy a house together. For many Northsiders, even that modest dream was out of reach, and getting by was a constant struggle, especially in winter. Extended families crammed themselves into flimsy housing built on the cheap as the resort was coming up. Poverty was a reality for many, and disaster was a door knock away in the form of an eviction notice when rent went unpaid. Or worse. Few had the resources to weather a bad spell or a family tragedy.

ONE EVENING IN DECEMBER 1919, Thomas Noble Monk was happy to catch a ride home from work with a buddy. Monk, the patriarch of a large family, had been a top student, the high school valedictorian who earned a place at Temple University, in Philadelphia. Despite his education, the best work Monk could find was a job as a janitor. His days were long and hard. If he resented his fate, he never let on. On this day in December, Monk was in the passenger seat of his friend's truck, heading home to Pleasantville, New Jersey, a suburb just over the bridge from Atlantic City, when a streetcar hit the truck broadside. Monk was killed instantly. He left a wife and seven children under the age of twelve, the youngest of whom, Wilson, was four months old. The Monks suffered after Thomas's death. His widow, Rosita Rebecca Monk, worked as many jobs as she could cram into her long days, cleaning for white families, taking in laundry, and ironing and starching till the wee hours. Rosita got a small settlement from Thomas's death, and she used it to buy a white stucco house on a quiet stretch of West Park Avenue in Pleasantville. Wilson remembered it as a "beautiful home with four bedrooms, a living room, dining room, a bath upstairs, a kitchen and a cellar." As hard as Rosita worked, it wasn't enough, and she eventually lost the house. The family moved to the Northside, and there Rosita's seven children, when they grew old enough, sought out whatever jobs they could land to bring in cash to keep them all afloat.

Rosita's youngest worried over his mother, a tiny wisp of a woman who couldn't hit five feet if she stood on her tiptoes on a soapbox. Like his mother, Wilson was earnest and determined. Unlike his mother, he had a gentle voice that he was reluctant to raise. He excelled in school and reveled in the attention of his teachers. In fourth grade, he was the only student to dress in his Sunday best for the class picture, grinning in pure delight for the camera. For that, he took a ribbing as the teacher's pet. He didn't care. Wilson would always be a sharp dresser.

As much as he loved school, the eighth grade was as far as he got. Although his father's time at university was a proud chapter in the family history, at age fourteen Wilson dropped out to go to work. He would always regret skipping high school, but there was no other choice. "Three months to hurry, nine months to worry," the saying went, a reference to Atlantic City's June-through-August working season. Wilson liked to say that, for him, the worrying season lasted ten months, at least.

Over the next few years, Wilson strung together a series of jobs to help Rosita pay the bills. He mopped floors and peddled Fralinger's famous saltwater taffy—twenty-five flavors—to vacationers. When he was lucky, he waited on well-heeled white folks at eateries along the Boardwalk. In the spring of 1941, he was hired behind the counter at Apex Community Drugstore, at the corner of Indiana and Arctic Avenues. Apex was a classy alternative to Woolworth's and the other lunch counters, where Northsiders weren't welcome to eat alongside whites. At Apex, whose advertisements promised "first-class luncheonette service," there was a place for anyone on the red vinyl stools, and a toasted sandwich set you back ten cents.

Everything was first-class when it was done by Sarah Spencer Washington, a self-made millionaire who rose from humble Virginia roots to found an empire under the name Apex. She would become one of the city's great philanthropists. A visionary of her time, Washington moved to Atlantic City in 1913 and opened a hair salon and school. Struck by the lack of hair products for black women like herself, she decided to try her hand at making some. It didn't hurt that she had studied chemistry at Columbia University, a highly improbable accomplishment for a black woman of that era, which followed an equally improbable degree in business administration from Northwestern University. In 1920 she created Apex News and Hair Company, reasoning that beauty was always a good business to be in. She was right: her Apex Beauty Colleges would go international, with forty-five thousand agents and franchises in a dozen U.S. cities and as far away as Johannesburg, South Africa.

Her initiative gave black women the power to own their own businesses and expand their possibilities beyond domestic work. Her laboratory and factory on Baltic Avenue made scores of products to straighten, curl, and shine black hair, plus a full line of cosmetics. Madame Washington, as she was known, thumbed her nose at the highbrow hotels that refused service to Negroes by opening Apex Rest, an upscale Northside hotel for African Americans with fifteen rooms, tennis courts, "large spacious lawns" for croquet, and a dancing pavilion catering to "select families and tourists," as her ads boasted. The "select" was no doubt a riposte to the perceived superiority of a white society that spurned her people. She followed that with other Apexes: a golf club for African Americans and a working farm fifteen miles outside the city that provided eggs, vegetables, and fruit to her many entities. When she made an offer to buy a house in a nearby white community, she anticipated racial prejudice and hid her identity by fabricating a group of buyers whose names included Mr. Truth Eternal, among other cheeky monikers.

Madame Washington was one of the most successful entrepreneurs of her day, black or white, but she wasn't alone. Other Northside women showed economic know-how in the early decades of the twentieth century by opening up boardinghouses, restaurants, and other businesses to supplement the family income, all of them catering to black tourists and entertainers working the so-called Chitlin' Circuit of black clubs and juke joints that spanned the South and extended north. Segregation opened up possibilities in black communities even as it limited opportunities outside. Mertina Madison's mother, Marie, helped her sister Alma Washington (no relation to Sarah) cook up beef stew and chicken and dumplings at the original Wash's, a six-seat eatery on North Kentucky Avenue that eventually spawned several much larger incarnations and grew into an Atlantic City institution. The efforts of the emerging black business class were all the more notable because they occurred outside the usual channels of credit, since white bankers would not lend money to Negroes.

For Wilson Monk, Atlantic City truly was the place to be. He tested life in New York for a year, living with an uncle before deciding that everything he wanted was right at home. Soon, he would have another reason to stay.

IN THE SPRING OF 1941, Wilson cut a dashing figure cruising the streets of Atlantic City behind the wheel of a two-seat Bantam roadster, delivering prescriptions for Apex Community Drug Store. Even whites ordered their medicines from Madame Washington's shop. One day, the order came to deliver to an extra-special customer. Wilson checked the name, paused, and checked again. The slip said Nucky Johnson, the infamous Republican political boss reputed to be the richest man in town. Wilson made the delivery—and drew belly laughs from his friends when he told them how much he had gotten as a tip: zero.

Apex was Wilson's "steady," his go-to job. On weekends, he waited tables at Heilig's, where a good day might bring in enough in tips for him to slip his mother a little extra. At the time, Rosita could use whatever cash she got. She was raising her three-year-old grandson, Billy, for her daughter Vivian, who was trying to get back on her feet after a rough divorce. Whenever he could, Wilson walked his nephew to the afternoon tennis practices that Rosita insisted upon, despite the cost. The little boy, dressed in the snow-white shorts and shirt his grandmother had washed and pressed for him, beamed at his adored uncle on those walks. Rosita had a washing machine, a luxury on the Northside, and took in laundry for whites and the Community Synagogue on South Maryland Avenue, not far from the Boardwalk. Wilson moonlighted at the synagogue as an "all-around man," doing whatever work needed doing.

On those rare times when Wilson was off work, he had only to step out of the rooms he shared on Kentucky Avenue with Edward Wilson, a buddy from Apex, to be at the heart of the action. If there was one certainty on the Northside it was this: Wilson Monk turned heads. He was tall and thin and knew how to wear a suit. His pencil-thin mustache was carved in a precise line, setting off his high cheekbones and caramel skin. Despite his intense working life, the nails on his long, fine-boned fingers were perfectly tended, a shiny wristwatch always on his wrist. He trailed a wake of cologne and minty mouthwash, and his multiwatt smile was a surefire lady-killer. He didn't circulate much, though, taking his meals at his mother's and spending his free time with little Billy. But sometimes Wilson joined friends like Edward Wilson and Cecil Hill for an occasional dinner of short ribs, or maybe a bourbon and ginger ale at one of the Northside clubs.

More than a few girls had a crush on Wilson Monk, but there was only one who won his heart, a lovely Lena Horne look-alike he spied one day in 1937. Wilson was sitting on the porch rail outside his mother's house on North Ohio Avenue when he saw her: petite with a café au lait complexion, rosy cheeks, and long, dark, curly hair. His mother called him inside for something, and when he got back to the porch a few seconds later, she was gone. It would be two more years until he saw her again, this time in a house just across the street. Her name was Mertina Madison.

That day was January 5, 1939, and the occasion was a party for Mertina's friend Vernon Hollingsworth. The young women had been friends since they were schoolgirls dreaming of strappy shoes. Vernon's fête was organized by her boyfriend, who was Mertina's brother. William Charles "C Baby" Madison doted on Vernon and planned the bash for her eighteenth birthday at his family's house. His mother, Marie, adored Vernon and treated the striking young woman "like a princess," Vernon said, even though her skin was several shades darker than the Madisons'. For this, Vernon was ever grateful, though her father was always suspicious of C Baby's motives, believing a courtship between a light-skinned man and a dark girl to be impossible.

The night of the party was bitter cold and stormy. C Baby wondered what had happened to his friend Wilson, who was late, and sent his pal Cecil Hill to pick him up in Cecil's car. When Wilson walked in the door, crisply turned out, despite the weather, in a camel-colored overcoat and green porkpie hat, Mertina was speechless. "He's a done deal," she told herself. "We made eye contact, and that was it." Wilson and "Mert" went steady after that, which by Madison family standards was rather sporadic, since Mertina's father, Charles Madison, didn't let his baby girl out of the house much. C Baby was just as strict as his father, making sure his little sister—Mertina was younger by one year and eleven months—didn't get into any trouble with his good friend.

In any case, "we were so poor we didn't have money to go to a movie. But that was the beauty of being with Wilson," Mertina recalled. The best things were free, such as dressing up for a stroll arm in arm along the Boardwalk. One time a kid was handing out coupons for Lorstan Studios, and Wilson and Mert decided to have a portrait taken together. They posed and paid fifty cents for one photograph. "We decided we should each have one," Mertina said. In a rare splurge, "we each paid for our own."

ONE EVENING IN EARLY JUNE 1941, Wilson Monk stopped by as usual to see his mother. Rosita was distressed: A telegram had arrived addressed to her youngest son. The contents were no surprise. Young men across New Jersey and the nation were being called up for military service. Wilson had registered for the draft the previous autumn, shortly after President Roosevelt signed into law the Selective Training and Service Act requiring able-bodied men from ages twenty-one to thirty-five to serve for at least one year. At the time, military service carried little risk. The vast majority of Americans (79 percent in one Gallup poll) wanted the country to stay out of the war in Europe, and isolationists in Congress were determined to keep it that way. "Your boys are not going to be sent to any foreign war," Roosevelt repeatedly promised, though he was now adding, "unless we are attacked." Concerns that America would be drawn into the conflagration multiplied with each German victory. Fears mounted later in June when Adolf Hitler broke a nonaggression pact he had inked with Joseph Stalin and invaded the Soviet Union.

Wilson Monk wasn't thinking about the possibility of being sent to a far-off battlefield. To him, the draft notice meant only one thing: a steady paycheck. Even after Labor Day, the usual season of worry, he would be working. "It meant that I would be making thirty dollars a month, and that was good money then," Wilson said. On June 10, his bag packed, he promised Rosita and Mertina that he would be home for Christmas. Mertina kissed Wilson good-bye and wrapped him in a tight hug. None of them could know that, six months later, a surprise Japanese attack in Hawaii would seal Wilson's service for the next four years. For now, joining the army—the only branch of the armed forces accepting Negroes—seemed like a grand adventure with pay.

Wilson Monk reported for duty at Fort Dix, New Jersey, joining 1.4 million enlisted men nationwide, 74,309 of them black. One week later he was sent on to Fort Eustis, Virginia, for basic training. Wilson's introduction to the South wasn't pleasant. As a black man, he was accustomed to the small daily indignities that marked his interactions with white people. There were places where he couldn't eat or drink, shop windows in which he wasn't allowed to peer, and a beach where he was barred from swimming. But that treatment seemed generous now. Nothing had prepared the soft-spoken young man for life in a segregated army, or for life in the even deeper South, home to most of the army's training camps. Black men were lynched there. In some places, they could be charged with rape if they were caught *just looking* at a white woman. Failing to step aside for a white man on a public sidewalk could land a black man on a prison chain gang or in a coal mine as a modern-day slave. Across the South, the mere presence of a black soldier was reviled by many whites, who looked upon their uniforms as a provocation, a demand for acknowledgment in a world that was carefully constructed around the premise that white people were superior and colored people knew their place in the background. It was a world where, in 1941, social equality was as impossible to imagine as a schoolhouse where black and white children were taught side by side.

Life on an army base offered no insulation from the slings and arrows of prejudice. In fact, it was worse in some respects because many of the officers were white southerners expert at inflicting humiliation with a particularly vile racist tongue. Southern officers were the majority in the peacetime army and contributed to the racist attitude that infused army ranks at every level. The generals in Washington believed early on that the best men to command Negro units were white men from the South, where three-quarters of the country's black population lived.

The U.S. Army was thoroughly Jim Crow, with little contact between the races except for the white officers put in charge of Negro units. White and black enlisted men trained, dined, slept, and socialized with their own kind. There were separate clubs, clinics, and blood banks. New York recruit Charles Orrett was stunned to learn that if the Negro sections in the two movie houses on base were full, black soldiers were forbidden to sit on the white side, even if there were empty seats. "I never knew what discrimination meant until I went to Fort Eustis," he said.

One Sunday, Wilson Monk and some friends went to Richmond and caught the last bus back to base at eleven o'clock. As they settled in for the eighty-mile ride, Military Police officers boarded the bus and told the black soldiers to get off. They stayed put. "We wanted to know why," Wilson said. The MPs returned with local cops, and this time the black soldiers complied. When they did, white soldiers took their seats and made it back to Fort Eustis on time. Wilson and his friends couldn't get another bus until Monday morning. They risked punishment for going AWOL and spent a long cold night seething in a Richmond bus station.

Most northern recruits like Monk had expected a racial divide when they went south. What they hadn't counted on was the bald-faced hostility that hit them head-on at each turn in their journey as soldiers—even in their own camps. Wilson Monk quickly learned the new rules. Besides segregated movie houses, black barracks often were the farthest to reach. Equipment that was in short supply for everyone before the war began in earnest would remain that way for the black soldier. Negroes could buy candy and gum at the PX, the Post Exchange, but forget about lingering over a soda. One day in basic training, as a black recruit grabbed the baton during a relay race, an officer from Georgia whooped, "Look at that nigger run!" Wilson had never heard that slur used so freely in his life as he did at that base. The insults stung, and hardened into a patina of rage over time. These men expected better from their government. They expected better from a military that urged them to fight for democracy and the rights of white people living in faraway places.

As bad as it got at Fort Eustis, Virginia wasn't the Deep South. For men like Wilson Monk, the worst was yet to come.

CHAPTER 2

Too Dumb to Fight

The negro is . . . by nature subservient and naturally believes himself inferior to the white. He is jolly, tractable, lively and docile by nature, but through real or supposed harsh or unjust treatment may become sullen and stubborn. . . . He has not the physical courage of the white. He simply cannot control himself in fear of some danger in the degree that the white man can.

—ARMY WAR COLLEGE STUDY, 1925
WASHINGTON, D.C.
SUMMER 1940

I n the summer of 1940, Americans were swinging to Glenn Miller's "In the Mood" and tuning their radios to a hit parade topped by Bing Crosby, Frank Sinatra, and Ella Fitzgerald. Fans were flocking to movie houses to see Gene Autry in *Carolina Moon*, and the new matinee star was a rabbit called Bugs Bunny.

The war in Europe seemed far away, even with the news in June that the Nazis had taken France, the latest in a long line of military conquests beginning with Poland the previous September. Great Britain suffered a humiliating defeat and eleventh-hour evacuation of 340,000 troops from the French port of Dunkirk, and found itself utterly alone as a German invasion loomed. On the other side of the world, the Japanese march through China seemed unstoppable, with Peking and Shanghai occupied and the empire setting its sights on territories farther afield in Southeast Asia. In Washington, DC, isolationists were determined to keep the nation out of the inferno, even as it appeared to many that the country was hurtling toward another world war.

"These are ominous days," President Franklin Roosevelt declared in May, calling for the greatest military mobilization and rearmament the nation had ever seen. It was an essential undertaking given that America's military had slowly wasted away since the Great War. As Hitler reveled in his victories, the U.S. Army was in a pathetic state, with a fighting force of only 190,000 men—smaller than Switzerland's. The army still used rifles from 1903 and favored *horses* as a means to move men in battle. Some 3,500 of those horses were paired with 450 tanks— nearly all the armor the army possessed—in war games. The results made clear what Germany's modern fleet of heavy tanks would do to a cavalry regiment. The firepower of the tanks, though outdated, amazed onlookers. In any case, America's sole tank brigade could hardly defend New York City, much less go to war. To make matters worse, there were almost no warplanes. Those facts were of little importance to opponents of American involvement in the ever-worsening conflict they dismissed as Europe's war. Among them were prominent Republican legislators, businessmen, and celebrities such as the aviator Charles Lindbergh, who blasted Roosevelt's "defense hysteria." They also opposed a move to revise the law to allow America, officially neutral, to sell arms to the warring countries that badly needed them, most of all Britain.

At the time, Roosevelt and his advisers believed that the greatest threat to America came from Nazi Germany, not Japan. With the bulk of the U.S. fleet in the Pacific, they deemed a Japanese invasion highly unlikely (though they presciently did not rule out a surprise attack on Hawaii). Yet after the defeat of France, there was profound doubt among Roosevelt's team that Britain could survive through 1940. After the French surrender, one high-ranking officer bet that the end would come for England within six weeks. In London, Ambassador Joseph Kennedy reported that the situation seemed hopeless. It looked even worse in July, when the first German bombs fell in the south of England, ahead of the devastating Blitz of London that began in September.

Roosevelt was among those who believed that if Britain were defeated and its navy no longer protected the North Atlantic, the next target for Germany would be North America, with a possible invasion route through Newfoundland and the Gulf of Saint Lawrence. To the president, rearming Britain was nearly as important as rearming the United States. It was a position that many in his War Department did not share, at least not at first. In late summer, Roosevelt negotiated a secret deal with British prime minister Winston Churchill, exchanging fifty aging American destroyers for ninety-nine-year leases to occupy nine strategic British bases, one of them in Newfoundland. Although the president considered the move "the most important event in the defense of the U.S. since Thomas Jefferson's Louisiana Purchase," it was hardly the behavior of a neutral country and could very well have prompted Germany to declare war—something America was decidedly not ready for. Yet Roosevelt firmly believed that Britain could withstand a German onslaught with America's help. "If Great Britain goes down," Roosevelt said, "it is no exaggeration to say that all of us in the Americas would be living at the point of a gun."

The North Atlantic wasn't the only weak spot in America's defense. To the south, war planners identified the unprotected Gulf Coast as the nation's "soft underbelly," along with the Caribbean approaches to the strategically vital Panama Canal. The bulge of eastern Brazil was considered a likely point of attack if Germany moved into western Africa, which was not that far away across the Atlantic. While these frightening calculations were unknown to ordinary Americans, Roosevelt hoped to use them to persuade a reluctant Congress to write some fat checks. After more than a decade mired in the worst depression the country had ever seen, the country could ill afford to build a war machine, much less contribute to Britain's. Even so, despite a loud outcry from critics, the president got his wish. Congress granted a billion-dollar revamp of the armed forces. Still, it would take the United States, which had practically no munitions industry, at least eighteen months to build sufficient stocks to challenge Germany, which had rearmed years ahead of its rivals with the latest weaponry.

Roosevelt's mobilization would involve more than fifteen million men and women from every corner of the country and every race and social class. In the coming months and years, Americans would buy war bonds hawked by Bob Hope, rip stamps out of ration books to purchase sugar and meat, and plant victory gardens like First Lady Eleanor Roosevelt's.

BLACK SOLDIERS HAD BEEN largely purged from the military during the mass downsizing that followed the end of the Great War. By 1940 there were only 4,179 black soldiers in the army and 5 black officers, 3 of them chaplains and the remaining 2 sharing the same name: Benjamin O. Davis. The elder would soon become the nation's first black general, an honor accompanied by the nagging imputation among African Americans that it was an award to an Uncle Tom. The younger Davis would go on to become a commander of the famed Tuskegee Airmen.

Even before the Revolutionary War, when runaway slave Crispus Attucks became the first American to die in the Boston Massacre in March 1770, African Americans looked upon their service to their country with pride, hoping loyalty and sacrifice would advance the case for better treatment of the race. This war was no different. The nation's leading civil rights organization, the National Association for the Advancement of Colored People, had been fighting for years to ensure a fair place and equitable treatment for black soldiers in all branches of the military. So in late summer 1940, when Congress began debating one of the most sweeping facets of Roosevelt's war plan, the nation's first peacetime draft bill, black leaders saw a prime opportunity to influence the agenda. It was an election year, and the black vote would wield clout like never before.

The first battle was waged over the insertion of a clause guaranteeing equal rights to all soldiers, something war planners opposed. Their policy for a future war envisioned a limited role for Negro recruits, setting a 10 percent quota in line with the black percentage of the population. They were to be assigned almost exclusively to segregated labor and service units, just as they had been in the last war. Military planners had long believed Negroes to be intellectually and physically inferior to white soldiers. How that perception developed is a lesson in what happens when racism meets pseudoscience. Add to that the selective memories of white officers who led black soldiers in the First World War, and the result was a policy of discrimination that penalized black recruits before they saw their first day of boot camp.

The attitude toward the Negro is perhaps best summed up in an influential 1925 Army War College study that deemed African Americans unfit for combat and helped shape the War Department's treatment of the black soldier:

> The negro is profoundly superstitious. He is by nature subservient and naturally believes himself inferior to the white. He is jolly, tractable, lively and docile by nature, but through real or supposed harsh or unjust treatment may become sullen and stubborn. . . . He has not the physical courage of the white. He simply cannot control himself in fear of some danger in the degree that the white man can. His psychology is such that he willingly accepts hard labor and for this reason can well be employed in labor troops or other non-combatant branches. The negro is unmoral. He simply does not see certain things as wrong. The negro is one of the most secretive in the world. While the negro undoubtedly

has a state of mind bordering on resentment against the white, this feeling is numbed by his easy going nature. The negro's [*sic*] growing sense of importance will make them more and more of a problem, and racial troubles may be expected to increase.

Those findings would be repeated over the years in War College reports, training materials, and other documents. An undated War Department memo proclaimed the Negro to be "mentally lazy, not retentive. Ruled by instinct and emotion rather than by reason. Has to be made to face facts, prone to escapism. Likes pomp and ceremony. Stubborn no end. . . . Difficult to assume responsibility. Lacks mechanical sense. Has keen sense of rhythm which can be put to good advantage in drills of all kinds (marching, gun, crew). Lies easily. Can *only* be led, not driven."

Cowardice was one of the most persistent stereotypes that followed the black soldier, regardless of the facts. The concept that African Americans inherently lacked bravery dated back to slavery, when southerners propagated the myth that the few courageous and intelligent Africans had enslaved their countrymen, and the slaves sold in America were "only the childlike and cowardly dregs," writes historian and anthropologist Robert B. Edgerton. A British journalist in Alabama during the Civil War found "something suspicious" in the southern insistence that "we are not afraid of our slaves" while maintaining curfews, night patrols, and constant vigilance for any stirrings of rebellion. "As time passed," writes Edgerton, "evidence that black Americans had fought courageously in America's earlier wars was not only ignored but was also systematically denied by influential military officers and government officials."

Bad science contributed to the impression that racial differences accounted for lower intelligence among blacks. "It is generally recognized that the pure blood American negro is inferior to our white population in mental capacity," the War College study concluded, quoting from another source that found this was due to the smaller size of the black brain, supposedly weighing thirty-five ounces as opposed to forty-five ounces for the white brain. "The negroes are descended from slave[s] imported from West Africa. Their characteristics, physically, were formerly quite uniform and show them to be very low in the seals of human evolution." Those findings were reminiscent of an 1869 government report that found the Negro soldiers "too animal to have moral courage or endurance." The author, a doctor, also relied on brain size and weight to conclude that the Negro soldier was simple-minded.

As to why black soldiers were unfit for jobs as mechanics and specialists, the army cited their "apparent lack of inherent natural mechanical adaptability." Further "proof" of black inferiority was found in low scores among black recruits on the Army General Classification Exam. Despite its nickname, the "IQ test," it measured not intelligence but knowledge gleaned from the education and cultural experiences of whites. The army's reliance on the test came despite the warning of the psychologists who designed it that it wasn't meant to gauge pure intelligence; nor was it intended to compare the abilities of men from disparate backgrounds. It was no surprise that, given the odds against them, 84 percent of black recruits tested in the lowest two categories out of five. (Sixty percent of whites tested in the top two categories.)

It was certainly true that literacy in America was a problem: The median education level for all men in 1940 was 8.3 years, and one out of eight was illiterate. Among poor southern blacks, the situation was far worse, with four out of five dropping out by fourth grade. In many parts of the rural South, schools for black children were abysmal, and often there were no options beyond seventh grade. The average per capita expenditure in eighteen southern states to educate a black child was eighteen dollars, as opposed to forty-four dollars for a white child.

Yet there was ample proof that many men with little formal education made fine soldiers. In fact, when a nonverbal test was given to black troops, 30 percent of those formerly in the lowest category moved up, with some scoring in the top level. A highly successful 1943 army literacy program showed that when given the chance to learn, black recruits excelled. Out of 150,000 soldiers who attained a functional standard of literacy, nearly 87,000 were black. The program also showed no substantial differences in learning ability between the races, though a slightly greater percentage of blacks completed the program than whites. Eighty percent of the men enrolled graduated and "went on to become good soldiers," a review of the program showed.

Later in the war, a group of Negro riflemen who volunteered as replacements in white combat units won praise for their performance. As a group, the men had tested in the second-lowest category on the army test, and yet "in courage, coolness, dependability and pride, they are on a par with any white troops," one commander said. He went even further, saying they fought "with a fierce desire to meet with and kill the enemy, the equal of which I have never witnessed in white troops."

War Secretary Henry L. Stimson admitted that the army adopted tough literacy requirements to limit the number of black recruits. His insistence that black soldiers couldn't be trusted to fight infuriated African Americans, particularly the black press, which railed against Stimson's "Negro-is-too-dumb-to-fight" policy. In the years preceding the outbreak of war, test scores combined with racist studies shaped the attitudes of future officers and policy makers. The tests became a "hazard to effective training," wrote Ulysses S. Lee, an official army historian and author of *The Employment of Negro Troops*. Officers learned they could use the low scores to explain away any problems tied to their leadership, from messy barracks to low morale. In some cases, officers ignored the specious evidence that blacks were less intelligent and competent, and were rewarded with good results. The test "is not worth a damn with colored troops," said one antiaircraft artillery commander. "Despite the ratings, I have the best group of soldiers in the army right here in this regiment."

Another factor the army considered in its recommendations concerning black soldiers was their performance in past wars. The 1925 War College study wasn't alone in demeaning this record, emphasizing that when good service occurred, it came under the command of whites. In fact, black soldiers had a proud legacy of service to their country. Nearly 5,000 black soldiers, slave and free, served in George Washington's army, including three who crossed the Delaware with him in 1776. A number of black units fought with distinction, including a 226-man regiment from Rhode Island that held off an attack by 1,500 Hessians. That unit was commanded by a white colonel, but another unit, led by a black colonel, the so-called Bucks of America, won praise and a silk banner from John Hancock. Although Negro troops collected accolades for their service, there was little change. Despite hopes to the contrary, enslaved African Americans remained in bondage.

In the War of 1812, a volunteer battalion of 600 freedmen "served creditably" in the Battle of New Orleans, the army concluded. As in the Revolutionary War, many states in the Civil War were aghast at the practice of arming Negroes. Once again, need trumped prejudice, and many of the 420,000 black soldiers and sailors served with valor in the Union forces and state militias. Twenty-five received the newly minted Medal of Honor, the nation's highest award for bravery. The first was Sgt. William H. Carney of the Fifty-Fourth Massachusetts, the volunteer Negro regiment famed for storming Fort Wagner in an epic battle that left half its troops dead or wounded. (Their story was retold in the movie *Glory*.) After the fall of Richmond, another black regiment, the 5th Massachusetts Cavalry, was given the privilege of marching into the Confederate capital to cheers by the city's ecstatic African Americans. The commander of the First South Carolina Volunteers, escaped slaves who were the first blacks to see combat, reported that his "colored men fought with astonishing coolness . . . They behaved bravely, gloriously, and deserve all praise."

After the war, the army scaled back, retaining only four black regiments of a total of sixty-seven. The Negro troops were sent to the western frontier, as far away as possible from the South, where their presence enraged whites. The men dubbed "Buffalo Soldiers" by the Native Americans they battled served "faithfully and effectively," the army said. Eighteen of the men received the Medal of Honor. Their performance was stellar enough to change the mind of Gen. William Tecumseh Sherman, who recommended that the army end segregation. Five Buffalo Soldiers and a sailor later were awarded the Medal of Honor in the Spanish-American War.

Black sailors served aboard integrated navy ships from the Revolution to the Civil War, during which time four sailors were awarded the Medal of Honor. One of them was Robert Smalls, a runaway slave who hijacked a Confederate steamer in 1862 and later won a commission as an officer and commanded his own ship. His heroics persuaded President Abraham Lincoln to allow Negroes to serve in the Union Army. The bravery of black sailors serving under Oliver Hazard Perry in 1812 impressed the commodore, who hadn't wanted them in the first place. "They seem absolutely insensible to danger," he said after the Battle of Lake Erie, a turning point in the war against the British.

In the First World War, a nationwide draft allowed African Americans the greatest possibilities to serve their country in meaningful positions. Yet this was not to be, as the vast majority of the nearly four hundred thousand black troops were assigned duties as cooks, janitors, and laborers, regardless of their ability or education level. Among the relatively few black fighting troops sent to France, one regiment, the 369th Infantry Regiment—the legendary Harlem Hellfighters—of the 93rd Division, racked up "one of the bravest records achieved by any organization in the war," the *New York Times* reported in February 1919.

Shortly after the 369th arrived in France, they were orphaned. Gen. John J. Pershing, the commander of the American Expeditionary Forces, was only too happy to hand over unwanted Negro troops to the beleaguered French Army, which had begged the Americans for help on the front lines. The 369th fought under French command, wearing French uniforms. They were called Men of Bronze by their respectful French comrades, and Hellfighters by the Germans, who whispered in their trenches about the ferocious dark-skinned fighters, giving rise to an almost mythic fear of the black soldier that would carry on into the next world war. Before the 369th arrived at the mud-soaked front, the excellent regimental band had dazzled the French with jazzy renditions of familiar songs, including "La Marseillaise," the national anthem. Led by the Broadway arranger James Reese Europe, a lieutenant, the band brought together some of Harlem's finest musicians and, it is said, introduced jazz to a very appreciative France. The black soldiers proved hugely popular with French villagers, especially the ladies, who warmly welcomed them into their homes—to the great dismay of many white Americans.

War Department officials were nearly as obsessed as white southern soldiers with preventing contact between Negroes and foreign white women. Commanders worked to keep black soldiers in their camps under lock and key, issuing orders such as this one in May 1918 to a black regiment: to avoid talking to or even being "in the company" of white women, regardless of the wishes of the women. Two months later, a document drafted at Allied headquarters and distributed by a French colonel to French troops warned that blacks were not the equal of white men and had a "tendency toward undue familiarity" with women. "Don't spoil the Negroes," it warned. The French ignored these orders, often with indignant delight, and endeared themselves to the black Americans. White soldiers carried home stories of the French saluting Negroes and women entertaining them. Returning black soldiers would pay a steep price for these wartime freedoms.

One of the most famous Americans in France during the war was Eugene Jacques Bullard, who was a teenager in Georgia when he stowed away aboard a ship bound for Scotland. He eventually settled in France and joined the Foreign Legion as an infantryman in 1914, and was seriously wounded in the Battle of Verdun. He recovered and became an accomplished aviator, shooting down two German planes. Nicknamed the Black Swallow of Death, Bullard tried to enlist when the United States entered the war but was rejected, even though there was a desperate need for pilots. He received fifteen medals from the French, including the most important one, the Legion of Honor.

Writing in the NAACP magazine *The Crisis*, W. E. B. Du Bois lauded the "thousand delicate ways the French expressed their silent disapprobation" of American discrimination, giving birth to "a new, radical Negro spirit." On the return voyage to New York, one soldier offered a crisp salute to the Statue of Liberty. When asked why, he responded, "[B]ecause France gave it."

But it was in battle that the black soldiers proved their mettle, most notably the Hellfighters, who spent 191 days on the front lines—the most of any American unit—fighting side by side with white French *poilus*. The regiment earned a total of 550 decorations from the French and, more reluctantly, from the Americans. Their shining moment came one long night in May 1918, when a band of Germans, twenty-four or more by some accounts, surprised two black soldiers in a remote trench. Though wounded and vastly outnumbered, the duo fought fiercely, armed with rifles and grenades. As the raiders attempted to capture Pvt. Needham Roberts, his partner, Sgt. Henry Johnson, ended the battle when he unsheathed his bolo knife—the only weapon he had left—and began slashing at his opponents. "Every slash meant something to me," Johnson said later. In the morning, four Germans lay dead with many more wounded (and apparently dragged away by their battered comrades). Johnson and Roberts were the first Americans in the war awarded the French Croix de Guerre. The story, called the "Battle of Henry Johnson," was picked up coast to coast by white newspapers and magazines, which rarely recorded the exploits of colored soldiers. The southern writer Irvin S. Cobb, renowned for his racist scribblings, was so moved by the story of "Young Black Joe," as he called it, that he wrote these words, which he no doubt believed to be the highest compliment: "Hereafter n-i-g-g-e-r will merely be another way of spelling the word American."

It wasn't always apparent that the regiment would perform so effectively. The 369th was "a victim of indifference, verging on contempt, displayed by Pershing's headquarters. Untrained men adrift among junior officers and noncommissioned officers who were utter strangers, could not fight well," wrote Bernard C. Nalty, an official U.S. Army historian. Yet the 369th, led by supportive French commanders, exceeded all expectations. Kudos came from unexpected quarters, including, finally, Pershing, the general who had handed them over so readily to the French: "I cannot commend too highly the spirit shown among the colored combat troops who exhibit fine capacity for quick training and eagerness for the most dangerous work."

Theodore Roosevelt, the ex-president whose Rough Riders were arguably bailed out in Cuba by the black Tenth Cavalry, would call Johnson "one of the five bravest soldiers to take part in the Great War." There were many who believed that Johnson deserved the Medal of Honor, the quintessential symbol of valor. That award would go to another 369th member, a white lieutenant named George Robb, who refused to leave his unit despite being severely wounded in another battle. As bravely as he fought, Robb would later say that he didn't deserve the award. Politics, he said, prevented black soldiers from receiving the honors due them.

Black troops were barred from marching in the Allied victory parade in Paris. Instead of accolades, what many Negro soldiers got after the Armistice was an order to stay behind in France and bury thousands of bodies. Fifty-seven black soldiers and sailors were awarded the Medal of Honor by 1902. No African American would receive the highest decoration again until Korea, in another forty-eight years.

As for Henry Johnson, the once-legendary Hellfighter never healed from battlefield injuries and died eleven years after the war in poverty, a forgotten man. Eight decades later, President Clinton posthumously awarded him the Purple Heart. Six years later, Johnson received the Distinguished Service Cross, the nation's second-highest honor. His final tribute came on June 2, 2015, when President Barack Obama awarded the soldier called the "Black Death" the Medal of Honor. "[I]t's never too late to say thank you," the president said.

THE SECOND WORLD WAR would see record numbers of African Americans serving their country. Between 1940 and 1945, more than one million black soldiers would don uniforms. Waves of black migrants would leave the rural South seeking jobs in defense-related industries, their presence straining the precarious frontiers of race relations across the North. Black leaders were determined that these strivers would have a place in the booming war economy and that, above all, the black soldier would have a position of respect in the U.S. Army.

Their demands weren't new. Charles Hamilton Houston, the NAACP's special counsel, had warned the president of the importance of giving black soldiers a fair shot. If war came, Houston wrote in an October 1937 letter, "the Negro population . . . will not again silently endure the insults and discriminations imposed on its soldiers and sailors in the course of the last war." He went further the following year, writing to the *New York Times* that "Negroes in the next war are not going to be content with peeling potatoes and washing dishes." For Houston, who ceaselessly lobbied the War Department and the White House, the issue was personal. Houston had served as a first lieutenant in the army in France in the First World War, an experience that left him deeply scarred by what he called the "hate and scorn showered on us Negro officers by our fellow Americans." He was left so embittered that he never sought any of his service medals.

Houston hailed from a middle-class Washington, DC, family and graduated from an excellent all-black high school before attending

Amherst College. He would go on to earn a degree from Harvard Law School, where he was the first black editor of the *Law Review*. The high-achieving Houston never lacked in self-confidence, which made his wartime exposure to discrimination all the more difficult to swallow, as the perpetrators were usually ignorant white southern "crackers." Those experiences fueled a lifelong desire, he said, to fight "for men who could not strike back." His goal now, as another world war approached, was to prevent the rebirth of the Jim Crow army.

Unlike in 1917, this time around Houston and other black leaders at least had a place at the table. They made the case directly to Congress, asking how black soldiers could be expected to fight for democracy when their people back home were being oppressed and even lynched. Since the late 1800s, lynchings had remained a gruesome crime for which the perpetrators nearly always went unpunished. Often the leaders were lawmen. Victims could be hanged, burned at the stake, or killed in other macabre ways, their bodies often torn apart by white mobs, including children, intent on keeping fingers or ears as souvenirs.

Lynchings had averaged about two hundred a year, but saw a decline in the 1920s and '30s. The reasons for the drop are unclear, but Walter White, the longtime NAACP chief who had investigated the murders, believed it resulted from increased awareness and publicity, led by activists and the crusading black press, that rained condemnation on the South. He and others thought that black migration played a role, as well as the Great Depression, which spared neither race the effects of joblessness, poverty, and suffering. But the new push for equal rights ahead of the 1940 election, including a just role for the black soldier, strained the boundaries of southern tolerance. Sociologist Howard W. Odum wrote that "the South and the Negro in the early 1940s faced their greatest crisis since the days of Reconstruction." It was hard to imagine hatred toward African Americans could be more intense than it was during the decades after the Civil War, when the *Lexington Times* in Missouri opined against black suffrage this way: "No simian-souled, sooty-skinned, kink-curled, blubber-lipped, prehensile-heeled, Ethiopian gorilla shall pollute the ballot box with his leprous vote."

Yet the 1940s would see spikes in violence meted out as payback to black southerners for stirring up trouble. Black soldiers in uniform were a favorite target. Virginius Dabney, a progressive southern writer and segregation opponent, blamed "a small group of Negro agitators and another small group of white rabble-rousers" for what he called the coming "racial explosion." Over the vehement objections of southern legislators, Congress approved a final draft bill that included the phrase for which black leaders had pushed hardest: "There shall be no discrimination against any person on account of race or color." It was a hollow victory, however, because the new law included two convenient clauses that allowed the War Department to sidestep the nondiscrimination order. The first provision set forth that draftees must meet an unspecified "physical and mental" standard. The second was more practical, allowing the army time to build sufficient "shelter, sanitary facilities, water supplies, heating and lighting arrangements, medical care, and hospital accommodations, for such men." In other words, sufficient time to exclude "such men," meaning Negroes, until a full-on Jim Crow system of segregated facilities was up and running. African Americans rushed to recruitment centers, only to be told there was no place for them. By the end of 1940, the draft had added only 539 black soldiers to the army.

Even in this climate, the army was the most hospitable branch of the service to the black soldier. The clubby and much smaller Marine Corps resisted all pressure to diversify, though a dozen black marines had served in the Revolutionary War. Marine commandant Maj. Gen. Thomas Holcomb would speak out over the next two years against the "absolutely tragic" idea of black enlistment. "If it were a question of having a Marine Corps of 5,000 whites or 250,000 Negroes, I would rather have the whites," he told the Navy Board in early 1942.

It was only marginally better in the navy, which allowed black men to work only as servants. Fifteen black mess men paid dearly after writing a letter to the *Pittsburgh Courier*, a widely read black newspaper with a national circulation, urging other black men to avoid the navy unless they intended to work as "seagoing bellhops, chambermaids and dishwashers." For their audacity, the men were thrown in the brig, put on trial, and kicked out of the service with dishonorable discharges.

Allowed to serve on the ground and on the seas as laborers and domestics, Negroes were barred from another realm: the skies. When America went to war, black pilots were not welcome in the Army Air Corps, the forerunner to the air force. It was a particularly sore spot for African Americans who wanted a piece of the glamorous world of aviation, made popular by swashbucklers such as Charles Lindbergh, the first man to survive a transatlantic flight in 1927. Captain Midnight and other fictional fliers dominated radio shows and comic books. Besides Bullard, the black expat airman in France, there were a number of pioneering black pilots at home, including Albert E. Forsyth, a doctor who made several long-distance flights in the early 1930s. Two black pilots tried in dramatic fashion to make the case for Negro airmen. Chauncey Spencer and Dale White climbed into a creaky old biplane on May 9, 1939, and took off from Auburn, Illinois, for Washington, DC. Forced to land in a farmer's field, they repaired a broken crankshaft and took off again, landing in Morgantown, West Virginia, where the airport manager ordered the black men to be gone before dark. Forced back in the air without a radio or proper lights, they made a dangerous landing as night fell in Pittsburgh, breaking regulations by tailing another plane onto the runway. They eventually made it to Washington, winning the admiration of legislators, including a Missouri senator named Harry S. Truman. For their efforts, Spencer and White captured the hearts of black America—but not a place in flight school.

The belief that black men lacked the aptitude and the agility to fly planes—and, for that matter, to operate any sort of complicated machinery—persisted in army documentation. A 1942 army report that deemed the segregation policy a success also found that an "apparent lack of inherent natural mechanical adaptability" meant that Negroes were best suited for nontechnical and labor units. Yet years of lobbying to create a Negro air corps, by black leaders, some white liberal Democrats in Congress, and, most important, Eleanor Roosevelt, had begun to pay off (although southern conservatives tried to squelch the effort by accusing the First Lady of having promiscuous sex with black men). The first cadets began training in early 1941 at the segregated Tuskegee Army Airfield in Alabama. Unlike white squadrons led by experienced airmen, the pioneering Ninety-Ninth Pursuit Squadron was led by a novice pilot. Black cadets missed out on a key opportunity to learn important skills from seasoned flyers. The Army Air Corps, meanwhile, made no guarantees that it would accept Negro pilots once they graduated. The individual squadrons that would later come to be known as the Tuskegee Airmen would eventually collect accolades for their bravery and performance in combat. Yet they were never able to shake the feeling that each time they took to the air, they were on trial. Seven decades after the war, Roscoe Brown, one of those celebrated pilots, marveled at a system that was "so silly and stupid, they would spend money to build a separate air base to keep blacks separate from whites."

HENRY STIMSON, THE NEW secretary of war, who adamantly opposed the entry of black airmen into the armed forces, had no intention of injecting any measure of equality into the draft. "I hope for heavens sakes [*sic*] they don't mix the white and colored troops together in the same units for then we shall certainly have trouble," he wrote in his diary.

Though he hailed from liberal-minded New York City, Stimson became one of the Roosevelt administration's most devoted followers of the southern creed of black inferiority. Southern politicians exerted unusually strong power over the War Department—and, by extension, the White House—controlling key panels such as the Senate Armed Services Committee. As a group, the southern delegation hailed from the more extreme pool of white supremacists, put forward by Democratic Party machines that controlled elections across the South. In this climate, the influence of more moderate white Dixie Democrats was vastly diminished. Black southern voters were shut out of the process entirely through the imposition of poll taxes they could not pay or literacy tests they could not pass. Some states outright banned black voters from primaries, and others sent armed men to polling stations to deliver a frightening message to any African Americans who had the temerity to attempt to cast a ballot. The winners of those elections rose through the ranks in Washington, creating a fearsome southern bloc that presidents such as Roosevelt were loath to cross.

In the 1940s, seniority rules allowed the South, with only 28 percent of the nation's population, to control up to 60 percent of House and Senate chairmanships, including the key posts that oversaw the military. In one example of the power of the southern legislator, plans were scrapped to distribute to soldiers *The Races of Mankind*, a pamphlet written by two respected Columbia University anthropologists that made the case for equal rights and disproved a scientific basis for racial differences. Rep. Andrew J. May of Kentucky, chairman of the House Military Affairs Committee, threatened to cut funds to the War Department if soldiers were exposed to the booklet. All copies were burned.

Stimson, a patrician son of the Ivy League, made no bones about how he viewed the black soldier and the pressure to increase his role in the revamped military. The seventy-three-year-old wealthy Republican was particularly opposed to advancing and promoting black officers, writing in his diary, "I saw the same thing 23 years ago when [President] Woodrow Wilson yielded to the same sort of demand and appointed colored officers to several of the Divisions that went over to France, and the poor fellows made perfect fools of themselves and at least one of the Divisions behaved very badly." It turns out that Stimson saw no such thing in the Great War. He had served only a short time in France, and with an all-white unit. He never fought alongside black troops, certainly not with the Ninety-Second Infantry Division—the Buffalo Soldiers—the "fellows" to whom he referred in his diary. The purported failures of the Ninety-Second Division were used by war planners to justify the discriminatory policies evolving in the run-up to the Second World War. In fact, the Ninety-Second had a mixed record in France, with twenty-one men receiving the Distinguished Service Cross, which like all high decorations was rarely awarded to black soldiers. The poor performance attributed to some elements of the Ninety-Second is widely accepted by historians to have been the result of shoddy leadership by white southern officers, scapegoating, and poor training.

How bad was the training? Army policy, stunningly, called for the forty-two thousand black combat troops to train *as little as possible with weapons* before heading overseas. In some cases, men were put on the front lines after only a few hours of training. Many soldiers didn't even know how to dig a trench. They were given the worst equipment, and their white officers, many of them ejected from white units, were usually hostile southerners deemed the best-suited to "handle" Negroes, which is how army commanders often put it. The commander of the Ninety-Second blamed black troops for ruining his career. His negative reviews of the black men he led, along with those of other white officers, were cited in the 1925 War College study and were instrumental in shaping army policy.

Many contrary voices were lost in the din, among them a colonel who was with the Ninety-Second in France and later commanded black soldiers in Cuba and the Philippines. Col. Vernon A. Caldwell told the Army War College that the practice of segregating units in France "has not been wise" and advised following the French example and mixing black and white troops in the same units. In a future war, he said, Negroes will be "an important military asset." Also lost to time and indifference were the positive reviews accorded to units of the Ninety-Third Division under French command, notably the Harlem Hellfighters.

One overseas commander chided the War Department later in the war for wasting an opportunity to use its "vast reservoir" of black troops. "There is not one iota of doubt in my mind that you people in Washington are building a mountain out of a molehill when you speak of 'The Negro Problem in the army,'" he wrote. "My God, these men are human and only waiting to be led. They are actually eager to do what is right."

SHORTLY AFTER ROOSEVELT SIGNED the draft into law on September 16, 1940, a trio of black leaders took their plea for an integrated military directly to the White House. Black organizations pressing for racial justice had been steadily gaining influence in Washington, led by the NAACP. Since its founding in 1909, the NAACP had become a significant voice in national politics, with membership reaching fifty thousand by 1940. By the war's end, it would be ten times higher.

The provisions in the draft law made it far too easy for the War Department once again to build a fully segregated military. Alarmed by the shape of the new law, the NAACP's Walter White appealed directly to Eleanor Roosevelt to arrange a meeting with her husband. The First Lady was a faithful friend of black causes and exerted considerable influence with her husband—he liked to say that he couldn't control her—though she had failed to persuade him to support federal anti-lynching legislation that the NAACP desperately wanted. In the coming years, Mrs. Roosevelt would prove to be an instrumental force behind the gains that black soldiers and civilians were to make.

As concerned as he was about the evolving segregation policy, White was unaware of the extent of the circumscribed role the army envisioned for the black soldier. A secret 1937 manpower plan still in place called for more Negro inductees than in the First World War, but they were to be funneled only to certain branches that performed support roles, such as dump truck companies and port battalions. Gone was an earlier provision that had called for dozens of separate Negro units to be attached to white troops in the infantry, cavalry, and field artillery.

The First Lady arranged a meeting at the White House on September 27 with her husband; Walter White; T. Arnold Hill, former leader of the National Urban League; and the black union leader A. Philip Randolph. Navy secretary Frank Knox was there, but war secretary Stimson was not; he sent a deputy in his place. Hill had written up a list of demands to present to the president. The top item was the "immediate and total abolition in the armed services of segregation based on race or color." Other points called for the inclusion of black recruits in all branches of the service, the assignment of army officers regardless of race, the commissioning of black professionals as officers on the same terms as white civilians, and the appointment of black members to draft boards.

Roosevelt had a folksy way of making his visitors believe that he was on their side, and the black leaders left the meeting hopeful. They were roundly disappointed two weeks later when the White House dropped a bomb: Rather than encouraging more contact between the races, the new War Department policy would ban the mixing of "colored and white enlisted personnel" in the same units. White officers would command black troops, except in the case of the four existing Negro regiments, which could retain their black officers. To make matters worse, Roosevelt's press secretary Stephen Early, a southerner who resented the black leaders' demands and the First Lady's interference, later issued a statement that made it seem as if White, Hill, and Randolph had agreed to the plan.

Stimson, Knox, and their many allies had won. Gen. George C. Marshall, the army chief of staff, summed up the prevailing thinking when he said that "vexing racial problems" had no place in war planning. "Experiments within the army in the solution of social problems," he wrote, "are fraught with danger to efficiency, discipline and morale." The blow rippled across black America, which had set high hopes that a measure of equality would accompany the coming war, which was being fought, after all, in the name of democracy and freedom. Yet those ideals as they concerned African Americans would have to wait, just as they had in previous wars. "White House Blesses Jim Crow," blared a headline in *The Crisis*. It was a crushing loss, but it soon became clear that the men in Washington had gone too far. If Roosevelt planned to win an unprecedented third term, he was going to need the votes of black folks.

Since the early 1900s, African Americans had fled the rural South each year by the tens of thousands. By 1940, more than two million black migrants had settled in the North, a number that would double in the coming decade. Whole families, with grandparents and children, piled onto segregated train cars with as many possessions as they could carry, heading to faraway places. Many, fearing reprisals from their employers, fled under the cover of night. These newly empowered and enthusiastic voters, many casting ballots for the first time, found themselves in the unusual position of being courted by both presidential candidates.

Republican challenger Wendell Willkie took full advantage of Roosevelt's betrayal of the black soldier, blasting the president at every turn. Willkie was an unusual nominee: a straight-talking farm boy turned wealthy lawyer-businessman who had never held public office. He was a Democrat until he sought the nomination and fashioned himself as the true civil rights candidate, promising voters of color an administration free of discrimination. His egalitarian rhetoric attracted a number of heavyweight supporters, among them the boxing champ Joe Louis. Some influential black newspapers endorsed him as well, though most stayed loyal to Roosevelt. After Emancipation, black America had traditionally stuck with the party of Abraham Lincoln, but Democrats gained ground as African Americans moved north. Roosevelt's promises to expand opportunities in post-Depression America attracted black votes that helped win him the White House in 1933. The New Deal programs that followed helped solidify that support among grateful African Americans.

In 1940 the candidates offered voters a contrast in styles. At age fifty-eight, the graying Roosevelt seemed older than his years, grandfatherly and wise, his speeches a combination of charm and wit. Felled by polio, FDR forced himself to walk in public with painful heavy steel braces. Willkie, a decade younger than his rival, had a hulking frame that supported a watermelon-size head dotted with laser-like blue eyes and a mop of dark hair. Reporters called him a "shaggy bear." Each had a personal style that endeared him to his supporters and impressed opponents.

The president, aware of the anger the draft law had stoked among African Americans, sought to make amends with a series of blatantly political moves. Days before the election, he announced that more black recruits would be admitted to all branches of the service, though their units would remain segregated. He promoted Col. Benjamin O. Davis Sr. to become, at age sixty-two, the nation's first black general, and he named William H. Hastie, the first black federal judge, to head the newly created Office of the Civilian Aide to the Secretary of War. Hastie was charged with managing "the equitable and orderly integration of Negroes into the army," though his office had little real power to follow through with that mission. His boss, Secretary Stimson, fumed in his diary that "the Negroes are taking advantage of this period just before the election to try to get everything they can."

Polls showed the race too close to call, but in the end, Roosevelt became the first president elected to a third term. He took thirty-eight states and 54.7 percent of the popular vote to Willkie's 44.8 percent. Among Roosevelt's most steadfast supporters were working people, immigrants, and black voters. As the country moved closer to war, the messy business of building an army hobbled by segregation, racial quotas, and inherent injustices began to take shape. It was, in the end, an army thoroughly infused with Jim Crow.

CHAPTER 3

"This Is a White Man's Country"

The nation cannot expect the colored people to feel that the U.S. is worth defending if they continue to be treated as they are being treated now.

—First Lady Eleanor Roosevelt, January 1942
Richmond, Virginia
December 1942

The telegram came when he was at work. Its single page ordered Henry Parham to report for induction on December 23, 1942, into the United States Army. It was a day Parham had known was coming ever since he signed up for the draft nearly two years earlier, as he was required to do by law. Though many men were eager to fight for their country, others were not. For them, the enticements of military service—a call to duty, a steady paycheck, a chance to see places far from home—did little to outweigh the risks. For the African Americans among them, the choice was even less appealing. Army life promised racism, discrimination, and segregation, sometimes worse than back home. Those young men committed to serving their country had already volunteered at the recruiting office before they were drafted. Parham hadn't been one of them.

His reluctance to serve wasn't rooted in the difficulties of a Jim Crow army or a lack of patriotism. His reasons were more practical. His job as a porter at the bus station in downtown Richmond,

Virginia, paid him a sum that provided, for the first time in his twenty-one years, a dose of security. His people skills accorded him a dose of respect. There were other perks, too, like the twenty-five-cent tips that paid for a meal, and a pass to ride a National Trailways bus anywhere he wanted to go. Parham traveled to New York City sometimes to see his older brother, Leander. But usually he didn't go far, taking the sixty-mile trip from Richmond back home to the family farm in sleepy Greensville County.

Henry Parham liked to say that he was born in a place so small that it didn't have a name. His family's land was near Jarratt, a speck on the Virginia map slightly larger than one square mile. When Henry was born in November 1921, the area was dominated by sharecrop farms. Most of the land was owned by whites, who rented out plots to black farmers whose descendants had tilled those same fields and picked the same cotton since the days of slavery. Even when Emancipation came, many African Americans stayed, be it for a lack of options, money, courage, or all three. Across the South, sharecropping was a way of life, a close cousin to enslavement that often left already poor black families so deep in debt that there was little hope of their ever emerging.

When the Civil War broke out in April 1861, Virginia was home to more slaves than any other state in the Confederacy. Although 60 percent of the state's enslaved men fled to fight for the Union Army, a half million African Americans were working on plantations when the war ended four years later. Gen. William Tecumseh Sherman raised hopes that grants of land would offer a fresh start when he doled out forty acres each to a number of former slaves (plus the odd mule from army stocks). After Abraham Lincoln's assassination, however, new president Andrew Johnson crushed those expectations when he ordered all land under federal control in southern states returned to the prewar owners. Left with no land and no compensation, illiterate African Americans whose only skill was picking cotton or curing tobacco were left with little choice but to submit to the system put in place by the new Freedmen's

Bureau: sign work contracts with their former masters or face eviction from their homes. Sharecropping was born.

In vast swaths of the rural South, little changed for decades from the post-slavery days, when Jim Crow laws took root and flourished across the South. A new slavery emerged. Despite the name, there was often little "sharing" of the crop. Black farmers weren't allowed to sell their own yield, and thus had no leverage with white planters who, at the end of each harvest, calculated what they owed their serfs—or more likely what was owed to *them*. Money rarely changed hands. It was a life of subsistence or worse. Sharecroppers with no shoes warmed their feet in the urine of the mule pulling the plow ahead of them. Floggings, rapes, and other routine violence still went unpunished, just as they had during slavery. A British journalist who toured an Arkansas cotton plantation in 1934 described the "nightmare" life of the black sharecroppers there, who were "treated worse than animals, worse than farming implements . . . They are dressed in rags, they have barely enough food to keep them alive; their children get no education." Schooling of black children, illegal under slavery, was supposed to be provided on a "separate but equal" basis. In fact, education was highly optional. With few rural schools to opt into, and with the planting season requiring all available hands, illiteracy was widespread.

In Virginia, sharecropping was most prevalent where the most important crops were grown: cotton, peanuts, and tobacco. Greensville County planted all three, with tobacco more prolific in the northern end, where tiny Jarratt straddled the border with Sussex County. It is unknown whether the slaves of Greensville County had a life that was typical of or gentler than the norm. Records show that twenty-three of them were granted their freedom between 1790 and 1825, out of the presumably hundreds of slaves there. One extraordinary man born a slave in 1834 was elected to the Virginia House of Delegates forty-five years later. Henry D. Smith was among about one hundred black men who served in the state legislature after Congress ordered the former Confederate states to allow Negroes the right to vote and hold office. (The rise of Jim Crow laws ended this practice by 1890; Virginia wouldn't see another black legislator until 1968.)

Henry Smith bought the 965-acre Merry Oaks plantation near Jarratt, where he had worked as a slave, from his former owner. How he managed to accomplish such a feat is not recorded, though the self-educated ex-slave was certainly clever. He also ran a brandy and whiskey distillery and married three times, fathering at least seventeen children. He was no doubt well known around Greensville County. One man certain to have made his acquaintance was an African American named Benjamin Wells, who would go on to own his 154-acre farm and become patriarch to a sprawling family whose many offshoots included the future soldier Henry Parham. The stories of Smith and Wells are emblematic of how some poor yet enterprising sharecroppers turned the miserable hand they were dealt into relative prosperity.

Wells was born in Greensville County around 1888 and, as a young man, married Emma Jane Parham, Henry's cousin. Their children came along every two years or thereabouts until there were eleven. Wells fathered other babies on the side—his philandering tolerated by his stoic wife. Wells was a sharecropper, but struck a deal with the white man who owned his land, the details of which his children never knew. What they did know was that the white man instructed Wells to keep careful records concerning his farm. This was done with precision in a book maintained by the seventh Wells child, Claresa, who logged every transaction down to the purchase of a bar of soap. The arrangement was unusual, because landlords typically controlled all the record keeping, which made it easier for them to cheat their tenants at the end of the season. Wells apparently made regular payments to the owner, so that by 1946, when Elizabeth, the eighth child, was married at age sixteen, the farm was paid off and Wells was the sole owner.

There were smaller farms owned by men named Parham, and it was around these plots of land that the lives of Henry and his many cousins orbited. Henry's unmarried mother, Susie Parham, came from a family of sixteen. When Henry was young, Susie placed him and his older sister Mary in the care of her sister Lucy, and left in search of better-paying work as a maid in the homes of white people. Lucy and her husband, Johnny Grezy, took care of young Henry as if he were their own son. Susie's niece Emma Jane Parham Wells tended to young Henry and the other cousins who trooped in and out of her busy wood-frame house. There were other uncles, aunts, and older cousins to watch over him, too, so many that Henry never missed having a father. "I consider myself fortunate," he said in 2010. "I had someone to love me."

If any Greensville County families had electricity and running water in the 1920s, Henry never knew them. People lit kerosene lamps, and water came by means of daily walks to the well. Each morning, Emma Jane balanced a stone butter churn atop her head that she used as a bucket. With two more aluminum buckets dangling from each arm, she led her daughters like ducklings, each weighed down with her own bucket, on the quarter-mile walk to the family well and back. "My mama walked straight as an arrow. She would kneel down, and we'd take that churn off her head. It was heavy," Elizabeth recalled eight decades later. In the winter, when the pump to the well froze, the women would build a fire and heat some water to get it working again.

The farm kept everyone well fed. Eggs came in vast quantities, and every so often were taken by a mule-drawn wagon to Emporia, the county seat a good ten miles away. There they were traded for necessities the family could not make, such as soap powder. There was no idle time on the farm. Games of hide-and-seek and jump rope were rare treats. Even the little ones worked from early morning to dusk, with an hour off twice a day for meals. By day the children tended the fields of peanuts, cotton, soybeans, tobacco, and sugarcane, plus a kitchen garden that grew vegetables. By moonlight they fed the pigs, cows, chickens, and mules. One of the mules powered a churn that pressed sugarcane, which Benjamin Wells cooked into a thick molasses and stored in a barrel with a spigot that the neighbors tapped. The sweet scent of Emma Jane's molasses biscuits wafting through the rows of cotton was enough to drive the kids mad. Meat came in the form of rabbit and squirrel, which Henry, his cousins, and the faithful hound they raised from a pup hunted in the woods. Thanks to those outings with his twelve-gauge shotgun, the future Private Parham would ace the rifle range in his army training, hitting ninety-two shots out of one hundred. Though his family was poor, the food was plentiful and delicious, the adults vigilant, and the children happy.

School days revolved around the planting season, beginning after the harvest in October or November and ending when it came time to plant in April. The Parham and Wells children walked two and a half miles along dirt roads, muddy in the winter, each way to the Merry Oaks School. "We had to do that in rain, snow, and sleet," Elizabeth said. Although blacks outnumbered whites in Greensville County, there was no bus provided to the Negro schools, a hardship not limited to rural Virginia. In Atlantic City, New Jersey, the driver of the white school bus often stopped to let Wilson Monk hop a ride to his school. Henry Parham and his cousins had no such offer. Winters seemed to go on forever, and school shared a sordid association with cold and hardship. "I cried every morning. My fingers were so cold," Henry said, clenching his fingers into fists at the memory.

The Merry Oaks School likely took its name from the old plantation bought by the ex-slave Henry Smith. Grades one through seven shared three rooms heated by a single struggling stove that managed to warm the place just as the school day was ending. As limited as their education was, Henry and Elizabeth were the fortunate ones. Many rural enclaves had no schools for black children, and those that did often crammed dozens of children into a single decrepit room with no desks or chairs. Although states that maintained separate schools were legally bound to ensure they be on par with white schools, the law was never enforced. A hero came in the person of Julius Rosenwald of Chicago, president of Sears, Roebuck and Company and one of the leading philanthropists of his time. Rosenwald believed there were similarities between the treatment of Jews in Germany, where his parents were born, and that of southern Negroes. In the early twentieth century, he forged an extraordinary partnership with the former slave and educator Booker T. Washington, who urged him to put his money toward building badly needed schools for black children. The styles varied, but many Rosenwald schools were small white clapboard structures with tall windows facing the sunniest direction.

The Rosenwald Fund was among the ten richest foundations in America, and was responsible for the building of 4,977 schools across the South between 1912 until its end in 1932, with the death of its founder. The money for each school came from three sources: Rosenwald, state governments, and local black families. It was important to Rosenwald that the community share in the creation of a school. Virginia was home to 364 Rosenwald schools, 13 of them in Greensville County. The Merry Oaks School, where the Parham and Wells children went, was almost certainly a Rosenwald school, though records use another name. The simple clapboard building had three rooms and three teachers, which was grand compared to another nearby Rosenwald beneficiary, the Orion School, in which sixty students shared one classroom. Henry enjoyed his studies, passing all his years until he reached the end, at grade seven. That was usually the point at which formal education finished for the children lucky enough to have made it that far. Many dropped out by the fourth grade, and illiteracy was not uncommon. High school—if there was a high school—charged fees their families couldn't pay and required transportation they couldn't provide. So, at age thirteen, Henry went to work on the farm.

When Henry was growing up, race relations in the South were a tricky combination of public separation and private accommodation. Personal relationships could be cordial, if not outright friendly. The man living next door to the patriarch Benjamin Wells was white, and for most of the time that they were neighbors, they got along fine. Black and white children often played together—some were best friends—though they never sat side by side in a classroom or in a church pew. When they got older, those ties frayed. They ate in separate restaurants, drank in separate bars, and watched movies on different floors of the cinema. If they were black, they learned to practice subservience and deference toward whites.

The year before the slave-turned-entrepreneur Henry Smith died in 1901, Virginia passed a law segregating streetcars, following a pattern as Jim Crow laws, also called Black Codes, swept across Dixie. What was once single was now double: two waiting rooms in public buildings, two ticket windows, two toilets and drinking fountains. Courthouse witnesses swore their oaths on separate Bibles. Etiquette laws varied, but typically required a Negro to show humility in the presence of a white person—move to the side on a public street, remove his hat, lower his eyes, and respond to questions with a "Yes, sir." Black women weren't spared the rule that required all Negroes to stand if their section on a bus was full, even if there were empty seats in the white section. Northern black recruits heading to southern army camps by train burned with rage when they were told, somewhere around Washington, DC, to move to the Negro car, always hard by the filthy coal engine. Jim Crow evolved with the times, eventually separating taxis and airport waiting rooms (though not airplanes; the skies remained integrated).

As in slavery days, the reasons given for the need to subjugate African Americans often revolved around the divine. The *Richmond Times* insisted in 1900 that "every relation of Southern life" be segregated on the ground that "God Almighty himself drew the color line and it cannot be obliterated." Four decades later, the Swedish sociologist Gunnar Myrdal wrote that "segregation was becoming so complete that the white Southerner practically never sees a Negro except as his servant" or in other "caste situations." It is one of the strange ironies of southern history that during the brutal days of slavery, when blacks were the lifeblood of the economy, there was far more contact between the races and less of the sort of unfocused white rage directed at African Americans that would skyrocket during the Jim Crow years. At the turn of the century, writes journalist and historian Isabel Wilkerson, "it appeared that young whites, weaned on a formal kind of supremacy, had grown more hostile to blacks than even their slaveholding ancestors had been."

Following the Civil War, Congress insisted on the rule of law in the conquered South, and African Americans enjoyed the fleeting right to vote, work, and live in relative safety. With the end of Reconstruction and the withdrawal of federal troops, however, newly empowered southern states promptly began reestablishing white supremacy. As hard-line southern Democrats supporting racial apartheid won elections by suppressing black voters, Mississippi governor Adelbert Ames remarked that "a revolution has taken place . . . they are to be returned to a condition of serfdom. An era of second slavery." Historian C. Vann Woodward calls this a time of "cracker fanaticism," referring to the influence of lower-class whites on the new social order. By 1900, Jim Crow laws were firmly in place across the South and mob violence became a semiofficial institution aimed at keeping blacks in their place. Such was the mood that William C. Oates, the former Alabama governor, observed in 1901: "When the Negro is doing no harm, why, the people want to kill him and wipe him from the face of the earth."

Nearly four thousand African Americans were lynched in the United States between 1877 and 1950. Most of the victims were not accused of any crime before they were sentenced to mob justice for offenses usually of a dubious nature, such as "seeking employment in a restaurant," "using offensive language," and "trying to act like a white man." Mobs often tortured their prey and mutilated the body. It was enough to earn the country the moniker the "United States of Lyncherdom," as coined in an unpublished 1901 essay by Mark Twain. Although vigilante violence was a part of America from the founding, and frontier justice was a staple of the "Wild West," by the turn of the twentieth century lynching had become an "integral part of southern culture," writes historian W. Fitzhugh Brundage, with few white victims. Mob violence toward blacks varied greatly across the South. Georgia was the lynching capital, with 586 killings by 1950. Virginia saw the fewest, with 76 dead. Most black southerners knew a lynching victim or had heard of one. Mobs sometimes terrorized entire communities, forcing blacks to watch lynchings and then ordering them to leave town.

Greensville County's only recorded mob killings made nationwide headlines because one of the two victims was white. On March 24, 1900, a convicted murderer named Walter Cotton was strung up at noon on Courthouse Square; his body was then riddled with bullets. A grainy photo reprinted in a Virginia magazine a century later shows what may be Cotton's body hanging from a tree, surrounded by a crowd. Cotton had escaped from jail and, while on the lam, carried out a crime spree with a white man from Boston named Dave O'Grady. What happened next is disputed. O'Grady was hung either "by the colored people of the town" or by a mixed crowd. In any case, the executions "aroused the entire county," with "the whites talking of proceeding to Greensville and dealing with the Negroes according to the rules of the South," the *New York Times* reported.

RACIAL VIOLENCE IN PART fueled black flight out of the rural South. While African Americans flooded northern cities, southern cities such as Richmond also saw an influx of black migrants. By the early 1940s, Richmond was booming. There were jobs aplenty, and a steady flow of workers from the countryside looking to earn a better wage. The air was perfumed by the sweet smell of tobacco, which stuffed the city's warehouses and fueled Richmond's rebound during the Great Depression. The outbreak of war in Europe prompted a rocketing demand for, among other things, smokes. Much to Richmond's benefit, the federal government bought most of the 1939 tobacco crop to sell to Britain on credit.

The city attracted businesses from other parts of the country, happy to relocate to a state with right-to-work laws, which restricted the ability of labor unions to organize workers. At the time, unions were spoken of in the same derisive breath as Communists. The majority of the city's cigarette makers were black women, who resisted with suspicion the best efforts of male-dominated trade unions to enlist them. By late 1941, other elements of the wartime buildup were feeding the economy. More than 350 million pounds of war supplies would be shipped through the city over the next few years, thanks in part to the new, modern Deepwater Terminal at the Port of Richmond. The cavernous theater known as the Mosque became the War Department's Anti-Aircraft Command headquarters in April 1942, directing most domestic antiaircraft operations and the newest addition to the army's defensive arsenal: barrage balloons. Military convoys clogged the main north–south arteries. On weekends, the downtown streets teemed with tens of thousands of servicemen, and a thriving industry popped up dedicated to sheltering, feeding, and entertaining them. Jim Crow expanded, too. Of the city's three armories, two were turned over for the use of white troops, with the third designated for Negroes.

Segregation reigned on jam-packed streetcars and buses—more crowded than ever with gas rationing and, later, a ban on pleasure driving. Black passengers had to push their way to their section in the rear through a "mass of tired, sweating, and irritable white people standing in the aisle," writes local historian Walter S. Griggs Jr. Northern black soldiers offended by Jim Crow deliberately took front seats, a move that annoyed authorities who refused to ease the seating rules, even during wartime. One time, an African American soldier weary from a long train ride was turned away from a whites-only USO lounge. One observer wrote that the black man, with tears in his eyes, remarked, "This is what I get for being a soldier."

After years of moving around in search of decent work, Henry Parham's mother, Susie, settled in Jackson Ward, a thriving African American neighborhood in the heart of Richmond lined with black-owned shops, restaurants, and nightclubs. Jackson Ward counted as one of its own an extraordinary black businesswoman, Maggie Lena Walker. Like Sarah Spencer Washington in Atlantic City and the beauty entrepreneur C. J. Walker in Harlem, Maggie Walker was a trailblazer, the first American woman of any race to open a bank, an inconceivable feat in 1903. St. Luke Penny Savings Bank allowed those in the emerging black middle class to buy their own homes for the first time, since white banks wouldn't lend to them. (It was a practice that would continue in America for decades.) Walker, the daughter of a slave and a white abolitionist, also founded a newspaper, and a department store that charged lower prices than the white stores. Walker's twenty-eight-room brick town house on East Leigh Street was a short walk from the apartment that Susie Parham shared with her sister Lucy, daughter Mary, and eventually her younger son, Henry.

The four Parhams lived in two rooms on the second floor of a tidy beige brick row house. There was no kitchen, but there was no need for one. Long workdays meant the family never sat down to dinner together. The women took their meals at the homes where they worked as maids. Henry was busy with a string of jobs. He was a janitor before he landed the porter job at the National Trailways bus station downtown at North Ninth and East Broad Streets. Richmond was a junction point for troops coming from Norfolk and other points north and south, and the bus station was a busy place. The job required nineteen-year-old Henry to develop skills he had never needed in Greensville County. He was a fast learner. He became a master schmoozer popular with the white bus drivers. His constant smile and gregarious nature were appreciated by the steady flow of passengers coming and going. Tips were an important supplement to his seventeen-dollar weekly salary. On a good day, he could count on ten to twenty-five cents for each bag he handled, plus some coins tossed his way from the white cab drivers to whom he steered new arrivals. He even counted a few of those white drivers among his friends. His best customer was a regular who passed through each week, pressing thirty-five cents in Henry's palm. That was enough to buy a breakfast of eggs, bacon, and coffee. "I knew how to deal with people," Henry recalled. "That's how I made my money."

When it was the capital of the Confederate States of America, Richmond was an important slave-trading center and an early enforcer of laws regulating racial apartheid. One ordinance specified that slaves and freedmen who crossed a white person "shall pass on the outside; and if necessary to enable such a white person to pass, shall immediately get off the sidewalk." Later, Richmond invented a novel method of segregating its neighborhoods block by block, based on whether prospective residents were allowed to marry their neighbors. If they were "forbidden to intermarry" with the people already living there, they had to look elsewhere for a home. (Laws barring intermarriage also existed in the North.) If Henry Parham, who had never known another way of life, was bothered by Jim Crow, he never let it show. "You learn to deal with that," he said. "I always knew how to treat people, and I was highly respected."

On November 15, 1942, Henry turned twenty-one. One month later, Uncle Sam came calling. "They got me," he said, as he read the telegram from the draft board, signed by the president. Henry's feelings had evolved since he had reluctantly registered for the Selective Service. America was now at war, and newspapers carried headlines about far-off battles. American and British troops were fighting Germany for control of North Africa. The Russians were desperately trying to stop the Axis advance at Stalingrad. That six-month battle, which would turn the tide against Germany in the East, came at a huge price: one million Russian soldiers killed and ninety thousand German troops dead from starvation. The suffering of the Jews of Europe drew sympathy from African Americans and, much to the annoyance of the Roosevelt administration, led to comparisons between Nazi Germany and Jim Crow America. Civil rights activist Roy Wilkins wrote in his autobiography, *Standing Fast*, that "Negroes did not need us at the NAACP to tell them that it sounded pretty foolish to be against park benches marked JUDE in Berlin, but to be *for* park benches marked COLORED in Tallahassee, Florida."

Black America had another reason to cheer the war: the nation's first hero was a black navy mess man named Doris "Dorie" Miller. Miller was collecting dirty laundry aboard the USS *West Virginia* in Pearl Harbor on December 7, 1941, when the first wave of Japanese bombers struck the heart of America's Pacific fleet in Hawaii. When his ship was hit, Miller rushed to the bridge and helped pull the mortally wounded captain to safety. Then he jumped behind an antiaircraft gun and didn't stop firing until he ran out of ammo. "As he did so, his usually impassive face bore the deadly smile of a berserk Viking," writes historian Gordon W. Prange. Reports say Miller hit between two and four planes. Miller, shy and modest, said he thought he took out one. Still, this son of a Texas sharecropper, who had never been taught to use the big guns—navy regulations forbade artillery training for blacks— was "blazing away as though he had fired one all his life," an officer said later. Initially, Miller's heroics were credited only to "an unidentified Negro messman." The navy apparently preferred that the title of first hero go to Capt. Colin Kelly, a white bomber pilot who died in battle three days after the Japanese attack.

By the time the navy released Miller's name three months later, under pressure from the black press and the NAACP, a campaign was already under way to award the unassuming Miller, whose rank was cook third class, the Medal of Honor. Miller received the Navy Cross, the third-highest award at that time, much to the displeasure of navy secretary Frank Knox, who had fought Roosevelt's wishes to open up the navy to black sailors. Despite the obvious fact that Miller was an awfully good shot, he remained a mess man, which is what he was on Thanksgiving Day 1943 when his ship, the USS *Liscome Bay*, was torpedoed. He was among 644 men killed. But Miller achieved something the president himself had failed to do. Thanks to Miller, Knox and the Navy Board finally succumbed to pressure to allow black recruits to train as gunners, ammunition handlers, and radio operators, just like white men—that is, as long as the Negro units remained separate.

Pearl Harbor changed everything. When the country went to war, it was with the support of America, white and black. "This nation has sinned . . . but it has not sinned as Germany has sinned." Those words, written by W. E. B. Du Bois in 1918, were even more relevant in December 1941. Du Bois and other black leaders had believed strongly that a valiant wartime effort by Negroes in the Great War would result in a better future for the entire race. Those hopes were dashed in the cruelest fashion when African Americans were subjected to a torrent of postwar hatred and violence. Still, as the country entered the Second World War, African Americans saw an opportunity to serve their country and, through loyal service, advance the cause of civil rights. They could have borrowed Du Bois's 1918 rallying cry, "*First* your Country, *then* your Rights!" This was not to say that the contradictions of fighting for freedom no longer rankled in a nation where, as Henry Parham observed, "we weren't being recognized as one hundred percent citizens."

The African American poet Langston Hughes supported the war, even as he relentlessly railed against racism and segregation in writings such as this one titled "NAACP":

> *I'm a cook or dishwasher in the Navy.*
> *In the Marines I can't be either.*
> *The Army still segregates me—*
> *And we ain't run by Hitler neither!*
> *The Jim Crow car's still dirty.*
> *The color line's still drawn.*
> *Yet up there in Washington*
> *They're blowing freedom's horn!*

African Americans began flashing a variation on the omnipresent "V for Victory" sign in early 1942. Their version formed a *V* with each hand, "the first V for victory over our enemies from without, the second V for victory over our enemies from within," wrote cafeteria worker James G. Thompson in an eloquent letter to the *Pittsburgh Courier*. Criticized as unpatriotic, the Double V campaign highlighted the festering issues on the home front for black America even as attention moved abroad.

By the time his draft notice arrived, Henry Parham had come to see military service as an important duty. "We had been attacked," he said years later. Not that there was a choice: "I went there or I went to jail." Henry left for the induction center at the Blues Armory on December 23, 1942, telling his mother that he wasn't coming home for Christmas, even if they let him. No sense delaying the inevitable. It was time to get going, begin the next phase of his life. In Richmond, people worried that German submarines operating off Virginia Beach could steam up the James River and fire on the city. German airpower was a great unknown, and average Americans commiserated at lunch counters and on assembly lines that perhaps the Nazis had the capacity to send bombs raining down over here, as in Britain. With no air-raid sirens working yet, wailing police cars and fire trucks alerted the public to the first test blackout at 9:01 on the night of February 9, 1942. Richmonders congratulated themselves on an effort well done, but the army later concluded that enemy bombers "would have had little difficulty in picking their target." Flags began appearing in city windows with a blue star for each son sent off to war. Those stars would turn to gold when the news came that those sons would never come home.

Across the country, men of all races were flooding into induction centers. By the end of 1942, there were 4.5 million Army recruits, nearly 500,000 of them African American. During the Great War, southern draft boards had been notorious for their unfair treatment of black men, denying exemptions given to white men in similar circumstances.

Under pressure from black leaders to equalize the draft, President Roosevelt appointed a black assistant director of the Selective Service in 1940. Even so, similar charges of inequity plagued the system this time around, too. A Red Cross field director in Arizona reported that southern draft boards had "shown great prejudice" in enlisting black soldiers who should have been excluded for reasons ranging from medical issues to dependent families. Wartime racism was fraught with contradictions: the black soldier wasn't wanted in the first place, and then he was held to a higher standard than the white man. It was a pattern that would repeat itself in multiple venues throughout the war.

Conscription remained unequal right down to the composition of local draft boards. Fourteen states maintained all-white panels. When a group of black pastors appealed to Tennessee governor Prentice Cooper to appoint blacks to that state's board, he refused. "This is a white man's country," he said. "The Negro had nothing to do with the settling of America."

At the induction center, there was no question that Henry Parham would pass the medical exam. In robust health, he weighed a solid 179 pounds, and his proud stature made him appear taller than his five feet nine inches. Within hours, Henry and other draftees had boarded a train, arriving after midnight at Fort Meade, Maryland. There, he was chosen for a select outfit charged with a strange mission, the details of which he would learn later. On January 2 there was another train to board, this time headed south. Curtains were drawn on the windows: Dixie whites were known to shoot at train cars carrying Negro soldiers.

CHAPTER 4

Sentinels of the Sky

=====

There are no signs of barrage balloon equipment. . . . There is considerable opportunity left to take advantage for a surprise attack.

—Japanese spy Takeo Yoshikawa Pearl Harbor, December 6, 1941
Camp Tyson, Tennessee
December 1942

After more than a year of training, Wilson Monk was fit and strong, but no wiser about his army assignment when he boarded a train and left Fort Eustis, Virginia. Unlike his first trip south from his home in Atlantic City, this journey required no change to the Negro car at the Dixie border. He was already there, tolerating the fumes from the belching coal engine, the only place for a black man to sit, even one in uniform. Monk was the farthest south he had ever been, and his unease grew as the hours passed. Sharing his car were forty-five black recruits from Fort Eustis, their anxiety a palpable presence on the long journey, even as they buzzed about the adventure ahead. For most of them, barely out of their teens, it was their first time away from home.

They disembarked on September 21, 1942, in a peaceful corner of northwestern Tennessee, where green fields and forests had given way to a sprawling army base called Camp Tyson. There, they were met with a puzzling sight: oblong balloons bigger than buses floating high in the sky. Were they manned blimps? Moving closer, they saw no signs of a cockpit, only wires anchoring the balloons to the earth.

Camp Tyson was America's first base built for the purpose of training men to fly barrage balloons, the army's newest weapon. These unmanned gasbags, piloted by a team on the ground, were destined to hover in numbers over strategic sites, forming an aerial minefield deadly to enemy planes. The mission of the balloons would change over the coming months, but for now, the men would learn everything about these balloons and how they worked.

Their teachers had trained at Camp Davis, North Carolina, beginning in the spring of 1941, when the War Department organized the barrage balloon program. Henry County, Tennessee, was selected to be the new home of the balloon school for its remote location off air routes and its variable weather ideal for balloon training. One year before the Fort Eustis men arrived, construction had begun on a miniature two-thousand-acre city connected by five miles of railroad tracks and ten miles of roads. There were barracks for enlisted men and officers, kitchens, social clubs, a theater, a library, and a hospital. The $11.7 million price tag covered a plant to make hydrogen. An expansion in 1943 would more than triple the size of the camp.

It was easy to get lost there, amid the identical streets and 450 white buildings, a layout replicated more or less at dozens of army bases that had sprung up across the country over the past year. The unfortunate sterile look of the camps had even prompted First Lady Eleanor Roosevelt to suggest that a bit of paint might spruce things up.

The Fort Eustis men were among more than eight thousand soldiers, black and white, who would arrive over the coming months. The black soldiers found their new home comfortable enough, even as they moved into their segregated barracks and ate their first meals in their segregated mess hall. It would be an existence apart for the Negroes of Camp Tyson, just as it was for the half million African Americans in the army in December 1942. The vast majority of those troops were consigned to service and labor units, where they would drive the trucks, load the ships, and clean the latrines that kept the army running.

The Tyson men were fortunate to have been assigned there, as the army had made a significant investment in the barrage balloon program. They couldn't have known that skeptics within the War Department had questioned the wisdom of a defensive line in the sky. Perhaps with that opposition in mind, Tyson's commanding officer, Brig. Gen. John B. Maynard, implored new arrivals in a letter to remember their "distinctive honor and special responsibility. This is the only barrage balloon training center in the United States Army, and it is your task to achieve results that will light the way for those who follow us." Maynard's admonition could have added the words "and for your race." No matter, the Negro soldiers knew they were being tested.

"Every man thought it was an important job because it wasn't commonplace," Monk said seven decades later. "As big as the army was, it only had a few barrage balloon battalions. Everyone took his job seriously."

When America entered the war, barrage balloons were flying in Britain, Germany, Japan, and Russia. In the London area, hundreds of balloons floated above Big Ben, Tower Bridge, Parliament, and other key sites, trailing thin steel cables powerful enough to shear off a wing. At night, their sausage shapes were outlined by sweeping searchlights prowling the inky sky for German bombers as they popped through the clouds. If all went well, the antiaircraft guns that took aim from the ground knocked out the bombers before they could drop their lethal cargo.

The success of the balloons was measured not by how many planes they took out but by how many they kept away from a target. As a defensive barrier, a curtain of balloons flying in a staggered sawtooth pattern forced pilots higher, fouling the aim of their bombs. Flying higher also made those planes better targets for the big guns on the ground, which were not as effective at hitting targets at lower altitudes. To fool Nazi spotters, the balloons were sometimes lowered during the day. In an attack on the Battersea power station in London, two German

dive-bombers didn't see the gasbags until it was too late. After striking a nearly invisible cable, one Stuka, a twisted heap of metal, "disin-
tegrated in the air," *Scientific American* reported. The second bomber,
attempting to flee, hit another balloon on the way up. The magazine
breathlessly described what happened next:

> There was a rending, tearing sound as the plane went
> through the fabric, followed by a terrific explosion as the hy-
> drogen in the barrage balloon ignited. The airplane, ablaze,
> went spinning over and over toward the shambles below.
> The pilot could be seen by watchers, sitting in the cockpit,
> solid with flames, as he gave his life for his Führer.

A third bomber—there were twenty-four in all—slammed into a
cable and was "blown to pieces," *Scientific American* reported. It was no
surprise that Luftwaffe pilots loathed the balloons, fearing that their
already hazardous cables were electrified. British propaganda maintained the mystery, hinting that the balloons, dubbed the Sentinels of
the Sky, packed a secret punch. In fact, many of them did, and testing
was under way on a deadly booby trap to arm the American balloons.

BARRAGE BALLOONS CAME LATE to America, and the delay proved
costly. In early 1941, in the months before the United States declared
war on Germany, Japan, and Italy, the threat from Nazi planes along
the Atlantic coast was considered the primary threat facing America.
President Roosevelt and his War Department believed the Japanese
had neither the military might nor the nerve to cross the Pacific, especially with the U.S. Pacific fleet based in the middle of the ocean. The
"Japs wouldn't dare attack Hawaii," declared Gen. George C. Marshall,
the army chief of staff. Underestimating Japan was a grave mistake.

Another was the failure to raise barrage balloons in time to protect the fleet as tensions with Tokyo boiled over.

Japan began preparing for war against America in 1940, after Roosevelt cut off steel and oil exports in protest of the empire's conquest of French Indochina. Japan's expansionism and alliance with Nazi Germany were seen as threats to American interests in the Pacific. Roosevelt had warned against a move south into territory controlled by the defeated European powers, but Tokyo had ignored the warning. With 90 percent of its oil coming from the United States, Japan was desperate for other sources, and looked to the oil-rich Dutch East Indies (today's Indonesia) as a solution.

To get there, Japan needed to hit America hard, before its primary adversary was rearmed for war. A bold sneak attack was planned to sink the U.S. Pacific fleet where it lived, in a curved harbor on the south side of Oahu. The hills overlooking Honolulu offered a prime view of comings and goings at Pearl Harbor, and it was from these heights that a diligent Japanese spy named Takeo Yoshikawa set to work in the spring of 1941, sending messages back to Tokyo.

Yoshikawa's bosses were particularly interested in barrage balloons. Five days before the attack, Tokyo demanded daily reports about the ships moored in the harbor and the defenses in place to protect them. Japan wanted to know if there were balloons aloft or "if there are any indications that they will be sent up." On December 6, Yoshikawa sent a final message home: "There are no signs of barrage balloon equipment. . . . There is considerable opportunity left to take advantage for a surprise attack."

The Americans, who had broken the Japanese code, intercepted these messages, but did not translate them until it was far too late. So it happened that early on a sleepy Sunday morning, the first wave of Japanese planes struck. When the attack was over, half of the American fleet was in flames, 2,403 people were dead, and another 1,178 were wounded.

As early as 1923, the army had investigated using barrage balloons at Pearl Harbor and the Panama Canal, installations deemed vulnerable to air attack. They had been used with success during the Great War, flying over sites in France, Britain, and Germany. After the war, the chief of the Army Air Service recommended balloons as an inexpensive barrier to keep planes so high they couldn't drop bombs with accuracy. After bickering within the army over which division would run the program, the Coast Artillery Corps won, at least at first. Some test balloons were commissioned, but the program lost steam, and funding, and wouldn't be reconsidered until 1937, after reports that the British and French had set up substantial balloon programs. American war planners wouldn't fully embrace the idea, however, until word got back to Washington in late 1940 that the balloons were effective at diverting bombers from important sites in Britain, namely war plants.

The British were particularly impressed with the performance of the balloons. In one example, German planes stopped attacking balloons flying over Dover in August 1940 after replacements were soon flying in place of those lost. The enemy concluded that the risk simply wasn't worth it.

After Pearl Harbor, amid all the speculation and recrimination about what could have been done to avert the disaster, one fact appeared clear: barrage balloons could have thwarted the attack. An army report five months before the strike had said as much, concluding that barrage balloons "would hamper the activities of low-flying enemy aircraft, and if properly placed would deny him the opportunity of pressing to low altitude with dive bomber attacks." Torpedoes dropped from planes inflicted the greatest damage to ships that day. The report further cited the balloons as a "mental hazard to enemy bombers," particularly at night and in low visibility. That point would prove instructive in later years, when the balloons went to war in Europe.

Back in October 1940, the chief of the Air Corps had recommended that the army acquire 4,400 barrage balloons and send 200 of them to

Hawaii. Three high-ranking army officers who had spent time in Britain said that the United States should obtain the balloons as soon as possible. The following February, there were three balloons in Hawaii (though they weren't flying) with 40 more slated for delivery in June and another 44 more coming in September, according to a letter sent by War Secretary Henry L. Stimson to the navy secretary. (Stimson said the army was planning on a total 2,950 balloons, far fewer than the original Air Corps request.) In any event, the first barrage balloon unit, the 301st Coast Artillery Battalion, which was activated in June 1941, wouldn't see duty until after Pearl Harbor, when it was rushed to Panama. It would be another fourteen months before balloons were flying in Hawaii.

So what happened to the balloons that were supposed to be aloft beginning in the summer of 1941? When asked that question during congressional hearings after the war, General Marshall dodged the matter. "We had not been able to procure them up to that time," he said. He didn't know why, he added, suggesting vaguely that there had been issues obtaining funding from Congress. Asked later if he knew about the decision not to use balloons at Pearl Harbor, Marshall testified that he presumably did, though he could not remember.

In the end, the balloons were rejected because they were seen as a hindrance to friendly planes. Although proven to be an effective defense against exactly the type of threat facing Pearl Harbor, the Army Air Force and the navy considered it too much of a bother to fly around them. Yet, after the worst attack on American soil, the army's barrage balloon program became a top priority, and the available balloons, along with reinforcements from Britain, were rushed to sites of strategic importance.

BALLOONS HAVE INSPIRED THE imagination for centuries. Their mythology spans the globe, from paper fire lanterns floating aloft in ancient China to supposed shaman balloon flights in pre-Inca civilizations. Modern ballooning traces its roots to eighteenth-century

France and a duo named Montgolfier. When the brothers discovered what happened when they filled paper bags with heated air, there was no stopping them. Their first flight of an unmanned balloon, in June 1783, was followed three months later with another launch, at the palace of Versailles. With Louis XVI and Marie-Antoinette looking on, a balloon in an appropriate royal shade of blue rose fifteen hundred feet and flew for eight minutes. Leaking hot air for two harrowing miles, the balloon touched down with no harm to its passengers: a sheep, a rooster, and a duck. Suddenly the desire to rise to great heights in a precarious wicker basket swept through Europe like a runaway, well, balloon, which is essentially what it was. There were few controls and zero possibility of navigation.

The balloons of the 1800s were as stylish as the frilly Victorian fashions of the day and delighted surprised spectators as they glided above the meadows and valleys of France, England, and Germany. These silken flying eggs were resplendent in their bright billowing shells adorned with intricate artwork, golden accents, and royal symbols. Paid passenger rides featured decadent spreads of rich foods, fine champagne, and spirits. It didn't hurt that some pilots were attractive women like the petite brunette Sophie Blanchard, who captivated Paris with her solo flights in a tiny silver gondola. As the crowds paying to see them multiplied, the balloons and their launches grew more elaborate. Pyrotechnics were added to night ascents, only sometimes resulting in a tragic end for their skippers, including the unfortunate Madame Blanchard. Romantic tales were spun from some of these accidents, adding to balloons' mystique.

Yet where some saw *amour*, others saw war. After Benjamin Franklin watched the first flight of a hydrogen balloon in Paris from his carriage window in 1783, he imagined giant gasbags carrying ten thousand men to battle. The British feared an airborne invasion throughout the Napoleonic Wars, all the while poking fun at the vessels at the center of their angst. In one cartoon a French aeronaut blows soap bubbles while proclaiming, "We will take Gibraltar in de air-balloon." In the end, the balloons' application turned out to be more sober. Napoleon formed the world's first military balloon brigade and sent *L'Entreprenant* to spy on his enemies in the Battle of Fleurus in June 1794. The balloon's appearance as if by magic was said to have terrified Austrian troops, while their less-impressed officers sniffed that the use of such a craft in war was utterly unsportsmanlike. The French balloon flyers, clad in spiffy blue uniforms replete with two pistols and a saber, considered themselves the swashbucklers of their day. Napoleon took his balloon air force, la Compagnie d'Aérostiers, to Egypt, "counting on the very sight of balloons to put terror into the heart" of his enemies, writes historian Richard Holmes. In fact, the British decimated Napoleon's forces, including the balloons, before they were even unpacked.

Napoleon soured on the corps after that, though he ordered the release of a grand balloon to celebrate his coronation in December 1804. The ornate orb disappeared somewhere beyond Rome, though the huge gilded crown that it towed was said to have landed on the tomb of Nero, the brutal emperor who sent scores of Christians to their deaths. The French emperor was not amused.

It didn't take long for balloon fever to cross the Atlantic, with the launch of the first American drone of sorts—an unmanned balloon—in Philadelphia in May 1784. The new age of flight inspired Americans to dream of the possibilities. Showboating balloonists dazzled crowds with daring stunts: There were ascents with an alligator strapped to a passenger's back, and on horseback with "the poor animal standing on a platform below the balloon," writes historian Eileen F. Lebow. Some daredevils jumped from the basket and were saved by a primitive parachute—a risky trick.

Before the advent of the transcontinental railway in 1869, entrepreneurial aeronauts studied the potential of cross-country balloons to move mail and people across vast distances more quickly than by horse and wagon. One of them, John Wise, had even loftier ideas in mind when he formed the Trans-Atlantic Balloon Corporation in 1885, hoping one day to cross an ocean. "Our children will travel to any part of the globe, without the inconvenience of smoke, sparks and seasickness,—*and at the rate of one hundred miles an hour*," wrote Wise (emphasis in original). Those intentions were dampened somewhat after Wise attempted to fly the hydrogen balloon *Atlantic* from St. Louis to New York and ended up crash-landing 809 miles later in a spectacular storm, narrowly missing a splashdown—and likely drowning—in Lake Ontario. Other mishaps would reveal how impractical a goal it was to attempt long-distance flight in vessels that couldn't be steered. Bags of hot air anchored to the earth were far easier to control.

The outbreak of the Civil War gave sky-seeking pioneers an idea. Taking a cue from Napoleon's air corps, a leading aeronaut named Thaddeus S. C. Lowe climbed into the basket of a balloon at the Columbia Armory in Washington, DC, and rose five hundred feet. From there, he dictated a message via a telegraph line attached to the White House. Dated June 16, 1861, from the balloon *Enterprise*, the telegram informed President Abraham Lincoln that, from his perch, he could see nearly fifty miles around, "a superb scene" that afforded a view of troop encampments across the Potomac River in Virginia. The stunt was Lowe's second attempt to capture the president's attention. His first effort, two months earlier, involved flying the *Enterprise* from Cincinnati to the White House, a trip that went awry when the wind blew him south to a landing in rural South Carolina, where he was arrested for being a Union spy. Lowe, who like other balloonists of the day enjoyed being called "Professor," managed to get away. One version of his escape had him protesting successfully to the illiterate locals, who were suspicious of the writings found in his basket. Another story said he was eventually recognized and released. Whatever the truth, Lowe had time to contemplate a different approach as he and his balloon were sent packing north.

Lowe wasn't alone. Other aeronauts were rushing to prove their services to the Union, with the contest descending into a jealous catfight.

Chief among them was the publicity-loving John LaMountain. He lived up to his outsize name by making a series of flights beginning in July 1861 that were far more dangerous than Lowe's ascents. Untethered, he flew in a free balloon up to three miles high over Confederate territory. Despite creating major excitement and headlines with his derring-do, LaMountain lost the battle to the better-funded and better-connected Lowe, who dismissed his rival as "unscrupulous."

President Lincoln eventually agreed to let Lowe form the first balloon regiment under the aegis of Gen. George B. McClellan, commander of the Potomac Army and an enthusiastic champion of balloons. Lowe's first ascent in a military balloon in August 1861 provided information that allowed Union guns to be accurately fired at enemy positions without the gunner seeing his target. "This was an ominous first in the history of warfare, by which destruction could be delivered to a distant and invisible enemy," writes Richard Holmes.

Balloons had been proposed, and rejected, in earlier American battles. The U.S. government's protracted war against the Seminoles in Florida in 1835 inspired an idea of nighttime balloon flights to spot tribal campfires. Later, during the Mexican-American War, John Wise suggested dropping torpedoes from balloons. Finally, the aeronauts would have their war.

Lowe's Military Aeronautics Corps eventually counted eight balloons in its fleet, with names such as *Constitution* and *Intrepid*, the latter of which was decorated with a giant eagle carrying a portrait of General McClellan in its beak. The balloons varied in size, with the largest ones, like the *Intrepid*, able to hold thirty-two thousand cubic feet of gas and carry five passengers. Their cables were long enough to climb to five thousand feet, though they usually flew lower. Sporting the Union Stars and Stripes to ward off friendly fire, the two-foot-square passenger baskets barely reached a man's knees, which likely explained why many Union officers declined Lowe's offer for a ride. Several generals who eventually went aloft with Lowe, including the gung-ho McClellan, became supporters of the balloon as a tool of war. But the corps didn't travel light, and moving them around was a headache. The balloon units took with them a ground crew of fifty soldiers, and wagons loaded with supplies towed by eight horses. The balloons were tethered to whatever surface was available near the front lines, from wagons to boats.

The balloon men also required bulky hydrogen generators towed by horse cart. Hydrogen, the lightest substance on earth, was the favored gas because it had far greater lifting power than hot air. The discovery of hydrogen in 1766 had been a boon to ballooning because the gas could be produced on the go through a chemical reaction; Lowe used one of the oldest methods, which involved diluted sulfuric acid and bits of iron. A major downside was that contact with a spark caused the hydrogen to explode. Coal-fired gas was an alternative that proved practical when gas mains began appearing in cities around 1820, but it lacked the buoyancy and mobility of hydrogen.

Like Napoleon before him, Lowe saw a psychological advantage to the balloons. The sky spies enraged the rebels, who sensed they were always being watched and unloaded their guns at the balloons, to no avail. On one occasion a runaway balloon drifted into enemy territory at Yorktown, but fortuitously veered back across Union lines, where it crash-landed on a tent, to cheers from the troops. Although no Confederate marksmen succeeded in downing a balloon, skeptics contended the gasbags made a fine target for the enemy, a charge that would resurface in future wars.

Lowe considered balloon surveillance a significant coup in the new age of warfare that was more mobile than ever before. Through heat and bitter cold, the aeronauts spent monotonous hours aloft with only the heaving of the expanding and contracting silk canopy for company, an experience that one journalist aboard found "extraordinarily tense and disturbing." At other times, the balloon flyers witnessed some of the bloodiest battles ever to involve Americans, with inconclusive outcomes that left thousands of men dead, dying, or wounded. They provided important information on troop movements, supplies, and re-inforcements. Telegraphy was the preferred means of communicating to the ground, but when this wasn't possible, flags or hand signals were used, or messages were dropped in canisters and then telegraphed or hand-delivered.

Aerial spying came with complications. Battlefield smoke and dust obscured events, and enemy troops took measures to hide their move-ments or deceive the aeronauts. What's more, the basket was unstable, bobbing about in the wind. Yet on a clear day a balloonist could see for up to thirty miles through a telescope, reconnaissance that had been impossible before. During the Seven Days Battle around Richmond, observers tracked troop movements in the rebel capital from a farm seven miles away.

Not to be outdone, Confederates raced to make their own balloons. Given that they were short on cash and materials, their efforts were primitive in comparison, with one ragtag balloon crafted by covering cotton with tar and pumping it with hot air. One of the war's most ro-mantic tales was spun when, it was said, southern ladies rich and poor, swelling with patriotism, handed over their silk dresses to the cash-strapped Confederate cause. From these frocks rose "a great patchwork ship of many varied hues," a rebel officer wrote. The majestic balloon supposedly lifted the spirits of Confederate troops demoralized by the state-of-the-art Union gasbags.

In truth, the "Silk Dress Balloon" never existed, though its roots can be traced to a more mundane, if no less patriotic, craft. A smaller balloon of many colors appeared over Richmond in the spring of 1862. Named *Gazelle*, the Confederate balloon certainly cheered troops and civilians worrying over a Union attack. The *Gazelle* was the work of a rebel engineer in Savannah, Georgia, who had taken his own money to buy twenty bolts of scarce dress silk, which he used to make a bal-loon. With tensions rising around Richmond, Union and Confederate balloons went head to head on June 27, 1862, for the first and only time in the war. At a modest thirty feet tall, the *Gazelle* rose three hundred feet; meanwhile, five miles away, at double her size, hovered the *Intrepid*. Armed with binoculars and telescopes, their crews could only gape at one another. The *Gazelle*'s demise came soon after, when she was shot down by a Union gunboat. The commander of the Union ship reported that the fleeing rebels left everything behind, "including a balloon made of silk dresses."

Lacking the Union's capacity to generate gas in the field, the Confederate balloon campaign never matched that of its rival. In the end, the Union balloons were relatively short-lived, too, flying two and a half years until the corps was disbanded in mid-1863. Their end was foreordained after McClellan, their commanding general and champion, was routed in the ferocious battle for Richmond in July 1862 and eventually lost his command. Lowe's civilian team lacked support in other quarters of the Union Army, which regarded the balloons with skepticism and their flyers as undisciplined whiners. The generals whom Lowe took up in his balloons were indeed supporters, but their numbers were relatively few.

Were the balloons effective? Lowe thought so. After the Union defeat at Bull Run in July 1861, Lowe calmed nerves in Washington, DC, by reporting on enemy movements. A crowning success, he believed, was spotting the rebels' nighttime evacuation during the Siege of Yorktown in May 1862, which gave Union troops time to overtake them. Lowe also believed that the intelligence provided during the Richmond campaign had saved scores of Union troops from massacre.

For their part, Confederates were thrilled to see the balloons gone, no longer having to camouflage their camps or engage in time-consuming ruses such as building fake cannons from tree trunks. Rebel artillery officer E. P. Alexander puzzled over why the Union would ditch such an effective tool. "Even if the observers never saw anything," he later wrote, "they would have been worth all they cost for the annoyance and delays they caused us in trying to keep our movement out of their sight."

A lone monument in Richmond recalls the long-forgotten balloon corps, dedicated to the "intrepid and patriotic" balloonists on both sides who "against ridicule and skepticism laid the foundation for this nation's future in the sky."

Around the world, balloons remained an instrument of war in countries from England to Japan. They were said to have helped Napoleon III score a victory over the Austrians at Solferino in 1859. (Events might have turned out differently for the first Napoleon had he used them at Waterloo.) Austria sent unmanned balloon bombs to Venice in 1849, and shortly after, the Russians flew them during the Crimean War. During the Siege of Paris in 1870, balloons were the only means for the trapped populace to communicate with the outside world—a function that Ben Franklin had envisioned a century earlier. Even in war, the balloons added a *morceau* of romance; engravings depicted brightly colored orbs ferrying important people such as the interior minister Léon Gambetta out of the blockaded city. Georges Clemenceau, the mayor of Montmartre, sent a letter via balloon to his American wife, Mary, urging her to "take care not to catch cold. You know your chest is not strong." Balloons being balloons, that one made its way not to western France, where Mary was living, but to enemy territory in Bavaria. Over the course of the four-month siege, 2.5 million letters were sent out of Paris. Carrier pigeons brought news back into the city, printed in miniature on photographic film developed for the purpose.

The balloons bedeviled the Prussians, who quickly discovered they were tough to shoot down with their rifles. So they therefore set to work developing the world's first antiaircraft gun, a weapon with a long, skinny barrel mounted on a wagon that tilted upward at a sharp angle. Although its bullets had a greater chance of hitting the balloons, even if a slug punctured the skin, it had little effect on a gasbag of low pressure. In any case, the French found a way to foil the new gun by flying their balloons after dark. Of the sixty-six balloons sent aloft during the Siege of Paris, only one, the *Daguerre*, was downed. A surprising fifty-eight flights landed in friendly territory, carrying 102 passengers to safety. (Despite the best efforts of the aeronauts, the Parisians surrendered in January 1871.)

Other European countries from Spain to Sweden embraced military balloons, and their appeal spread east to China. Japan and Russia each flew observation balloons during their war in 1904–5. In an astute display of early marketing, balloons promoted as copies of the military gasbags flown during the 1899 Boer War in South Africa flew across England emblazoned with "Hudson's Soap."

At the turn of the century, the Germans were still puzzling over how to take out the French balloons, which were now even stronger. Over time, balloon skins, called envelopes, evolved from silk and cotton to varnished fabrics. In one test in 1909, German army riflemen and machine gunners fired 7,500 rounds in vain at a giant tethered balloon flying at four thousand feet. Frustrated, the Germans once again sought help from Krupp Works, the master armament maker that had built the Prussian gun used in Paris. Krupp developed an incendiary shell that, unlike a cold metal slug, set the hydrogen alight. Krupp's mobile high-angle guns would see action in the coming world wars, and the targets would include more than balloons.

Even as military aeronautics proceeded, the lighter-than-air world hadn't lost its fun side. At the World's Fair in Paris in 1878, a 118-foot-wide balloon—the largest the world had ever seen—gave fifty passengers at a time a tethered ride at 1,600 feet. Balloon racing evolved into an elite sport, drawing competitors from across the globe, along with deep-pocketed sponsors and enormous crowds. The grand-daddy of them all was the annual Gordon Bennett Cup, in which the world's leading aeronauts competed for a silver trophy provided by James Gordon Bennett, the playboy publisher of the *New York Herald*. The first American to win the cup in 1907, during its second year, was army flyer Frank Purdy Lahm, who sailed his balloon from Paris to

England and returned home a huge celebrity. Lahm would play a role in the next chapter of American military balloons.

Balloons didn't have the skies to themselves for long. The early twentieth century saw rapid innovations in other flying craft, from airplanes to a new type of gasbag: the airship. Unlike balloons, blimps were powered not by wind but by engines that ran on steam, electricity, and, later, gasoline. Airships would rule the skies for the next two decades, ferrying mail and people in large gondola-shaped cabins suspended under a giant bag filled with hydrogen. With a crew of three dozen or more, they crossed great distances. Plans were hatched to send them to the North Pole and other places where aircraft had never gone.

Whereas the French led the world in balloon making, it was a German who commanded the airship era. Count Ferdinand von Zeppelin saw the vast potential of motorized blimps to transport people during peacetime and weapons during wartime. He was inspired in part by the Union Army balloons he saw in America, where he spent a few years as a young Prussian Army observer. His company built a fleet of airships in the first two decades of the 1900s named after him, and zeppelin mania swept Germany, with thousands of people clamoring to ride in one of the giant sausages—measuring more than four hundred feet long and thirty-nine feet wide—that ferried people across the country and even to Denmark.

When the Great War erupted in Europe in August 1914, Germany had a substantial head start on the production of military airships, which Count Zeppelin had boasted could fly in any weather, day or night. The 115 Zeppelins that served with the German forces spied on enemy troop movements and dropped bombs in France. Zeppelins were soon sent to bomb London, though advancements in airplanes would later make the much-slower airships impractical for that purpose.

America's entry into the airship age was hardly smooth sailing. The first military craft ordered up in 1909—far smaller than the zeppelins—were grounded after a series of mishaps. As it became clear that the nation was going to war, the program assumed more urgency but saw little more success. One ship built in 1917 was a leaky gasbag so heavy that it could barely get off the ground. It was wrecked after only three flights.

The U.S. Navy, which was put in charge of the program, looked to the British Sea Scouts for inspiration. Smaller than the zeppelins, these were simple craft composed of an airplane fuselage hung below a cigar-shaped envelope with a fin. The pressurized bags were said to make a sound like "blimp" when flicked by a finger. The name stuck. The navy ordered sixteen similar ships, the majority built by the Goodyear Tire and Rubber Company. In the years to come, Goodyear would become the nation's leading maker of airships and military balloons.

Meanwhile, the first class of eighteen navy airship pilots finished training in September 1917. A few were sent to war in France, where they flew patrols in French blimps. The others flew airship missions from seven bases from Cape Cod to Key West, trolling along the Atlantic coast for German submarines. Though they spent 13,600 hours on patrol, they never sank a U-boat, but neither did any other navy aircraft.

The most successful sky spies during the First World War were not airships or airplanes but the hundreds of balloons flying over the trenches that snaked through northern France and Belgium, and over the battlefields that claimed millions of lives. The sight of a balloon floating above a quiet sector of the Western Front meant only one thing: hellfire was coming.

As in past wars, the balloonist's job was to direct artillery fire from the ground on enemy positions and collect intelligence on troop movements and supply lines. But with ever-deadlier weaponry, technology made that job all the more perilous. Improvements aboard the balloons gave commanders more information in real time. Telephone lines enabled observers to transmit information directly to commanders. The crude sketches of the past were useless after the advent of cameras, which delivered to officers accurate pictures of enemy positions to pore over. Unmanned propaganda balloons were sent over enemy lines, infuriating German officers, who complained that the leaflets they dropped maligning the emperor were out of bounds.

Craig Herbert, a seventeen-year-old U.S. Army balloonist who would suffer a German gas attack and other close calls, described in his memoir, *Eyes of the Army*, what the observers saw: "Hardly a train could move within five miles of the trenches, or a group of men come up for relief, or digging begun on a series of emplacements or batteries, but a pair of eyes would take notice of it."

The balloons, at about two hundred feet long and fifty feet wide, made plum targets for the latest instruments of war: airplanes. Observers bobbing in wicker baskets at four thousand feet had to have nerves as strong as the steel cables that anchored their bags to the ground. The British fliers called themselves "balloonatics" for good reason. Yet so-called balloon busting was extremely dangerous for the pilots who dared. Antiaircraft and machine gunners on the ground opened up with a vicious barrage that downed many planes. In fact, the British sometimes set traps, launching balloons with straw figures as bait to attract planes. The danger was so extreme that German aces who kept score of the aircraft they downed counted balloons as one and a half times a plane.

Still, the knowledge that the pilots were taking major risks was little comfort to the men hanging under a bag filled with thirty thousand cubic feet of hydrogen, particularly when a German Fokker came screaming through the clouds with guns blazing. If the plane's incendiary bullets and shells hit, the bag exploded. To make matters worse, pilots picked off parachutists as they bailed. One study found that balloonists suffered the most nervous breakdowns of all combatants.

In the early days of the war, the balloonists had no way out when menaced. Parachutes were installed only after several observers were killed. Surprisingly, nobody thought airplanes would attack balloons. The chutes came packed in cones that hung from the side of the basket, and were automatically triggered when an aeronaut jumped. Balloon men leaped into the void with little more than a prayer and a rope attached to the chute.

Sometimes these so-called guardian angels didn't open, and other times bits of the flaming balloon carcass incinerated the helpless flyer before the ground crew could separate them. It was no surprise when British doctors concluded that two such bailouts were as much as a balloonist's nerves could take. Even so, some flyers couldn't get enough of the highs. Up in the air, one English balloonatic confessed, "[A]ll fear disappeared. I felt happy, exhilarated, even at the most hectic of moments."

When Europe went to war in 1914, Germany had a supreme advantage over France and Britain, with a well-equipped balloon corps ready for service. Its *Drachenballon*, or "dragon balloon," was far superior to the balloons of its rivals, with a new sausage shape and a bottom fin resembling a puffy diaper that made it far steadier than the spherical balloons that worked so well in flight but that jerked like crazy tops when tethered to the ground. These so-called kite balloons—*drachen* also means "kite"—were copied by the Allies as soon as they captured one. In 1915, French engineer Albert Caquot designed an even better balloon, a teardrop-shaped bag even more stable thanks to a top fin and a pair of bottom fins that, when deflated, resembled, in the words of one writer, a sad beagle. The Caquot could tolerate wind gusts of fifty miles per hour and soared to thirteen thousand feet, though the war balloons flew much lower. The Germans then copied that one, and the Caquot remained the standard for the rest of the war, with Goodyear and other companies making versions for the U.S. Army.

The Americans scrambled to train a balloon corps when it appeared the nation would be drawn into the European war. The army's balloon school, which had been mothballed at Fort Omaha, Nebraska, was reopened in late 1916, and Frank Lahm, the racing champion, was put in charge. Army balloons hadn't seen action since 1898, when one gasbag took a brief turn in Cuba during the Spanish-American War. Airships had replaced balloons in the hearts of military planners, but upbeat reports from Europe about the performance of balloons changed minds at the War Department. (On a much smaller scale, navy ships and the Marine Corps also flew observation balloons.)

Balloon cadets were still in training in September 1917 when Gen. John J. Pershing, commander of the American Expeditionary Forces, wired Washington: KITE BALLOON SITUATION ON FRENCH FRONT VERY SERIOUS. FIFTY COMPANIES URGENTLY NEEDED. It would be another six months until the first American unit got a balloon aloft in France, but the army would never meet Pershing's demand, topping out at thirty-five companies. Second Balloon Company served the longest, 251 days straight, until the Armistice on November 11, 1918. By that time, there were 6,811 American balloonists in France, most of them at the front. They would clock 3,111 hours in the air, bailing 116 times. One observer, Lt. Glenn Phelps, jumped from balloons five times, earning the Distinguished Service Cross. (Fourteen other balloonists also received the military's second-highest honor.) There were many mishaps, but, astonishingly, only one balloon jumper was killed by his burning balloon.

In the final days of the war, with defeat assured, German planes went after the hated gasbags with a vengeance. By all accounts, the balloons performed optimally, though infantry troops and villagers complained that they drew German shelling. That was no doubt true, but the intelligence provided by the sky spies was considered so important that artillery officers who had spurned the balloons grew to prefer them to any other means of observation. With constant telephone contact to the balloon, commanders had the best information available. Radio contact was less reliable in airplanes, which in any event weren't available in numbers required for observation. That would change as advances in airplanes rendered the observation balloon obsolete and prompted a radical change in the mission of military balloons in the future.

Perhaps the highest praise came from the Germans, who told a high-ranking American officer after the war that of all the U.S. units, the "most efficient and effective" were the balloon companies.

As soon as the fighting stopped, recreational ballooning resumed, with some of the most enthusiastic competitors being the "Bag Vets," as the army balloonists called themselves. Although improvements in technology had made the sport safer than during the Montgolfier days, ballooning was still outrageously dangerous. Contest rules that required flights no matter the weather made it all the more hazardous. The 1923 Gordon Bennett race in Belgium ended with a half dozen balloons wrecked, many of them struck by lightning. Among them was the U.S. Army's entry, whose two crew members were among five killed. The navy's balloon narrowly missed a water landing and was one of the few to touch down safely in a Dutch turnip field.

Military training flights were no less risky. A navy balloon that left Long Island in December 1920 ended with the desperate crew of three wandering in the frigid Canadian wilderness for four days before they found a lone, wary trapper to help them. The following March, a navy balloon with five men aboard disappeared over the Gulf of Mexico. Their last message, relayed by carrier pigeon back to their base in Pensacola, Florida, said they were falling.

Yet balloons could still pull off amazing feats, such as when the navy's *Goodyear III* balloon landed on the deck of a fortuitously placed ship, at night, off the coast of France during a 1925 race. Three army aeronauts in 1934 reached 60,000 feet in the *Explorer I*, parachuting to safety from 22,000 feet when the balloon ruptured. The *Explorer II* set an altitude record in 1935 when it sailed to 72,000 feet. The stratosphere has remained a balloon destination to the present day.

After the war's end, airships grew ever bigger and faster. Millions turned out along the East Coast in the autumn of 1923 as the mighty USS *Shenandoah* made a victory lap. The American-made blimp, copied from a zeppelin shot down in France, was state-of-the-art at 680 feet long and 78 feet wide; its cotton shell was lined with so-called goldbeater's skin, an airtight coating made from the membranes of cattle intestines, the secret to the durability of European balloons. The envelope was painted with a silvery varnish that reflected the sun.

The summer of 1929 saw the mother of all flyovers when the zeppelin Graf mesmerized people around the world. Americans rushed outside as the monster airship, nearly 800 feet long and 110 feet wide, rumbled above them on its route from New Jersey across the Atlantic Ocean, over Europe, and on to Asia and then over California, where a boy named Louis Zamperini, the future Olympic star and prisoner of war, would remember the sight as "fearfully beautiful."

A serious pitfall of airships was their tendency to catch fire and crash with alarming regularity, taking passengers and crew down with them. One of the worst such accidents befell a blimp built for the U.S. Navy, which split in two on a test flight in England in 1921, killing sixteen American men—the navy's airship elite—along with twenty-three British airmen. Four years later, the *Shenandoah* cracked up in a storm over Ohio, killing fourteen of the forty-three men aboard.

A zeppelin launched the airship heyday, and it was a zeppelin that ended it. Newsreel captured the moment when the *Hindenburg* exploded in flames over Lakehurst, New Jersey, in May 1937, shocking audiences again and again. A spark likely caused by static electricity ignited the hydrogen, killing thirty-five of the ninety-seven passengers. U.S. military airships had switched to much safer helium gas more than a decade earlier, after the *Roma*, a 400-foot-long blimp bought from Italy, crashed into high-voltage lines in Norfolk, Virginia, and caught fire, killing thirty-four.

Why wasn't helium used all along? Nearly as light as hydrogen, helium isn't combustible. Yet unlike hydrogen, which is relatively cheap and easy to produce, helium must be extracted from natural gas, and quantities were limited. At that time, America had a monopoly on the world's supply, with the discovery of deposits in the early 1900s around the Texas Panhandle and neighboring states. (U.S. law banned export of the gas.) After the *Hindenburg*, the commercial airship era sputtered to an end.

Military airships carried on, even after the worst crash of all time, in 1933, when seventy-seven servicemen died aboard the USS *Akron*. During the Second World War, two hundred navy blimps armed with bombs and machine guns patrolled the coasts for enemy subs. In the early days of the war they were particularly effective in the Atlantic, where German U-boats had been terrorizing American merchant ships, many of which were loaded with supplies for Britain. In January 1942, the month the navy blimps began patrols, forty-three ships and more than a thousand lives were lost to U-boat attacks.

When the U-boats moved south, fanning across the Caribbean and down to Brazil, the navy gasbags followed. By the end of the war, the blimps had escorted 81,000 ships. Although airplanes posed a far greater danger to the subs, airships were credited with keeping the U-boats from surfacing.

THE PEARL HARBOR CATASTROPHE reverberated far beyond Hawaii, with Americans fearing a foreign attack for the first time. Suddenly, the West Coast appeared vulnerable to a full-fledged Japanese invasion by land or air, a prospect all the more unnerving with many vital defense-related factories and navy yards dotting the 1,300-mile coastline. The Los Angeles area alone was home to eight plants that produced almost half the military's airplanes and nearly all its bombers.

As if to drive the point home, a Japanese sub surfaced on February 23 near Santa Barbara and fired thirteen rounds at oil installations. There was barely any damage, but jittery nerves were blamed for the so-called

Battle of Los Angeles the following night, when the army fired thousands of antiaircraft rounds at "unidentified planes" cruising toward the city. Newspaper headlines the following morning trumpeted the news of the many Japanese planes dispatched to a fiery end—except that there were no enemy planes. Although some thirty witnesses swore they saw planes in the sky, investigators concluded that a military weather balloon had set off the commotion. There were many other false reports of enemy planes and ships heading toward the mainland. Even Eleanor Roosevelt got a scare en route to Los Angeles, when her plane received a false report that bombs were falling on San Francisco.

The men in Washington who had reckoned that Germany posed the greatest threat from the east were now scrambling to beef up defenses in the west. They pondered over how to spot a Japanese aircraft carrier force approaching in the thick fog that often shrouded the Pacific coast. Tens of thousands of troops were rushed across the country, and barrage balloons hurried to key sites in Panama and on the West Coast.

For America's cities, balloons were envisioned as protection should the enemy develop bombers that could travel long distances. (Germany had developed a model for a long-range bomber that could reach New York City from the French coast, but eventually abandoned the effort as too complicated.) In January 1923 the chief of the Army Air Service had recommended balloon barrages over the White House, the Capitol, and important bridges and viaducts. By early 1941, War Department plans called for nearly 3,000 barrage balloons to be used for continental defense. Beyond Pearl Harbor, other important sites were left with little protection when war broke out. Only one military police unit with a few submachine guns was guarding the Sault Ste. Marie Canal and locks between Ontario and Michigan, a crucial shipping route for iron ore necessary for war production. Although known to be a weak spot in a potential air attack by Germany from the north, infantry troops and a barrage balloon unit weren't sent there until April 1942.

The need for improved coastal defense was proved further in

June, when German U-boats dropped off agents armed with TNT on beaches in Jacksonville, Florida, and Amagansett, Long Island. Their job was to carry out sabotage attacks and generally stir up trouble. The agents soon were rounded up by the Coast Guard and the FBI, but the incidents revealed a disturbing vulnerability. Barrage balloons were soon flying on Long Island.

Despite a very real threat to the coasts, there was still opposition to the balloons. Much of it was familiar, such as the charge that the balloons tipped off the enemy to the location of the installations under guard and foiled camouflage efforts. The navy insisted the gasbags posed a danger to its planes. "We had that trouble all the time," General Marshall said after the war. Marshall, the army chief of staff, flew to San Diego shortly after Pearl Harbor to "straighten out" the problem with the barrage balloons, which he called "the only fairly effective defense" of a major B-24 bomber plant there.

The army, meanwhile, tested various sorts of balloons. The early ones were nine-hundred-pound behemoths at about ninety feet long (the length of two yellow school buses) and thirty feet wide. Made by Goodyear, B.F. Goodrich, Firestone, and other companies, they roughly resembled the teardrop-shaped Caquot observation balloons of the previous war. These models came with additional ribbing, sometimes with sharklike fins along the sides, and floppy lobes that, when viewed from the front, gave the impression of an elephant charging. When the balloon was ready to lift, the crew detached the mooring lines that secured it to the ground and attached the bag to a quarter-inch steel cable linked to a motorized winch. The balloon was raised to five thousand to six thousand feet, though it could fly twice that height. When the balloon was aloft, its cable was transferred to an anchorage so the winch could be used to hoist another balloon. Larger balloons required crews of up to a dozen men. Taking cues from British design, smaller low-altitude balloons were later developed, and eventually even smaller ones flying at a few hundred feet that could be handled by four men. An early plan to use high- and low-altitude balloons together was scrapped in favor of the lower-flying gasbags, which were intended to float in the clouds whenever possible. The purpose was to deny enemy planes the use of cloud cover and to shield the balloons from fire. In 1942 a barrage of fifty-four balloons was considered ideal protection, with thirty-six the minimum. The smallest balloons were versatile, able to fly from the masts of ships or from vehicles to protect troops in the field. A Coast Artillery Corps colonel concluded in 1942 that a barrage flying at full strength "is probably the most dependable defense against air attack, within the operational altitude of the balloons, that has ever been invented."

Borrowing a page from the old observation balloons, military planners considered, and eventually rejected, a proposal to fly balloons at twenty-five thousand feet equipped with a platform from which a crew of men with machine guns could be mounted. A plan to develop small balloons to protect marching columns of troops was tossed for fear the bags would attract the enemy to an infantry deemed "already too large and unwieldy." Those concerns were heightened by the risk of chemical gas attack, which had been a problem in the First World War. Planners were also considering the concept of balloon-carried bombs, something the Japanese had already mastered.

In the early days of the war, the barrage balloon program suffered the same supply problems that hobbled much of the army. Not only were actual balloons lacking, but so were parts for hydrogen generators, winches, and other gear. Undersize cable was pilfered from stocks of old observation balloons, which were also used for training. A U.S. Marine balloon unit headed to Samoa in February 1942 took the only hydrogen generator at Camp Tyson. To make matters worse, the American-made balloons were often faulty, and allowed in air that fouled the hydrogen and weakened the envelope. The gas used to fill them became an issue, again, after reports that hydrogen-filled British balloons burst into flames under fire. Roosevelt had asked Congress in 1941 to expand the country's helium-producing capacity, at that time limited to one plant in Amarillo, Texas. Original plans called for the balloons to be filled with helium, but limited supplies and the need to produce gas remotely meant hydrogen was the only practical choice. Yet there were risks. The explosion of a navy free balloon on a training flight in New Jersey in May 1943, killing three crewmen, was blamed on hydrogen that had been fouled by air. In the end, though, navy investigators recommended that hydrogen continue to be used for manned balloon flights because helium supplies were insufficient.

The gasbags, virtually unknown in 1941, crept into the vernacular and peppered popular culture. Readers could tuck into a mystery called *The Body in the Barrage Balloon*, and for kids there was *Bobo, The Barrage Balloon*. The clever Bobo, the largest balloon on the Pacific coast, was heralded for bravery after capturing an enemy plane and, somehow, a sub. The press bestowed countless nicknames upon the bags, from sky elephants to rubber cigars to flying beer bottles. One newspaper columnist of questionable taste labeled overweight women "walking barrage balloons."

People on the West Coast grew accustomed to seeing hundreds of the "silly rubber sky cows lazily mooing around in the air above," wrote an Associated Press correspondent, who predicted that "not long hence, many cities on both coasts will take a barrage balloon as casually as a street car."

THE FIRST BARRAGE BALLOON was raised at Camp Tyson, Tennessee, on September 4, 1941, although vast numbers of men wouldn't begin arriving at the army camp until the end of 1942. More than thirty barrage balloon battalions or equivalent units trained at Tyson during the war. Each battalion counted an average of forty-two officers, eleven hundred enlisted men, and fifty-four balloons. These units were white, with the exception of four Negro battalions. All the top officers were white. In the strange world of Jim Crow, other minorities such as Native Americans, Chinese Americans, and U.S.-born Japanese served in white units.

Wilson Monk and the other Fort Eustis men were assigned to the

320th Coast Artillery Barrage Balloon Battalion, which would eventually comprise 1,366 enlisted men from across the country, with a large number hailing from the states ringing Washington, DC. The name changed later, with "Coast Artillery" dropped and "Anti-Aircraft" added when the Antiaircraft Command took over the balloon program. It was a natural union; barrage balloons worked closely with antiaircraft guns, just as the observation balloons had during the First World War.

Tyson's four Negro battalions—the others were the 318th, 319th, and 321st—were a source of tremendous pride for black America. Reporters from the black press, along with the white media, descended on Henry County, Tennessee, to write stories about "our boys" and the "silvery sausages" they were training to fly. The Baltimore-based *Afro-American* newspaper chain likened the troops to the pioneering Tuskegee Airmen. Unlike the "glamorous" Negro pilots, correspondent Francis Yancey wrote, "these sky fighters keep both feet firm on the ground as they skillfully jockey elephantine monstrosities of destruction thousands of feet high in the sky." The *Pittsburgh Courier* extolled "these colored battalions [that] have won the praise of the entire camp. . . . They march well, they drill hard and work hard, and what is more important, their enthusiasm is unbounded."

That enthusiasm was sorely tested on exhausting twenty-five-mile hikes the men endured in the thick woodland that surrounded Camp Tyson. Basic training was the toughest nine weeks the recruits who arrived in December 1942 had ever lived through. Reveille at 6:25, followed by endless calisthenics and laps around the base. One of the hardest tests of stamina for the men was the Infiltration Course, which sent them crawling through a gamut of obstacles, pressing their rifles against their bellies and whispering prayers. If they cracked under pressure, a cover of barbed wire prevented them from jumping up and getting hit by the machine-gun fire that *rat-a-tat-tatted* overhead. Whether the rounds were real or blanks, the men never knew. The goal was mental conditioning, prepping them for battle.

Regular training wasn't much easier. Henry Parham dreaded the 2:00 a.m. wake-up calls signaling a hike until dawn. The Richmond porter was muscled from days spent hefting bags, yet it seemed impossible, at least at first, to attain a twelve-minute mile with a sixty-odd-pound pack on one's back. There were inevitably a few stragglers, who returned to base in the back of an ambulance. Truth be told, some of the men were hardly in fighting shape, tilting the scales too much the wrong way. The army didn't seem to mind. "Apparently the theory is that the heavier the ground crew the less likely the balloon's escape," the *Afro-American* wrote with a wink in an article headlined "Handling Barrage Balloons No Task for Namby-Pambies." Yet by the end of their training, the men would complete a four-mile hike in forty-eight minutes, staggering into their barracks and falling on their cots.

Over the next eleven months, they would learn to shoot M1 rifles, hurl grenades, fight a man hand to hand, and live in the rough. The woods ringing the base served as a setting for nighttime training, bivouacs where they pitched dog tents shared by two men and, sometimes, a snake. All-night hikes were led by a punishing lieutenant from Buford, Mississippi, who worked the men until they were near collapse. "Broke 'em down! Broke 'em down!" he'd yell when it was time for a break, his men struggling to suppress their laughter at his very particular use of grammar. "He was really behind me education-wise," said Arthur Guest, a 320th sergeant, "but in wartime it didn't matter if you went to school or not"—at least not if you were white.

The training was combat-worthy, and serious. "We learned how to handle ourselves. Learned how to fight," said George Robert Hamilton, a 320th draftee. "We'd been taught how to wrestle with another man, how to get the best of each other, how to take a gun away."

Hamilton never bristled at the rigors of base life. Tall and lanky with razor-sharp cheekbones, the twenty-year-old looked every bit the part Cherokee that blended with his African heritage. Born in tiny Spindale, North Carolina, the youngest child of nine, Hamilton knew how to hunt and work the small farm that kept his family fed on a crop of corn and potatoes. He was working as a night watchman at a furniture warehouse in High Point, the closest city, when he got his draft letter in December 1942. He had no idea what the war was about, and he was ambivalent about serving. He knew his way around a rifle—but little else. He trained as a gunner and learned to master an M2 Browning, a .50-caliber machine gun mounted on trucks and jeeps from which the smallest, mobile barrage balloons flew. These thirty-five-foot-long bags were called VLA, for "very low altitude," because they topped out at forty-four hundred feet, though they usually flew at two thousand feet or lower.

Balloon training involved an intensive six weeks of classes. British instructors boosted the teaching ranks, showing the men how to inflate the balloons with care so as not to spark the hydrogen, which they learned to produce at the base gas house. To avoid static electricity, woolen clothes were banned, a frigid prospect in February, when "the chilling cold seemed to penetrate through our bones," one Tyson soldier wrote. The purity of the hydrogen was tested regularly for the presence of oxygen, which at a certain concentration makes the gas highly explosive. The rookies learned to build beds on which the balloons rested when hauled down, covered with a net and camouflaged. They patched holes in the envelopes made of neoprene, a synthetic rubberized cloth of two-ply cotton. A final coat of an aluminum compound reflected the sun and minimized heat, preserving the hydrogen.

They also learned to handle the balloons' secret weapon: small, four-pound bombs. If the cable strike wasn't enough to down a plane, the hope was that a blast of TNT would do the job. The armed-cable system worked in two parts: When a plane made contact, the cable snagged the wing. Trapped, the plane rapidly lost speed. One pilot compared the effect to that of hitting a brick wall. The impact could shear off a wing or cause the plane to stall and crash. The second part of the system involved the bomb. At impact, a link near the top of the cable armed with an explosive charge cut the cable from the balloon. As the cable parted, a parachute opened. At the same time, near the bottom, a link cut the cable from the anchorage and a second parachute opened. One of these drogue parachutes was smaller than the other, and together the chutes dragged a bomb attached to one end of the cable onto the plane. The bomb detonated. The intention was to blow a hole in a wing or ignite the gas tank. Not all barrage balloons had armed cables, but those that did included the balloons that would dot the battlefields of Europe.

"To be snagged by one of these cables means certain destruction," wrote Yancey, the *Afro-American* reporter. Investigators at Camp Tyson found the system to be "lethal in almost all cases when the cable is hit by the wings or fuselage of a plane." Still, fine-tuning the explosives was ongoing in early 1943, when the army reckoned that the four-pound bombs could blow a hole in a plane's wing but would not necessarily take it down unless the gas tank was hit. To do that, the explosives had to pack the same punch as a far more powerful seventy-five-millimeter artillery shell. Yet the Army Corps of Engineers concluded that the bombs were sufficient because the "mental hazards" posed by the balloons alone "would be the greatest deterring effect with the lethal device as secondary."

As far as the Tyson men knew, they were handling a half pound of TNT each time they touched those canisters—and they were careful doing it. They could rest easier knowing the balloons would not be armed during routine training. Yet there was another challenge that was perhaps more daunting: the wild weather that often made the balloons as impossible to control as a bucking bronco hundreds of feet in the sky. For this reason, weather forecasting was taught over twelve weeks, twice the length of the other courses. Wind force and speed were closely monitored by the crews as they struggled to keep the balloons' noses into the wind "since that's the safest way for a rubber cow to fly," observed an Associated Press correspondent, who went on to explain how to do it:

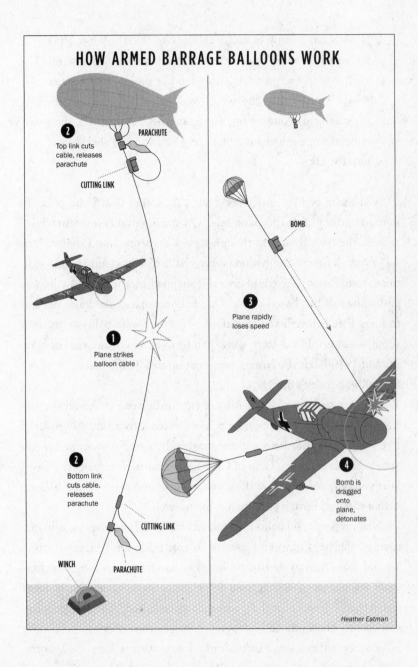

HOW ARMED BARRAGE BALLOONS WORK

2 Top link cuts cable, releases parachute

PARACHUTE

CUTTING LINK

1 Plane strikes balloon cable

2 Bottom link cuts cable, releases parachute

CUTTING LINK

WINCH

PARACHUTE

BOMB

3 Plane rapidly loses speed

4 Bomb is dragged onto plane, detonates

Heather Eatman

It takes some doing to keep a rubber cow into the wind. She's anchored by wires from her sides which attach to guy wires anchored in the ground. To switch her means nudging her slowly around into the wind. Sand bags must be shifted, she's nudged around a bit, more sand bags are shifted, she's nudged some more. Just the wrong balance, and she'd be off into the air.

Add gusts of fifty miles per hour that sorely tested the balloons flying at around five thousand feet. On stormy nights, men struggled to keep the bags flying "as though they were protecting London," the AP wrote. Though the balloons were built to withstand these conditions, sometimes they could not, and snapped their cables. A runaway gasbag had to be chased down. One balloon that broke loose made it to Lake Erie before it was shot down. Not only were balloons in short supply—some of the bags were hand-me-downs from the London Blitz of 1940—but the largest ones cost up to $10,000 apiece, or about $140,000 in today's dollars.

When a balloon went missing, a rip cord disengaged, and the bag slowly deflated. One balloon set a speed record, traveling 190 miles at 104.4 miles per hour before it was snagged by a tree an hour and forty-nine minutes later on a farm in Croydon, Indiana. The farmer, a Great War veteran, donned his 1917 army overcoat and guarded the balloon with a shotgun until Tyson men came to fetch it.

News reports said balloon breakouts amused Tennesseans, who discovered the bags limp and splayed in cornfields for a hundred miles around. But a flyaway gasbag was not always so funny. Although the steel cable was meant to detach from an errant balloon, sometimes it didn't and wreaked havoc. Trailing wires short-circuited high-voltage wires and caused blackouts and property damage from Mexico to Canada. Fifty-seven balloons in Seattle broke free during a June 1942 storm. The fugitive bags "went on an offensive rampage" over Vancouver, news reports said, snapping power lines and touching off fears the city was being invaded. The same month, Canadian legislators raised the alarm for balloons to protect the coasts from enemy attack. The balloons were blamed for similar problems abroad. Swedish radio reported later in the war that drifting balloons of unknown origin caused a train wreck and power outages in two countries.

Balloon men wore rubber gloves under leather gloves, the inside layer to guard against shock from static electricity and the outer layer to protect their hands from the cables that could shred skin like paper in high winds. The protections didn't always work. During one fierce electric storm at Tyson, lightning struck a balloon cable. The winch operator was killed when he touched the mooring lines to ease the balloon down. There is no mention of his death in army records, but several 320th men witnessed it. "The balloon man's lines caught static [electricity]," said Henry Parham, explaining how the wires were supposed to be handled. "When you brought them down, you had to let the four mooring lines hit the ground before you could touch them, or the static would knock you out." Or worse. A far more common misstep was to catch an arm or foot in the mooring line of a rising gasbag, after which the hapless balloon man was yanked high in the sky until his crew could pull him back down.

Elsewhere, the balloons were up to other tricks. In the Pacific, Japanese planes dropped balloon bombs in an effort to take out American flyers. No damage was reported by the new enemy air mines, which consisted of an explosive attached to a free balloon, but "mysterious aerial explosions" were reported over the ocean.

Much later in the war, the Japanese would reprise the idea by sending balloons to crash-land, and start fires, in the Pacific Northwest. A specially trained unit of soldiers would be sent to hunt them down, and they would be African American.

CHAPTER 5

"We Were Like Little Dogs"

I'd rather see Hitler and Hirohito win the war than work beside a nigger on the assembly line.

—White protester, Detroit, June 1943
Camp Tyson, Tennessee
April 1943

On a sunny morning in April 1943, Wilson Monk and three friends left Henry County behind and boarded a train bound for Memphis, the city on the Mississippi River where Cab Calloway, Louis Armstrong, and Muddy Waters were regulars in the Southside clubs. Black musicians were doing astounding things on Beale Street, cradle of the blues and incubator for the sultry soul that would come to be known as the Memphis sound. Memphis sure beat sleepy little Paris, the closest city to Camp Tyson. In Paris, a single USO club—the one for Negroes—was the only option for the thousands of black soldiers needing to blow off steam. If they wanted a drink, and they usually did, they were out of luck: Henry Country was dry. On Beale Street, the liquor flowed as smooth and easy as the music. In April 1943 you could catch Amateur Night at the Palace Theater, or see the beautiful Lena Horne in *Cabin in the Sky* at one of the ten movie houses—out of forty—that admitted Negroes.

With weekend passes in hand, the Tyson men settled in for the three-hour ride, content to trade balloons, nocturnal hikes, and mess hall eats for some blues, barbecue, and a bourbon or two. What they found was a city where black men were not welcome in most places. Their first stop was a diner near the station, where someone suggested they play some songs on the jukebox. Monk placed a fifty-cent piece on the counter and asked the man on other side for change. The man glared back, opened the cash register, and threw a handful of nickels back at him. "If you wasn't in uniform," the man said, "you wouldn't get a damn thing from me."

Later that day, the Tyson men watched, incredulous, as a long line of German prisoners of war filed into a restaurant where black men were not welcome. *The enemy can eat there but we can't.* It was an often-repeated scene: African Americans were turned away at restaurants throughout the South, and sometimes in the North, but German and Italian POWs were welcome because they were white. During the war years, 425,000 Axis prisoners were interned in the United States, some 800 of them at the Memphis Army Depot.

Many of the POWs were vocal in their preference for life in America over fighting on the front lines, and their enthusiasm and compliance granted them liberties. They worked for pay at jobs, often on farms across the Midwest and the South, where most of the six hundred POW camps were situated. Their privileges, often far and above what was required by the provisions of the Geneva Convention, drew the wrath of not only black soldiers but also some whites, who considered the prisoners' lives far too cushy. Some camps earned the moniker the "Fritz Ritz." At Camp Claiborne, Louisiana, German POWs could move about freely and use the same facilities as white soldiers. They got passes into town—a privilege denied to black troops, who were confined to barracks built on swampland in the worst part of the sprawling base.

Black soldiers seethed as German prisoners shared cigarettes and jokes with the white soldiers guarding them and struck up conversations with the locals. Many of these encounters occurred at transit points, where black soldiers were decidedly not welcome, but where enemy troops could grab a bite before boarding their next train—in whites-only cars. A soldier named Davis Cason Jr. recounted how he found a meal in "a dingy, dinky place" near the train station in El Paso, Texas, after bypassing the bustling station restaurant where "there sat the so-called enemy comfortably seated, laughing, talking, making friends, with the waitress at their beck and call. If I had tried to enter the dining room, the ever-present MPs [military police] would have busted my skull." Elsewhere in Texas, Tech. Sgt. Richard Carter was sickened when he spotted "American MPs and some of Hitler's bully boys . . . having a ball together, wining and dining" in the train station restaurant. Carter had just been roused from a nap on a station bench in withering heat. A "typical southern cracker cop" had rapped the soles of his shoes with a billy club and hollered, "You niggahs can't sleep in heah," Carter said, imitating the cop's country drawl.

The largest court-martial of the war sprang from accusations that resentful black soldiers at Camp Lawton in Seattle had attacked Italian POWs, killing one by hanging him from a tree and wounding many others. In 2008 the army threw out the convictions, citing a cover-up and a trial that was "fundamentally unfair" to the soldiers, who were denied access to records and their lawyers.

Seven decades after the war, memories of POW privileges still touched a nerve with black veterans. "It really hurt us," said Wilson Monk, shaking his head at the memory of the cordial, if not outright back-slapping, treatment afforded many German prisoners. Monk was hardly naive; he expected this kind of treatment in the South. Even his northern hometown was a hardly a bastion of racial equality. Burned in Monk's soul was the day when, as a boy, he had watched as the Ku Klux Klan paraded in full white pointy-hooded regalia along West Park Avenue in Pleasantville, New Jersey, past his family's home, and set fire to a cross in a field down the street. Still, the treatment in Memphis stung. Maybe it was because he was now a soldier enlisted in the fight for freedom and democracy.

Monk didn't know it at the time, but he was lucky his uniform had at least gotten him change for the jukebox. For many soldiers, their army khakis marked them as a target. Tensions had been high across the South for many months as thousands of black recruits poured into army bases built to take advantage of year-round training in temperate weather. Southerners loudly protested the influx of so many Negroes, and the Southern Governors Conference of 1942 unanimously objected to their presence, with the Alabama chief executive calling it a "grave mistake." Northern black soldiers were dragged off buses for refusing to sit in the back, and any white soldiers who took their side were threatened by drivers, who often carried guns. When a private at Camp Claiborne objected to being called "nigger," the train conductor who used the slur shouted, "Yes, you are a nigger, a goddamn nigger. You are down below the Mason-Dixon Line and you are all nigger boys down here." Simply walking the streets was fraught with indignities, and even ceding a place on the sidewalk for a white person wasn't always enough. A white woman in Alabama spat on Lt. Earl Kennedy, he said, "for having my black skin in an officer's uniform."

In one of the army's most outrageous Jim Crow episodes, an order came down at a Pennsylvania camp warning that "any association between the colored soldiers and white women, whether voluntary or not, would be considered rape. And the penalty would be death." After howls of protest from William H. Hastie, the civilian aide to the war secretary, and the NAACP, the War Department revoked the order.

WHITE ANTIPATHY TOWARD black soldiers had existed as long as there had been black soldiers. From the Revolutionary War onward, many whites opposed arming Negroes. During the First World War, white southerners reacted with outrage and violence when Negroes reported for duty, their uniforms seen as an implicit demand for respect. When two thousand black troops from New York arrived in Spartanburg, South Carolina, in October 1917, the authorities warned that there would be trouble. The sight of so many black men in uniform "with their northern ideas about racial equality" was "like waving a red flag in the face of a bull," the mayor told the *New York Times*. Their white commander understood that the simple act of his men standing at attention "chest out, shoulders back, chin up—a pose of strength, dignity and pride—would likely offend the southern Jim Crow mentality," writes historian Peter Nelson. Mounting hostility eventually prompted the War Department to send the black troops to France, where the New York 369th Infantry Regiment found glory as the Harlem Hellfighters.

During the so-called Red Summer of 1919, race riots flared in some thirty cities from New York to Knoxville, leaving thousands dead, black and white. At that time, it marked the greatest period of racial strife the nation had ever seen. "Mobs took over cities for days at a time, flogging, burning, shooting and torturing at will," wrote historian C. Vann Woodward. "When the Negroes showed a new disposition to fight and defend themselves, violence increased."

The primary provocation for the violence was the return of white soldiers, who reclaimed jobs taken by blacks who had migrated North in their absence. For their part, black soldiers who had tasted equality in France were no longer prepared to tolerate discrimination and limited work opportunities. Many black vets saw themselves in the Eddie Cantor song "How Ya Gonna Keep 'Em Down on the Farm (after They've Seen Paree"). Soldiers were allowed to wear their uniforms for up to three months after being discharged, and many black veterans did so. For some, it was a show of pride in their service. Others were too poor to afford new clothes. In 1919, seventy-seven black men were lynched, at least ten of them veterans in uniform. Two were burned alive.

Southern whites sometimes lay in wait for returning soldiers at railroad stations and ripped off their uniforms. Law enforcement officials often took part in the attacks, and even when they didn't, their silence provided official sanction. A sore point among whites was news that Negroes serving abroad were treated well by European whites. Stories had filtered home about the warm welcome the French accorded to black soldiers, of salutes and, worst of all, romances with white women. Mississippi senator James K. Vardaman called for vigilantes to keep watch over "those military, French-women-ruined Negro soldiers."

The police chief in Sylvester, Georgia, blamed "a bitter feeling against colored soldiers" for one breathtaking act of violence committed against a black veteran in uniform. Daniel Mack had refused to yield his place on a Georgia sidewalk to a white man in April 1919 and was thrown in jail for two days. At his arraignment, he caused further outrage by declaring, "I fought for you in France to make the world safe for democracy. . . . I've got as much right as anybody else to walk on the sidewalk." He got a dressing-down by the judge, who told him, "This is a white man's country and don't you forget it." Before he could serve out his sentence of thirty days' hard labor, a mob dragged him from his jail cell, beat him, and left him for dead. Mack somehow survived.

Two decades later, a black man still invited violence when he donned an army uniform. In April 1941, a black soldier was found hanging from a tree at Fort Benning, Georgia, his hands tied behind his back. Base officials at first called the death a suicide. Nobody was ever charged. Billie Holiday evoked the macabre world of lynching each time she performed the haunting "Strange Fruit," her best-selling record that recalled a double lynching of two black men:

> Southern trees bear a strange fruit,
> Blood on the leaves and blood at the root,
> Black bodies swinging in the southern breeze,
> Strange fruit hanging from the poplar trees.

Pastoral scene of the gallant south,
The bulging eyes and the twisted mouth,
Scent of magnolia sweet and fresh,
And the sudden smell of burning flesh.

In the fall of 1941, William Hastie unsuccessfully urged his boss, the war secretary, to speak out against the rising incidents of violence directed at black soldiers, including the killing of black troops at Fort Bragg, North Carolina, and the shooting of black soldiers at Fort Jackson, South Carolina. "Day by day, the negro soldier faces abuse and humiliation," Hastie later wrote. "In such a climate resentments, hatreds and fears and misunderstandings mount until they erupt in sensational violence."

Life in northern camps often wasn't much better. Racial clashes flared repeatedly at Fort Dix, New Jersey, an embarkation point for troops heading overseas that doubled as a reception point for inductees. Northern black draftees were shocked by their first taste of life alongside southern troops "and their use of a well-known epithet to describe all people darker than they are," the *Afro-American* newspaper reported. The slights were many, and often petty, such as black soldiers being barred from the PX except during certain hours. "We might as well have been in the heart of Dixie," one of them said.

The mounting wave of discontent culminated in a riot that broke out off base in April 1942 as black and white soldiers queued outside Waldron's Sports Palace. What happened next is unclear. In one version, a black soldier wanting to use a telephone took offense when a white MP told him he couldn't leave the line. In the ensuing violence, some fifty shots were fired and three soldiers lay dead, two black privates and one white MP. The post's public relations officer later explained opaquely that the melee was triggered by "some persons with a little too much race consciousness getting off track." The situation remained unchanged one year later, when the *Afro-American* reported that the base was still a "veritable powder keg." The incidents certainly belied the findings of a 1942 report by the Army General Staff that concluded that the policy of segregation had "practically eliminated the colored problem, as such, within the Army."

Even when violence wasn't an issue, northern communities some-times opposed the arrival of black soldiers, even in places where there was already a sizable African American population. A base for a black Army Air Forces tactical unit failed to find a home after vehement pro-tests from officials in Syracuse, New York; Columbus, Ohio; and Wind-sor Locks, Connecticut. Yet for the black soldier, the South remained the center of strife and rage. "The South was more vigorously engaged in fighting the Civil War than in training soldiers to resist Hitler," said Grant Reynolds, who made the remark about his first posting at Camp Lee, Virginia. He later resigned as chaplain at Fort Huachuca, Arizona, in protest of the racism he experienced there.

One of the worst places for a black man to be stationed was Camp Stewart, Georgia, which was among a dozen military bases shaken by racial disturbances in 1943—a year that far surpassed 1919 as the bloodiest for the Negro soldier. Black troops there wrote a letter to the *Pittsburgh Courier* in February complaining that "Camp Stewart was nothing but a slave camp for the colored." Four months later, a false rumor that white soldiers had raped a black woman and killed her hus-band was the tipping point for black soldiers, who seized guns on the evening of June 9 and refused orders to disperse. "It looked like a small Battle of the Bulge. Instead of Americans against Germans it was black Americans versus white Americans on an Army post that perpetuated segregation and prejudice," recalled William Purnell Shelton, a young black officer, after the war. Over the next three hours, men rushed to arm themselves, exchanging fire with Military Police. "It was more or less guerrilla warfare," the *Afro-American* reported. One MP was killed, several others wounded, and five thousand shots fired.

An inquiry blamed the revolt on "an outgrowth of long pent-up emotions and resentments" caused by, among other things, fears for personal safety among Negro troops and "a feeling of desperation . . . to fight back against existing abuses without regard for the consequences." The base commander, Col. William V. Ochs, blamed "troublemakers and agitators" for the problems, which had been brewing since mid-1941 but had intensified with the transfer of two units comprising northern black troops who had come from postings in more hospitable places and refused to abide bad treatment.

The 369th Infantry Regiment from New York, which had returned from the Pacific to a most unwelcome reception at Camp Stewart, was not part of the revolt, but at the time, members of the unit had been writing letters home detailing instances of abuse. Complaints at the post dubbed a "hellhole" by one black newspaper included Negro barracks that were little more than "leaky garages," petty humiliations, and fabricated offenses that resulted in beatings by white officers and imprisonment. Black officers protested that they were denied the promotions and privileges accorded to white officers. Concerned parents of 369th men sent outraged letters to the War Department.

"We demand the removal of the 369th . . . to some northern camp," wrote Mr. and Mrs. J. L. Bowman of the Bronx on May 3, 1943. "We on the home front are not going to sit passively by watching such undemocratic treatment of our colored men in any branch of the service."

Adele W. Timpson of Mount Vernon, New York, sent a letter to the White House urging the president to take action at Camp Stewart. "These boys should be protected not penalized for their long faithful service." She had included a letter dated April 25 written by her nephew, Cpl. Wilbur "Tim" Timpson, who said troops had not been paid since February:

It looks like these people just don't want to pay us. Conditions here are really something that can't be explained. We hardly get enough to eat to keep a bird alive and there is no need for it. The average [white] soldier here has hardly had education and most of them from

four years in school to no time at all. We aren't liked here at all
since we are the most educated soldiers in the camp and know right
from wrong. These white officers here have the boys afraid of them
and . . . [they] look up to them as if they're Gods or something.

The problem at Camp Stewart went all the way to the top. Talking points issued to officers of black troops in July 1943 included the following passage: "Most slave owners were good-hearted, Christian people who liked for everyone around them to be happy. They were, as a rule, good to their slaves." And this one: "Some of you may not understand why you can't go everywhere white folks go in Georgia. It's because the law says so. . . . The laws of Georgia may not be like the laws of New York, or the District of Columbia, or Pennsylvania, or Illinois; but that makes no difference."

Racial strife rocked the nation in 1943, with 242 riots erupting in 47 cities. Most of the violence broke out during a long hot summer that served as a fuse, igniting a powder keg of racial animosity. In Los Angeles, white soldiers and sailors attacked young blacks and Latinos in the so-called Zoot Suit Riots. In Newark, the stabbing of a black teenager by white youths provoked days of fighting and stone throwing. Much of the anger had simmered since African Americans had moved into tens of thousands of jobs once open only to whites. Those work opportunities were the result of an executive order signed by President Roosevelt in June 1941 banning discrimination against blacks in the defense industry.

The president's action, however progressive, was not the product of forward-thinking leadership at a crucial time for the nation. Rather, it was the result of shrewd political pressure that African Americans were just beginning to wield. In this case, A. Philip Randolph, the influential leader of the Brotherhood of Sleeping Car Porters, called for a march on Washington to protest bias in the defense industry, which under Roosevelt's massive rearmament program had become a jobs jackpot for whites. As draft letters began landing in the mailboxes of thousands of black men in 1941, companies benefitting from fat government defense contracts flatly refused to hire black tradesmen, machinists, or mechanics. Leaders of American industry adamantly refused demands by the NAACP and other pressure groups to expand their workforce. "Negroes will be considered only as janitors," the general manager of North American Aviation declared. The response was the same at Standard Steel, which told the Urban League: "We have not had a Negro working in 25 years and do not plan to start now." The black press closely followed the national shutout of their own at steel plants, bomber factories, and assembly lines. In a meeting at the White House in June 1941, Randolph told the president bluntly that "time was running out."

Randolph, charismatic and movie-star handsome, led the charge to open the doors to black workers. He was two decades ahead of his time when he "invited" the president to address "a throng of 100,000 Negroes" that he planned to assemble at the Lincoln Memorial. The threatened demonstration stunned Roosevelt, who feared violence would break out if thousands of black men, women, and children descended on the nation's capital and camped in the streets. The District of Columbia was Jim Crow territory, and nobody expected restraint from the police. Where Randolph would get one hundred thousand marchers was a mystery to Roy Wilkins, the assistant secretary of the NAACP, who recounted in his autobiography what happened next: "A tall, courtly black man with Shakespearean diction and the stare of an eagle had looked the patrician Roosevelt in the eye—and made him back down." Whether Randolph was bluffing was never known, but Wilkins wrote that if he were, "what a bluff it was." Roosevelt signed the order, and Randolph called off the march.

The White House downplayed the importance of Executive Order 8802, which also created the Fair Employment Practices Commission to ensure the law was followed. The commission had no enforcement power, however, and could do little more than twist arms and hope

for the best. Still, after exhortations from leaders, including the president, to make use of every available American, black workers poured
into jobs previously denied them, and black leaders were jubilant.
Years ahead of the civil rights movement, Randolph's effort showed
the potential power of uniting behind a cause backed by the threat of
public spectacle.

By 1943, American production was booming, with eighty-six thousand planes produced, more than double the number of the year before.
Detroit was turning out tanks at the rate of four thousand a month, compared to four thousand a year in Germany. Allied manufacturing led by
America topped Axis output by three to one. An admiring Joseph Stalin
called the United States "the country of machines," many of which were
flowing to the battered Soviet Union. In October, equality in hiring was
a subject of a presidential "fireside chat." Tens of millions of Americans
tuned their radios to hear Roosevelt urge employers to hire Negroes,
women, and older people to keep the war economy moving. "We can no
longer indulge such prejudices or practices," he said.

Since Roosevelt had ordered that African Americans be given a fair
shot at war economy jobs, black employment doubled in one year. An
estimated fifty-three thousand jobs opened to blacks, hardly equal to
white levels, but a breakthrough nonetheless. Six million women went
to work during the war, many of them black domestics now employed in
factories. The presence of so many Negroes in places where they hadn't
been before strained the already taut high wire of American race relations. Waves of rural black and white southerners inundated northern
cities ill equipped to absorb the deluge. Black workers content to have
jobs were dismayed at living conditions that crammed families into un-
healthy slums—the only places where Negroes were permitted to live. It
was a formula repeated in cities across the country, and by the spring of
1943, ill will had bubbled into fury. At a shipyard in Mobile, Alabama,
white welders attacked blacks who had been promoted to work alongside
them, sending eleven blacks to the hospital. "It gives one a feeling that,

as a whole, we are not really prepared for democracy," Eleanor Roosevelt wrote in her syndicated newspaper column "My Day" on June 20.

Discontent had been rising steadily in Detroit, which was struggling to meet the needs of five thousand arrivals each month. Thousands seeking jobs in automobile factories converted to war production were without a permanent roof, sleeping in tents, churches, and even jails. A plan in early 1942 to build public housing for black workers touched off what would be a series of racial skirmishes that foreshadowed a breathtaking rebellion that rocked the city the following year.

The trouble began in early June 1943, when twenty-five thousand workers went on strike at a Packard plant after three black employees won promotions. A "fiery orator" with a thick southern accent screamed, "I'd rather see Hitler and Hirohito win the war than work beside a nigger on the assembly line," reported the NAACP's Walter White, who arrived on the scene to help maintain calm. It was too late. With white-supremacist groups from the Klan to the Southern Voters League working to stir up antiblack sentiment, Detroit was ready to explode. On a Sunday afternoon marked by rising temperatures and short tempers, scuffles broke out between whites and blacks at a park called Belle Isle. A false rumor ricocheted among the African Americans that whites had thrown a black woman and child to their deaths off a bridge leading to the park. For the next thirty hours, until several thousand federal troops and tanks intervened, mobs raged through the city. "Race War in Detroit: Americans Maul and Murder Each Other as Hitler Wins a Battle in the Nation's Most Explosive City," bellowed *Life* magazine. Eight pages of disturbing pictures showed bloodied black men being chased, surrounded, and beaten by whites armed with lead pipes and bottles.

In the end, twenty-five blacks and nine whites lay dead and six hundred injured. Seventeen of the black victims were killed by policemen. Of the fourteen hundred people arrested, twelve hundred were black, even though most of them reportedly had been attacked first. Despite the many problems in Detroit, bigotry did not reign in all quarters of the city. The United Automobile Workers union refused to tolerate whites who would not work with blacks on its assembly lines, and there were few problems. It was a lesson in what could happen when discipline was imposed. It is an example that another organization renowned for discipline, the U.S. military, could have followed, thus avoiding the pain, violence, bureaucracy, and phenomenal expense of maintaining segregated armed forces.

Roosevelt's war team shrugged off calls to equalize the military by continually arguing that it wasn't the job of the War Department to change America's social climate. "Experiments within the army in the solution of social problems," said Gen. George C. Marshall, "are fraught with danger to efficiency, discipline, or morale." To those arguments, William Hastie retorted, "If the army says it has difficulty in making its orders stick, then I say . . . it's a hell of a poor army." A disgusted Hastie resigned his post in January 1943. The distinguished former judge had never cracked the insular shell of the War Department, which despite his efforts was determined to remain firmly planted in the world of Jim Crow.

Disturbances flared throughout the summer of 1943, many of them resulting in deaths. Gossip was rampant, such as a false report that Negroes planned a nationwide riot on July 4. Problems at southern bases prompted an idea, apparently not fulfilled, to give northern black soldiers a booklet on local manners and customs similar to the guides given to troops headed overseas. After rioting in Beaumont, Texas, there was local support for "men on horseback or nationwide martial law." (When it was later revealed that the cause of the riot—a white woman's rape allegation against a black man—was untrue, some white citizens contributed to the rebuilding of black businesses.)

It was another fictitious rumor that touched off a riot in Harlem on a sweltering night in August. Harlem had evolved into America's black capital, a metropolis sheltering and comforting generations of southern

Wilson and Mertina Monk used a fifty-cent coupon to have this portrait taken in Atlantic City during the war. In a rare splurge, they then decided to get a second, so that each of them could have one. "We were so poor, we didn't have money to go to a movie," Mertina said. The Monks were married for sixty-eight years. *Courtesy of Wilson and Mertina Monk*

In this July 1939 photo by Russell Lee, a black man in Oklahoma City drinks from a watercooler marked COLORED. *Library of Congress, Prints & Photographs Division, FSA/OWI Collection (LC-USF34-9058-C)*

One year before rioting rocked Detroit in 1943, white protesters demonstrated to prevent blacks from moving into a federal housing project, planting a sign informing them that they were considered unwelcome. *Arthur S. Siegel/Library of Congress, Prints & Photographs Division, FSA/OWI Collection (LC-USF34-9058-C)*

Waverly Woodson served as a medic in the 320th Barrage Balloon Battalion, and was among the first African Americans to land on Omaha Beach at 9:00 a.m. on June 6, 1944. Twice wounded by shrapnel, he treated hundreds of men for more than thirty hours before he himself collapsed. *Courtesy of Joann Woodson*

In December 1942, one month after Henry Parham turned twenty-one, a draft letter landed in the mailbox at his home in Richmond, Virginia. "They got me," he said. *Courtesy of Henry Parham*

Wilson Monk, in front of a barrage balloon, most likely at Camp Tyson, Tennessee. *Courtesy of the Monk family*

Camp Tyson, in northwestern Tennessee, opened in 1942, and thousands of men were trained there to fly barrage balloons. The army's newest weapon was sent to strategic sites, most notably battlefields in Italy and France, to form aerial curtains against enemy aircraft. *National Archives and Records Administration*

"Barrage Balloon Training Center," Camp Tyson, Tenn.

A wartime postcard from Camp Tyson, Tennessee. *Courtesy of Bill Davison*

An enormous barrage balloon is raised at Camp Tyson in June 1942. The early models were nine-hundred-pound behemoths, about ninety feet long—the length of two yellow school buses—and thirty feet wide. *National Archives and Records Administration*

Lt. Col. Leon J. Reed was the commanding officer of the 320th Barrage Balloon Battalion. Though he hailed from South Carolina and attended the Citadel, Reed broke with southern tradition by treating the black men under his command with respect. In the words of one soldier, he was "a hell of a fine fellow." *Courtesy of Charlotte Reed*

At a 1942 demonstration in Washington, DC, four men from a black barrage balloon unit set a balloon aloft. Viewed from the underside, the balloon appears to be laced up like a corset. As it rose, elasticized ropes allowed the envelope to expand, along with the gas inside. *Roger Smith/ Photographs and Prints Division, Schomburg Center for Research in Black Culture, the New York Public Library; Astor, Lenox and Tilden Foundations*

A postcard of the *Aquitania* in lower Manhattan with the spire of the Woolworth Building in the background. During the two world wars, the Cunard liner transported thousands of men, including the 320th Barrage Balloon Battalion, to Great Britain. *Courtesy of Graham Newell*

CUNARD R.M.S. AQUITANIA   TONNAGE 45,650

Artist Peggy Beeton captured the only known image of 320th men performing at the Village Hall in Checkendon, England, on New Year's Eve 1943. Six men gave a concert of Negro spirituals after prayers by the battalion chaplain, Rev. Albert White. *Oxfordshire Record Office*

Jessie Prior in Wales gave a pocket-sized New Testament to Wilson Monk before he left for Normandy. She told her beloved American GI: "With loving thoughts and best wishes. May God protect and return you 'safely home.' Friend for ever." *Linda Hervieux*

migrants, and inspiring a dazzling marquee of artists, poets, and musicians. It was "the most complex of Negro communities," wrote the black journalist Roi Ottley in 1943, "a test tube in which the germs of Negro thought and action are isolated, examined, and held up to full glare to reflect Black America."

Yet in the summer of 1943, Harlem was a "cauldron of brooding misery and frustration," wrote Walter White, who, like Ottley, lived there. There were in fact three Harlems wedged into four square miles, and between two rivers, in Upper Manhattan. The Italian and Spanish Harlems stretched north from the top of Central Park to West 125th Street, giving way to Negro Harlem, which veered northwest for another twenty blocks. Mirroring the larger city flanking it, Harlem was a community of extremes, where the elegant row houses of Sugar Hill, hub of the Harlem Renaissance two decades earlier, gave way to dismal tenements farther south, "where thousands exist in basement dungeons," Ottley wrote. By the 1930s, with a population that had mushroomed 600 percent in three decades, Harlem had become the nation's largest and most overcrowded slum. The Depression had hit African Americans disproportionately hard, and even after the economic situation had eased, job choices were limited to the typical porter, waiter, and maid. It wasn't unusual to find an elevator operator with a PhD (an "indoor aviator" as one Harlem doctor put it). Jim Crow was alive and well in liberal New York City, with Harlemites turned away from some theaters and nightclubs even on their own turf. White-owned department stores along West 125th Street refused to hire black clerks, and the defense plants not far away on Long Island that begged for white workers had no place for men and women with dark skin.

Months of newspaper headlines recounting bad treatment of black soldiers had enraged readers. The travails of Harlem's own 369th Infantry Regiment at Camp Stewart were chronicled by the *New York Amsterdam News* and other local papers. The people of Harlem found a uniting force in "the indignities and dangers suffered by Negro boys in uniform," wrote James Baldwin, who observed that a posting in a war zone was preferable to one in the South:

> Everybody felt a directionless, hopeless bitterness, as well as that panic which can scarcely be suppressed when one knows that a human being one loves is beyond one's reach, and in danger. This helplessness and this gnawing uneasiness does something, at length, to even the toughest mind. Perhaps the best way to sum all this up is to say that the people I knew felt, mainly, a peculiar kind of relief when they knew that their boys were being shipped out of the south, to do battle overseas. It was, perhaps, like feeling that the most dangerous part of a dangerous journey had been passed and that now, even if death should come, it would come with honor and without the complicity of their countrymen.

And so when a story circulated that a black soldier in Harlem had been shot and killed by a white police officer, people were primed for vengeance. "Harlem had needed something to smash," Baldwin wrote. Marauding groups looted white-owned stores and preyed on white men who found themselves amid the mayhem. Six people were killed, 550 arrested, and 1,400 businesses destroyed or damaged. The future Harlem congressman Adam Clayton Powell Jr. later blamed "the whole sorrowful, disgraceful bloody record of America's treatment of one million blacks in uniform."

Never before had problems facing the black soldier gotten so much attention. The *Afro-American* demanded that the president do something to correct the situation at Camp Stewart (a future home of the 320th Barrage Balloon Battalion) and other problematic bases. "We say to Mr. Roosevelt that the war on the home front has lasted long enough," the newspaper declared. "He can end it. He ought to do it now. We expect him to do it."

What the president did was nothing. His position toward civil rights was described by a biographer as one of "benevolent neutrality." Roosevelt was reluctant to cross the powerful southern Democrats he needed to pass his wartime agenda. To his credit, he didn't hold back a key member of his inner circle who would make a difference: his wife. Since the early days of the Roosevelt administration, African Americans had found a friend in Eleanor Roosevelt, who crisscrossed the country during the war to promote issues important to her, particularly equal opportunity.

The First Lady's evolution into a politically savvy, peripatetic ambassador for her husband's administration transformed her into perhaps the most loved—and hated—person in America. Mrs. Roosevelt's exhaustive travels "began to resemble a crash course on the struggle of blacks against oppression," wrote one black historian. Black leaders tapped her access, and she obliged them. Beyond creating a path for black pilots in the armed forces, she was instrumental in the decision to open the defense industry to African Americans. Her activism sparked the wrath of southerners, who, according to an FBI report, considered her to be "the most dangerous individual in the United States." (The First Lady had asked the FBI to find out the truth behind so-called Eleanor Clubs, which supposedly encouraged southern Negroes to stand up to their white bosses. The clubs turned out to be a regional legend.) In response to the 1943 riots, the southern press blamed the First Lady for inciting trouble by "coddling" Negroes. "It is blood on your hands, Mrs. Roosevelt," scolded the *Jackson Daily News*.

In fact, Eleanor had begun offending white southern sensibilities long before her husband's election as president, when, on her first trip in the autumn of 1924 to his beloved spa retreat at Warm Springs, Georgia, she was horrified by the treatment of African Americans there—and didn't keep those feelings secret. She asked relentless questions about living conditions for Negroes, offending the local white sensibilities. "We didn't like her one bit," one southern lady sniffed.

The year before the riots, Mrs. Roosevelt was filled with regret after she failed to save Odell Waller, a poor black sharecropper in Virginia executed on July 2, 1942. Waller claimed he had acted in self-defense when he killed his landlord, but an all-white jury convicted him in twenty minutes. The verdict was striking because, in the same county, in an eerily similar case, a white farmer who had shot a black sharecropper dead was found not guilty in fifteen minutes, again by an all-white jury. In both cases, the jury was composed of people who paid a yearly poll tax. The tax was one of the methods employed throughout the South to prevent poor blacks from voting, holding office, or serving on juries. The results of such laws were stark: between 1908 and 1942 in Virginia, 156 black men were executed compared to 23 white men. Waller sent the First Lady a handwritten note asking for help. "I never had a chance to make anything not even a good living," he told her. Eleanor tried without success to get Waller's sentence commuted. She failed, and was shaken by the result. "I could hear tears in her voice," said Pauli Murray, a civil rights activist who listened in on the phone call when Eleanor broke the news to Philip Randolph.

Throughout the war years, Mrs. Roosevelt found herself a national ombudsman of sorts on behalf of aggrieved African Americans. It was an exceptional transformation for a woman who, four decades earlier, as a young sheltered wife, had called her servants "darkies." Black soldiers wrote her asking for help, and she often forwarded their pleas with a personal note attached to high-powered members of her husband's administration. One of those letters, in February 1943, came from a black sergeant with the 349th Aviation Squadron who complained that Negro troops at Carlsbad Army Airfield in New Mexico weren't allowed to use the recreational facilities or transportation available to whites. The base movie theater allotted only twenty seats in the last row to Negroes, who weren't permitted to sit in the white section even if some of the thousand seats there were empty.

Keeping millions of soldiers occupied was a difficult undertaking in the best of circumstances, but in the Jim Crow army, it was nearly impossible. Movie houses, social clubs, and other places where off-duty soldiers could relax were supposed to be provided on an equal basis to each race. In practice, this was rarely the case. Some bases didn't allow black soldiers in the swimming pool or Post Exchange, and even if they were admitted to the PX, it was rare for them to linger over a soda as the white soldiers could. Most USO clubs were closed to black soldiers, who missed out on seeing acts such as Bob Hope and Rita Hayworth. Negro USO clubs were fewer in number and second-rate. Lena Horne, the black singer, actress, and pinup, walked out of a USO show for black troops in Alabama when she saw German POWs seated in the best seats. "Screw this!" were her parting words.

Life off base was hardly better. Black soldiers were restricted as to where they could eat and drink, and even before they got there, they were often refused rides by white bus drivers. Since the rules varied from place to place, the black soldier was always on edge, never knowing whether he would be welcomed or spurned. Even in the War Department in Washington, DC, the nation's only black general, Benjamin O. Davis, wasn't welcome in the whites-only cafeteria. As long as he worked there, he skipped lunch.

For soldiers honed to fight to the death for country and honor, morale was a key component in the development of loyalty and motivation. Confronted with so much abuse, black soldiers felt they could fall no lower. War Department surveys in March 1943 revealed a chasm of understanding between the races. The question "Do you think that most Negroes are being given a fair chance [in the war effort]?" drew a positive response from 76 percent of white soldiers, compared with 35 percent of black troops.

Problems with transportation and recreation were some of the leading reasons behind the level of dissatisfaction. After the Carlsbad sergeant apprised the First Lady of the situation there, Mrs. Roosevelt "fired off passionate missives" to General Marshall in such numbers that the army chief of staff assigned two staffers to manage the deluge, writes historian Doris Kearns Goodwin. It worked. In March, the War Department issued an order calling for all recreation to be equalized. Signs marking WHITE and COLORED facilities were removed. It would take another year for a similar directive to correct inequities on army buses—again after prodding by Mrs. Roosevelt.

AS THOUSANDS OF INDUCTEES began arriving in numbers at Camp Tyson in late 1942, Henry County appeared to be one of the more benign southern postings a black soldier could hope for. Southern officers had a bad reputation among black troops, but at Tyson the men found an ally in a surprising place: their own white commanding officer. Lt. Col. Leon J. Reed was a strapping career soldier from South Carolina who graduated high school at age fifteen and won a scholarship to the Citadel. He was well liked by his men. George A. Davison of Waynesburg, Pennsylvania, remembered his CO as "a hell of a fine fellow" quick to stick up for his men if he perceived unequal treatment. Later in the war, when white soldiers cut in front of 320th men in an early morning chow line with a curt "what are these niggers doing here?" Reed was roused from his bed, charged up to the interlopers, and told them that *his* men would be served first. "Colonel Reed, although from the South, hated the word 'nigger,'" Davison wrote in an unpublished memoir. It was another story with Reed's second in command, Capt. William "Wild Bill" Taylor, a true "Texas cracker" whose vocabulary was more limited. "He didn't talk to you like you were a man," said Wilson Monk. "It was 'boy this' and 'boy that.' He let you know right away where he was from, and there was no question in your mind where he stood on the blacks."

Off base, Tyson's African Americans found a kindly welcome among the small black community in the city of Paris, seven miles from camp. There were invitations to dinner, especially after church on Sunday. The infusion of so many eligible men thrilled the Paris girls, many of whom soon found husbands. Others, like Hattye Mae Thomas, nursed a couple of crushes, but mostly made many good friends. Hattye had come to Paris in 1937 to attend the Negro high school because she was barred from attending the whites-only high school in her hometown more than a hundred miles away in Grand Junction, Tennessee. She lived with her aunt and uncle, who at various times during the war rented a room in their comfortable house on Williams Street to three black lieutenants and their wives.

Invitations to the homes of local families were cherished because, otherwise, there wasn't much else for a black soldier to do in Paris. While there was a handful of black churches, there were no restaurants that would serve the congregants. The humdrum Negro USO club at the Negro high school was hardly a draw, and any of the 4,400 black soldiers who wanted to go had to take Tyson's Negro bus, which had only twenty-five seats. The white bus had one hundred seats and ran once an hour; the Negro bus less often, sometimes not at all. On base, black troops weren't welcome in the white social club, though white officers could use theirs, called Service Club No. 3. No matter what was going on at the club, a Tyson man with a weekend pass usually headed out of town.

Beale Street was always a popular destination, but for soldiers with limited time and money, only halfway to Memphis was Lane College in Jackson, where a soldier could grab a hamburger and a cup of punch and jitterbug and jive with pretty girls like Hattye Mae Thomas, who was a student there in 1943. Wilson Monk and his friends appreciated those dances organized just for them. With no colored hotels, they were also grateful for the hospitality of the black folks who put them up for the night in their homes. That scene was too tame for other GIs like Bill

Dabney and Cecil Curtis, who often headed north to a "wet" county, where they could find some whiskey. Usually the place was Paducah, Kentucky, a city at the junction of the Ohio and Tennessee Rivers about seventy miles from Paris. There, they sought out juke joints, the traditional refuges for African Americans across the South, which were sometimes no more than a shack with a jukebox.

William Garfield Dabney had met Harry Cecil Curtis Jr. in the PX at Camp Tyson, and was amused that, like him, Curtis came from the countryside near Roanoke, Virginia. Curtis was drafted at age twenty-one and assigned to the 318th Barrage Balloon Battalion, one of the four Negro battalions at Tyson. The two would become lifelong friends. Bill was the baby in his circle of army friends—and looked it—just as he had been back in Roanoke. In 1942 he had watched as, one by one, his buddies "got letters from the president" (as Cecil liked to say) and headed to the induction center. Though many of his friends dreaded army service, Bill, who was too young to be drafted, longed to join them. If you weren't called up, he explained many years later with a twinkle in his eye, "you were all but eliminated with the ladies. They thought you were a 4-F [military code for unfit for service], that you couldn't make the grade."

Bill was determined to make the grade, but persuading his grand-mother to sign the enlistment papers wasn't going to be easy. The young-est of nine children, he had left the family farm in Altavista, Virginia, at age twelve after his mother, Eleanor, died of pneumonia. Steven Dabney decided to send his youngest to live with his mother, Caretta Bailey, who lived by herself outside Roanoke. "I wanted to get out on my own, anyway, even though I was still young," Bill Dabney recalled.

Caretta was a strict churchgoing woman who insisted her rules be followed and who brooked no nonsense. She expected her grandson to work in the summers and pay her ten dollars a month in rent. If he didn't have the cash, she locked him out until he got it. When Bill was a junior in high school, his friends were drafted one after the other, leav-ing jobs on the railroad hauling coal out of West Virginia and making parachutes in the silk mills. Caretta wasn't ready to let her boy join the army so young. He was enrolled in a good school in Salem, and she wanted him to finish his last year. Eventually, tired of her grandson's entreaties, she relented and signed the papers. As a winter chill hung in the air, Bill headed to the recruitment center and told the officials there he wanted to enlist. He was inducted on December 9, 1942, and was sent to Camp Tyson, where he was assigned to the 320th Barrage Balloon Battalion. His decision to enlist drew reactions ranging from teasing to scorn as fellow GIs noticed the serial number on the teenager's dog tags: 13121160. The number one meant that he had signed up. *You volunteered?* For Dabney, the number one lost him the right to grumble or grouse about anything over the next four years lest he invoke sneers from the number threes, the draftees. "You didn't *have* to be here," they told him again and again.

One 320th man who decidedly did not volunteer was Albert Grillette Wood. He didn't resort to extreme measures to dodge service, like some of his friends in Baltimore who ate lye soap before their army medical exam. (Word had gotten around that the homemade concoction lowered the heart rate enough to get a reluctant draftee a 4-F.) Wood passed the exam and was inducted two days before his twenty-first birthday in December 1942. Baltimore was the farthest south he ever wanted to go. He was sent to Camp Tyson and was scared to leave the post, rattled by the stories he'd heard about black men in the Deep South forced to work on chain gangs.

Wood's fears were justified. After the Civil War and the end of slavery, a new incarnation of that institution rose up in its wake that rivaled or exceeded sharecropping in its sheer brutality. Over five decades, black men and sometimes women were charged with crimes they hadn't committed or with offenses created with the very purpose of ensnaring them—such as vagrancy, which could be applied to anyone without a job. Many innocents were kidnapped, turned over to the local sheriff, and then "leased" to employers. Coal mines that fed northern steel plants were a major source of "convict" labor. The "convicts" were presumably paying off their court costs and fines, but many of them were compelled to work far longer than their sentences stipulated. Others simply disappeared, their families never hearing another word about them. Scores died in squalid camps. While not slavery in name, convict leasing, which continued into the 1950s, writes journalist and historian Douglas A. Blackmon, was "a system in which armies of free men, guilty of no crimes and entitled by law to freedom, were compelled to labor without compensation, were repeatedly bought and sold, and were forced to do the bidding of white masters through the regular application of physical coercion."

During the war, chain gangs were used to exact revenge on black soldiers who challenged the Jim Crow code. In one extreme incident, eight black soldiers found themselves in zebra-striped jumpsuits, with a ball and chain around the ankle, after they challenged a bus driver who had punched a black woman passenger in the face near Aiken, South Carolina. The soldiers were among several passengers who protested the assault, including two white men. The driver summoned the police, who arrested only the black men. Earlier, the driver had ordered a black and a white soldier sitting together to separate. The soldiers were jailed, denied a phone call to their post, and put on trial before a judge, who took into account only the driver's story that he had been beaten, a claim the soldiers denied. All were convicted. Three paid a fine and were freed, but eight others were sentenced to thirty days' hard labor. Each had received a good-conduct medal for his military service, and one who was wounded in combat had a Purple Heart.

White soldiers who spoke up in defense of their black comrades often found themselves in trouble. When an earnest white private from New York City named Victor Barnouw tried to sit in a Negro train car in Virginia in a show of solidarity, he was quickly arrested by military police officers, who called the Columbia graduate student a "nigger lover" but puzzled over how to charge him. The exchange that followed at the guardhouse at Fort Pickett descended into absurdity when an MP told the others that Barnouw had admitted that he wouldn't mind if his sister slept with a black man. "Jesus Christ, you god-damn fool, don't you know there's a war on?" one MP replied, "and you'd let your sister sleep with a goddamn nigger!"

Much of the unrest at army postings in the South and beyond was caused by hostility between white MPs and black soldiers who believed they were unjustly targeted by the army's enforcers. While Wilson Monk was at Fort Eustis, Virginia, shortly after his induction in June 1941, a white MP was killed by a black civilian. "That is the second murder of its kind in two weeks [and] in New York last Sunday the same thing happened," Monk wrote in a letter to his mother. Two months later, black troops protested when white MPs were assigned to accompany them on a Sunday beach outing. When their demands for black MPs went unheeded, the men refused to go. "The officers got scared and sent for the riot squad of about 200 white MPs and then the fun began," Monk wrote. "The boys were finally cooled off and the trip was called off."

Southern civilian police also were notoriously hard on black soldiers. In Arkansas, black troops marching to a new encampment were ordered off the road by state police armed with submachine guns. When the white lieutenant leading them protested, he was nearly beaten to death. The troops scurried into a water-filled gully and continued their march, "forbidden to put our black feet on the white man's highway," one of them recalled. There were exceptions, such as the time Willie O. Howard, a private in the 320th Barrage Balloon Battalion, was headed home on furlough to a speck of a town called Olivia, in North Carolina. Howard and several other Tyson men were waiting to change buses in Greeneville, Tennessee, when a local sheriff drove by, circled back, and told the men to get in the car. The last place Howard, twenty years old, and the other black men wanted to be was in the back of that car, but they did as they were told. They were relieved when the sheriff told them he was taking them to wait at the police station, and then he'd drive them back to the stop to catch their bus. "He was concerned for our safety. If he hadn't done that, God knows what would've happened to us," Howard said in 2011. "We didn't have to be warned—we knew. If you were raised in the South back then, you knew."

Often, however, encounters with law enforcement didn't end that way. In Paris, two 320th men were returning to base on a Sunday evening when they crossed two MPs and two local officers. The white cops were looking for some men, and thought they had found them in the soldiers, one of whom was Samuel Lee Mattison. Hardened by a life spent in children's homes in Columbus, Ohio, Mattison had little patience for the white cops with whom he frequently tangled—men whom he considered racist, capricious, and malevolent. "All they did was beat up niggers," Mattison recalled in 2010. "Black men ain't no men. We were like little dogs."

At Hastie's urging, the War Department had banned commanders from using slurs and abusive language—an order that was thoroughly ignored. A report in November 1942 to the National Lawyers Guild about civilian violence against black soldiers warned about the corrosive effects of continual mistreatment, including the use of racial epithets: "To address a Negro soldier as 'nigger' is such a commonplace in the average southern community that little is said about it. But the mounting rage of the soldier himself . . . is of such stuff that bitterness and hatred are made. In such a climate resentments grow until they burst forth in violent and unreasonable reprisal."

For Sam Mattison, living under such conditions was like having a thorn stuck in a place he couldn't reach. His sense of outrage, easily triggered, was rooted in an acute sense of dignity traced to an early life of not having much respect. His mother, Nellie, had left her father's farm in Anniston, Alabama, with her six kids to join her husband in

Columbus, only to learn that Louieco Mattison didn't have a job to support them. And he wasn't good at keeping any he got later on. He drank whatever money was around and disappeared after Nellie died in childbirth in 1928. After that, nine-year-old Sam was in charge, watching out for his older brother, Louieco Jr., who had been disabled by a brain injury. The Mattison kids—three girls and three boys—were scattered in group homes across Columbus, and Sam struggled to keep the family in touch. At age fifteen, he ran away with a white boy named Jack, and soon regretted it. Leaving the home meant leaving school, which was the only place where he felt he belonged. Sam loved reading and the sound of the poems he created with his own hand. "I was very happy for knowledge," he said.

One day Sam saw his father in the market district, foraging among rotten vegetables in a trash bin. It was a fate that he vowed would never befall him. He learned to talk his way into any odd job he could get— anything that would win him a measure of independence and respect. He was driving a coal truck when he was drafted in March 1941, and while he wasn't eager to fight for a country that he believed didn't do right by his people, the army offered the stability he craved. So it was galling to Sam Mattison to find an utter lack of order and respect where he most expected it. Despite his quick temper, Mattison's nimble mind and social savvy got him promoted to corporal and then sergeant, heading one of the 320th Battalion's motor pools and winning the affection of his men, despite the irreverent nicknames he gave them, such as TNT and Pig Meat. Keeping cool in the face of daily indignities, however, was a constant battle—one that Mattison didn't always win.

So it was on this Sunday night, after a weekend away, that Mattison and his friend found themselves on a Tennessee street with four lawmen staring them down. Things quickly went south. Mattison told the cops he wasn't their man. Words were exchanged and then blows, four against one towering angry soldier. The city cops landed their billy clubs on each side of Mattison's head as a short MP took aim with his club. Mattison, a sinewy 156 pounds, pinned the club-wielding MP before the other man got off a whack, breaking two of the cop's fingers before the second MP pulled out his .45-caliber pistol and pointed it at Mattison's head. Terrified of being taken to the civilian jail—"they'd probably hang me"—Mattison was relieved to be hauled back to Camp Tyson, where he was locked up and court-martialed. At the trial, the short MP arrived with two bandaged hands, Mattison remembered, chuckling. Somehow, Mattison beat assault charges, though his pay was cut for one year.

A confrontation on a hot summer night in July 1943 didn't end so peaceably for another Tyson soldier, whose fatal shooting roiled the post and stoked resentment. An official report said a prowler had been spotted crawling near cottages where fifteen families of Tyson soldiers, all white, were living. Earlier that evening, a Mrs. Lovin reported seeing three colored soldiers walking along the highway, one of whom said, "[W]e will be back." Later, another woman reported a Negro "peeping" in her window. Her husband and two other soldiers stood guard outside the house and, shortly after 9:30 p.m., saw "a prowler approaching the house on his hands and knees." A report by the Tyson intelligence officer said the men tried to arrest the suspect, but he ran. They ordered him twice to halt, and when he didn't, Pvt. Murphy Price Jr. aimed his .22-caliber rifle and shot him once in the back. The man fell and died shortly after, before reaching the hospital.

The man killed, Herman "Hank" Hankins, was a private in the 320th Barrage Balloon Battalion. His fellow soldiers challenged the official version of events, saying that Hankins was shot at a white tourist cabin in another town. Tyson authorities apparently did not investigate the shooting further and never commented on the fact that Hankins was shot in the back. They did tell reporters, however, that Hankins had been released from the guardhouse two days before he was killed, implying that he had found trouble previously.

Hankins's death was first reported by the black press on August 14,

in articles that also listed the killings of two other black soldiers elsewhere, one of them a private in South Carolina shot in the back under
mysterious circumstances. Whatever happened the night Hankins was
killed, Tyson officials worried about repercussions and were keeping
a "very careful watch" on black troops. No charges were filed against
Murphy, a member of the 316th Barrage Balloon Battalion, one of
several white units at Tyson. The 320th men never learned who shot
their comrade, but they were convinced Hankins was murdered. "After
Hankins's death, I don't know that anybody went into Paris after that,"
said Wilson Monk.

In the months before Hankins's death, fears had been mounting
that Tyson was ripe for riot. A rumor spread that a white MP had shot a
black soldier and that post authorities had covered it up. A Tyson soldier
reported the shooting to the War Department in early July. There is no
mention of the incident in existing records, but whether it was true or
not, it stirred up bad feelings. The letter was one of several written by
Fred Hart, a first sergeant from McDuffie County, Georgia, who was
angry after being demoted to private. In a June 19 letter, Hart detailed
several recent incidents that had outraged black soldiers, most of them
involving law enforcement and the use of a certain epithet. In one, a
black second lieutenant who was driving in Paris was stopped by local
police and asked, "Nigger, where is your pass?" When he replied that
he was a commissioned officer and didn't need a pass, he was beaten
and jailed. In another, the wife of a black officer visiting her husband
on base was slapped in the face by a white MP when she asked to use
the telephone. Hart accused white MPs of deliberately causing black
soldiers to return late from leaves, and thus risk punishment, by allowing white soldiers to pass ahead of them in line at the gate. "There is a
tense feeling that there will be a race riot here," Hart wrote. Colonel
Reed ordered weapons locked up after six rifles were taken, Hart said,
describing the sentiment on base:

[T]hey feel they would rather die here than on a field of battle, they state they are tired of being mistreated and seeing the [colored] officers also mistreated and if some thing does not happen in the near future, there will be a riot not very long now. . . . Most men have stated that if an Officer or an MP draws any weapon upon them or thier wife or mother they will have to die right on the spot.

Another sore point among troops was the replacement of black officers by newly arrived white officers. Failure to win deserved promotions was a common complaint among black army officers. The rank of captain was the highest most of them could hope to attain, though few did. (There are three grades above captain before general.) At Tyson, an unidentified black officer expressed that frustration in an emotional letter in July:

There has been continual jim-crow, in the towns, on the busses, at the "Post" theatres, disrespect to officers by white military personnel, without punishment or cessation. All of this has been accepted due in great measure to the continued insistence of the colored officers for passive obedience.

Losing respected black lieutenants to white captains, the soldier wrote, had contributed to "sagging morale" among the officers and their men, who "have learned to love and respect their colored officers, and from time to time have expressed their relief to be out from under the thumb of officers who treated them as slaves. It is therefore a direct slap in the face of all loyal colored American to feel the rights, freedom, and rewards of a democratic government apply to white Americans only . . . The slogan seems to be 'You must <u>die</u> together, but you <u>cannot</u> live in freedom together'" (emphasis in original).

The letters were addressed to Truman K. Gibson Jr., who had

replaced Hastie as the civilian aide to the war secretary. Like his predecessor, Gibson, an Ivy League–educated black lawyer, was inundated with complaints from disgruntled black soldiers. Yet beyond protesting to army officials, there was little Gibson could do to correct the injustice.

On the afternoon of July 7, someone slashed a barrage balloon with a knife, an act of sabotage that a Tyson investigator concluded was likely the work of a black soldier in the 318th Barrage Balloon Battalion, disgruntled over a demotion. There were problems of a different nature three months later, when two black units from the Second Army arrived at Tyson ready to brawl. "They pointed to the insignia on their sleeves and said that they did not want anyone to 'mess with that' and, in effect, that they were going to take over Camp Tyson," an aide to Gibson wrote to the president of the *Afro-American*. In the most dramatic incident, troops took over a PX in a white area on base and hit a white major who intervened on the head with a beer bottle. In October, sixty-four black Tyson soldiers stole two army trucks and left base to hunt down "a white policeman who had murderously beaten up one of their number," the *Afro-American* reported. There are no details of the incident in existing records, but the men were captured, court-martialed on charges of misappropriating government property, and ordered to serve one to five years' hard labor. The black press called the sentence one of the harshest handed down by a military court for such an offense. Tyson was still on edge later that month, when Wilson Monk wrote to his mother in Atlantic City:

> *The colored troops here don't seem to get along very well with the white officers and white civilians. No colored are allowed in Paris, Tenn. or Jackson, Tenn. now. There have been quite a few run in's with soldier[s] of Cp. Tyson and city police. I haven't been out since my return from furlough so it doesn't make much difference to me.*

Sixty-seven years after the turbulent summer of 1943, Wilson Monk handed me a photograph that he had taken at Camp Tyson. Yellowed and faded, it showed a mound of dirt surrounded by flowers. He said it was the grave of Herman Hankins. Why Hankins's body was not sent home to his family in Danville, Virginia, was a question that haunted Monk.

PART II

CHAPTER 6

Last Stop, U.S.A.

———

*Even in the summer when it is light nearly 24 hours a day, the North Atlantic
is a cold ocean. The sun seldom shines.*

—LIFE, JULY 27, 1942
NEW YORK, NEW YORK
NOVEMBER 1943

A gauzy fog settled over the Hudson River, its wispy fingers curling
southward toward New York Harbor and the open ocean beyond.
Silhouetted in the fading light of a mid-November evening, the
Statue of Liberty beckoned to the thousands of soldiers crowding onto
ships that would take them to the battlefields of Europe.

Winter was coming and the air was frigid, the coldest it had been this
season as the great British liners crossed the perilous North Atlantic in-
fested with German subs hunting for prey. Darkness was falling as the
ferries arrived one after the other from New Jersey ports to the piers on
Manhattan's West Side. A short walk from Times Square, the docks between Forty-Sixth and Fiftieth Streets—Steamship Row—were home
to the grandest ships sailing the seas. The gems in this collection were
three mighty Cunard White Star liners, floating palaces converted to
mega–troop carriers, the finery of their previous lives stripped away.
These ships would shuttle a large number of the three million men sent
to Europe and North Africa through the Port of New York from 1942

to 1945. British prime minister Winston Churchill later said that the liners, the only vessels capable of moving the vast numbers of troops required, shortened the war by one year.

The mood was festive at Pier 86 as thousands of soldiers began arriving after dark on November 16, 1943. On the dock, a brass band played rousing tunes as the men stepped off ferryboats, their breath turning to clouds of steam as the temperature dipped below freezing. Smiling Red Cross ladies handed out doughnuts, milk, lemonade, and cigarettes. On their backs the men lugged enormous barracks bags packed with all they would need for the next step of their journey, which they approached with eagerness, anxiety, or, for some, dread. For these men, the shroud of secrecy that cloaked all military transport had been lifted a bit. While they were not told where they were going, their arrival in New York pointed to Europe—or maybe it meant Africa. In either case, it was likely they weren't headed to Asia, which for many of them was a relief—the Pacific front seemed so very far away. Others shrugged. *War is war.* From the dock came an earsplitting whistle. The mammoth ship anchored there bore no insignia. Her hull, once gleaming white, was now a somber gray, and her jaunty red smokestacks now an all-business black. A few men recognized her: She had graced the cover of *Life* magazine the previous year.

Pier 86 was home to the *Aquitania*, once the largest and most regal of the Cunard fleet, with a capacity of eight thousand soldiers and one thousand crew. She had been dethroned by the *Queens, Mary* and *Elizabeth*, which were faster and larger, with the ability to carry up to sixteen thousand troops each. The future president Harry S. Truman called them "Britain's three proudest passenger liners." The sinking of any one of them by the wolf packs of German submarines hunting in the dark Atlantic waters "would have amounted to the greatest single disaster in the history of the war at sea," wrote Alister Satchell, a Royal Australian Navy officer who served aboard the *Aquitania* throughout all her fifty-three Atlantic crossings between 1943 and 1945.

The *Aquitania* had been called the Ship Beautiful, the most fashionable liner until the *Queens* came along. She was the flagship of Cunard, named for a province of the ancient Roman empire. She was christened on April 21, 1913, one year and six days after the sole voyage of the *Titanic*, a liner to which she was similar in size, shape, and prestige. For the celebrities, royals, politicians, nouveaux riche, and Russian aristocrats of dubious title traveling between New York and the great ports of Europe, the *Aquitania* promised, in the words of one reviewer, "the last word in luxury and decoration." The liner offered enough power to light a city of one hundred thousand, along with fifteen hundred push bells should passengers find themselves in need of a blanket, fresh flowers, or a mint julep. Like the *Titanic*'s, the promenade decks were enclosed to protect the well-heeled from the turbulent Atlantic weather.

The ship, at 902 feet long, counted eight spacious first-class suites among a long list of features, with verandas and private bathrooms named after great painters and filled with reproductions of their works. The boutiques of the mahogany-lined Long Gallery were an essential stop for ladies needing to restock their trunks ahead of the Paris fashion shows and the London season. Fluted columns adorned the Pompeiian swimming bath, and the lounges and smoking rooms were hailed by one reviewer as "faultless as anything that has ever appeared on the Atlantic." Comparisons were drawn with the German *Vaterland*, the largest ship at the time, with the *New York Times* proclaiming the new British contender, though seven thousand tons smaller than her rival, the winner with a "greater symmetry of design" along with overall "shipshapeliness."

Once asked why the *Aquitania*'s decor lacked a nautical theme, its French architect replied that the wealthy American widows aboard preferred to imagine themselves at the Ritz. Dinner in the Grande Salle-à-Manger featured eight courses and some eighty delicacies ranging from endless oysters to French lamb chops to poached turbot to six types of roasted fowl. Masked balls followed, with dancing until the wee hours on a floor that was just a hint too small. Generous stocks of spirits, fine wine, and champagne heightened the appeal, particularly during Prohibition—at least for those who could foot the bill. Conveniently, there was a bank on D Deck.

Life was far different for those on the lower decks, many of them immigrants heading one way to New York. If things got rowdy, a shipboard police brigade was at the ready to ensure the top decks were undisturbed.

After the outbreak of the Great War, the British government requisitioned the *Aquitania* in May 1915, the same month her smaller sister ship *Lusitania* was sunk by a German torpedo, taking 1,195 civilians, including 100 children, down with her. (With 123 of the victims being American, the tragedy helped turn public opinion at home—the United States was still neutral in the war—against Germany.) Speed was the *Aquitania*'s savior for the first time—but not the last—in July 1915, when a torpedo missed her by mere feet. She was a workhorse, carrying up to thirty thousand wounded men home during a stint as a seaborne hospital. After the Armistice, the *Aquitania* was among only four Cunard liners out of twenty-two still afloat. The victims included the *Carpathia*, which had plucked the *Titanic*'s 705 survivors from the North Atlantic.

The *Aquitania* was the first passenger ship to leave Europe after Britain declared war in September 1939, steaming from Southampton to New York with what one journalist called "a special aura of mystery and adventure," along with two twelve-pound guns on deck. The 1,625 people aboard got a last-minute fright when U.S. ambassador Joseph Kennedy warned that German subs might attack the ship at any time.

Soon, the *Aquitania* was drafted again into His Majesty's Service, making her the only liner to serve in both world wars. For the servicemen aboard, the journey was an exciting brush with an exotic world. The great liners of the day were often in the news, and the comings and goings of their glittering passengers chronicled in the leading newspapers. The great ship certainly had seen better days, but even in her cheerless wartime attire, the *Aquitania* enchanted. She "looked like some huge city as majestic as she did gigantic," a private named G. A. Hanford wrote in his diary during the Great War.

After ferrying British soldiers in the Far East and Africa for two years, the ship had been running the Atlantic route for six months on the night 687 men of the 320th Barrage Balloon Battalion gathered at Pier 86, stomping their feet to keep warm. Their journey had begun ten days earlier, when they boarded a train in northwestern Tennessee. Everyone knew better than to ask where they going. The curtains on the windows were drawn, as much to keep their movements secret as to deflect hostility from southern whites as their train chugged north. Along the way, Willie Howard from North Carolina kept an eye out for car license plates to figure out where they were.

They arrived two days later, on November 8, at Camp Shanks in Rockland County, twenty-five miles north of New York City, one of three embarkation centers run by the Port of New York to send men and matériel where they were needed. During the Great War, bottlenecks had caused freight cars of essential goods to languish for weeks waiting for a place on a ship. Not so this time around. The Army Transportation Corps ran the operation with clockwork precision. A similar effort was going on heading westward from San Francisco and other Pacific ports. But the Port of New York—Last Stop, U.S.A.—was the country's largest, moving millions of men and many more millions of tons of tanks, planes, trucks, guns, rations, and clothes to war. It was, the *New York Times* proclaimed, "the mightiest port of war ever created."

At Camp Shanks, GIs underwent medical and dental exams and were given vaccinations. They were issued two pairs of boots, a wristwatch checked for accuracy, binoculars, and an M1 rifle. In a disturbing reminder of what lay waiting for them, there was also a gas mask and a set of skunky-smelling clothes chemically fortified against poison gas.

If they wanted it, they could buy life insurance or war bonds. For the lucky ones, the most prized handouts were passes permitting a quick trip to the big city. There, they found restaurants serving anything a serviceman might want, with nightclubs such as the Copacabana to repair to afterward. Taxi drivers refused tips from men in uniform, and bartenders poured free drinks. Store shelves heaved with goods, untouched by rationing that had pruned stocks in much of the country—or at least that's how the GIs remembered it in their halcyon haze.

For the men of the 320th, the lights of Midtown Manhattan were a distant glimmer from Pier 86, six blocks straight down Forty-Sixth Street. There had been no passes for them, no last fling, though few were aware that had been an option. During their nine-day stay at Camp Shanks, they spent free moments writing letters home that were heavily edited by army censors. They played football, saw movies, and drilled, marching and singing so well that the camp commander was sad to see them go. With a registration number chalked onto their steel helmets, they were ready. Their departure was solemn and silent as they boarded train cars heading to a New Jersey port and the penultimate step of their trip.

This voyage of the *Aquitania* was notable for a passenger list that included an unusually high number of African Americans—2,000 out of 7,409 troops. The remaining passengers included 800 army nurses, 670 Canadian personnel, and 20 bags of first-class mail. As the roster was called for boarding, the band broke into a rousing rendition of "Roll Out the Barrel." If the lighthearted tune was intended to boost the soldiers' spirits, it failed, and nerves began to fray. When a Red Cross worker asked a 320th man named Frasier if he'd like a coffee, Frasier could only sob, "Lady, I want to go home!" Everyone laughed, though many of them were just as daunted. Many had never seen the ocean until this day. A final glance toward the band, and they were off, stumbling up the gangplank.

. . . .

"GUEST!"

"Arthur!" replied Staff Sergeant Guest.

Skinny Arthur Guest staggered under a barracks bag that he swore must weigh one hundred pounds. He marveled at the hulking vessel before him with four giant smoking funnels. (Only three stacks were technically necessary, but the fourth added panache.) Guest had hardly imagined he would ever cross the sea on a great ship. He was born on a rented farm called Smithfield in Bonneau, a tiny town in Berkeley County, South Carolina. Smithfield's ten acres kept the Guest family fed and clothed, though sometimes it did neither. They grew corn, potatoes, and cotton, which was useful in the winter for plugging holes in drafty floorboards. The hogs they raised were sold, never consumed. Arthur wouldn't taste his first pork chop until he moved to Charleston at age twenty-one. He was the fifth of eight children, one of three boys who shared a bed. Little Arthur, called Raggy, was always in the middle. Water came from a creek, which also provided some small fish. On a bad year, the corn ran out by March, and with nothing left for grits, the family foraged and hunted squirrels. "We were just above the slavery line," Arthur Guest said in 2012. "I wonder how we survived."

When there weren't crops to plant or pick, the Guest kids went to school, though not for very long. Still, Arthur learned to read, and favored the Bible, which would serve as a guiding light for the rest of his life. He was working as a laborer at the Charleston Navy Yard in December 1941 when the Japanese attacked Pearl Harbor. He heard the news on the Philco radio at the house where he rented a room. "I'd never heard of Hawaii before that," he said. Arthur was drafted into the army, and reported for duty on December 21, 1942. Though his mother, Mary, wasn't happy about it, Arthur was content to pocket thirty dollars each month, which was better money than he had been earning.

Aboard the *Aquitania*, Arthur and the rest of his battalion saw little of the finery of the upper decks as they made their way down to the bottom. For many enlisted men, certainly for the African Americans, life aboard ship meant long, bleak hours in the former steerage compartments. They were outfitted with four rows of tight bunks that seemed barely habitable as the men of the 320th settled in for a voyage of indeterminate length.

Life elsewhere aboard ship wasn't much better for the typical GI. Nearly every open space, even the swimming pool, was strung with hammocks or metal bunks laced with canvas. But the F Deck, the very bottom, was remembered on an earlier crossing as a "hellhole" by a white soldier, who worried about being so far below the waterline if a torpedo struck. George Davison, a clerk in the 320th, was lucky to have an embarkment card for E Deck. There, he likely bunked with Wilson Monk and other members of the Headquarters Battery, which comprised weathermen, balloon inspectors, repairmen, and others with specialized skills. They considered themselves to be the battalion elite. Not that E Deck was a huge improvement, but at least it was one floor closer to the top.

Those of higher rank, meaning white officers, were treated to a taste of the *Aquitania*'s former high life. For them, there were the same luxe dining rooms and well-stocked libraries ideal for passing monotonous days at sea. The two Australian cipher officers aboard, who sent and translated the ship's coded messages, shared a spacious stateroom with three windows overlooking the promenade deck high above the sea. Tapestries the colors of peacocks hung from the bulkheads above two large beds. Perhaps best of all was the private bathroom, even if saltwater ran from the taps. A woman serving in the British Royal Navy recalled that the meals served in the officers' dining room were "quite miraculously good."

Belowdecks, admission to the mess was by ticket, with thousands of troops lined up for each seating in a hall that sat only two hundred. The wait was hardly worth it. The soldiers rated the chow somewhere between abysmal and frightful. The Americans were hard-pressed to pick the worse meal: oily kippered herring for breakfast or smelly mutton with cabbage for the second, evening meal. A group of black soldiers aboard the *Queen Elizabeth* eating similar fare performed a protest ditty:

What did we eat just yesterday?
Baaa—aaa—aaa
What will we get to eat today?
Baa—aaa—aaa!
And what will we eat tomorrow too?

Their audience knew the rest.

Willie Howard tried, and failed, to fall asleep the long night of November 16–17. The idea of being somewhere out at sea was utterly unnerving. He was in for a surprise in the morning. "We thought we were in the middle of the ocean," he said. "When I went up on deck, we were still in the harbor." Troop carriers usually left in the dead of night, but the *Aquitania* got under way at 12:30 in the afternoon, chaperoned by tugboats as she steamed toward the Narrows and out to sea. Decks from which the fashionable set once waved good-bye as their Grand Tour commenced were now crammed with young Americans beginning a far different adventure. For many of them, this would not be a round trip.

Huddled along the rails, they watched as the towers of Lower Manhattan retreated, the neo-Gothic spire of the Woolworth Building and other wonders craning toward the heavens reduced to dots. It was a view that sent a Cunard publicist into a near swoon: "It is the city, not the ship, that moves, seeming to withdraw itself from us like a reluctant hand in a long and lingering farewell."

For many African Americans, their parting view of Lady Liberty was a bittersweet reminder that they were off to fight, and perhaps die, to protect freedoms afar that they had never known at home. Wilson Monk prayed that he would see her again.

. . . .

THE SO-CALLED SHOOTING WAR waged in the waters of the North Atlantic began three months before the United States officially declared war on the Axis powers. By the middle of 1941, German submarines were picking off American merchant ships like ducks, dealing a devastating blow to vessels carrying crucial supplies to Britain. Before Pearl Harbor, the United States had been caught by surprise by the U-boat menace and hadn't prepared, either, for the possibility of an attack on the East Coast. The lapse was surprising given that German subs had terrorized Allied shipping during the First World War. Finally, in September 1941, President Roosevelt ordered armed convoys to protect American ships from what he called the "rattlesnakes of the Atlantic."

Even so, during the first four months of 1942, U-boats (short for *Unterseeboot*) sank some eighty ships off the East Coast. The slaughter was similar along the Gulf Coast, and in the South Atlantic and Caribbean, where U-boats threatened the transport of oil and minerals. The United States was fighting a "new kind of war," the president told the nation in February 1942. "The broad oceans which have been heralded in the past as our protection from attack have become endless battlefields."

After the fall of France, Germany moved U-boat operations to Atlantic bases there, closer to their hunting grounds. In port, thick concrete pens protected the boats from British bombing runs. The loss of shipping in the United Kingdom was hitting Britain hard: imports of food and raw materials had fallen to 30.5 million tons from 60 million before the war. Worried about his nation's "potential strangulation," Churchill said he would prefer a full-scale invasion to the "shapeless, measureless peril" posed by the craft dubbed Hitler's Grey Wolves.

When ships began making the Atlantic crossing in 1942 laden with a far more precious cargo—U.S. soldiers—the stakes were raised. At first, carriers such as the *Aquitania* traveled in convoys, without radar, alongside smaller warships that added much-needed firepower but slowed the journey. A convoy could go only as fast as its slowest ship. The *Aquitania*'s advantage was speed: at her usual twenty-three knots (about twenty-six miles per hour), double the speed of some convoys, she could outrun U-boats. The *Queen Mary* and *Elizabeth* were even faster, at thirty knots. War planners decided it was safer to send the big ships out alone.

Unbeknownst to them at the time, the *Aquitania* had narrowly escaped an attack on April 30, during a run from New York to Northern Ireland. Hans-Dieter Heinicke, the skipper of U-576, had already sunk two freighters off the East Coast and fired at four others when he spotted his most prized target yet: the *Aquitania* crawling at twelve knots in a convoy of seven ships. With no torpedoes left, "Heinicke could only grind his teeth in frustration," writes historian Clay Blair. German propaganda boasted that Nazi torpedoes had hit transports laden with troops. None of it was true, but the false reports made the ocean crossings all the more alarming for the GIs aboard.

Sent out on their own, the liners zigzagged to prevent subs from fixing onto their positions, and sailed under radio silence. Even electric razors were banned except in the ship's chart room, where they were switched on in an effort to jam a U-boat's radio frequency. Each voyage, with as many as sixteen thousand young American lives at risk, was exceedingly dangerous.

In May 1943, the same month the *Aquitania* began her solo travels, forty U-boats, the largest pack seen during the war, attacked a convoy off Halifax, sinking eleven merchant ships. Subs weren't the only threat, with German bombers targeting ships close to the European coast. A German plane had bombed Cunard's *Lancastria* off France in June 1940, taking the lives of at least four thousand British men. In the open ocean, a handful of small German battleships stalked victims. One of them, the *Admiral Scheer,* had fired on a British convoy near Iceland in November 1940, sinking five of thirty-eight ships.

Many of the casualties of German torpedoes were U.S. Liberty ships, cheaply built vessels meant to quickly replace those lost. What a torpedo would do to a ship like the *Aquitania*, the third-largest afloat, was unknown. Experts believed the ship's dense watertight compartments would prevent it from sinking, but those with long memories recalled that the *Lusitania* had sunk in only 18 minutes. (The *Titanic* had lingered for 160 minutes). "The British sailors said we could outrun a sub . . . [that] the only way we could get hit was from the side," recalled George Davison. "Well, that would be enough for me."

The *Aquitania*'s weapons included two three-inch guns at the bow and two six-inch guns at the stern. To counter air attack, American and British artillery crews manned twenty-millimeter cannon and forty-millimeter guns. Even with such defenses, the *Aquitania* would have been hard-pressed to defend herself against a warship. Simply put, she had to avoid crossing one. A frightening possibility was losing an engine and sitting, helpless, at sea—which is what happened in late 1942, when a mechanical failure in the mid-Atlantic sent the normally unflappable British crew scurrying to get the ship moving. A GI from Florida recalled the "immense relief" when the engine sputtered to life and "the old bucket leaned into her four stacks . . . and sped off into the foam again."

At times, Allied Liberator B-24 bombers provided air cover during daylight near the coasts. Lookouts kept their eyes on the water, searching for a telltale silvery wake. When the carriers began transporting German prisoners of war to the States, the POWs were sometimes penned topside and told to spot torpedoes—or floating mines, yet another hazard. But U-boats posed the greatest threat, and a clock reminded the quartermaster to change course every few minutes. If a torpedo was sighted or if radar fixed on a surfaced sub, the ship turned hard, jostling everyone aboard. Daily reports from the Admiralty in London, which intercepted U-boat communications, gave captains an idea of what they were up against. U-boats would remain a threat throughout the war, but by the spring of 1943 the Allies were gaining ground, sinking seventy-three subs between April and June. Allied ship production soon would outpace losses to the enemy. Still, at this point in the war

Germany could build replacements almost as fast as they were lost, and sixty-nine U-boats were released in the spring of 1943 to prowl again.

There was another enemy lurking, often just as deadly. The wild North Atlantic saw some of the world's worst weather, with gales during half the year, towering seas, pudding-thick fog, and, of course, icebergs. A harrowing article in *Life* magazine in July 1942 described the danger:

> There is wind and fog and horizontal rain. There is "general quarters" and a bated breath while depth charges go off. There is black night on a lonely ocean and the terrifying silver wake of a torpedo. There are German submarines and turquoise-blue and gold sunsets. Sometimes for somebody there is sudden explosion and cold water and a salty death.

Before radar was installed—in the *Aquitania*'s case, not until April 1943—several Allied ships collided in these lanes. In December 1939 the *Aquitania* had a minor brush with Cunard's *Samaria*.

Contemplating the myriad ways they could arrive at the bottom of the ocean sent many GIs like Arthur Guest to their Bibles. Others plotted their escape. Private Hanford hailed the *Aquitania*'s "magnificent supply of lifeboats" in his Great War diary. After the *Titanic*, Cunard had promised "lifeboats for all," to calm jittery nerves. Before the *Aquitania*'s maiden voyage in May 1914, newspapers featured the liner's new safety measure: two motorized lifeboats each equipped with a sound-proof room and a wireless operator. Cunard heralded the liner's water-tight compartments as a "ship within a ship" and "much more extensive" than regulations required. The improvements eased fears among the 4,200 passengers and crew. Yet with at least double that capacity during each world war, it was no secret to anyone aboard that if disaster struck, the lifeboats would be insufficient. In addition, Satchell noted that "the chances of a perfect launching of 80 lifeboats in the frantic North Atlantic amidst panic from a steeply listing ship would be remote." (Only six of the *Lusitania*'s twenty-two lifeboats were in the water before the liner sank, taking the remaining lifeboats down with it.) The convoys that escorted the smaller troop ships had a rescue rate of slightly more than 50 percent. There had never been a rescue attempted involving one of the big troop carriers, and in any event, as Wilson Monk noted, "We were out there on our own."

At Camp Shanks, troops had practiced climbing down a long cargo rope into a boat floating in a pool. Aboard the *Aquitania*, so-called boat station drills were carried out every morning, with an alarm sending men massing on deck. Around their necks they wore cotton life vests nicknamed Mae Wests after their bosomy effect when inflated. The men were ordered to wear the vests at all times. More than one man mused that the army hadn't provided swimming lessons, and many of them didn't know how to swim.

The skies were mostly clear and the moon slightly more than half full when the *Aquitania* began her trip. The moonlight that lent a shimmery romance to Atlantic crossings in happier times was no friend to the liners, which traveled under total blackout. When troop carriers began their service, the largest ships, the *Queens*, were barred from sailing under a full moon. The rule was soon abandoned as impractical with so many men to move. In fact, Cunard captains had protested the decision to pack their ships with so many men, concerned the weight made them unstable in seas where thirty-degree rolls weren't unusual. With a cross-Channel invasion in the planning for the spring of 1944, however, U.S. generals decided the ships to Britain would be filled to capacity.

On two clear days during her voyage, Allied planes provided a welcome escort, buzzing ahead of the *Aquitania* to scan the seas for trouble. Records show that the ship's course along the coast of Nova Scotia was diverted farther north than usual, perhaps to avoid the spot where a U-boat had torpedoed a ship the previous day. Some U-boats were using new acoustic torpedoes powered by electric batteries, which left no wake.

Mercifully, those incidents were not shared with the soldiers aboard, many of whom hadn't gotten their sea legs and would spend a long week retching into their steel helmets. Even the seaworthy found it hard to take. The already stuffy air was fouled not only by vomit but by putrid lavatories overtaxed from the aftermath of British wartime cuisine. With few options, the men made the best of it. Some wrote letters "home," popped them in used soda bottles, and threw them overboard. Others brewed a rather noxious homemade moonshine from medicinal alcohol. A ban on gambling was roundly ignored, and the men passed time belowdecks playing cards and shooting dice. Henry Parham knew his way around a five-card poker game and won some cash, but the real 320th cardsharp was a whippet of a man from Louisiana named Rudolph Valentino Frelo. Plying a con he'd honed at Camp Tyson, Frelo got a buddy to bet against him at dice and then let him win, luring others into his web. Then Frelo began winning, and kept winning. "He was a hell of a gambler," recalled Albert Grillette Wood. "He'd take money off officers, anyone."

Bill Dabney was in cahoots with his fast-thinking friend, checking Frelo's signals before placing his bets. Then Dabney would do the cleanup. "I was like the collector." By the end of the trip, Frelo had cleared two thousand dollars—though the windfall climbed to five thousand in the retelling, as Frelo's fame grew as large as the barracks bag he stuffed with his loot.

Cunard had heralded the *Aquitania* at her launch as its steadiest ship, relatively free of vibration. Her powerful engines, fed a daily diet of nine hundred tons of coal, prompted one British lord to crown her the "Rolls Royce of the seas." Few of the passengers aboard in November 1943 would have believed that tale. Even with a speed reduction to 20.5 knots, and even in seas that were not unusual for late autumn, the ship pitched. Walking was an exercise in coordination, as were meals taken by those whose stomachs could stand it. If he didn't hold his plate tight with one hand at all times, Floyd H. Siler, a 320th man from North Carolina, said it would slide clear to the other end of the table. If needed, the *Aquitania* could push her speed to 28.5 knots, making the ride even rockier. Anti-sub tactics didn't help, with every zig and zag jerking the men this way and that.

One evening an alarm sent the men rushing topside, where they heard the boom of depth charges, sub-sinking bombs encased in metal that they nicknamed trash cans. After a few tense hours on deck, the men returned below, never knowing if they had actually crossed a U-boat or if it had been a false alarm. The point was made. Fear of another enemy encounter overshadowed the journey like an unwelcome stowaway. "We weren't alone on the *Aquitania*," said Henry Parham. The worst was yet to come.

After four days at sea, panic erupted on the night of November 21 when the ship was pounded from all sides. Four tiers of bunks were ripped loose, sending men crashing to the floor. The clang of metal mixed with shouts and terrified wails. Lights flickered, and men stumbled to their feet, unsure what to do, where to go. They fumbled for life vests as the 320th chaplain, Albert M. White, tried to restore calm. The Harvard-educated preacher from Philadelphia had already protested being quartered below the waterline. Now, as the ship heaved and pitched, White had to control his own jangling nerves as he tried to help others. Pinned in the bottom of the ship, "we thought we'd been attacked," said Wilson Monk. The men were sure their compartments would be locked and they would slowly drown. Eventually, word spread that it was only a storm and they should settle in for a rough ride. The passengers later learned that it was a ferocious gale—force nine out of twelve—that had pummeled them with waves upwards of thirty feet high. Such a storm could tear mess tables and lifeboats from their moorings.

Had they known about it, a crisis the following day would have rattled them far more than the weather. Six German Junkers Ju-88 planes armed with a new type of bomb attacked a convoy south of the *Aquitania*. It was the most-dreaded type of assault. Glide bombs were a German innovation operated by remote control, which meant they could be dropped a distance from their target. The only defense was to shoot them out of the sky. The ship could have used an air escort that day, but there wasn't one. The possibility of air cover had increased in late October, when neutral Portugal allowed British air bases in the Azores. The *Aquitania*'s captain, Charles Ford, had complained earlier that month that air escorts were provided more often to the larger ships, which carried twice as many troops, though he believed the *Aquitania* was more at risk because she was slower.

During the battalion's crossing, four U-boats were sunk west of Ireland, south of the ship's route. The *Aquitania* was lucky—a streak that would carry her through the war, despite some close calls. There had been three tense moments in October 1943 alone, a month that would see 175,000 troops safely ferried to Britain. In the first, on October 1, an Allied Liberator B-24 had bombed a U-boat three miles from the ship. Six days later, the *Aquitania*'s guns fired at a German Focke-Wulf FW-200 Condor—a bomber that had sunk many freighters—which then shadowed the ship, sending radio messages. One week later, she outran a sub, U-129. One U-boat captain wrote in his memoir, *Iron Coffins*, that he had traveled in the same waters as the *Aquitania* seven times. Twice, she narrowly missed floating mines. In January 1944 a violent hurricane caused substantial damage, with nearly fifty-foot waves washing overboard anything not nailed down, and many things that were, such as iron railings. Lighter vessels had been sunk in similar storms, but the former Ship Beautiful, though battered, survived.

The rolling hills of northern Scotland were dusted with snow when the *Aquitania* docked at Gourock on November 24, seven days and 3,300 miles after leaving New York. The ports of Gourock and Greenock were among the most important during the war, serving as transit points for 1.3 million American troops, war casualties, and civilian survivors of sunken ships. One of the most tragic was the *City of*

Benares, a liner loaded with evacuee children heading to Canada, when it was torpedoed on September 17, 1940. Out of ninety children, only thirteen survivors were brought to Gourock.

For hundreds of years these ports north of Glasgow had built the ships that enabled the expansion of the British Empire across vast swaths of the globe, flourishing in particular with the sugar trade in the 1700s. This was a homecoming of sorts for the *Aquitania*: she and other grand liners were built nearby, in Clydebank, at the John Brown and Company shipyards.

After taking an approach around the northwestern tip of Ireland, the *Aquitania* had turned into the Firth of Clyde and then along the west coast of Scotland, a route so breathtaking that many passengers would never forget it. With their destination kept a secret until the very end, many men were surprised to learn where they had ended up. Some had bet on Italy. The day was crisp and clear when Wilson Monk caught his first view of Gourock, his gaze extending from the quaint port town to the mountains in the distance: "It was a beautiful sight."

Some men expected to see destruction, yet before them unfurled a scene so peaceful it could have been drawn from a storybook. In fact, German planes had bombed these ports over two nights in May 1941, killing some two hundred fifty people and destroying thousands of homes. To thwart U-boat attacks, a giant net attached to buoys spanned the northern end of the Firth of Clyde, protecting the ships anchored there. Barrage balloons bobbed above barges moored in the harbor, a sobering reminder of why the Americans were there. The pocket-size resort town of Gourock was known among officers for its exacting golf course perched on the hills overlooking the bay. Visiting Allied servicemen fancied the pubs, which closed at 10:00 p.m., after which time ghostly shapes could be seen moving about the streets. Mystified Americans quickly learned the wisdom of tying a white handkerchief around the upper arm, the better to be seen during blackouts.

For the men of the 320th, there were no pub stops. Scotland was a mere blip in their long journey. After disembarking, they marched to trains waiting for them and headed south. But on this trip, the train car curtains were open. A black soldier could gaze out the window for as long as he wished. It was a harbinger of the life that awaited them. For the next seven months, these African American men would experience freedoms they had never known.

CHAPTER 7

A Taste of Freedom

The general consensus of opinion seems to be that the only American soldiers with decent manners are the Negroes.

—George Orwell, December 1943
Abersychan, South Wales
February 1944

A fter more than four long years of war, a devout and sturdy Welsh-woman took pen to paper and opened her heart to an American she'd never met.

My Dear Mrs. Monk,

How are you? I expect you will be very surprised receiving this letter from me. I feel I must write you, and tell you how very delighted we are meeting Wilson and having him in our home. . . . Mrs. Monk, you have a son to treasure, and feel very proud of. We love him very dearly, and will do anything in the world for him, all we regret is we cannot have him home more, but duties won't allow, he does come as often as possible. We have told him he can look upon our home as his home while in our country, and I will try to fill your place, if only in a small way. But don't worry too much about him, while he is here, we shall take every care of him, if ever he is ill, or in any way wanting us, we shall be there, we look upon him now as our own.

Mother to mother,
Very sincerely with loving thoughts,
Jessie Prior xxxxxx

Jessie Prior's correspondence with Rosita Monk in Atlantic City would endure far longer than the three months that Wilson would spend in a village called Abersychan. Jessie, like Rosita, was barely five feet tall, but stocky where the American was slight, with pale eyes and matching hair streaked with gray. At forty-five, she had never seen a person of color in her life—like most people in Britain— until the U.S. Army began sending thousands of African American troops to her corner of southeast Wales in the autumn of 1943. With her only child, eighteen-year-old Keith, far away at war, Jessie had found a surrogate to mother in a lanky American with soft brown eyes, and genteel manners.

He is such a gentleman. Every night my husband goes along to the hall, just to know before going to bed that he is alright. We have spent such happy times together, and he sings so very nicely. . . . We do pray he will stay with us for a long time. It will be terribly hard parting with him. . . . I shall always and for ever look upon him as one of our family.

In Britain, the arrival of the Americans was big news. The arrival of *these* Americans was huge. "One day Hollywood came to town. The Americans were glamorous compared with our soldiers," recalled Ken Clark, who was a ten-year-old boy in the village of Talywain when the black GIs arrived. "They had lovely smooth uniforms with insignia and gleaming teeth."

The "tan Yanks" were the first soldiers to arrive in villages ringing Pontypool, the principal town in the heart of an industrial belt of factories and coal mines. At first there were no white American soldiers to challenge the black troops, sparing the people of southeast Wales the friction and strife that usually accompanied the mixing of resentful southern white Americans and soldiers of color.

During the war, more than 130,000 African Americans passed through Britain and were welcomed by people who noted their courteous demeanor and friendly smiles, not just the color of their skin. The reception was a magnificent surprise. All the worries that the black soldiers had carried with them on their journey across the Atlantic faded away. This was a land where they could be themselves. They made white friends, enjoyed cake and tea in their homes, attended their churches— and they found themselves the object of fascination among a group that had been nothing but trouble for them in the past: white women.

Ollie Stewart, a well-traveled correspondent for the *Afro-American* newspaper chain who would settle in Paris after the war, no longer able to abide American racism, described the reaction of those early days in Britain: "The English people show our lads every possible courtesy and some of them, accustomed to ill will, harsh words, and artificial barriers, seem slightly bewildered. They never had a chance to leave their Southern homes before, and therefore never realized there was a part of the world which was willing to forget a man's color and welcome him as a brother."

It was nothing short of miraculous for Arthur Guest of the 320th Barrage Balloon Battalion, a deeply religious man from South Carolina destined to become a preacher. "It was a spark of a light," he says. "You can see a different way of living." Every last man of the battalion, even those who hailed from northern states and thought they knew a gentler America, felt it. Here, whites-only train cars didn't exist. There were no colored-only bathrooms. Dark faces weren't turned away at restaurant doors. The black Americans were greeted most places with a cheery "Hello, Yank," and often an invitation to supper. Working-class people in the Welsh villages shared their meager rations and the yield of their small kitchen gardens. Here, they were *Americans* first.

By the time the men of 320th stepped off train cars in Pontypool on February 21, 1944, the locals were long accustomed to the rigors of wartime life that stunned the Americans. There were nightly blackouts that made it nearly impossible to walk or cycle home from work. Black curtains covered the windows and doorways of houses and pubs, and the volunteers of the Home Guard remained on alert at all times for the enemy that might arrive from the sky.

Yet the war had also brought life to this corner of Wales. The winter sky was dark with dirty smoke as factories, some hidden underground, turned out tons of steel, iron, and the weapons of war. The bitter smell of sulfur lodged in the back of the throat. On low-cloud days a soupy brown curtain hung over the horizon, stinging the eyes. The coal mines that had sustained generations of families, only to forsake so many of them during the hard times between the wars, were back in business. Welsh ports protected by balloon barrages were important centers of transport. The mountains that ringed the valleys served as an ideal training ground for troops preparing for the land invasion of Europe—which everyone, including the Germans, knew was not long off.

The people in southeast Wales lived their lives prepared for the worst, but war landed in their midst only one time. On November 30, 1940, a lone German pilot dropped his cargo behind the Congregational Church off High Street in the heart of the village the GIs learned to pronounce as "Abber-sucken." The bomb reduced a pair of houses and the fire engine house to rubble. The fire chief was dug out of the ruins alive, along with a canary found in its cage.

The army had warned the GIs in advance about the privation they would find in a country that had been at war since September 1939. Heading south from Scotland by train, after their ship had docked in Gourock, the 320th men thumbed through *A Short Guide to Great*

Britain, a thirty-eight-page how-to produced by the War Department in part to head off their complaints. "You are coming to Britain from a country where your home is still safe, food is still plentiful and lights are still burning," the guide read. "So stop and think before you sound off about lukewarm beer, or cold boiled potatoes, or the way English cigarettes taste. If British civilians look dowdy and badly dressed, it is not because they do not like good clothes or know how to wear them. All clothing is rationed. . . . Old clothes are 'good form.' "

It was into this world of scarcity, and among the inhabitants coping with it, that the black soldiers settled. In villages, churches, and pubs, they were able to forge close ties with their hosts. It was the first time they reaped benefits not shared by the larger white regiments that would be confined to the sprawling Polo Grounds in the village of New Inn, outside Pontypool. The soldiers marveled over the sheer number of pubs and their place in the community—not mere watering holes as in America, but meeting points where men lingered at any time of day, exchanging news. A card game was always going, and it was there that GIs whose games were pinochle and blackjack learned to play three-card brag, a sixteenth-century-era forerunner to poker. Wilson Monk and his friends preferred shooting darts. If there was a piano—and sometimes even if there wasn't—Bill Dabney was singing:

There'll be bluebirds over
The white cliffs of Dover,
Tomorrow
Just you wait and see.

There'll be love and laughter
And peace ever after,
Tomorrow
When the world is free.

In Abersychan, Wilson Monk was billeted in the basement hall of Trinity Methodist, a stately church of large gray stones. It was there he met Godfrey Prior, a milkman who was as tall and lean as his wife, Jessie, was stout. "Goff" played the organ and led the choir with his throaty baritone. He was surprised when the young American stopped him one day and asked for permission to attend Sunday services. *Would it be all right?* Goff, unaware that congregations did not mix in America, told the visitor he was certainly welcome. Goff and Jessie shared many things, but not the same parish. Jessie worshipped up the road, at Noddfa Baptist, a simple church of clean sharp angles on a hill fronted by tombstones mossy and black with age. To the Americans, it looked like a graveyard in a fairy tale. It was there, most likely, that Sam Mattison cuddled with a girl named Jean among the graves.

Sam, a young sergeant in the 320th, spied the brunette one day as she passed on her bike. "Hello, pretty lady," he called out. Simply being able to flirt with a white woman, without fear of retribution, was a delight. But then Jean invited Sam home to meet her family. Decades later, he was still astounded: "You didn't go to a white person's house!"

Or to their churches. Back in Columbus, Ohio, where he grew up, a white boy from school invited him to join his family at their church one Sunday morning. As Sam walked in, murmurs rippled up and down the aisles. Someone asked him to leave, and his white friend burst into tears. Even at eight years old, Sam expected such treatment. So when he was given a red-carpet welcome in Wales, he said a loud amen. Many of the black GIs became regular congregants. They also joined the local choirs, where they performed their own hymns and spirituals, to the delight of the white worshippers.

The Priors lived a short walk from Trinity Methodist, across High Street and through the little victory gardens planted in Glansychan Park. It was in their tidy house of beige stone on Old Lane that Wilson Monk spent much of his free time, sometimes bringing his friend Earl

Davis from Philadelphia along to Sunday dinner. Wilson was a grateful recipient of the Priors' hospitality, which Jessie chronicled in her letters to New Jersey:

This afternoon I made cakes to send to my son Keith, and I took some over to Wilson for his tea, bless him. I shall know tomorrow when he comes home how he enjoyed them. I expect Mrs. Monk, you like myself has had many sleepless nights over your son leaving home, and shed thousands of silent tears. You and I, mother to mother, know what the feeling is. This wicked war was never meant to be, the suffering, separation, broken hearts, and loss of near and dear ones, is dreadful. I wonder often just what God thinks about it all.

For the 320th, the early days in Britain were a sort of paradise. Still, the specters of war and racism were never far away. On the war front, a major confrontation on the European mainland was looming. And although the Americans brought with them their Yankee spirit and energy, they also carried the baggage of home. Yet this time the burdens of discrimination were felt not only by the young black men accustomed to bearing the brunt. Consternation over race issues permeated the highest levels of the British government, and spilled over into the cities, towns, and villages across England, Wales, and Northern Ireland where the Americans were clustered.

The decision to send U.S. troops to Britain was negotiated by President Franklin Roosevelt and Prime Minister Winston Churchill at the White House over the Christmas holidays in 1941. The Nazi threat to Britain showed no signs of ebbing, and Churchill had been lobbying for American reinforcements. Finally, he would have his wish. At first, Roosevelt's advisers had opposed helping Britain, but gradually they lined up behind a Germany-first strategy, which meant devoting more resources to the fight against Hitler than to the Pacific war against

Japan. After studying the tactical possibilities, American war planners concluded that Britain was the best launching pad for a land invasion of Europe intended to drive deep into the heart of Germany.

Over the next three years the densely populated central and southern parts of the country would become, in the words of Gen. Dwight D. Eisenhower, "one gigantic air base, workshop, storage depot, and mobilization camp." The island all but heaved under the weight of shiploads of matériel, and strained to meet the needs of some two million Americans deployed there in what was called Operation Bolero. "It was claimed," Ike wrote with a wink, "that only the great number of barrage balloons floating constantly in British skies kept the islands from sinking under the seas." The American occupation of the United Kingdom would rank second only to the fighting war with Germany in terms of its impact on this unsuspecting land.

As supreme commander, Eisenhower led the Allied Expeditionary Force from a quiet cottage on the edge of London, away from the bustle of the city and the social obligations that he so disliked. He had his work cut out for him. The British adamantly disagreed with the Americans about the timing of a cross-Channel invasion. In fact, Churchill, wary of a bloodbath, had opposed an invasion route through northern France. In a test run, a small-scale amphibious assault had already been tried there, at Dieppe in August 1942, with the resulting rout and slaughter of 60 percent of the Canadian-led invading force—more than nine hundred dead and four thousand wounded or captured—attesting to the enormous difficulty of a frontal attack against a well-entrenched foe. The prime minister was also mindful of the one million Britons killed in the Great War when he told Eisenhower, "We must take care that the tides do not run red with the blood of American and British youth, or the beaches be choked with their bodies." His advisers believed that an invasion of the Continent from France should occur when the Germans were all but defeated. Casting a wary eye on Stalin's ambitions in eastern Europe, Churchill wished to see Anglo-American troops marching into the Balkans and Austria.

In Russia, Joseph Stalin was pushing strenuously for a second front in Europe as soon as possible, to draw German firepower away from his beleaguered country. With more than seven million dead, the "colossal sacrifices of the Soviet armies," Stalin wrote to Churchill, could not compare with the "modest" losses sustained by Anglo-American forces. The Russian leader suspected the English-speaking leaders were leading him on, content to prolong the massacre in the east to spare their own skins. In fact, Roosevelt wanted to get on with things. With morale flagging at home and desperation infecting the occupied countries, FDR ordered his generals to plan a ground assault to take place in 1942. But America wasn't ready. It simply wasn't possible to transport enough soldiers across the sea in the numbers needed for such an operation, which also required mammoth quantities of matériel yet to be produced. The British weren't ready to act on their own, either. Gen. George C. Marshall, the U.S. Army chief of staff, proposed an invasion plan for 1943 that would allow for the production of sufficient numbers of airplanes, tanks, specialized weaponry, and, in particular, landing craft. In the end, nothing was possible until the spring of 1944.

During the buildup, a more limited landing occurred in Sicily in July 1943, followed by an invasion of the Italian mainland. It was a victory for Churchill, who wanted to neutralize Italy as a Nazi ally. A foothold in southern Italy would also allow the Allies to resupply their lines from coastal ports and move bombers based in Britain to airfields on the Continent, closer to the enemy targets they were relentlessly bombing every day. The prime minister believed the war-weary Italians would quickly surrender, and they did, though the Germans would fight doggedly there for almost two more years. That operation had repercussions for the men of the 320th. Italy was the first major combat test for the American barrage balloons.

As relieved as British officials were to receive the first waves of white American troops, they fretted over the next influx: black Americans. Both countries struggled with the politics and logistics of making it work. The British referred to it as the "colour problem." Even so, writes historian Graham Smith, "few in power realized how the black presence in Britain would affect almost every government department, almost every facet of British life and almost every aspect of Anglo-American relations." In preparation, cables flew back and forth between Washington and London during 1942, all under the utmost secrecy. British officials at first believed that no African Americans would be sent. When it became evident that this was not so, they asked the Americans to keep their black troops at home. Britain wasn't alone. Also opposing the entry of black soldiers was a diverse list that included Alaska, Hawaii, Iceland, Panama, Venezuela, Bermuda, and even Liberia. Australia cited its whites-only immigration policy. Among the reasons given for opposing the entry of African Americans was the higher pay they received compared to the local men, fears of miscegenation, and racial tensions with white Americans. The War Department mostly ignored these demands, except in Trinidad, where black troops were replaced with Puerto Ricans after the British complained that the black Americans' "self-assurance" would influence the islanders. In Jamaica, white Americans caused offense when they insulted the locals and expected southern-style privileges. Young Jamaicans organized themselves in bands to fight them.

In Britain, the government was concerned about how their citizens would react if white Americans attempted to impose southern-style segregation in their towns. Jim Crow was alien to their way of life, and they feared the reaction when the British public saw that black troops were assigned the dirty work of building airfields and digging ditches. They worried about violent reactions from white southern soldiers if Negroes were welcomed with dignity. And they predicted, correctly, that Britons would take the side of the black GIs.

Reluctance to tackle the issue directly by Churchill's government would lead to much dithering over how to handle the matters raised by America's race problem. The result would be confusion. Still a colonial powerhouse, Britain also worried about the impact on its territories. But to its credit, the U.S. government stood its ground. The black troops were on their way—and among them were the men of the 320th.

The first white American troops landed in Northern Ireland in January 1942. They were soon pouring into the rest of the country, even before there were enough camps built to house them, in "the biggest influx of foreigners in most places since the coming of the Normans," writes historian Norman Longmate. The British government had kept quiet about the American wave that was coming, and the unwitting populace had no idea what was about to hit them.

Only sixteen months earlier, their nation had stood alone as German bombs pummeled London in the Blitz. Many feared German tanks and foot soldiers would be next. (Defying the advice of his generals, Hitler had instead sent his forces east, to Russia.) The arrival of so many fresh young faces was rousing to most Britons. It gave them hope. "Morale on the airfield and in the workshops got a tremendous uplift," said one Great War vet, "and the feelings of despondency at once changed to 'Now we can't lose.'"

Because the ordinary Briton had never met a Yank, their perceptions were gleaned entirely from the cinema. On the big screen, the United States seemed a luxurious paradise, where every American had a big house staffed by servants. It was a nation of "wise-cracking he-men and alluring blondes," writes Longmate. Many people, and not just children, envisioned cowboys and Indians battling it out on the plains. And machine-gun-wielding gangsters lorded over Chicago, wherever that was. "They ought to win easily as they are all so used to guns," one Belfast man told his son after Pearl Harbor.

Over the next three years the "GIs"—a nickname perhaps derived from the military term "Government Issue"—would alter life in Albion for the good, and bad. Britons were struck by their friendliness and found their cheerfulness to be "as good as a tonic," said one man in southeast England. "For a while the people forgot about the war." The presence of so much youthful effervescence after so much deprivation "was certainly something our drab, dreary old town needed," recalled a woman in North Wales.

Besides their Yank exuberance, the Americans brought fun in many forms. The American Red Cross opened clubs around the country and staged dances and concerts. To their delight, the local girls were invited en masse and picked up in army trucks untouched by gasoline rationing. With the Americans also came a windfall of imported delicacies unseen since before the war: oranges, grapefruits, and sweets. Sharing their bounty was the least the Americans could do when invited to dine by families living on rations. On the street, the GIs doled out Lucky Strikes and Camels and, to children, strange skinny sticks called Juicy Fruit. "Got any gum, chum?" asked the kids who trailed the Americans everywhere. ("Got a sister, mister?" replied the cheekier GIs.)

The Americans greeted every holiday with merry excess, at least in the eyes of their hosts. They threw parties for the children, with plenty of candy, turning Christmas into something of a bonanza. One little girl in Norfolk thought that Santa Claus "spoke with an American accent . . . and called all little girls 'honey.'" For Mother's Day, homesick soldiers showered a mum of choice with gifts. "They were horrified at the casual way we treated birthdays and anniversaries," remarked one Welsh woman.

Some Britons had the impression that Americans were always "on holiday," and it surprised them to see so many Yanks filling church pews that had long sat empty. Ten-shilling notes dropped into the collection plate at a Roman Catholic church near Preston, in the north of England, were much appreciated. A little seaside church down south in Plymouth was able to pay off a thousand-pound debt thanks to the four tall sergeants who manned the collection at Sunday services.

Senior American officers showed a warmth toward lower-level workers unheard of in the ranks of the British services. Two telephone installers clad in overalls working in a house in Birmingham were surprised to be invited to dinner by the U.S. colonel living there, along with a dozen U.S. officers. Yank informality sometimes backfired. It wasn't unusual for a private to tap a British officer on the shoulder in a pub with a hearty "Hey, bud," only to receive a cold stare from the rank-conscious Englishman in return. Chided by their commanders, lax GIs eventually offered crisp salutes to anyone in uniform, even hotel doormen.

The only group immune to the Yanks' charm were the young British men, especially Tommies peeved that GIs were paid three times more than they were. They were especially resentful of the riches that the Americans could lavish on their new girlfriends. For the women, an American boyfriend ensured not only a steady supply of sweets and cigarettes but the best prize of all: nylon stockings. These were heaven-sent for fashion-conscious women who had survived years of rationing by smearing a gravy preparation on their bare flesh and finishing it off by drawing a "seam" up the back of their legs. Newfangled and durable nylon stockings were a blessing. Why the U.S. Army stocked such a healthy supply of them is an enduring mystery of the war.

But amid this amusing clash of cultures loomed a far more troubled divide. The vitriol directed at people of color by so many white Americans was a shock to the British. In one of the first widely publicized incidents in March 1942, a group of U.S. Marines outside a London restaurant accosted Samson Morris, a black corporal from the Caribbean serving with the British forces.

"You're not going in there to eat with us," a marine told Morris.

"I am a British subject from the West Indies and you are not in America where you lynch us people," retorted Morris.

More marines entered the fray until there were six, and one grabbed Morris by the collar. A policeman intervened before the situation got out of hand.

Black Americans had not even arrived in Britain, and already America's "colour problem" was sparking conflict in a country that had never experienced such unrest on its native soil. It also had the potential to cause problems in the empire's far-flung colonies. How would support of discrimination play in such places as India, which had an active independence movement? "The British Empire is on the whole, a coloured empire, and it is hardly necessary to emphasise what the reactions might be in the Empire if we took a wrong course on this subject," cautioned Viscount Simon, who as lord chancellor was a member of Churchill's War Cabinet.

When a police report of the Morris incident was circulated in the top levels of Churchill's government, there was considerable hand-wringing over what to do. Some officials urged that the Americans be told that such behavior had to be curbed. Reluctant to upset their much-needed allies, the Foreign Office opted to present the report to the U.S. chargé d'affaires "with an appropriate hint." That kind of toothless reaction would characterize the government's response to the many racially charged incidents that were to come. Ordinary citizens would prove far more dynamic in defending the rights of men of color.

The Roosevelt administration was worried as well. The last thing Washington wanted was a public airing of such sensitive issues at a time when pressure was mounting to equalize responsibilities between black and white troops. Any misstep was sure to be exploited by the NAACP and other pressure groups, by the increasingly influential black press, and by white liberals led by the president's own wife. For their part, the British were loath to embarrass the Americans over their weak point. (The Germans and the Japanese had no such reservations, exploiting the race problem in their propaganda.)

ONCE THE BRITISH GOVERNMENT knew that black troops were indeed on their way, they wanted to know how many to expect. Rumor had it there could be up to one hundred thousand. Then a cable from London signed by General Marshall told the War Department not to send any black troops. Eisenhower waded into the confusion, responding that, yes, black troops were coming to Britain, but in reasonable numbers and in service units—and so they did. The first African Americans arrived in Britain a few weeks later, in May 1942.

That didn't stop the British government from quietly trying to stop their deployment, or at least restrict their numbers. Leading the way was Foreign Secretary Anthony Eden. At a meeting of Churchill's War Cabinet on July 21, Eden raised the potential problem of Britons "showing more effusiveness to the coloured people than the Americans would readily understand." His private secretary, Oliver Harvey, perhaps betrayed his boss's true feelings when he wrote in his personal diary that same day, "It is rather a scandal that the Americans should thus export their internal problem. We don't want to see lynching begin in England." The British Cabinet decided to raise the matter in talks with Gen. Marshall and Harry Hopkins, Roosevelt's close friend and frequent emissary, who were in London.

In Washington the following month, a young British official named R. I. Campbell told Hopkins that the prime minister was "genuinely concerned" about the "serious and difficult" problem posed by the presence of black GIs. Hopkins reassured him that the estimate of one hundred thousand Negro troops was "fantastic." (It was correct.) Campbell also met with Marshall, and in a telegram to London, summed up the Americans' dilemma:

The difficulty he says is that 60% of United States army engineers are coloured and provide most of their organised dock labour. Politically the army must accept coloured men on equality with white and the former are quite unsuitable for combatant duties. Engineers, fighting units of which have to be included in field formations, are in serious danger of being over-darkened.

Eden, in a telegram to the British ambassador in Washington, said that "our fears were in considerable danger of being realised," with blacks comprising up to 10 percent of American troops expected in Britain. "The last war had shown that our climate was badly suited to the negroes," Eden wrote, trotting out an old canard heard during the First World War to restrict black soldiers.

Eden then took up the matter with the U.S. ambassador in London, John G. Winant, who told him that "he did not think that the climatic argument would have much effect." At Winant's urging, Eden agreed to drop the subject until after the upcoming U.S. elections. Churchill's War Cabinet nevertheless endorsed his weather-and-health theory. Finally, Roosevelt put an end to the matter, writing in a cable to Winant on September 10 that black troops must be sent to Britain "of necessity" despite "many complications." He also sent the nation's only black general, Benjamin O. Davis, to Britain to investigate reports of racial tension.

The Roosevelt administration's fears about riling the NAACP were soon realized when, hearing of Eden's efforts, the group sent a telegram to Churchill asking for an explanation. British officials agonized over how to respond, and ultimately did nothing, not even sending a reply.

All in all, the "coloured problem" may have been one battle more than Churchill was willing to fight. Asked in Parliament if he would "make friendly representations" to U.S. military authorities to rein in menacing behavior toward British troops and civilians of color, the usually frank Churchill demurred. He called the question "certainly unfortunate" and added, "I am hopeful that without any action on my part the points of view of all concerned will be mutually understood and respected."

The black press was not happy with Churchill's answer but was grateful for the question. "The white Southerners were making a nuisance of themselves, just as they do over here," opined the *Afro-American*. "The difference is that in England, the British people are not going to stand for American Southerners telling them how to treat their guests." A cartoon depicted a bowler-hatted John Bull berating Uncle Sam, with a caption that quoted the parliamentarian who had questioned the prime minister: "The color bar is not a custom in this country."

To white American soldiers, usually from the South, the lack of "proper" racial awareness in Britain was appalling. Even Capt. Harry C. Butcher, Eisenhower's naval aide and confidant, who was raised in Iowa, remarked that the British "know nothing at all about the conventions and habits of polite society that have developed in the U.S. in order to preserve a segregation in social activity without making the matter one of official or public notice." White GIs aimed to "reeducate" the British about the Negroes, spreading stories that black men were savages collected in Africa and taken directly to Britain to do menial labor. The instigators were often officers, who were as a rule better educated than enlisted men.

Some of the fiction constructed around the black troops had an almost comical edge. "They'd tell all kinds of tales about the black soldiers," says Willie Howard of the 320th, "tell them [we] had tails like a monkey, and some of those English girls believed it. They went looking behind for tails." A black sergeant invited to dine with an English family was repeatedly offered a cushion for his hard chair. He later learned that a white American had warned them that without a cushion, a Negro with a tail would grow "excited and dangerous."

The mayor of a university town who was warned about the disturbing strangers began crossing the street to avoid them. One morning he nearly collided with a black GI and was startled when the soldier excused himself with a crisp, "I beg your pardon, sir." The mayor struck up a conversation and was astonished to learn that the well-spoken soldier had a college degree. He had been told that black men could only bark. Still, even after such hysterical warnings, Britons were hospitable to their black guests. "Our biggest enemy was our own white troops," says Howard.

Black soldiers loyal to the cause wondered how much vilification and abuse they were expected to endure from their own countrymen. If it hadn't been clear to them before in America, it was obvious now in this white country that there was nothing natural about the hatred and discrimination that had marked their lives. Albert Grillette Wood of the 320th later said he "felt like a king" in this part of the world, but the conduct of his fellow Americans left him bitter. "Discrimination hurt me more than anything in the world," he said seven decades after the war. "And I had to fight for these sons of bitches?"

THE AVERAGE BRITON HAD never thought about, much less discussed, the hot-button issue of race. Despite the nation's colonial reach, which encompassed vast swaths of Africa and South Asia, and extended to the Caribbean, Britons knew little about the lives of people of color. The ordinary Briton did not know much about the pioneering role British merchants had played in the trading of slaves that built American plantations, though he likely knew that slavery, illegal in Britain, had been outlawed in the empire's far-flung territories in 1834.

Guides printed by the British government to enlighten people about American ways sidestepped the race question, except for one pamphlet, *Meet the U.S. Army*, which offered this advice: "Any American Negro who comes to Britain must be treated by us on a basis of absolute equality. And remember never to call a Negro a 'nigger.'" The American evolution of racial nomenclature—whether to use "Negro" or "colored," the preferred terms of the day, with "black" considered by many to be disparaging—hadn't taken place in Britain, and many were unaware that such a term might cause offense. "In 1942," writes Longmate, "'darkie' was a term of affection, and the word 'nigger' was used without intention to offend; discrimination on racial grounds was not so much rejected as never even considered." The same went for trinkets with stereotypical images of people of color, which were not uncommon in British homes.

In Wales, twelve-year-old Ken Rogers was fiercely proud of a coin bank he had gotten as a gift when he was five years old. It featured the torso of a black man in a red uniform with a jet-black face. On the back was a lever that, when pressed, raised a hand that shot a coin into an open mouth rimmed by huge red lips. The bank had a name, too: "Jolly Nigger." One day, Ken invited a black GI he had befriended to his family's home in Pontypool. The soldier walked across the room to the mantel where the bank was displayed, and picked it up. He looked at Ken and smiled. "One day, son," he said, "that name will cause a lot of trouble."

"What did he mean by that?" Ken asked his father after the soldier had left.

"I don't know," his father said.

There was no official government policy regarding the "colour problem," leaving military, law enforcement, and civilian leaders to manage on their own. A British army officer attempted to fill the vacuum by issuing his own guidelines, which supported his preference for U.S.-style Jim Crow. And Maj. Gen. Arthur A. B. Dowler demeaned the "negro character" in a way reminiscent of some of the U.S. Army's own reports. In what came to be known as Dowler's Notes, the officer noted the black man's "simple mental outlook," lacking "the white man's ability to think and act to a plan." Still, he warned, black men will take advantage of a white man's weakness: "Too much freedom, too wide associations with white men tend to make them lose their heads and have on occasions led to civil strife. This occurred after the last war due to [too] free treatment and associations which they had experienced in France."

Dowler counseled "sympathy," but warned that "white women should not associate with coloured men." He told British soldiers that efforts to befriend Negroes "may be an unkind act in the end." A similar message had been sounded during the First World War, when U.S. Army officers warned that black soldiers would return home from France spoiled and "uppity." Though Dowler asked that the Notes be kept confidential, they were widely circulated, seemingly with the imprimatur of official military policy.

When the British government finally acted, it made matters more confusing. In September 1942, the Home Office sent out a spirited appeal to chief constables nationwide to reject any demands put to the police to enforce the segregation of public places. "It is not the policy of His Majesty's Government that any discrimination as regards the treatment of coloured troops should be made by the British authorities," read the letter, marked "Confidential." It continued: "The police should not make themselves in any way responsible for the enforcement of such orders."

The minister of information, Brendan Bracken, made a rousing, and unusually public, case against discrimination that same month in an essay in the *Sunday Express* headlined "Colour Bar Must Go." Bracken chided his countrymen for harboring hidden racial prejudice, which he said should "should die a natural death as many prejudices have done in the past. . . . If we have learned at least one thing from the two great wars of this century, it is to be less insular and to regard ourselves less as a nation set apart."

Shortly after, the secretary for war, Sir P. J. Grigg, entered the fray and took the polar opposite line, privately urging his fellow members of Churchill's War Cabinet to observe the American's army's practice of racial separation. The natural inclination of Britons to treat black men as the equal of whites, he wrote, put the nation at risk of losing the respect of the ' "average white American." Colored troops, he said, "probably expect to be treated in this country as in the United States, and markedly different treatment might well cause political difficulties in America at the end of the war."

Addressing the issue as it pertained to British troops, Grigg said morale might suffer if white women had any "unnecessary association" with black Americans. He proposed no official discrimination, but he favored directing army officers to "educate" their men and women regarding the U.S. Army attitude *without the issue of overt or written instructions*" (emphasis in original). Grigg hoped that such knowledge would allow his soldiers to "regulate their conduct as not to give cause for offence either of the white or coloured troops."

The Foreign Office supported Grigg's sentiments but tempered with Bracken's egalitarian language. The subject was aired at a War Cabinet meeting on October 13, which was dominated by the recommendations of another official, Sir Stafford Cripps, whose ponderous title, Lord Privy Seal, belied the power he wielded in Churchill's inner circle. Cripps borrowed from Dowler's Notes when he wrote in a memorandum that people of color were not considered equal in the American South but "inspire affection and admiration" like children. He warned against embarrassing the Americans in their "great experiment" in race relations. Although he said social gatherings with black GIs need not be ruled out, he suggested that British troops be instructed to remain friendly to black soldiers but to avoid close relationships with them. White women, he urged, should not "go about *alone* in the company of a coloured American" (emphasis in original).

As the Cabinet member with the most substantive proposals to buttress his viewpoint, Cripps had the advantage. The Cabinet decided to issue a revised memorandum that largely embraced his ideas. Senior British army officers were to pass along these points orally to subordinates and to the women's army corps. Aboard one warship, this directive translated to a commander telling his men that "the

American regards a Negro as a child and not the equal of the white race. Please conform to that."

Churchill's only known comment on the subject came after he was told that a black staffer in the Colonial Office was not allowed in a restaurant after protests by white Americans. "That's all right," replied the prime minister, "if he takes his banjo with him they'll think he's one of the band."

In the end, the Cabinet concluded that "it was desirable that the people of this country should avoid becoming too friendly with co-loured American troops." Though instructions on how to avoid such friendliness were not spelled out, the stage was set for individuals to in-terpret the directive as they saw fit. Numerous officials, particularly in the Colonial Office, supported equal treatment of African Americans. Yet in the end it was the loudest voice that prevailed and effectively opened the door to British compliance with, and sometimes participa-tion in, Jim Crow.

MOST OF THIS BACK-AND-FORTH was ignored by average Britons. Some were offended by the admonitions, and many not only treated African Americans with respect, but opened their arms to them. The British press, too, opposed discriminatory treatment toward black GIs. When a vicar's wife in North Somerset urged her neighbors to refrain from inviting black soldiers into their homes and for ladies to "of course have no social relationship with coloured troops," the *Sunday Pictorial* wrote:

> Any coloured soldier who reads this may rest assured that
> there is no colour bar in this country and that he is as wel-
> come as any other Allied soldier. He will find that the vast
> majority of people here have nothing but repugnance for

the narrow-minded, uninformed prejudices expressed by the vicar's wife. There is—and will be—no persecution of coloured people in Britain.

Instances of segregation drew condemnation in the press, such as an incident in Bath in which "four perfectly sober, and quite polite, coloured soldiers" were refused service in a bar. A letter writer to the local paper called the incident a "scandalous act." The *Times* printed a poignant letter from an Oxford man who said a black soldier entered his snack bar and "very diffidently presented me with an open letter from his commanding officer explaining that [name deleted] is a soldier in the U.S. Army, and it is necessary that he sometimes has a meal, which he has, on occasion, found difficult to obtain. I would be grateful if you would look after him." The incident left the manager "feeling ashamed that in a country where even stray dogs are 'looked after' by special societies, a citizen of the world, who is fighting the world's battle for freedom and equality, should have found it necessary to place himself in this humiliating position. Had there been the slightest objection from other customers I should not have had any hesitation in asking them all to leave."

The kindness extended to them shocked the black Americans. "This is a great country here and the people are very friendly. We like them very much," wrote one sergeant in a letter home. "I have met a great number of friends and when you have a friend here you've got a friend. I am living the happiest days of my life."

Eisenhower understood that the British had different attitudes on race than Americans, and told his top commanders, "It is the desire of this Headquarters that discrimination against the Negro troops be sedulously avoided." Of course, that did not mean integration. The policy was "separate but equal." Eisenhower assured reporters on background in July 1942, "The colored troops are to have everything as good as the white."

Eisenhower warned his generals that they should not tolerate racist talk (even though Ike sometimes used the word *nigger* in private conversation). "It is absolutely essential," he ordered, "that American officers and soldiers carefully avoid making any public or private statements of a derogatory nature concerning racial groups in the United States Army." He also took the progressive step of overturning a press ban on reporting incidents of racial tensions.

Privately, Eisenhower believed the race issue was a distraction at a crucial time when his energies were needed elsewhere. When a New York journalist boldly told the supreme commander that he had an obligation to change the way his men thought about race, "I told him he was a damned fool, that my first duty is to win wars and that any changes in social thinking would be purely incidental," Eisenhower told the NAACP's Walter White.

Ike left it up to his local commanders "to use their own best judgment" to carry out his directives while preventing clashes between black and white GIs. The result was a series of orders by subordinates that wove a crazy quilt of Jim Crow across Britain. Towns and villages were designated either black or white. In other places, whites were allowed in the local watering holes on certain nights of the week, and blacks on others. Passes were issued to prevent mingling, and MPs were charged with enforcement. These much-hated rules stoked resentment and often provoked violence when soldiers restricted to base were determined to find something to do while off duty. Further scratching off the veneer of Ike's order, Gen. John C. H. Lee ordered that army dances and other entertainment be organized by unit, which effectively prevented race mixing, though he cautioned that color lines should never be mentioned as the reason. If questioned, Lee said organizers should claim "limitation of space and personnel."

The emerging American policy was a confusing hodgepodge of contradictions and double-speak. Eisenhower's deputy chief of staff, Brig. Gen. John E. Dahlquist, assured confused British officials that "non-discrimination is exactly the policy which has always been followed by the United States Army." Dahlquist also claimed that placing certain areas out of bounds was never determined "on the basis of color."

A year after Dowler's *Notes*, an American colonel took a similar tack in a two-page memo titled "Leadership of Colored Troops," which instructed U.S. officers "not to focus undue attention on the color question," but to display "no hesitancy" if problems arose. The author, Ewart G. Plank, advised that "under the right officers and conditions, colored troops are capable of doing excellent work." He urged that "all personal prejudices must be forgotten," then ticked off a list of "peculiar characteristics of the colored race" that revisited the same old tired ground: "Colored soldiers are akin to well-meaning but irresponsible children. As such they have to be given the best possible care by their officers and at the same time be subjected to rigid discipline. Generally they cannot be trusted to tell the truth, to execute complicated orders, or to act on their own initiative." After protests from black soldiers as well as some whites, Lee ordered all copies be collected and destroyed.

The confusion trickled down to other institutions. The American Red Cross social clubs scattered across Britain were forbidden to divide by race, but hired all-black or all-white workers with the expectation that soldiers would segregate themselves. An army colonel directed that those clubs "staffed by colored hostesses" should provide "music and entertainment . . . more to the taste of colored personnel." As for housing and feeding soldiers, the races ought not to be "needlessly intermingled."

Race relations were a blight on the record of the American Red Cross, which provided cheer, snacks, and a touch of home wherever in the world a GI found himself. Even so, those smiling Red Cross women weren't always so welcoming to black soldiers, as the sailors aboard the USS *Mason* learned. At Eleanor Roosevelt's urging, the *Mason* was the navy's attempt to expand racial opportunity with a crew that was nearly all black. When the ship docked in Plymouth, England, in October

1944, the bedraggled crew had just survived the worst Atlantic storm of the war, in a crossing from New York during which six vessels in their convoy sank and the *Mason*'s deck split. The men heard there were hot dogs and Coke at the Red Cross canteen, but when the got there, they were refused service. The sailors were pointed to the Negro canteen a few blocks away, where the woman on duty apologized for serving them cookies and Kool-Aid.

Three years earlier, the Red Cross had outraged African Americans when it banned black blood collection at a time when donations were being sought for Britain. Although it was widely understood that there was no biological difference between the blood of different races, the Red Cross nevertheless went along with the U.S. surgeon general's wishes on the grounds that whites would refuse black blood. The slight was all the more egregious, given that it was a black scientist, Charles Drew, who had developed a pioneering technique to preserve blood plasma in mobile blood banks that would save countless soldiers on the battlefield. The Red Cross eventually reversed the ban, but kept black blood apart from white blood.

In camps, the army carried on its "separate but equal" policy, with blacks and whites bunking and eating apart. An order that transportation be separate meant that black soldiers who worked deep in an English forest testing detonation cap shells alongside whites—a dangerous job—were not allowed to climb into the same trucks with them at the end the day. Truman K. Gibson Jr., the civilian aide to the war secretary charged with safeguarding the rights of black soldiers, complained that the army was instituting segregation in a country with no tradition of it. "Any system that attempts to keep men rigidly apart increases distrust and suspicion," he wrote to the assistant war secretary.

One of the few units of black women sent to Europe experienced the cruel reality of the U.S. Army undoing the best efforts of the citizenry. Upon arrival in Birmingham, some seven hundred members of the 688th postal battalion drew cheers and applause as they marched

through the streets, proud in their flawless starched uniforms. The
sight of white people happy to see them was overwhelming. Later, the
women were barred from a public swimming pool by the local council,
at the request of the Americans.

The black war correspondent Roi Ottley wrote that white southern soldiers aboard his ship bound for Liverpool had assumed that Jim
Crow existed everywhere. They were flabbergasted to find out that ac-
ceptance was much more the British rule. In his article "The Englishman Meets the Negro," George W. Goodman, former executive secretary of the Urban League in Washington, DC, recorded the wonder on
the white side of the color line: "As honestly devoid of color prejudice
as the average Englishman is in Great Britain, just as honestly amazed
were some American whites to find there were English-speaking white
people in the world who could not make themselves hate another individual because he was colored."

The 320th Barrage Balloon Battalion arrived in this new world, in the
Oxfordshire hamlet of Checkendon, on November 24, 1943, three days
after they had landed in Scotland. It was there that the 320th men raised
their first pint alongside white men in the two village pubs, the Black
Horse and the Four Horseshoes. On Sundays, they were invited to the
Village Hall to sip tea and play games with the local girls. There were
dances organized in their honor, to which the GIs generously contributed, bringing large cans of army-issue peaches, and other treats.

"They always had massive amounts of food that we didn't have,"
recalled Barbara Dennett Holtom, who was eight years old when the
soldiers came to town. "Meats, vegetables, and hams. The tinned
fruit was what I used to love." They also dazzled the locals on the
dance floor, teaching the girls how to jive, jitterbug, and Lindy Hop.
Those evenings were as innocent as the gatherings had been for the
Camp Tyson men back at Lane College in Jackson, Mississippi, with

punch the strongest brew served. That was enough for soldiers such as Wilson Monk and Arthur Guest, who had sweethearts waiting for them back home.

Waverly Woodson, a 320th medic who would become the battalion's most famous member, found a dancing partner in a young woman who worked at the post office. She became a good friend—as did her husband, a fighter pilot stationed not far away. It was a friendship forged despite the best efforts of white Americans to prevent such liaisons. "As I danced with the postmistress, she asked me why our officers were saying such bad things about us," recalled Woodson, who'd left his premed studies in Pennsylvania to volunteer for the army. "She couldn't understand it. Sometimes there were fights in the pubs and clubs between black and white Americans. Whites would come into a pub where we were sitting and they would ask the landlord, 'Why do you let these people in? They don't belong here.' Often they went away and came back with reinforcements."

There were few cameras, and photographic chemicals were scarce, so barely any wartime pictures were snapped capturing village life. A single sketch exists of 320th men performing onstage at Checkendon Village Hall. Local artist Peggy Beeton recorded the scene on New Year's Eve 1943, when six musicians from the battalion gave a concert of Negro spirituals, following prayers led by the 320th chaplain, Rev. Albert White, and a nativity play performed by the village Women's Institute. At midnight, everyone joined hands and sang "Auld Lang Syne."

When the two village pubs weren't enough, some men ventured farther afield, breaking the rules of their limited weekend passes and skipping off to London. Theolus Wells hopped a train to the capital with some friends in the 320th. There, in the biggest city he had ever seen, it was another world of pub crawls and dancing. Nicknamed "B," the twenty-one-year-old from Orangeburg, South Carolina, was often mistaken for the heavyweight champ Joe Louis—an error he used to his advantage, especially with the ladies. The "Brown Bomber" was one of the few African Americans well known in Britain, where he boxed in exhibition bouts while in the army. In 1937, Louis's fifteen-round match with the Welsh boxer Tommy Farr in New York City had people across Britain glued to their radios. Yet even Louis couldn't escape Jim Crow. When the boxer tried to see a movie in Britain in early 1944, he was told he had to sit in a special section. The well-connected Louis called "my friend" General Lee and complained that the Americans "had no business messing up another country's customs with American Jim Crow."

In towns where both black and white soldiers were billeted, the white troops were astonished to learn that the girls actually *preferred* the black soldiers, whom they found exotic, handsome, and exceedingly polite, never catcalling after them like the white GIs. The 320th men reveled in the attention, treating their dates to double features at the Empire picture house in Pontypool, and an evening at the Palais de Danse, where orchestras played throughout the war. In Abersychan, the men and their guests enjoyed fish and chips wrapped in newspaper and served up hot at Mark Belli's shop on High Street. (Belli's also had a "temperance bar" that served lemonade, a remnant of Britain's fleeting movement to ban alcohol, which was decidedly less popular with the GIs.) In Checkendon, the beech forest was the favored locale for assignations. It wasn't unusual for fourteen-year-old John Cox and his pals, while they were out hunting rabbits, to spot ladies' knickers hanging from a fence post.

In their letters, white soldiers fumed to people back home over a world where they were second choice. "They shipped in some of them black boys and the people act as if they never saw any of them before," one private wrote. "The gals go for them in a big way here. They think they're cute."

"I have seen nice looking white girls going with a coon," wrote another private. "They think they are hot stuff. The girls are so dumb it's pitiful. Wait till Georgia gets those <u>educated</u> negroes back there again." One lieutenant noted that the locals "think that the niggers are quite a novelty and wonder why we raise hell upon finding them in the same hotel or dance floor. In many cases it has been necessary to lay down the law."

The red line for the average white southern man of that era was interracial sex. The Nobel Prize–winning Swedish sociologist Gunnar Myrdal, who studied American discrimination, wrote in 1944 that what the South feared most in extending voting, educational, and other equal rights to African Americans was the belief that such freedoms would inevitably lead to marriage between the races. The South "will never, never permit intermarriage," *Life* magazine wrote in an editorial two months before D-Day, noting the irony of a discussion about civil rights "in the midst of a war for freedom." Anti-miscegenation laws in seventeen southern states would endure as late as June 1967, when the Supreme Court, in the aptly named *Loving v. Virginia*, declared them unconstitutional.

The reactions of southern GIs to mixed couples ranged from expelling blacks from dances, hotels, pubs, and other public places, to beatings meted out when a black soldier protested. The incidents were well chronicled in the press, and became some of the most memorable wartime stories for many Britons. "We got really scared they had so many fights," said one woman in Devon. In southeastern Wales, there were knife fights in the pubs, mystifying the locals, who couldn't fathom what the Americans were doing to one another.

In one of the worst clashes, a battle broke out in Lancashire in June 1943 when white MPs, one of whom was drunk, challenged black GIs outside a pub. The locals took the side of the blacks, who fought back with bricks and bottles. Eventually, seven servicemen were wounded and thirty-two black soldiers court-martialed. In other instances, black soldiers rebelled when they were refused entry to pubs because they didn't have passes on a particular night. Violence erupted in the western town of Paignton one night in October 1943 after several black soldiers, fed up with bad treatment in town by white soldiers, armed themselves, returned to town, and exchanged fire with MPs. In such cases, the black soldiers were usually court-martialed on charges ranging from rioting to mutiny to attempted murder, and handed sentences that local people considered excessively harsh.

Fifty-six racial clashes were reported between November 1943 and February 1944, an average of more than four each week, most occurring in the congested southern half of the country. It wasn't only black soldiers who suffered. Some white soldiers kept a list of names and refused to dance with young women who attended the Negro dances or admitted going to town on "coloured nights." Pettiness knew no bounds, as a little white girl in Herefordshire learned when she showed her prized black doll to some white GIs. They grabbed it, placed it on a post, and bombarded it with snowballs.

When reports of racial strife made their way to her mailbag, Eleanor Roosevelt told War Secretary Stimson in a letter, "I think we will have to do a little educating among our Southern white men and officers." The First Lady visited troops in Britain in the fall of 1942, prompting Stimson to urge the president to impress upon his wife that she ought not to publicize the superior treatment accorded to Negroes there.

Not all efforts at integration led to conflict. Contact between the races could breed tolerance, and sometimes even understanding. It had worked on some union-monitored assembly lines in Detroit. In Britain, one white southern soldier who spent time with black GIs found that he was no longer appalled by the very concept of integration. When he heard about a proposed all-volunteer infantry division mixing black and white troops, he said he'd like to volunteer. "Then I wouldn't feel like such a goddamned hypocrite when people over here ask why, in fighting a war for democracy, the United States sends over one white and one Negro army." (The integrated unit was never formed.)

A white soldier from Georgia stationed in central England found that he preferred the "Negro" Red Cross club to white clubs elsewhere. There, he was free to speak with black GIs, some of whom he befriended, something he would never have done in front of his white friends. The story of the Midlands Red Cross club revealed what could happen when the army applied strong leadership and discipline to enforce civility. When a large contingent of white soldiers was stationed in the area, their commander, a southerner, told them that the only club in town was run by a Negro and staffed by Negroes. Anyone who had a problem with that should stay away. He warned them that if any man started trouble, he would be immediately court-martialed. There were no problems. In fact, many white troops from various units who had avoided the club began going there. What they found was a friendly place that welcomed them.

Several months after the bloody riot that rocked Detroit in June 1943, a white soldier marveled over the racist cataclysm that had engulfed his hometown. "It looks very different from over here," he observed, adding, "Don't the people back home realize that they are playing Hitler's game?"

EVEN BEFORE THEY BEGAN abusing their black countrymen, white Americans were rapidly wearing out their welcome. GIs offended their British hosts by scoffing at the absence of electric refrigerators, telephones, radios, and other comforts typical in their lives back home. They were appalled by the condition of their billets lacking hot water, showers, and sometimes indoor plumbing. Little more than half of all British homes at the time had indoor bathrooms, and even if they did, a bath was a weekly luxury. The Americans proclaimed British cuisine revolting. The dreary mutton aboard ship now seemed a relative indulgence. Perhaps the least favorite was the gray bread made from potato flour. The humble potato was a wartime staple, the most popular "meat substitute" in *War-Time Cookery*, a 1940 recipe booklet that encouraged British housewives to stretch their scarce food stocks. In it, potatoes are the base for, among other things, a sort of cheese, pudding with macaroni, and suet paste.

Even Eisenhower acknowledged built-in GI hubris: "Every American soldier coming to Britain was almost certain to consider himself a privileged crusader, sent there to help Britain out of a hole." The average GI, a secret British survey found, "thinks the country is inexcusably old-fashioned", with "the agonizingly leisurely shopkeepers, the uncomfortable hotels, the outmoded lavatory equipment, the funny trains, the cut of the women's clothes, the style of the men's haircuts, the left hand drive, the slovenly business offices, and dozens of other things."

White troops shared their criticisms freely—and loudly—in restaurants, pubs, and just about everywhere else. Speeding army trucks flattened hedgerows and sent cyclists and pedestrians leaping into ditches. The soldiers flouted the boldface advice "Don't Be a Show Off" recommended in another army booklet, *Instructions for American Servicemen in Britain 1942*. Britons began to find the Yanks' swagger annoying, their ways wasteful and extravagant. "Brag, conceit and cocksureness were the features most disliked in Americans," concluded a survey taken by the British government in January 1943.

In Checkendon, a white soldier fired two shots clean through the weathervane atop Saint Peter and Saint Paul, the church on the village green. (He was eventually tracked down and made to pay for the repairs.) After drinking at the Four Horseshoes, a group of rowdy white soldiers left an unwelcome calling card on their way home. "They took everyone's gates off and piled them in the road," recalled Gus Gray, who was nine years old. "This didn't endear them to anyone."

Public drunkenness was out of control from Liverpool to London, and trysts in doorways and gardens tested the patience of just about everyone. "Overpaid, overfed, oversexed and over here," was the new label pinned on the occupiers. Less than one year after their arrival, the GIs could do nothing right. Even the fat from the richer U.S. Army rations was blamed for clogging the filter beds of public drains.

With some exceptions, soldiers of color who cherished the treatment extended to them did not engage in this sort of behavior, according to multiple sources, including British officials, civilians, and visiting American observers. More than 75 percent of African Americans came from humble southern homes lacking the comforts commonplace in white homes, and they cherished their circumstances in Britain. Economic conditions also created a bond. Black Americans earned half the income of white Americans, while Britons earned about one-third that of white Americans.

"The general consensus of opinion seems to be that the only American soldiers with decent manners are the Negroes," wrote George Orwell in the *Tribune*, a leftist weekly. Mistreatment of blacks at the hands of white Americans only enhanced their popularity. In early 1944, nearly two years after the first black troops arrived, the NAACP's Walter White found during a tour of Britain that they were still welcomed, particularly in places that had experienced racial violence. Some pub owners were said to have practiced reverse discrimination by barring white soldiers.

That only exacerbated the tension. White GIs unused to having their behavior challenged pushed back. This in turn made Britons even more protective of the black soldiers. On one occasion, a black GI was sitting on a train in Wiltshire County, in southwestern England, when two white Americans boarded, spotted him, and refused to share his car. As the white GIs hovered in the passage, a British sailor made a show of offering the black American a cigarette and striking up a conversation with him, which the other travelers joined. One evening at a dance in the same region, an MC announced, "The management wishes white American soldiers attending the dance to leave." The "laughing couples fell silent, then applauded," a news report said. Earlier, white GIs had asked the black men to leave.

In Wales, underdogs held a special status. Black GIs found defenders in the many coal-mining families who had been left impoverished during the economic downturn between the world wars, suffering hunger, humiliating bread lines, and derision from their countrymen. "They were considered inferior by the English because they would work long hours for less money," says Ken Clark. "They identified with the black Americans because they were also oppressed."

The British media also championed the black men's cause. Newspapers covered good deeds performed by black GIs, such as the heroics of two soldiers in Liverpool who were awarded medals for rescuing a dockworker who fell into the water. American military justice was denounced in the press, from the pulpit, and by ordinary citizens for its brutality and bias against black soldiers. Since Parliament had granted U.S. authorities powers to police their own, death sentences handed down in sexual assault cases, which were not capital crimes in British courts, drew demands for clemency.

One case that gripped all of Britain was that of a black GI named Leroy Henry. Late on the evening of May 5, 1944, a black soldier knocked on the window of a house in a town near Bath. A woman left the bed she shared with her husband, popped her head out a window, and asked the soldier what he wanted. "I'm lost," replied the GI. "I've got to get to Bristol tonight." The woman, thirty-three years old, opened the door, invited him inside, and then agreed to show him the best route to find transportation. After some time, her husband wondered where she had gone and found her walking in the street. She told him that the black soldier had pulled a knife and raped her.

Leroy Henry was arrested shortly after and admitted to assaulting the woman. It seemed an open-and-shut case. Except at his court-martial three weeks later, Henry testified that he had signed a confession only after a brutal interrogation during which he was abused, threatened, and so cold from hunger that he passed out. The truth was, Henry said, that he had met the woman twice before and had paid her for sex, one pound each time. On the night of his arrest, he had arranged a tryst with the woman, who surprised him by demanding two pounds. They argued, and Henry refused to pay her. When he was picked up by police, Henry had no knife on him. A doctor testified that the woman showed signs of recent sex but not of a struggle.

Although the prosecutor conceded it was "rather odd" for the woman to leave her husband and her bed and accompany a stranger outside at such an hour, he explained to the court that "in our relations with the English they do things that we don't do, and many of us will be able to teach our wives lessons." Henry was quickly convicted and sentenced "to be hanged by the neck till dead."

It was one month before the invasion of France, yet Britons had Leroy Henry on their minds. In letters, newspaper columns, and petitions, they pressed to see justice, insisting that Henry would not be in such a predicament if he were white. American officials denied bias, as they had in other cases. A later study indicated otherwise: while black soldiers represented 8 percent of all personnel in Europe, they comprised 21 percent of servicemen convicted of crimes, and 42 percent convicted of sex crimes. Those figures appear particularly stark when considered alongside the many accolades showered on African Americans during their time in Britain.

Petitions with tens of thousands of signatures to free Henry made it all the way up to Eisenhower, who swiftly overruled the conviction for lack of evidence and reinstated the soldier to full service. Had there been no public outcry, Henry would very likely have been executed. He was saved by the British public, who knew about the case only because Foreign Minister Eden had insisted that when British civilians were involved, U.S. courts-martial be held in public.

Another barrage of petitions helped free a black soldier named Joseph Ballot. During his trial for assault in the southern city of Portsmouth, no mention was made of rape and no evidence presented of a sex crime. Yet Ballot was sentenced to life in prison, "no doubt on account of his color," wrote the local woman who circulated a petition to free him, even as German bombs fell. "A white American sailor, tried for murder, received a sentence of only ten years?!" she wrote. "We are asking ourselves why we stood up to the nights of terror in 1940 and 1941 if it was not for the freedom, justice, and rights of all men?"

Not all Britons were so moved. "Their form of justice may be stern, but it is undoubtedly necessary," one man wrote to the *Gloucester Echo*. "When that justice is applied . . . to the upholding of the protection of young English womanhood, it should evoke thanks, and not squeals of ignorant protest."

The use of courts-martial against black soldiers appeared to many observers to be "used to break the spirit of Negro soldiers, particularly those who knew their rights and insisted upon exercising them," wrote Walter White. He cited the case of two black privates who objected to being called "niggers" by a white MP captain and who drafted a petition to their commander noting that the army barred the use of racial slurs. Although that very rule had been emphasized by Eisenhower on British soil, the two GIs were court-martialed and sentenced to ten years' hard labor. Their sergeant wrote a letter of protest to their commander that was ignored, so he appealed to the commanding general, and was himself sentenced to six months' hard labor for violating army regulations.

Even Parliament became involved in the struggle for racial justice. After two black soldiers were hanged for rape, legislators grilled the foreign secretary about whether white soldiers faced the same penalties. And the fate of a cricket legend from Trinidad almost prompted the House of Commons to criminalize any form of discrimination perpetuated against British citizens. The treatment of Learie Constantine made national headlines after he and his family were kicked out of a London hotel after Americans complained about their presence.

The British press was particularly offended by attacks on people of color from the colonies who, like Constantine, had volunteered to serve in the empire's armed forces. "WHAT ARE WE GOING TO DO ABOUT THIS?" blared the *Sunday Pictorial* in a boldface headline in

August 1943, after a black airman from Barbados was beaten in Suffolk by two white American soldiers after he asked a woman to dance. In an emotional letter reprinted in the newspaper, the victim, Sgt. Arthur A. Walrond, asked, "Is it fair, is it just, to ask me to risk my life nightly over enemy territory" while being subjected to constant indignities. "I came to this country as a volunteer for air crew duties under the protection of the British government, and I demand as far as it is humanly possible that I get that protection and its corresponding consideration."

Hours after he signed his missive, Walrond, twenty-nine years old, climbed into his Stirling bomber, headed out on a raid over Germany, and never returned.

British officials debated their response to the Walrond incident for months. A lieutenant colonel proposed asking U.S. military authorities "to let their troops know that whatever may be their feelings toward their own coloured troops, they must treat all British coloured troops as they would treat British white troops." But a higher-up in the War Office concluded that since Walrond was missing in action, "no useful purpose would be served." The matter was dropped.

"This man was a hero," the newspaper scolded. "He died that the Empire might live." Few of these cases led to official action, but the publicity likely helped deter future incidents.

Equity in the empire was not subject to the same scrutiny, and when Roosevelt tried to press the matter with Churchill, it was shrugged off. Many Britons didn't see a parallel between British behavior in the colonies and the white Americans' treatment of black soldiers, even when it was pointed out to them. At a London dinner party with high-level officials, Walter White mentioned that there would be certain "difficulties" if he dined with the ranking British official in India at the man's club. "Why should it be embarrassing?" one guest asked. "Because," replied the NAACP chief, "the club boasts that no person of colored blood has ever crossed its threshold. And I am a Negro." White, whose light hair and blue eyes enabled him to pass as white, wrote, "There was no further discussion that evening of the race question."

AMID THESE TENSIONS AND simmering social and political disputes, the American soldiers prepared for the great invasion to come. The wait was long, the work hard and tedious, and the conditions rough. For the men of the 320th, the warm reception they experienced during their early days in Checkendon gave way to the starkness of army living. Their barracks, metal tubes of corrugated steel called Nissen huts, did little to keep out the raw English chill. In another few months, the beech forest surrounding their camp would be abloom in a lush carpet of bluebells. As November turned to December, the incessant rain left the turf sodden, and the battalion's daily ten-mile hikes were a slog. Mud was an ever-present feature of the English winter, sucking at shoes and marooning trucks. In a February 1943 cartoon in *Stars and Stripes*, a World War I veteran of the trenches tells a distressed GI, "I know mud pretty good, mate, but this sort's new to me." Cheers went up when the soldiers learned they were to get a second pair of woolen socks.

Henry Parham remembers shivering during the long winter of 1943–44. The meager coal ration that filled only half his helmet left the little iron stove in the center of the hut hungry for more. Chopping wood was not allowed. Cold showers were the norm, unless crafty GIs managed to rig the plumbing. Parham had grown up amid the drafty shacks and rustic outhouses of Greensville County, Virginia, but this was something else. "It was miserable to sleep in a cold barracks," he recalled. "Once you got up during the day, you'd have to march and drill to keep yourself from freezing."

American ingenuity sometimes came up short. Men at a bomber base in Great Ashford poured aviation fuel into their stove and blew it out, along with the chimney pipe and part of the roof. For the men of the 320th, relief came in the form of invitations to spend an evening in a warm, cozy house.

The men had plenty of work to distract them. Sixteen days before the battalion left Tennessee, their mission had abruptly changed: they were to take with them to Europe smaller balloons called VLAs, for "very low altitude." More versatile than the larger balloons they had been trained to fly, the British-designed VLAs required one-tenth as much inflation gas, about 3,300 cubic feet at flying height. Their smaller size (thirty-five feet long and fourteen feet wide) allowed them to be safely tethered to boats and vehicles traveling up to forty miles per hour. When hoisted in tandem with a second bag, they could reach 4,400 feet, the same altitude as the larger balloons.

The VLA advantage was clear: The bags, already inflated, could accompany soldiers in landing crafts on the cross-Channel invasion, now set for early June 1944. At 125 pounds, the balloons could be maneuvered by a smaller crew of four men, and transported by jeep. And fewer hydrogen tanks were required to refill them, a crucial advantage on the battlefield.

The change in mission meant that the men of the 320th were obliged to master new equipment and techniques. They spent the final months before their deployment in specialized classes and training exercises. Upon arrival in Checkendon, they discovered that much of their gear hadn't made the journey with them. The missing equipment would delay their training on the balloons and thwart a plan to take over a harbor barrage at Cardiff, in South Wales. The 320th had been set to relieve a Royal Air Force balloon squadron there, and an important training opportunity was missed. Differences in equipment made it impossible for the battalion to borrow British gear, though the RAF would supply crucial hydrogen tanks to the Americans in the months to come.

By mid-January, when the battalion moved to a temporary camp in Chepstow, Wales, enough equipment had arrived for daily four-hour drills on balloon inflation. This they would be required to execute in minutes on the battlefield, using portable tanks of potentially explosive hydrogen. "These balloons will move right along with the troops, even over rugged cliffs and through high-voltage lines," Lt. Col. Leon Reed, the 320th's commanding officer, told a reporter. "The soldiers have ways of overcoming the worst possible obstacle. This we know, for we run an obstacle course as part of the simulated battle training—and it's plenty tough." Physical training was stepped up, with drills in the use of bayonets and hand-to-hand combat. Daily hikes were increased to twenty-five miles. Selected officers were trained in signal communications, map reading, aircraft recognition, and waterproofing of vehicles. After the 320th moved to Pontypool one month later, three dozen balloons dotted the skies above the Polo Grounds.

As invasion planning evolved, the balloons were pegged to go ashore early in the assault. Landing under enemy fire was always challenging, but the cumbersome equipment the balloons required also meant the crews would be easy targets as they struggled to haul their gear to shore. They had to lighten their load. One glaring problem was the thousand-pound gasoline-powered winches used to hoist the balloons. The men experimented with a lighter design, and ended up rejiggering a telephone wire reel they appropriated from the Signal Corps, to which they added two handles. The new fifty-pound winch could easily be carried ashore by one man. To save room on the landing craft, many balloon crews were reduced again, by one, to three men.

Meanwhile, the ultra-top-secret invasion-to-come turned out to be the worst-kept secret in the British Isles. So many senior U.S. officials were caught spilling details that a nervous Eisenhower complained that the security lapse "practically gives him the shakes," recalled his aide Butcher. One loose-lipped general alerted fellow diners at Claridge's hotel in London in April that the invasion would happen before June 15. Ike demoted the officer, his classmate at West Point, and sent him home. When an ill-packed envelope containing documents related to

Operation Overlord, the code name for the invasion of Europe, broke open in a Chicago post office in March, alarmed War Department officials scrambled to determine whether the secret was out and, if so, whether spies were to blame. In the end, an officer in London had accidentally addressed the packet in question to his sister. In the strangest twist, terms related to the invasion began appearing in the crossword puzzles of the *Telegraph* newspaper, including Utah, Omaha, and even overlord. When questioned by British intelligence agents, the unassuming physics teacher who had created the puzzles called it an astounding coincidence. Berlin had learned the meaning of Overlord thanks to the work of an Albanian spy working as a valet in the British embassy in Turkey. Yet Hitler's forces still had no idea when, or where, the assault would take place.

After three months in Wales, the majority of the 320th Battalion boarded trains in late April and headed to what would be their last stop in a country of which they had grown immensely fond. Here, in scores of jam-packed holding camps called "sausages," which had popped up along the southern English coast, they would wait. But first there was a final training exercise, the most realistic, and dangerous, to date. The battalion piled into boats for maneuvers off the coast of Devon, landing on May 4 at Slapton Sands, a beach similar in topography to the Normandy beaches where Allied forces would land in one month's time.

There, the 320th joined thousands of Allied soldiers prepping for the invasion of France. Conditions were elaborately set to mimic what the men could expect: There were drills unloading landing craft in rough seas, under live fire shot high over their heads. Six days before their arrival, disaster had struck when nine German E-boats on patrol due north in Lyme Bay stumbled upon Exercise Tiger, a mammoth rehearsal involving thirty thousand American troops destined to land on Utah Beach. The speedy German craft surprised the convoy and opened fire. In the worst catastrophe to befall U.S. forces in Europe, enemy torpedoes sank two of eight American landing ship tanks, killing seven hundred fifty servicemen. Yet none of the men of the 320th even knew it had happened. Fearing German discovery of D-Day preparations, the disaster was covered up, even from many of the soldiers who were there.

Back at the marshaling areas on May 6, the battalion split between crowded camps in Torquay and Dorchester. Unlike previous billets, these posts conspired to keep the men from leaving, with rings of barbed wire and armed guards. With Nissen huts and tents stretching as far as a man could see, soldiers packed elbow to elbow were keenly aware of the undertaking that awaited them. Here, there were interminable queues for everything from showers to chow. There were no weekend passes, no evening sing-alongs or dart contests in the pubs. Outside communication was forbidden, and train service and other transport severed. They were effectively cut off, isolated. No visitors were allowed, obviously, though some wily GIs and Tommies managed to sneak away for a last-minute rendezvous with sweethearts who knew where to find them—proving that leaks were unstoppable, even in the last days before an operation that could determine the fate of the world.

With precious few diversions, they set about writing letters home, and flipped through their new pocket French phrasebooks, practicing a few lines. *Parlez-vous anglais, mademoiselle?* They struck up games of cards and craps and wagered with the odd blue-green bills printed for use as currency in France. Jim Crow, always close by, plotted to stamp out any last morsels of freedom. One afternoon, white GIs broke up a softball game, incensed that black men had been allowed to play. Willie Howard could only shake his head. Would German shells know who was black and who was white?

The prisonlike atmosphere only antagonized jittery men nursing second thoughts about soldiering. For most of them, though, it was anticipation for the battle ahead, rather than misgivings, that kept them on edge, pacing and chain-smoking their weekly ration of Lucky

Strikes. They imagined what combat must be like: the blasts, the fire, the smells. It was the waiting that was the hard part.

During those final days, Wilson Monk worried over the future, his thoughts turning to his lovely Mertina. In the photograph that he kept close at hand, Mert is smiling, with rosy cheeks and bouncy brown curls. They were planning a wedding in Atlantic City as soon as he could get himself home. And he *would* get himself home. As the hours dragged by, Wilson thumbed through a palm-size New Testament with a taupe cover. The little book had been a farewell present from Jessie in Abersychan, a talisman she hoped would keep her adopted American alive through the next adventure. On the first page, Jessie had penned a dedication in her careful hand:

With loving thoughts and best wishes. May God protect and return you "safely home."
Friend for ever
Jessie Prior

PART III

CHAPTER 8

The Greatest Hour

If a Nazi bird nestles in my lines—he won't nestle nowhere else.

—CLEVELAND HAYES, 320TH BARRAGE BALLOON BATTALION
SOMEWHERE IN THE ENGLISH CHANNEL
EARLY MORNING, JUNE 6, 1944

Waverly Woodson squinted into the distance. From the deck of the boat, he could see little. A thick cloud blanket hung overhead, and the heavy air pressed in from all sides. Drenched fatigues clung to Woodson's weary limbs. For hours now he had peered into the blackness. A stripe of pink brightened the eastern horizon. First light. In the dark, choppy waters of the English Channel, Woodson found serenity, even beauty. It would be one of his last tranquil moments on this very long day.

It was a strange place to find peace. Above, the sky hummed with Allied planes, and all around, thousands of vessels of every size steamed toward France. On Woodson's ship, men were gray with seasickness. Their single army-issue vomit bag was long used up, so they heaved into their steel helmets, then tipped them over the side to be rinsed in the cresting swells. When that effort proved too much, they heaved wherever they could. Puddles of sick pooled at their ankles. The metal boat pitched forward and back with each roll. *Dying would be better than this.* Some of them said that.

The storied Channel had thwarted generations of marauders to keep Britannia safe, at least most of the time. The Roman emperor Caligula's soldiers mutinied rather than sail these waters thick with mermaids. On this day, the invaders were heading in the opposite direction, their mission to conquer a continent systematically crushed by an enemy for whom freedom meant very little. To Woodson, freedom meant a great deal. He had lived it fully for the first time in a friendly village in Oxfordshire, where he'd met white people pleased to be his friend and a postmistress happy to dance with him. That might not have seemed like much to other men, but Woodson would never forget it. For him, there was no ambivalence entwined in fighting for his country, even if that country didn't support equality for all its citizens. If you asked Woodson, he would tell you: This was a war in which he believed with all his heart. He was in this boat, in this war, to defeat the Nazis and their brutally racist worldview.

The noise, varied and constant, grew louder as a swarm of B-17 Flying Fortresses and B-24 Liberators droned above the fleet. In the distance, the thunder of explosions echoed, and every man prayed their aim was good. The Allied bombs were seeking to smash the enemy bunkers, pillboxes, trenches, hideaways, and deadly obstacles spanning the French coast. Hitler had built this vast system of fortifications—the "Atlantic Wall"—which he imagined would seal western Europe from an assault exactly like this one. It was a tactical error. The Führer's other epic mistake was underestimating his opponents. Allied fighters were better trained and supplied, and far more committed to victory than the German High Command expected. On this early morning, as the largest armada ever assembled was speeding toward the coast, the twenty-three thousand American and British paratroopers dropped behind enemy lines hours earlier in a chaotic operation were already working to foil Nazi defenses.

Deafening booms shook the men to their soaking boots as the great battleships opened fire, each blast of their guns lighting the murky dawn with flame and smoke. The noise was almost impossible to believe. To Ernest Hemingway, who was aboard a small boat in the Channel that day, it "sounded as though they were throwing whole railway trains across the sky." The powerful concussion reverberated through the fleet and "struck your ear like a punch with a heavy, dry glove." An Associated Press reporter in one of those boats initially mistook the men's violent trembling for fear. Yet these men were ready. This was the day for which they had trained for years. For the British with bitter memories of being driven back into the sea at Dunkirk in 1940, the wait had been far longer. The bombardment was an awesome display of might. Lt. Gen. Omar Bradley, commander of the First U.S. Army, had promised his troops "the greatest show on earth." The GIs and Tommies watching from the sea were certain that no enemy could survive it.

For Woodson, this journey to France was a most unexpected chapter in his young life. Odds were low that a black man would be in this landing. Yet Woodson was used to defying expectations. Unlike many of his friends in West Philadelphia, Woodson hadn't waited for a draft notice. He'd left his premed studies at Pennsylvania's Lincoln University, where he was in his second year, and enlisted in the army on December 15, 1942. His younger brother, Eugene Lloyd Woodson, had signed up, too, and was stationed in Texas with a unit of the Tuskegee Airmen. It was a source of tremendous pride for their parents, and the doings of the Woodson brothers would become regular items in the black newspapers back home.

Waverly Bernard "Woody" Woodson Jr. looked far younger than his twenty years in his first army portrait, clad in his olive-drab uniform and garrison cap trimmed in red, a tentative look on his round face. In a later photograph, Corporal Woodson oozes confidence, his dark almond eyes almost twinkling, a sprig of a mustache accenting a thinner face. He had studied German in high school and could speak it pretty well, and had won a spot in the Anti-Aircraft Artillery Officer Candidate School after scoring high on an exam heavily weighted to favor whites. He was one of only two African Americans in an otherwise all-white class. Before he finished the course, he was told there were no officer positions open to him in the AAA corps. It was a common story for black officers, who saw their opportunities limited by quotas and ceilings on the ranks available to them. Restrictions were placed on their assignments, such as not being allowed to serve in units with white officers junior to them. Instead, Woodson was sent for training as a medic and assigned to the 320th Barrage Balloon Battalion. He was one of five unit medics on this boat, all of them black.

It was after dark on June 5, 1944, when the medics left England aboard a landing craft tank. The LCTs were large steel barges with a deckhouse and space belowdecks for a crew of a dozen men. Woodson's LCT carried one Sherman tank, two jeeps, three trucks, and some fifty-five men, mostly from the Twenty-Ninth Infantry Division, along with navy crew. The LCTs were the largest boats that would land directly on the beaches on June 6, though the bumpy ninety-mile ride from England pushed every boundary of misery. The boats ranged in size all the way down to the smallest, the LCVPs (landing craft, vehicle, personnel), with room for about three dozen men packed tight. Hemingway, who was aboard one, called it an iron bathtub, which was generous, considering that the sides were made of plywood and offered little protection against enemy fire.

The smaller craft were not capable of crossing the open ocean and had been ferried from port aboard the big ships. Ten miles or so offshore, small cranes called davits lowered the boats into the bucking Channel waters either with their passengers already aboard, or else empty. In the latter case, the men scrambled down mesh ladders and jumped aboard the pitching tubs, a hazardous undertaking in five-foot swells. Some ankles snapped and limbs were crushed as the boats smashed against the hulls of the mother ships.

In spite of turbulent seas, the order to go had been a relief. Woodson and the four medics had endured several uncomfortable days aboard this metal bucket, jockeying for space with the five dozen men. Behind the boat carrying the medics, the rest of the 320th Barrage Balloon Battalion was scattered among more than 150 landing craft. Thousands of barrage balloons had been inflated in England by Royal Air Force crews and then tethered to ships and the smaller craft for the journey to France. Floating high above the ships, the balloons formed a miles-wide aerial curtain, their shining silvery shapes carved in relief against the flat pewter sky. Their job was to protect the fleet from German dive-bombers, which would be loath to tangle with the lethal balloon cables. Once ashore, the men of the 320th would rush the balloons onto the beach, transferring the protective veil to land.

Most of the 621 men in the 320th's assault force were headed to a five-mile-long, crescent-shaped patch of sand once known as Beach 313. The Americans had renamed it Omaha, and it was one of the five beaches the Allies had to seize on June 6, in the seventeen hours of daylight available to them. War planners expected a bloodbath on Omaha, the most challenging terrain, where enemy guns lay hidden in scrub-covered bluffs as high as one hundred seventy feet.

Omaha is where the medics were headed. They would be the first African Americans ashore—if they made it to the beach alive.

FOR GENERAL EISENHOWER, THE days leading up to the invasion were the stuff of nightmares. After weeks of calm weather, the forecast for the coming days was bad. Ike had delayed the landings, originally set for June 5, by one day. There were only three days this month that promised the necessary conditions: a bright moon for the paratroopers and a low tide at daybreak for the infantry. If the assault, code-named Neptune, was pushed back another day, to June 6, and the weather didn't turn, that would leave only June 7. After that, the assembled forces would have to wait until the second week in July. It was enough to strain the chain-smoking, coffee-chugging supreme commander's every last jangling nerve. You couldn't hide a fleet of five thousand ships. Somehow, they had managed to do exactly that, but how long could their luck hold out?

On the evening of June 4, Ike's team finally got a welcome bit of news: a break in the weather on June 5 was expected to prevail into the sixth. Urged on by chief planner Gen. Bernard L. "Monty" Montgomery and the rest of his team, an exhausted Eisenhower made the call: D-Day would be Tuesday, June 6.

The Germans had long expected the Allies to storm the Continent, but they never expected the invasion to take place under such conditions. Rain and gale-force winds were lashing the coast as Ike made the decision to go. German forecasters had not predicted the narrow interval of decent weather. It would be a costly mistake. In another bad call, Hitler and his commanders were betting on a landing at the Pas-de-Calais, within sight of the white cliffs of Dover, the narrowest point of the Channel. There were many reasons why the Allies had ruled out landing there, not the least of which was that it was where the Germans expected them. It was the most heavily defended position on the coast.

There were plenty of arguments against staging the assault at Normandy, which lay to the southwest. The only available port, at Cherbourg, could not handle the amount of matériel the Allies would require to support the invasion. They would have to ferry supplies from the sea. The topography was rough, with offshore rocks and jagged cliffs of granite, sandstone, and limestone. Extreme changes in tide posed problems. The three hundred to six hundred yards of sand exposed at low tide would be almost entirely swallowed up within five hours. Many of the men landing at high tide on D-Day would find themselves with little more than a strip of sand to navigate. Omaha was the worst: a narrow battlefield perfectly enclosed and well protected by natural obstacles that made the man-made impediments more effective. The only way off it was up, over the well-defended bluffs.

Despite those challenges, the German commander Erwin Rommel

suspected that Normandy could be in Eisenhower's playbook. The beaches there reminded him of those in Salerno, in southern Italy, where the Allies had landed months earlier. There is no evidence that Rommel acted on his hunch, though he was already beefing up a veritable fortress along the eight hundred miles of coast under his command, from the Netherlands to Brittany. The shrewd general, whose early victories in North Africa had earned him the nickname the Desert Fox, was still stung by the hard-fought Allied victory there in May 1943. This time, Rommel would push the invaders back into the sea. Displeased with so many weak spots in Hitler's Atlantic Wall upon his arrival in France in November 1943, Rommel ordered a frantic buildup. By June 1944 about 80 percent of the fifteen thousand planned fortifications were completed. Land mines were a particular obsession of Rommel's, and he wanted to lay as many as 100 million of them along the Atlantic coast. By June, some 1.7 million mines seeded the Normandy beaches, bluffs, and *bocage*, the grid of wall-like hedgerows inland that would bog down the Allied infantry in the weeks following the landings. There were large pancake mines that could blow off a tank's treads and small S-mines, the dreaded Bouncing Betty, which leaped into the air when stepped on and gutted victims with a spray of shrapnel. In *The Longest Day*, Cornelius Ryan recounts the gruesome sight of a soldier, an S-mine victim, lying on the ground, spitting up ball bearings.

Rommel's net extended into the sea, with a ring of floating mines offshore. For the vessels that made it through, a lethal forest awaited. The beaches were cluttered with twisted iron and jagged steel, five-foot-high crosses called hedgehogs, plus tetrahedra and other terrors borrowed from a geometry textbook. There were concrete cones and wooden sawhorses and stakes topped with more mines or, worse, with shells even more sensitive to the touch. Thick aprons of barbed wire blocked exit points, and automatic flamethrowers spat clouds of fire down the scrubby paths leading to them. Rommel had designed most of these medieval-looking instruments himself, believing that if the invaders could be stalled on the beach and culled by the guns on the heights, the assault could be stopped there within forty-eight hours. In this view, Rommel diverged from his boss in Normandy, Field Marshal Gerd von Rundstedt, who thought the defenses should be kept mobile, for quick reactions to whatever the Allies cooked up. Four years earlier, von Rundstedt had outwitted the Maginot Line of French fortifications on the German border by leading his troops around it through Belgium. He considered Hitler's Wall an "enormous bluff" that would delay, but not stop, a determined enemy.

In any case, the Wall was not finished by June 1944. Hitler's bluster that his "fortress" was impregnable belied reality. The same was true for the Führer's boasts that the Reich was winning the war. Night after night Allied bombers pummeled Germany, destroying so many defense plants and oil refineries that Germany was losing its ability to recover. The Luftwaffe, the German air force, could not build enough planes to replace those lost, and gasoline stocks were critically low. On the ground, the Allies were closing in on Rome. To the east, the Soviets shook off a long, brutal winter and were marching through Poland. By mid-July, the Red Army would kill or capture three hundred fifty thousand Germans.

There had been other D-Days during the war—the *D* simply means the day of an operation—in North Africa and Italy and in the Pacific. But this would be the big one. If the invasion succeeded, Eisenhower's team knew it would be only a matter of time before the Allied troops were marching through Berlin. Normandy was where they would land, and new technology would help them do it. There were tanks dressed in canvas skirts that could swim, and artificial harbors, called Mulberries, that could replace a port. In one of the most thoroughly choreographed assaults in the history of war, the British would land on two beaches to the east, Sword and Gold, with the Canadians at Juno in the center. The Americans would land to the west, on Omaha and Utah. Between those beaches, American Rangers would scale the hundred-foot-high sheer cliffs at Pointe-du-Hoc and knock out the big German guns that were believed—erroneously, it turned out—to be there. Success depended on surprise. Allied counter-intelligence had worked hard to confuse the enemy. In an operation called Fortitude, they invented fake army divisions to keep the Germans occupied elsewhere, with supposed plans to launch an invasion near Calais and in occupied Norway, and with radio channels broadcasting their supposed chatter. German reconnaissance planes observed legions of mock aircraft, machinery, and landing craft, along with the very real ships that were converging in southern ports in preparation for the true invasion. Constant bombing around Calais kept attention focused there.

In one of the most colorful ruses, in the hours before the Allied soldiers began landing on the beaches, hundreds of rubber dummies outfitted like miniature paratroopers were tossed from airplanes over Normandy, setting off explosives as they touched down. These helped sow confusion among the German defenders while, at the same time, real airborne troops were parachuting into villages and fields behind the invasion beaches. These landings were messy and disorganized, with troops arriving far from their targets and separated from their companies. Many men drowned in lowlands the Germans had flooded to thwart such an operation. Despite those setbacks, the airborne action left the enemy puzzling over the scope of the assault. German commanders believed the attack was a sideshow to the main event that was sure to unfold near Calais. One man who might have guessed the truth was asleep in his bed in Germany. Rommel had left Normandy on June 4, tucking under his arm a box of gray suede shoes for his wife, whose birthday was on June 6. The Desert Fox believed the invasion was still weeks off. "How stupid of me," he would say later. "How stupid of me." His absence contributed to the chaos that engulfed the German command on D-Day morning. Their disorganization would save the lives of countless young Allied men.

A few miles from Allied headquarters, in Portsmouth, where Eisenhower had made the most important decision of his life, the marshaling camps called "sausages" were close to bursting. The ports were clogged with thousands of ships that had begun loading a week earlier in a one-hundred-degree heat wave, and the nearly two hundred thousand men slated to go ashore in the first waves were fed up. Breakfasts of steak and eggs and other decadent meals served up to keep them quiet weren't working. Ike's command to go was a relief. From the loudspeakers of ships came pep talks. Even the humble Eisenhower, not known for his grandiloquence, cheered them on: "Soldiers, sailors and airmen of the Allied Expeditionary Force! You are about to embark upon the Great Crusade. . . . The eyes of the world are upon you. The hope and prayers of liberty-loving people everywhere march with you."

WHILE AWESTRUCK SOLDIERS WATCHING from the sea couldn't believe it was possible for those onshore to survive the mighty guns of so many warships, in reality, damage from the predawn bombing was slight. Allied firepower barely touched the concrete-and-iron German fortifications overlooking Omaha Beach. It was the concussion from the blasts that pummeled the men inside, killing a few but mostly rattling them. The 329 bombers assigned to Omaha had overshot their targets, hampered by low cloud and fears of hitting their own troops less than two miles offshore. Not one of their thirteen thousand bombs had knocked out the lethal guns aimed at the men about to land at H-Hour, 6:30 a.m.

The Germans held their fire until the landing craft dropped their ramps with a hard splash. That was the signal. Machine guns spraying twelve hundred bullets per minute opened up, slaughtering soldiers before they touched the water. Mortar shells rained down on boats, setting ammunition afire. Half the swimming tanks that were supposed to put firepower on the beach early in the assault were set loose too far from shore. They sank like giant boulders, drowning many of their crew. Some tanks made it to the beach only to be hit by shells, their

In this rare close-up of members of the 320th Barrage Balloon Battalion in action, Cpl. A. Johnson of Houston, Texas, with help from two men in his crew, walks a VLA (very-low-altitude) balloon toward a winch on Omaha Beach. The VLA balloons flew as high as two thousand feet. *National Archives and Records Administration*

Men from the 320th haul a barrage balloon through a partially cleared minefield in France on August 14, 1944. *From left to right:* Arko Shaw, Alvin Smith, Jessie Sumlin, and James Shrapshire. *National Archives and Records Administration*

A barrage balloon hovers over Omaha Beach on June 12, 1944, as Lt. Gen. Omar N. Bradley shakes hands with Gen. George C. Marshall while Gen. Henry H. Arnold *(right)* looks on. *National Archives and Records Administration*

Crouched in a foxhole on Utah Beach, Willie O. Howard dreaded the nightly visits from the German planes they called "Bed Check Charlie." First, flares would light up the beach "like a football stadium," the 320th veteran said. That meant a visit was imminent. *Courtesy of Willie O. Howard*

Private First Class James L. Simmons Jr. of the 320th was killed on Omaha Beach on June 6, 1944. His little sister, Charlotte, remembers when an army man in a brown car drove up to the family's house in Upper Marlboro, Maryland. "I heard my mother crying," she says. "That's when I found out my brother died." *Courtesy of Charlotte Simmons Chase*

Davison, Clayborne, Coles
Archer, Abney, Scott, Brown, Chebester, Hopher
Madrie, Johnson, Cripps, Murphy, Barnes, Pendexter, Cross
Wasler, Davis, Small, Lt. Alrid, Ector, Frazier, Thomas
TAKEN IN FRANCE JULY 1944 320TH AVIATOR

320ers
Invasion Group
of Normandy Beach

George Davison wrote the names of his buddies from the 320th on this snapshot from July 1944. He noted his own place in the back row. *Bill Davison*

Malchi Adkins strikes a pose, likely in Hawaii. Back home in Charles City County, Virginia, Adkins had left school after the seventh grade to work in wood pulp plants before being drafted into the army. *Courtesy of the Adkins family*

Albert Grillette Wood displays his wartime portrait. The hatred he experienced in the army left him bitter. "Discrimination hurt me more than anything in the world," he said. "And I had to fight for these sons of bitches?" *Linda Hervieux*

First Lt. Theophile F. Lavizzo, one of the few black officers in the 320th, landed with his men on Utah Beach on D-Day under heavy fire. For the leadership he demonstrated, his superior recommended him for the Bronze Star. He never got it, and never learned why. *Courtesy of Ted Lavizzo*

First Lt. Grant Gordon of the 320th was the only African American in his officers' training class. Limited by quotas and shut out of the top ranks, black officers had no choice but to accept the army's Jim Crow system. After the war, Gordon became the first black school principal in Milwaukee, Wisconsin. *Courtesy of Geoff Gordon*

First Lt. Theodore E. Corprew was the medical officer of the 320th. He grew up in a family of twelve in Norfolk, Virginia. In 1936, he graduated from Meharry Medical College in Nashville, where black doctors were not allowed to treat white patients. After the war, he moved to Washington, DC, where he pursued a long career as an obstetrician. *Courtesy of Barbara Corprew*

Wilson Monk gets a peck from Mertina at their home in Silver Spring, Maryland. When Mertina set eyes on Wilson in 1941, she told herself, "He's a done deal." They married on December, 6, 1944, shortly after he returned from Normandy. *Linda Hervieux*

James Hardy Sims landed with the 320th on Utah Beach. During the war he had brushes with "nasty" southern whites who weren't happy to have black soldiers stationed among them. Today when he wears his World War II cap, white people often stop him, shake his hand, and thank him for his service. *Péralte Paul*

Henry Parham greets fellow veterans at Allegheny Cemetery in Pittsburgh on Memorial Day 2011. Parham landed on Omaha Beach on D-Day. In May 2013, the French government awarded him the Legion of Honor. *Linda Hervieux*

Virginia natives William Dabney and Harry Cecil Curtis Jr. trained together at Camp Tyson, Tennessee, and remained lifelong friends. Dabney was awarded the French Legion of Honor in June 2009 for his service on D-Day. *Linda Hervieux*

Samuel L. Mattison had a difficult upbringing in children's homes in Columbus, Ohio. In the army, he had little patience for the racism and hatred inflicted on black troops. "Black men ain't no men," he said. "We were like little dogs." *Linda Hervieux*

Arthur Guest shares a laugh with his wife, Marthena, at their home in North Charleston, South Carolina. The couple had been married sixty-seven years when this photo was taken in 2012. Guest landed on Utah Beach with the 320th on D-Day. *Linda Hervieux*

Wilson Monk holds a gas mask canister he found in Normandy in 1944, painted with the names of his friends. *Linda Hervieux*

Waverly Woodson, the 320th's hero medic, is buried at Arlington National Cemetery. Each May, around Memorial Day, his widow, Joann, arranges red roses beside his grave and drops to the grass and prays. *Linda Hervieux*

burning hulls sending up thick clouds of smoke that obscured the scene of horror from the men yet to land. On some parts of Omaha, the guns were more forgiving, and infantry platoons survived largely intact. Elsewhere, there was little more than carnage.

Some of the first troops on the beach were the combat engineers and demolition teams tasked with clearing paths through Rommel's obstacle forest. The tide caused half the teams to land late, with many ending up far off target. They were hard-pressed to do their job blowing up obstacles with boats loaded with infantrymen arriving on their heels. With so many tanks out of commission, there was little protection. They were slaughtered within the first thirty minutes of the invasion, suffering among the highest casualties on June 6. Some of the more sadistic German gunners waited until the engineers had set up their explosives before pulling the trigger. With the tide rising about one foot every ten minutes, soon those deadly obstacles they had failed to demolish, topped with mines, would be underwater, and invisible to navy coxswains as they brought their boats to shore packed with troops.

In the Channel, chaos reigned. Some of the smaller boats couldn't handle the swells and were swamped miles from shore, sinking quickly and drowning many men. Coxswains struggled to find landmarks through black billows of smoke, not realizing the current had carried them east of their designated landing spots, sometimes miles off course. Some boats unloaded too soon, plunging the men in water over their heads. Many were unable to shake off their enormous packs, some upward of one hundred pounds, and were pulled under and drowned. Some flopped forward, top-heavy, the gray life belts ringing their waists unable to save them. Relentless fire pelted those who made it onto the sand. They crowded behind Rommel's obstacles or collapsed from exhaustion where their feet touched the earth. But the beach was no place to stay. Weak from seasickness and heavy in waterlogged clothes laden with sand, they staggered toward the shingle, a sloping embankment of chunky off-white stones about ten yards from the high-water line. The shingle was angled just enough to act as a low wall offering cover from the enemy guns. The respite was temporary: It wouldn't take the Germans long to figure out how to hit the soldiers clustered there.

AS THE BOAT CARRYING Woodson and the medics approached Omaha Beach, all eyes were on the water. Around them, men bobbed in a sea made red by their own blood. Those still alive waited to be pulled from the drink by boats that might never come. The skippers of the landing craft had been ordered to ignore their cries for help, and men in motor launches with megaphones dissuaded those with second thoughts. "You are not a rescue ship!" hollered one of them. "Get onshore!" First, Woodson's craft hit a mine, which blew out the motor. Then another blast exploded on the right side, felling troops like matchsticks. The heavy fire kept coming. The LCT's forty-millimeter guns, which had been blazing moments earlier, now lay silent: the bodies of their gunners hung lifeless as if from a gruesome clothesline. A shell landed on the hood of a jeep, incinerating the four men inside. Woodson crouched beside a truck filled with medical supplies. Inside it, medic Warren Capers of Kenbridge, Virginia, sat behind the wheel. Shells missed the ship and exploded in the water, sending a shower of burning metal shards raining on deck. A soldier beside Woodson was hit and killed. Woodson's lower extremities burned. He reached down and brought a hand up covered in blood. "I am dying," he thought. One of the medics slapped dressings on his buttocks and inner thigh, ripped open by shrapnel. "Close," Woodson would say later, "mighty close." The medics tended to the few men still living. The helpless craft drifted to a stop. The ramp fell with a bang, and to Woodson's surprise, the tank came alive. It rolled down the ramp onto the beach and turned right. The men followed it, splashing down in four feet of water. Woodson and medics Eugene Worthy and Alfred Bell, both from Memphis, hit the beach and ran, slugs popping mini-geysers of sand at their feet.

Woodson looked back and saw the tank's turret in flames. No men were coming out. It was 9:00 a.m.

In the shelter of the shingle, Woodson unpacked a tent roll he had pulled out of the water. Now there was a medical station. The rising tide carried in the dead and threatened to drown the living. Under constant fire, the medics dragged the wounded and the dead out of the shooting gallery at the water's edge. Their Red Cross brassards made them easy targets for German snipers hiding in the bluffs, who ignored the rules of war and fired on many medics that day. There were too many men who needed saving. Their cries for help would haunt Woodson.

On Omaha, war was a great equalizer. "At that time," Woodson would say later, "they didn't care what color my skin was." Throughout the day and night and into the next day, Woodson worked through his pain to save lives. He pulled out bullets, patched gaping wounds, and dispensed blood plasma. He amputated a right foot. When he thought he could do no more, he resuscitated four drowning men. Thirty hours after he set his boots on Omaha Beach, Woody Woodson collapsed.

SOMETIME AFTER THE MEDICS landed, Bill Dabney plunged from a flat-bottomed metal boat into the waist-deep water, holding his rifle above his head, and staggered toward Omaha Beach. He breathed in a bitter mix of cordite and burning gasoline. Deafening booms mingled with the incessant *brrrppp brrrppp* chatter of the machine guns and the *sip sip sip* of their bullets skipping across the fine golden sand. Hot metal hit Dabney in the leg. He taped up the wound and kept going. A barrage balloon about the size of a Volkswagen Beetle had been clipped to his belt, but now it was gone. The teenager from Roanoke, the baby of his group once teased for volunteering to serve, was now Corporal Dabney, a balloon crew chief. He was in charge of getting himself, three other men, and that gasbag to shore. *Where did that damn balloon go?* He couldn't worry about it. Now it was time to save himself.

Dabney was among the 320th's assault force, in which the 621 men were divided among four batteries, three of which were bound for Omaha Beach. The men were further separated into crews of three or four, each in charge of one balloon. Each crew traveled aboard a landing craft crammed with infantrymen, and each one operated as an independent unit: The crews would land together and get their balloons in the air as soon as the infantry neutralized the worst of the enemy fire—or, at least, that was the plan. The reality was far different. Under punishing fire, the men scattered, desperate to find shelter. Dabney fell to his knees and raced to dig a foxhole with the entrenching tool he pulled from his pack. Other men chucked the little shovel, unbuckled their helmets, and used those to move gobs of sand. "It didn't take you long to dig a hole when you were getting shot at," Dabney said.

Like Dabney, some of the 320th men carried their balloons with them aboard the smaller craft. More balloons would be transported to shore, already inflated, aboard boats set to land later in the day. For the next month, until hydrogen stocks allowed the balloons to be inflated on the beach, the balloons would land this way, already inflated in England, with the 320th men plucking them from the landing craft. This system of handling the balloons was called the "plum tree," coined by the British who likened the process to, of course, picking plums from a tree.

In the Channel, the navy operated the balloons flying above the largest vessels. Some of the crews got little instruction on how to handle the balloons before they set off from port, and many of them were unhappy to have them. "It was like putting a tall billboard up saying, HERE WE ARE!" said one sailor. (At least they could take comfort in knowing that benign helium filled the navy balloons, rather than the combustible hydrogen used in the army balloons destined for the beaches.)

Worried that the balloons made a prime target for enemy artillery, some sailors cut them loose. It was a similar situation on land: Beach commanders ordered the first bags ashore to be set adrift or shot for the same reason, though it was a mistaken assumption. In a little-known secret of D-Day, German field artillery batteries had already set their guns to fire on particular locations well before the invasion. During practice exercises along the coast, the artillery men had determined the best aim points, and registered those positions. As the GIs hit Omaha, their 105-millimeter and 150-millimeter guns were ready to unleash a devastating blow. Some of them were concealed in fortifications unknown to the Allies. Reconnaissance planes had not spotted them camouflaged under nets or tucked in the rocky outcroppings that made this dramatic coastline so perilous to invaders from the sea.

THE 320TH MEN WERE slated to begin landing at mid-morning, after the heaviest enemy fire had been suppressed and it was possible to raise the balloons. But nothing went according to plan on D-Day. The Normandy operation may have been one of the most tightly synchronized battles ever, yet its clockwork precision went awry from the start. Infantry companies pulled off course by the eastward current, beach obstacles left intact, and untrammeled enemy fire—all these conspired to throw the invaders off track. They missed their landing targets and arrived in bunches, trapped by enemy fire. Burning tanks and trucks littered the waterline. There were no craters from the Allied preinvasion bombing in which to take shelter, as many men had expected. All around was a vast expanse of bloodstained sand littered with piles of wrecked radios, gas masks, ration tins, photographs, and guns big and small, some rifles still topped with the condoms put there to keep water out. Congestion was so bad on the western end of Omaha that commanders on the beach halted the landings there. The Germans observing the tumultuous scene from the heights thought they were winning.

GIs separated from their companies huddled along the shingle. On the western third of the beach, they sheltered behind a fortified seawall. To stop the slaughter, they knew they had to make it across hundreds of yards of sand and hidden mines, through sheets of barbed wire, and up the bluffs to reach the German pillboxes—all while under constant fire. Leaderless and lost, they were too scared to move. Eventually, men such as Col. George Taylor of the First Division arrived to take charge. "Get the hell off the beach!" he bellowed. "If you stay on, you're dead." The GIs began the treacherous push across the sand and toward the bluffs. Not until 11:00 a.m. would the anxious generals waiting offshore get the first bit of good news: there was movement off the beach. Yet the invasion timetable was hopelessly behind schedule.

That was bad news for the balloons. Two-ply rubberized cotton coated with aluminum was no match for the German guns. The idea was to replace a balloon as quickly as one was lost, maintaining a steady line of defense. That strategy had worked well in Britain early in the war, when the balloons had been used to protect defense plants from merciless German air attacks. Frustrated that they couldn't eliminate the balloons, enemy planes sought targets elsewhere. That was impossible, however, without balloon reserves at the ready and protection for the men charged with getting them in the air. Men like Dabney landed without their balloons or lost them to bullets, gravity, or who-knows-what in the race for cover. They zigzagged across the sand, trying to step in the tracks of the men before them who had made it clear of the Bouncing Betties.

It was bedlam on the beach, and still the boats kept coming, disgorging fresh stocks of men into the fury. Several hundred yards offshore, George Davison took refuge behind the ramp of his LCT as machine-gun fire pinged the flip side. All around, boats were being hit, "bodies being blown to bits, parts of men flying through the air like birds," he would write years later. Before the war, Sergeant Davison, a twenty-two-year-old clerk in the 320th, had been a jackhammer operator in Waynesburg, Pennsylvania. His parents had three blue stars in their window, one for each of their boys in the army. Their oldest, Frank, was a sergeant, and he would land in Normandy with the 515th Port Battalion a few weeks after D-Day. The brothers would meet by chance in August. The third son, Lawrence, was a private stationed in the Pacific.

A motor launch pulled up beside Davison's LCT. "Hit the beach!" barked a man with a megaphone. The launch passed two more times before the ramp finally fell. "Guys were screaming 'Let's hit it, men, give 'er hell!'" They didn't expect the water to be so deep. Davison grabbed onto a rack on the back of a truck just ahead of him as it rolled off the ramp. The truck sank like the two and a half tons of steel it was, and Davison let go. At five feet eight inches tall, he plunged into the fifty-six-degree surf, his gear a dead weight on his 180-pound frame. He recalled the entreaty that Brig. Gen. E. W. Timberlake had given his troops before they left England: "Keep your gun dry . . . and don't shit your pants." That was perhaps a more practical turn of phrase for the general known as Big Ed, whose soaring exhortations could whip young soldiers into a frenzy. The men under his command in the Forty-Ninth Anti-Aircraft Artillery Brigade were charged with shooting enemy planes out of the sky. The "Forty-Niners" fancied themselves as brash as their commander. Their unit insignia featuring a gold prospector clad in a cowboy hat, a moonshine bottle at his feet and a pistol in each hand, aiming at an oncoming plane. For the invasion, Timberlake's men included the 320th Barrage Balloon Battalion. The 49th's big guns would be teamed with a blanket of bullet-shaped gasbags. "We'll write our history in the skies," Timberlake told them.

The small musette bag slung around Davison's neck floated away, carrying with it a trove of cherished possessions, gifts bought in London and a nine-inch-long gold cigarette holder—"a real beauty." Davison could do nothing but watch it go. He paddled toward shore and prayed the machine-gun fire thwacking the water around him would miss. A wave gave him a hearty push and his feet touched ground. *Relief.* At least he wouldn't drown today. Davison's solace was short-lived. All around, men were cracking. Some crouched in the surf, clutching obstacles now submerged. Others sobbed, too scared to move, while others went berserk, screaming and walking crazily to nowhere. One soldier on his knees clutched rosary beads and prayed as if he were in church. "Get down!" his friend called out, but it was no use. Machine-gun fire cut the praying man in half. His friend, a Twenty-Ninth Division infantryman named Harold Baumgarten, got revenge: "I saw the glint of the German's helmet. I fired one shot and I killed him. Then my rifle broke."

George Davison ran for the shingle. "There was other guys there all pinned down by machine gun fire so I took a place between two men that were alive," he wrote. "Nobody said anything to each other, just laid there eating that earth." The shingle, it turned out, was no place to stay, either. German rifles could not hit men sheltering there, but mortars could lob shells over the embankment with seemingly eerie precision. "They could put a mortar down our shirt collars," said Morley L. Piper, who on June 6 was a young lieutenant with the Twenty-Ninth Division. A shell hit a man close to Davison. Covered in guts and blood, Davison started running in circles. A soldier popped his head out of a foxhole and shouted, "Get in here," and sense returned to Davison. "I made a couple of giant steps and rolled in the foxhole."

It had been a long two days for Davison. His LCT had begun its journey on June 4, turning back after Eisenhower postponed the invasion. By the time they set off for good, the men aboard Davison's craft were thoroughly wet and miserable. Davison eyed the ammo all around and imagined the fireball "if Jerry was to lay an egg on this." Shouts of a man in the water jolted the soldiers from their thoughts. Soon after, the navy crew hauled aboard a grateful British pilot who had ditched his plane after it was hit by flak.

One advantage of that bleak crossing was the company. Davison and his 320th crew shared their LCT with troops from the 1st Infantry Division. The men of the "Big Red One" were seasoned fighters who had landed in North Africa in 1942 and Sicily the following year. Their experience stood in marked contrast to that of the Twenty-Ninth Infantry Division, the other U.S. fighting force on Omaha, which was well trained but seeing battle for the first time. The 320th men, the only African Americans aboard, peppered the infantrymen with questions, and the "schooling" they got back was much appreciated. To their surprise, the white soldiers answered their queries with kindness. They were, wrote Davison, "the best group of men we had come in contact with anywhere"—even the ones, he noted, with southern accents.

Deep in the foxhole, Davison and the man who had saved him sat in silence. The cacophony raging above their heads faded into the background as Davison fixated on a spider that had burrowed out of the cool damp sand and settled in beside him—or maybe it was a small crab. Whatever it was, Davison hated creepy-crawlies. At any other time, his boot would have made fast work of the uninvited guest. But with so much death so close, Davison grew reflective. "If I let you live," he told the multilegged intruder, "maybe I get the chance to live."

While Davison was reconciling with his phobia, his 320th comrade Willie Howard was shivering in a landing craft bound for Utah Beach, fifteen miles west of Omaha. Cold and wet, Howard eyed a pile of wool blankets. "Those are for the dead," someone said. The boat beached, and Howard hit the water up to his armpits. A shell slapped down so close he could almost touch it. It didn't explode—a dud. Ahead of him were five hundred yards of soft grayish sand. The first wave of the U.S. Fourth Infantry Division had cleared the beach of the machine-gun nests and snipers concealed behind gently rising, willowy dunes. Unlike at Omaha, the pre-invasion bombing at Utah had been accurate and effective, hitting enemy strongpoints and sending many troops running. The threat was far from eliminated. A mile or more behind the beach, German artillery on higher ground had a clear shot at the beach. These well-fortified bunkers would be harder to knock out, and their shells would shower Utah on and after June 6, frustrating the Allied advance.

When the fighting was finished, they would call Utah the easy beach. Some infantrymen would complain that they were let down after three long years of training. Their preparations had included amphibious

landings on beaches along the Florida Panhandle with snipers at the
ready to rout alligators. Balloon crews from Camp Tyson had also
trained along Florida's Gulf Coast with the Thirty-Eighth Infantry
Division, "storming" three beaches in December 1942 called Red,
White, and Green. When the disappointed raiders of Utah learned
about what had happened on Omaha during the bloodiest day of fighting for the Americans in World War II, many would say a prayer of
thanks. Utah's 589 casualties were few relative to the toll on Omaha:
4,720 killed, wounded, and missing. No beach was like Omaha, but
that didn't make the taking of Utah any less important. A late addition
to the Overlord plan, Utah was vital turf in the strategy to seize the
heart-shaped Cotentin Peninsula and eventually capture the port of
Cherbourg. From the sea, some 21,328 infantry troops would push
inland to join the more than 17,000 American airborne troops who
had parachuted, or crash-landed in gliders, somewhere in the marshes
and fields beyond the beach. D-Day was a lesson in improvisation,
and American troops on the ground were highly adaptable. General
Timberlake had implored his junior officers in a written appeal to
take the initiative: "*Do something!* Yours must be the strength of desperation. Improvise, chisel, beg, borrow or steal. Your life, and that of
the thousands you are protecting, depends on your initiative drive and
energy. . . . WE *CAN* DO IT, BE A LEADER!"

Willie Howard would remember Utah as a convulsion of noise, fire,
and death. So would others in Battery C, the sole company of the 320th
Battalion on this mile-long beach. They began landing late morning,
one crew to a landing craft equipped with a balloon, which they unloaded on the beach. The twenty-five balloons brought ashore would be
cut loose, erroneously believed to be drawing enemy fire.

"The beach was covered with dead soldiers and you were step-
ping over them to get to dry ground," said Floyd Siler, a 320th man
from Bennett, North Carolina. Siler found a foxhole already dug and

jumped in. He would spend a sleepless night in that hole, shivering in his wet clothes. Howard's crew dug their own trenches as the big artillery guns blazed. The mortars had uncanny aim, if sporadic timing. A GI lulled by a quiet moment could find himself, after a gut-churning blast, maimed or worse. In another cramped foxhole, Arthur Guest prayed with Joe Evans as the bombs fell "like raindrops," but the future preacher wasn't scared. "I thought I would be better off living in the Promised Land." Yet God had other plans for him, he liked to say. While Guest was in Britain, his mother had died of cancer. A letter would come in a few weeks telling him that, and the melancholy of this day on this beach would come racing back. Theolus "B" Wells shared their foxhole, and he had dug it so deep he could barely haul all six feet two inches of himself out of it. Wells was the winch operator of their three-man crew. Like Arthur Guest, their chief, Wells hailed from South Carolina, from Orangeburg. Joe Evans was from Raleigh, North Carolina, and he handled the gas. Wells was surprised to learn that Evans was a religious man. It may have been a battlefield conversion. "When the bombs stopped," said Wells, "he was the first one to start the crap game. I said, 'You can't be shooting craps after all that praying!'"

Wells watched as a plane was hit by fire and the pilot jumped. "I'm an American!" the flier yelled repeatedly as he parachuted to the beach. It was a risky move among so many amped-up soldiers primed for action. Friendly fire killed many men during the invasion. On June 7 an American pilot who bailed over Utah Beach was machine-gunned by one of his own.

When the shelling eased, Willie Howard climbed out of his trench and joined white soldiers dragging bloated, blasted-apart bodies across the beach for burial. Later in the day, more than a thousand African American troops would land in quartermaster, port battalion, and truck companies. It would be their job to bury the dead.

. . . .

IT WAS THE WATER that surprised Henry Parham—so much water, water that drowned men before his eyes. Even some of the sailors couldn't swim. The water was up to Parham's neck when he landed off Omaha Beach. The thirty-odd men aboard his boat plunged down the ramp as an officer waved a .45 in the air, the pistol a threat to anyone who harbored thoughts about staying. It had been dark when Parham clambered down a wobbly rope ladder from a transport ship somewhere in the Channel and dropped into this boat, which bobbed off Omaha Beach for eight nauseating hours. It was around 2:00 p.m. when the order came to unload and the ramp fell. Soon enough, Parham was in a foxhole, water lapping at the edge. The man from Greensville County, Virginia, had never seen water like this. Other men in the 320th would never forget the water and the terror that it brought. Albert Grillette Wood from Baltimore would fear the sea for the rest of his days.

There were five narrow ravines called draws leading from the beach over the bluffs to the roadways beyond, and the Americans needed to control them in order to move men and machinery off the sand. The Germans knew this and ensured that the enemy wouldn't have an easy time of it. The draws ranged in sophistication from a paved road to a crude dirt track. They were heavily defended by German troops in concrete bunkers and by snipers hidden in the scrubby heights. By early afternoon, one of the draws, E-1, on the eastern side of Omaha, was open to trucks, if not yet to tanks. Later in the day, atop this draw, one 320th battery would set up a command post.

From his foxhole, George Davison relaxed a bit. He gazed toward the sea, at the barrage balloons floating above vessels as far as the horizon. *What a pretty sight.* Unlike the infantry that was clamoring to get off this beach, the mission of the 320th men was to stay put. Until they raised their balloons, and even after they did so, they were combat troops. The trouble was knowing where to aim their M1 rifles. The snipers picking off targets everywhere were all but invisible, secreted in the scrub. Many infantrymen left Omaha without firing a shot. Now and again the 320th men got lucky. Cpl. Jesse L. Sumlin of Fruitdale, Alabama, fired at an enemy soldier he spotted hiding and took him prisoner. Sgt. Israel W. Hughes of Middletown, Ohio, helped capture eleven Germans.

Davison heard a voice shouting names, a roll call, but nobody answered. Men were wandering, searching for their companies, their commanders, aching for direction. Davison popped his head out of the trench. "Hi, Davie," a familiar voice said. Looking straight at him from a nearby foxhole was Lt. Col. Leon Reed, the 320th's commanding officer. When Davison eventually emerged from his bunker, hungry and in need of a smoke, he saw bodies lying everywhere, some washed clean of their clothes. The smell of burned flesh scarred the air. Davison peered down a trench and spied a smiling Eugene Coles, the 320th's cheerful supply sergeant from New York City. Units of the 320th were scattered along Omaha, the majority landing without balloons, which were to follow on later transports, along with winches, 6,600 cylinders of hydrogen, reels of cable, and other supplies. Yet the turmoil of June 6 delayed the men and their matériel, much of which was lost. Two 320th jeeps and a three-quarter-ton weapons carrier sank after being unloaded in water that was far too deep. All the balloon crews were supposed to be on the beaches by evening, but the landings would carry on for four more days.

For the better part of June 6, the 320th men were entirely on their own as they searched for the other members of their small balloon crews. Colonel Reed would write later that the battalion "came through in grand style." That outcome was not evident early in the day as the 320th commander sought to round up as many of his men as possible. He needed to get those balloons in the air. Night brought with it the danger of Luftwaffe attacks. The American and RAF planes would return to their bases in Britain, leaving the beaches unprotected. Soldiers packed tight on the sand were sitting ducks if

German planes came hurtling out of the clouds, with machine guns blazing. Or a well-aimed bomb could obliterate the mountains of supplies offloaded at the shoreline.

Barrage balloons were most effective when used to protect a contained area. Unlike during the London Blitz, when the balloons were incapable of preventing massive high-altitude bombing over such a huge swath of territory, in Normandy they were an ideal defense. Floating over the beaches, they would force aircraft to fly higher, making it more difficult for them to drop their bombs with accuracy or to strafe the men below with machine-gun fire. The higher altitudes also allowed the powerful AAA guns on the ground to get a better shot at them. The balloons on the American beaches were set to fly as high as two thousand feet, and at least two hundred yards apart. (Minefields would force them closer together.) They would be most effective in cloud cover, leaving pilots guessing as to where the bags were lurking.

Early in the war, the Germans had been determined to defeat the balloons. They developed a knife-edge cable cutter called a *Kuto-Nase*, installed at the leading edge of a plane's wings. In one version, a V-shaped, bumperlike device was wrapped around the plane's nose and attached to the front fuselage. The cutter had mixed results. On some bombers it could slice a cable only at high speeds. It was not effective when mounted on the Junkers Ju-88, the twin-engine plane that would fly the most missions over the Normandy beaches. In the end, the Germans ditched the cutter, which added too much weight, slowing an aircraft and draining precious fuel.

The balloon's nearly invisible steel cable, which was basically piano wire, was nerve-racking enough to enemy pilots, but it was the four-pound punch they packed that was truly frightful. Before D-Day, the small bombs attached to the cables were a closely guarded secret. British propaganda hinted at electrified wires and other surprises. Early articles written about the balloons at Camp Tyson detailed the lethal cables that could shear off a wing, but only vaguely mentioned their "booby traps." The British-made bomblet, packed with eight ounces of explosives, was larger than a soda can and secured with a pin, similar to a grenade. When the pin was removed, the bomb was armed. When the device was fastened to the cable and sent aloft, the balloon was transformed into a floating mine. A plane that hit the cable became ensnared, as if caught in a spider's web, and risked stalling. The cable strike released the bomb, dragging it toward the wing. A well-placed hit could detonate the gas tank, though the true value of the bomb was not in its power, but in its deterrence factor. If the balloons did their job, enemy pilots would strive assiduously to avoid them.

A newspaper correspondent on Omaha Beach called the balloon curtain "one the most important missions of the war." Colonel Reed explained the balloons' function in one of the many interviews that 320th men would give over the coming months to curious journalists intrigued by one of the army's more unusual lines of defense. "The primary aim of a barrage balloon pattern is to keep the enemy planes above the barrage or around it, so that automatic weapons of the AAA [Anti-Aircraft Artillery] can get at them," said Reed. "Flying balloons looks like kids' play, but it is a scientific and intricate art."

The balloon men often referred to their bags as their "babies." That summer, they would regale the newspapermen with images of fish and birds caught in mortal nets. "If a Nazi bird nestles in my lines," said Cleveland Hayes, a private from Okolona, Mississippi, "he won't nestle nowhere else."

Now Hayes and the rest of the 320th would have the chance to find out exactly what those babies could do.

CHAPTER 9

Forgotten

———

Every man who set foot on Omaha Beach that day was a hero.

—Retired general Omar N. Bradley, 1983
Omaha Beach
Evening, June 6, 1944

In northern France, the days of June are extravagantly long. It is perhaps nature's way of compensating for the endless gloom of January. Approaching the summer solstice, the last embers of twilight glow until almost 11:00 p.m., sinking into a fitful darkness stretching barely six hours until the first hint of dawn appears. The copious hours of daylight worked to the Allies' advantage on June 6. By nightfall, some 57,500 Americans and 75,200 British and Canadian troops had landed on the five invasion beaches. After an unforgiving attack and thousands of dead and wounded, they held a tenuous foothold along fifty-five miles of heavily defended coastline. As darkness came to Normandy, one fact was certain: The Allies were staying. They would not be pushed back into the sea.

On Omaha Beach, exhausted GIs hoped the darkness would bring them peace, but that was not to be. The din never quieted, a sound track of ack-ack guns, hisses, blasts, and booms mixed with the moans of the wounded. Searchlights and flares lit up the sky. One soldier compared it to the Fourth of July. Scrunched in foxholes, the men tried to catch whatever rest they could. Most of them had already unpacked, or scavenged, boxes of K-rations, and devoured their contents, which usually consisted of something like a disc of pork loaf, sawdust-dry biscuits, and a few squares of bitter chocolate. If they were lucky, the four cigarettes and matches inside were still dry. George Davison of the 320th moved to a foxhole farther from the waterline. As night fell, he feared learning that the "dreadful stories" the men had been told about fearsome German defenses would prove true. Whatever happened, he wrote, they weren't moving. His commander, Colonel Reed, had told him, "This is where we make our stand . . . or die trying."

Davison thought about the tinned scrambled eggs in his musette bag lost to the sea. There were bigger problems than rumbling stomachs. Many of the wounded would not survive the night, outmatched by cold and shock. GIs gave up the blankets wrapped in their bedrolls to keep them warm, and medics struggled to keep them alive, hindered by limited supplies and their own fatigue. Some enemy troops took advantage of the darkness to make their escape, many of them second-rate fighters culled from Soviet and Polish prisoners of war. There were, however, plenty of highly skilled and fiercely loyal German-born troops from the 352nd Infantry Division that were still there. The Allied front was not the sturdy line that General Eisenhower had envisioned. The men who were dug in on and around Omaha Beach felt anything but secure. "The Americans controlled only the soil on which they currently stood and the ground that was within range of a hand grenade toss," writes historian Joseph Balkoski.

It was around 11:00 p.m. when a German plane popped out of the clouds and buzzed the fleet just above the barrage balloons. "Every ship in the English Channel opened fire on that single airplane," said a Twenty-Ninth Division private, "illuminating the sky with millions of tracer bullets." The plane survived the onslaught, circled, and flew away. Other versions have more than one plane in the sky that night. Seventy years after D-Day, the number of enemy aircraft in the air on

June 6 is still not known. Cornelius Ryan writes in *The Longest Day* that there were only two Luftwaffe fighters on the ground in northern France on the morning of June 6, and with them a pair of hungover pilots. As Ryan tells it, with so many German commanders out of France and little chance of an invasion in what they expected to be stormy weather, the Luftwaffe command had dispersed the squadrons far from Normandy to keep them safe from Allied bombing runs.

So, early on the morning of June 6, the phone rang at a lonely airfield near Lille, close to the border with Belgium. Lt. Col. Josef "Pips" Priller and his wingman shook off their booze-fueled fog and climbed aboard their Focke-Wulf FW-190 fighters. Hitler had vowed to send a thousand planes to defeat the invaders, but now it was down to two planes, and up to Pips to lead what he was sure would be a suicide mission. They took off at 9:00 a.m., heading west toward Le Havre, where they spotted the invasion force. "What a show!" Pips whooped. They ducked into the clouds before diving down at more than four hundred miles per hour over the British-held beaches, coming in so close that stunned Tommies could see their faces as machine-gun fire sprayed the sand. On the eastern edge of Omaha, the fliers turned and zoomed over the fleet above the barrage balloons before heading for home. That the scores of antiaircraft guns trained on them missed entirely was a testament to Priller's skill (or, as some infantrymen snarkily observed, the inaccuracy of the flak guns). In nine days' time, the German ace would score his one-hundredth "victory," shooting down an American Liberator.

Many popular histories of D-Day have repeated Ryan's account, published in 1959, of that two-plane morning assault. Yet there were other sorties on D-Day. Allied planes chased off three German FW-190 fighters during daylight. German records do not agree but place as many as 319 Luftwaffe planes in the sky. Other accounts say enemy planes flew up to two hundred fifty missions against the landing force. Whatever the truth, the German air response was surprisingly weak—and despite a tepid rally, it would remain anemic for the remainder of the battle for Normandy. American and RAF planes dominated the skies, flying fourteen thousand missions on June 6 alone. Although the Allied bombing just before the landings had proven ineffective at clearing German fortifications, the bombs dropped inland had shattered roads, rail lines, and vehicles vital to the German supply chain. Enemy troop reinforcements racing to the beachhead would find their paths blocked by debris, not to mention a steady rain of Allied bombs that would force their convoys off the roads during daylight.

Only four years earlier, Germany had boasted the world's most formidable air force, under the control of Hitler confidant Hermann Göring. Yet by early 1944, the Luftwaffe was operating on little more than hope, with rapidly dwindling stocks of planes, pilots, and gas. As the Führer's lust for territory sent millions of German troops eastward, the air force was stretched beyond its limits. As a result, the Germans were outmatched everywhere but at home. The Luftwaffe was unable to supply the aircraft needed on three fronts (against the Red Army in the east, and the Allies in Italy and France), and the situation turned all the more dire when Allied bombs began pummeling Germany day and night. Nearly half the Luftwaffe's 2,635 aircraft in the west were needed to defend the Fatherland, leaving the French invasion front open to air attack. By June 1944 the Luftwaffe did not control the skies anywhere, not even over Germany.

As the war intensified, severe shortages in raw materials forced air commanders to make tough choices. Rather than produce better aircraft, an early priority was set to pump out as many planes as possible to replace steadily rising losses. Many of these machines were of poor quality, and by early 1944 mechanical failure was one of the reasons blamed for the loss of nearly half of all planes produced. In any event, by 1943 the Allies were producing four times as many planes as Germany. The derring-do of Luftwaffe aces had once been the talk of the Allied air corps. Now those once-distinguished ranks were filled with poorly trained novices. In May alone, the Luftwaffe lost half its single-engine fighter planes and one-quarter of its pilots. Although a few aces such as Priller would fly missions in Normandy in subsequent weeks, most German pilots were little more than "cannon fodder straight out of flying school," writes historian Antony Beevor. By early 1944 the once-superior German planes were no match for the zippy new version of the American Mustang that could reach four hundred forty miles per hour. The Germans had failed to develop a bomber that could match the British Lancaster, which could drop four times as much explosive as the antiquated Junkers Ju-88. Göring's team had bet that Germany would win the war before its air power collapsed. Now it was too late.

In the weeks before the invasion, Allied intelligence had decrypted reams of important German communications that informed their invasion strategy. The intercepts decrypted at Bletchley Park in the English countryside helped plan bombing runs that destroyed so many Luftwaffe airfields in Normandy that when reinforcements finally arrived, fighter pilots would be forced to hide their planes in woods near intact stretches of road. Beyond the blow wrought by Allied bombs, the absence of the German air force on June 6 was the result of a perfect storm of bad timing, inept decision making, and poor leadership. Lulled into a false sense of security by the dismal weather, the Germans had failed to run reconnaissance flights for the first five days of June. If they had, Luftwaffe pilots would have seen the world's largest armada forming right under their wings. German intelligence intercepted coded messages broadcast by the BBC signaling to the French resistance that the invasion was close at hand. Told about these communications hidden in lines of poetry by Verlaine, commanders did not take them seriously.

In the early hours of June 6, even after it became clear to some lower-ranking German officers on the front lines that the long-expected invasion was under way, Field Marshal Gerd von Rundstedt still believed it was a diversion and that the real attack would come near Calais. By the time German reinforcement troops and planes were dispatched, they had lost crucial hours. Had the Germans been better prepared, the results could have proved catastrophic for the Allies. With thousands of ships massed in the Channel, and tens of thousands of GIs and Tommies flooding the beaches, the supply of targets was seemingly limitless. Despite the damage that Allied bombers had inflicted before the invasion, D-Day planners did not know the extent of the Luftwaffe's abysmal state. So they prepared for the worst. Their nightmare scenario had the Germans throwing every available fighter and bomber into the battle. The Allies predicted 1,350 enemy planes in the air on June 6, fortified by a special force of 500 fighters held in reserve especially for the invasion. All told, they foresaw the Luftwaffe flying as many as 1,800 missions. By D+1 (June 7), they anticipated 300 more fighters thrown into the battle.

On June 7 the Allied air chief, Sir Trafford Leigh-Mallory, confided in his diary that "we have had a very easy run as far as the Luftwaffe is concerned." Yet he believed the great Axis-Allied air battle could still happen. He was not alone. On the beaches, thoughts of an impending blitz terrified the men in the foxholes. They looked skyward, straining to hear the distant drone of a swarm of planes with black-and-white swastikas emblazoned on their tails. It was with dive-bombing and strafing attacks in mind that Colonel Reed, the commanding officer of the 320th, likely hurried to gather his men, scattered across five miles of beach, and salvage any balloons that had weathered the journey from England. There is no record of Reed's actions on June 6, other than the simply stated fact that the first barrage balloon was flying at 11:15 p.m. It served as a sentry over the eastern end of Omaha Beach near the crucial E-3 draw, which was the beach exit near Colleville-sur-Mer, still held by the Germans. The Americans would not capture it until the following day, and firefights raged throughout the night.

By dawn, the 320th had raised twelve balloons high over Omaha Beach.

. . . .

ELEVEN MONTHS EARLIER, AMERICAN barrage balloons had made their first appearance in Europe when the 103rd Barrage Balloon Battery landed in Sicily in the first waves of Operation Husky, the first of the multiprong Allied campaign to force Benito Mussolini to surrender and push the Germans out of Italy. The 103rd was among three balloon batteries that had left Camp Tyson, Tennessee, in the spring and summer of 1943 bound for North Africa, after its capture by the Allies. From Oran, Algeria, they traveled to Sicily, then to the southern Italian mainland, and finally to southern France, when the Allies launched their second invasion of that country in August 1944.

The Italian operations would teach balloon commanders a number of important lessons that proved useful in the Normandy planning. Chief among them was that balloon crews ought to carry as much equipment with them as possible, particularly winches and hydrogen cylinders. The chaos of the Sicily landings left balloon units stranded without their supplies, which in some cases took days to recover. They also learned that it was more effective to inflate their balloons after landing, with the exception of one balloon flying over the landing craft. (The opposite strategy would be employed in Normandy, where balloons landed inflated.) The ship-based balloons did not always deter German planes from attacking them, but the balloons served as an effective morale booster for the men on board.

These batteries differed from the 320th in that each consisted of at most three hundred men, or about one-third the strength of a battalion. Another difference was that these men were white. Of the more than thirty balloon units that trained at Camp Tyson, only four were African American. Of the black battalions, only the 320th was sent to war. It is unknown why the army selected an African American unit for its most important operation in Europe and arguably of the entire war.

Perhaps the War Department, which saw African Americans as intellectually and physically inferior to whites, deemed the flying of balloons to be a job that black men could "handle." Or perhaps pressure exerted on the Roosevelt administration played a role. Civil rights leaders, white liberals in Congress, and the First Lady had long urged an expansion of responsibilities for black soldiers beyond service and labor units.

The first combat test for the army balloons came on July 12, 1943, when they landed with the 103rd at Licata, on the southwestern coast of Sicily, where villages coated in ankle-deep dust and foxholes ridden with fleas and ants made a lasting impression on the balloon crews. The landings on the southern Italian mainland in September 1943 were particularly brutal, with German planes attacking the landing craft, and artillery fire pounding troops from the shore. The men of the 102nd Barrage Balloon Battery landed at Salerno too early, before the beach had been cleared of small-arms fire, and most of their balloons were destroyed as soon as they were inflated. As enemy guns raged, seven men improvised and grabbed the mooring lines of a surviving balloon and ran it up and down the beach to prevent the gunners from drawing a bead on it. For their efforts, the men received the Silver Star, the third-highest award for heroism in battle.

The balloons were credited with taking out a number of enemy planes in Sicily and on the mainland. The 104th Barrage Balloon Battery was flying a barrage from the landing craft on the night of September 9 when two German Messerschmitt ME-109 fighters hit balloon cables and crashed. In November, a plane hit a cable near Naples and the explosion of its gas tank destroyed the plane and the balloon. In Palermo, the 103rd reported taking out a couple of German planes. The balloons succeeded in their aim of keeping enemy planes at high altitudes. Army commanders lauded them for protecting the invading force, and a report concluded that "numerous instances were observed [where] enemy planes would veer off and drop their bombs from an ineffectual angle rather than risk contact with the balloon cables." After the Italian campaign, Lt. Gen. Mark W. Clark, who led the Fifth Army in the Mediterranean, wrote that "barrage balloons are a vital element of the defense of a vulnerable area, such as a port or landing beach."

THE MEN ON OMAHA BEACH awoke on June 7 to a landscape of utter devastation. The bodies of the dead and the charred skeletons of tanks, trucks, and landing craft told the story of the worst day of their lives. Steel hedgehogs and other obstacles stood defiantly at the waterline, and shards of barbed wire curled along the sand. Throughout the day, shells would fall and enemy fire would pepper the beach. Still, the landing craft kept coming, unloading more men and more supplies. Hulking LSTs (landing ship tanks), the largest troop carriers, beached on the sand, disgorging more tanks, more half-tracks, and heavy guns—more of everything. A Twenty-Ninth Division quartermaster unit with a bulldozer dug the first cemetery between the beach and the bluffs. The unit would bury 456 men while under fire.

During the morning of June 7, enemy fire claimed the twelve barrage balloons that members of the 320th Battalion had raised overnight on Omaha Beach. They would be replaced with new balloons carried by 320th men who would land over the next four days. By the evening of June 7, there were twenty balloons over Omaha and thirteen over Utah. Artillery fire would claim twelve of them. Over the coming days, as the picture of D-Day slowly came into focus, Colonel Reed would learn that three of his men were killed on June 6. Seventeen others were wounded. Countless acts of heroism large and small, from saving lives to tucking a blanket around a dying man, would never be recorded.

The Germans rushed three hundred additional planes to France and launched a series of attacks against the invasion force. On June 7, four fighters strafed Utah Beach at 10:30 a.m. Nine more fighters attacked by early afternoon, though the Luftwaffe paid a heavy price. Antiaircraft guns destroyed all but three of the planes. Over the next twenty-four hours, the Luftwaffe flew about six hundred missions, mostly over the ships, and suffered heavy losses. By the end of the first week, more than a thousand German planes were on the attack in Normandy. Soon, nearly six hundred would be lost.

"Every night Jerry visits the invasion coast of France," wrote James Hugo Madison, a newspaper correspondent who spent time with the 320th in July. "He comes to bomb or strafe the beach but he keeps a respectable distance above the lethal cables held erect along the shore line by barrage balloons. Not since the first night has he been able to drop to strafing altitude and that was before balloons were present in sufficient numbers." The balloons, he wrote, "keep the front door to the front lines open."

The job of handling balloons was a solitary task. Balloon crews of three and four men worked alone. In Normandy, they raised their balloons mostly at night, after Allied planes had returned to base. In the event that an alert was sounded during the daytime, indicating that a Luftwaffe attack was imminent, the balloons could be raised within a minute. Nearby, an AAA unit and its heavy flak gun—the 320th men were partial to the powerful ninety-millimeter—sat on the sand, its long barrel aimed at the sky. Daytime photographs of Omaha and Utah Beaches taken during the weeks after the invasion show bright silver orbs dotting the skies, evidence that the threat of enemy attack persisted.

The raiders that menaced the invasion front regularly in June and July were hardly the terrifying squadrons the GIs had imagined. Most of them were "single plane nuisance raids," as the army called them. The exception was an attack by one hundred planes during the night of July 28–29. Damage was likely minor, given that AAA records provide no details except to note that the target was shipping. American and RAF planes forced most enemy bombers to drop their cargo far from the coast, and flak guns consistently shot down Luftwaffe planes that reached the front.

Still, the men on the beach dreaded the nighttime visits they called "Bed Check Charlie." First came the flares that lit up the beach "like a football stadium," as Willie Howard saw it. Sometimes planes would follow; other times not. From his foxhole on Utah Beach, Theolus Wells says he was too young to have enough sense to be scared. But Willie Howard did; he hated the night. Their rifles at the ready, the 320th men spent long dark hours on alert for another threat from the air: parachutes. The men didn't know that Germany had given up paratroop operations in June 1941, after the battle for Crete, which the Reich had won, but with catastrophic losses.

During the long days and short nights of June, as many as 143 balloons floated high in the sky above the Normandy beaches. "Now and then a Jerry pilot takes his chances," wrote the correspondent James Hugo Madison. That happened one night when a Ju-88 hit a balloon cable and crashed offshore. The 320th men reveled in their first hit. Madison described what happened:

> In the early morning of June 16 one pilot came down to strafe. Before he could get his guns going, he hooked a wing on a flying cable. He realized his error too late, and headed out to sea in an apparent effort to avoid other cables in front of him. His whole plane was visible for an instant when the bomb on the cable crashed against his wing. Then the plane disappeared in the turbulent waters of the English Channel.

The Ju-88 was one of two or three planes the balloons took out, though the 320th was credited with a large number of possible hits as well in the early days of the invasion. On three occasions, the link that connected the balloon to the cable was severed for unknown reasons. This could happen if a plane struck the cable and escaped, or in the case of sudden tension caused by high winds. The bags were often flying under cloud cover and at night, making it difficult to discern what happened. The purpose of the balloons was to discourage pilots from descending below the balloon, and in this goal they succeeded. Battalion records show that only one plane managed to get below the barrage once the balloons were flying at full strength

The balloons "confounded skeptics," wrote a reporter for *Stars and Stripes*, "by their part in keeping enemy raiders above effective strafing altitude." The 320th Battalion drew substantial praise that summer from visiting newspapermen fascinated with their mission. "It seems the whole front knows the story of the Negro barrage balloon battalion outfit which was one of the first ashore on D-Day," wrote the military correspondent Bill Richardson to Eisenhower's staff. The 320th men "have gotten the reputation of hard workers and good soldiers," he added. "Their simple earnestness and their pride at 'being in on' the Second Front is obvious even to some of the most Jim-Crow-conscious southerners. As one paratrooper said to me: 'Well, they ain't exactly airborne troops, but they're doing a good job.'"

Richardson, who was the first editor of *Yank* magazine, wrote a series of private reports from the front lines. In one piece devoted to black troops in which he mentions the 320th, he lauds the "marvelous" performance of Negro soldiers and notes the surprise of white troops when they learned of it. "Innumerable soldiers and many officers said— and I quote rather generally and precisely—'By God, those bastards are doing all right. I didn't know they had it in them.'" Walter Bedell Smith, Eisenhower's chief of staff, flagged the balloon-related dispatch to his boss with a note that said, "Please read this."

Eisenhower landed on Omaha Beach on June 13. Photographs show him talking to black soldiers, many of whom were assigned to port battalions and quartermaster companies charged with off-loading and moving tons of supplies. Beginning in late August, those supplies were then trucked from the beachhead by African Americans who manned the Red Ball Express, the twenty-four-hour supply route that fed the front lines. Many of these service troops landed on D-Day and worked under steady fire. One of them was the 4042nd Quartermaster Truck Company, which transported blood plasma and other medical supplies to the beach under brutal conditions. They were praised for displaying "ingenuity" by salvaging some of their vehicles sunk during the landing and putting them back into service.

The 4042nd won a commendation from Eisenhower for extraordinary service on Omaha Beach. The other Negro unit so honored was the 320th. "Despite the losses sustained," the 320th commendation reads, "the battalion carried out its mission with courage and determination, and proved an important element of the air defense team."

As THE DAYS TURNED to weeks, the men of the 320th Battalion settled into a steady routine on Omaha and Utah Beaches. At dawn, they lowered the balloons using the lighter hand winch they had redesigned in Britain. After a balloon was back on earth, they'd remove the bomb, delicately, and replace its pin. They'd then throw a net over the balloon, and secure the mooring lines with sandbags or concrete blocks, seven on each side. Like a giant sea creature at rest, the gasbag heaved lightly in the breeze as if breathing. There was work to do when the balloons were down. The men unloaded a steady stream of supplies from the boats that landed constantly throughout the summer and fall. If it was a windy day when the latest balloons arrived, already inflated, it took the strength of several men to wrestle the bouncing 125-pound bags to berths that moved farther from the beach as the weeks ticked by. A balloon man who wasn't wearing leather gloves ended up with bloodied hands.

By the end of the summer, most of the balloons were guarding beach exits and an airfield not far from the top of Omaha. The men moved from foxholes to more spacious quarters in abandoned German pillboxes and tent camps in the fields above the beaches. Commanders tapped off-duty 320th men for other jobs. George Davison joined a patrol to rout a German sniper holed up at a farm near the beach. He also ferried messages from the beach several miles to Twelfth Army Group headquarters. Other assignments weren't so interesting. Sam Mattison was told to bury the stinking corpse of a bloated cow in a field near their billets. He stuck his knife in the festering mound to see what would happen; the results were exceedingly unpleasant. When his balloon was down, Bill Dabney spent countless hours in his foxhole watching Allied planes hurtling overhead. He enjoyed the show immensely, about as much as the local Calvados apple brandy. Allied bombs had leveled towns and villages across Normandy. The 320th men had few places to go when they were off duty in those early weeks, which was a change from their time in Britain. Contact with the French was limited, but soon enough, the local children who had eyed them warily at first discovered that the GIs were a font of treats.

As time passed, the homesick men dreamed of warm showers and steak dinners. "Dear Ma," Wilson Monk wrote on July 13, "Things over here are pretty hot but we're coming through 100%. I've been in a foxhole and haven't pulled off my clothes in nearly a week. I think if I were to jump in a feather bed now I'd sleep five years." Wilson Monk had only recently arrived on Omaha Beach. He was among sixty-six battalion reserve troops who had stayed behind in England and landed in Normandy on July 3. In a letter the following week, Monk complained to his mother about the mosquitoes and tucked a fifty-franc note into the envelope as a keepsake. Monk would send more souvenirs home to Atlantic City over the next two months, including a German helmet and a French knife. He found a German gas mask and later passed the gray-green metal canister it came in to his friend Malchi Adkins, who wrote in a clear, steady hand. In small block letters, Adkins painted the names of men in their headquarters battery around the canister in white paint, adding, "Scotland, Wales, England, France, June 1944." Seven decades after the war, Monk would trace a finger over those names, recalling his late friends, all of whom were inspectors like him, ensuring the balloons and the equipment were in top shape. They included

William "Tic" Ektor from Chicago, Eugene Smack from Philadelphia, Sam Small from New York City, and Forrest Redd from Cleveland, who would be godfather to Monk's only son.

By the end of July, Allied bombing runs had stripped Germany of nearly all its capacity to produce aircraft fuel. "We were fighting a poor man's war," one German general said, referring to his depleted tank fleet. The same was true in the air. By August, the skies over Normandy were quiet, with the Luftwaffe down to seventy-five fighters. By September, the once-mighty German bomber force that had been instrumental in Hitler's conquests was all but dead. The Reich would urge its surviving pilots to show "greater enthusiasm and courage" in the face of disaster, but it was too late.

ON THE MORNING OF June 7, Waverly Woodson performed one last act of bravery on Omaha Beach. Fighting his own exhaustion and throbbing pain, Woodson plunged into the surf and dragged four drowning soldiers to safety. They were British Tommies attempting to come ashore with the help of a guide rope that extended from the beach to their landing craft, anchored in deep water. The rope had broken, and several men were floundering. Woodson revived four of them, and taught the soldiers on the beach how to do the same and save the others. Later that afternoon, he collapsed.

Woody Woodson was taken to a hospital ship, where his shrapnel wounds were treated. Three days later, he asked to go back to the beach. Word of his heroics spread. Newspapermen interviewed him. They described the medic from West Philadelphia as shy and modest, and wrote stories saying that he had cared for more than three hundred men. An army press release lauded Woodson's heroism and said he had ignored his wounds and worked for thirty hours. Back home, the local paper called him "No. 1 Invasion Hero." *Stars and Stripes* wrote that Woodson and the other medics "covered themselves with glory on D-Day."

The headlines and plaudits kept coming. Woodson returned home a celebrity. He recounted his adventures during a nationwide radio broadcast. The black press wrote that he deserved the Medal of Honor, the ultimate symbol of heroism and self-sacrifice.

A sole piece of paper exists revealing that Woodson was in fact a candidate for the nation's highest honor. The note that passed from the War Department to the White House says that Woodson's commanding officer had recommended him for the Distinguished Service Cross, the second-highest award. In an intriguing twist, the note adds that the office of U.S. Gen. John C. H. Lee in Britain believed Woodson deserved the Medal of Honor, and the recommendation was changed to reflect the higher decoration.

The unsigned note, addressed to "Jonathan," was likely written by Philleo Nash, an assistant director in the Office of War Information. In it, he alerts Jonathan Daniels, a White House aide, that if Woodson was to receive the Medal of Honor, the award would rate presidential attention. "Here is a Negro from Philadelphia who has been recommended for a suitable award," writes Nash (emphasis in original). "This is a big enough award so that the President can give it personally, as he has in the case of some white boys."

In the end, Woodson and four other 320th medics received the Bronze Star, the fourth-highest award. Their commanding officer, Lt. Col. Leon Reed, got one, too. The Bronze Star, created in February 1944, was usually given for "meritorious service" rather than heroism.

What happened to Woodson's high honor? The records trail ends with the Philleo Nash note. Of the 433 Medals of Honor awarded during World War II, none went to the more than one million African Americans who served. Nine black soldiers received the Distinguished Service Cross. In the navy, one African American received a high award: Dorie Miller, the cook at Pearl Harbor who jumped behind an AAA gun he had never been trained to use and fired at Japanese planes until he ran out of ammo. For his efforts, Miller received the Navy Cross, the third-highest decoration at that time (it was later elevated to the second-highest). Among the fifteen men awarded the Medal of Honor for their service on December 7, 1941, one was Mervyn Sharp Bennion, the mortally wounded captain of the USS *West Virginia*, whom Miller had helped pull to safety before he began firing.

Woodson and Miller were not alone. Black soldiers performed valiantly in World War II despite the limitations placed on them by quotas, training that was frequently inferior to that of white troops, assumptions that they were less intelligent and courageous than white men, and outright hostility directed at them by officers and peers. "You can't make a first-class soldier out of a second-class citizen," a black corporal told journalist Roi Ottley. But in fact, often you could. Before taking command of the 761st Tank Battalion—the "Black Panthers"—Col. Paul L. Bates had been warned repeatedly that Negro troops would never measure up. "You don't know what you're in for," he was told. When they arrived at the front, Lt. Gen. George S. Patton Jr., commander of the U.S. Third Army, left little doubt that the Negroes were on trial. "I don't care what color you are, so long as you go up there and kill those Kraut sonsabitches," Patton told them. "Everyone has their eyes on you and is expecting great things from you. Most of all, your race is looking forward to you. Don't let them down, don't let them down!" The Panthers didn't disappoint: They fought in five countries and captured thirty towns. They spent more days in combat—183— than any other armored unit. Among their awards were eleven Silver Stars and sixty-nine Bronze Stars. President Jimmy Carter awarded the 761st a long-delayed Distinguished Unit Citation in 1978.

America's first black pilots of the 332nd Fighter Group and the 99th Fighter Squadron—the Tuskegee Airmen—flew more than fifteen thousand individual sorties in Europe. They spent the war treated as "pariahs," said airman Lee Archer. Spurned by many senior white officers, they were denied the benefit of training with experienced white pilots. The 99th's commander, Lt. Col. Benjamin O. Davis Jr., said in

1943 that each man carried with him a tremendous burden: "At all times every man realizes that the pleasures and relaxations that are available to men in other organizations are not available to him because his task is far greater, his responsibility is much heavier, and his reward is the advancement of his people." To many of the bomber pilots whom they escorted deep into enemy territory, the men of Tuskegee were invisible, save for the scarlet markings on their planes. "We had no idea that the Red Tails who were giving us the finest escort . . . were black men," said George Barnett, a B-24 pilot, long after the war. Most of America wouldn't learn of the black airmen's heroics until 1995, when a cable television movie sparked interest in their story.

Time would vindicate the men of the 92nd Infantry Division. Tracing their roots to the nineteenth-century Buffalo Soldiers who fought with distinction on America's western frontier, the 92nd was pilloried after the Second World War for incompetence and cowardice, as it had been in the First World War. Yet as in that earlier war, elements of the division fought with extraordinary courage on the front lines. One of those regiments, the 366th Infantry, was sent to fight seasoned German troops in Italy in 1944, in a high-stakes frontal assault, with only several days' training and inferior weapons. The division commander, Maj. Gen. Edward M. Almond, had "welcomed" the 366th into his fold with these words: "I did not send for you. Your Negro newspapers, Negro politicians and white friends have insisted on you seeing combat and I shall see that you get combat and your share of the casualties." (The division saw three thousand casualties.) Years after the war, a white colonel in the 92nd said Almond's views were hardly unique: "Hell, everyone in the army then was a racist." Despite an awards system that shortchanged black soldiers, the men of the 92nd collected scores of decorations, including 2 Distinguished Service Crosses, 208 Silver Stars, and more than 1,000 Bronze Stars.

In December 1944, more than two thousand black service troops answered an urgent call for volunteer riflemen during the Battle of

the Bulge. The surprise German attack in Belgium's Ardennes Forest
had left eighty thousand Americans killed, wounded, or captured—and
the army in desperate need of replacements. The black soldiers, many
of whom took demotions for the chance to serve as privates in combat
units, impressed their white commanders with their drive and ferocity.
Although assigned to segregated platoons, they were the first black men
to fight shoulder to shoulder with whites since the Revolutionary War.
They fought in the same infantry companies that crossed the Rhine and
pushed deep into Germany during the final months of the war. White
GIs came to respect their black comrades, belying the army's often-cited
concern that integration would weaken fighting units and lead to strife.
"We ate together, slept together, fought together. There were no incidents," said J. Cameron Wade, a truck driver turned rifleman who fought
with the Ninety-Ninth Infantry Division. The volunteers won praise
from their commanders, including Patton and Eisenhower. "I have never
seen any soldiers who have performed better in combat than you have,"
Gen. Charles Lanham told several black volunteers who received medals.
Yet many men wouldn't see the medals they were due until years after the
war. Two New York veterans received Bronze Stars in 2000.

During the Battle of the Bulge, several black field artillery battalions fought with courage. One of them, the 333rd, took the most casualties of any Allied artillery unit. To the east, in France, the 614th
Tank Destroyer Battalion fought off German defenders despite losing
half its men. The 614th became the first black outfit to win the Distinguished Unit Citation, and individual awards included one Distinguished Service Cross and four Silver Stars. Among the army's AAA
units in Europe, the 452nd Automatic Weapons Battalion ranked near
the top for shooting down the most German planes, in three countries.
Five black members, including two medics, won the Silver Star.

In Europe and the Pacific, black labor and support troops won accolades for carrying out supposed menial duties with bravery under fire.
On Iwo Jima, fourteen black members of amphibious truck companies

won the Silver Star for outstanding service in the face of brutal conditions. Black soldiers comprised 60 percent of the fifteen thousand Americans who suffered through blistering heat, monsoons, and disease to build the Ledo Road, the 271-mile supply route through the mountains of northeastern India and Burma. The role played by black troops was acknowledged for the first time by the Department of Defense in 2004.

Limited by quotas for much of the war, black women volunteered in numbers to fight for their country. An estimated four thousand served in the Women's Army Corps, and more than five hundred worked as army nurses.

The only black paratrooper outfit, the 555th Parachute Infantry Battalion, finished training too late to see combat, but was tapped for a unique mission called Operation Firefly. During the hot, dry summer of 1945 the Japanese sent paper balloons floating toward America's West Coast loaded with incendiary bombs. Their existence was kept top secret so as not to incite panic. The 555th—the "Triple Nickels"—became smoke jumpers, fighting fires in the forests of the Pacific Northwest, some of them caused by the Japanese balloon bombs. When they were off duty in Pendleton, Oregon, the men often found it difficult to find a meal, and only two bars would serve Negroes.

At Omaha Beach, the Hollywood director John Ford came ashore on D-Day with a Coast Guard camera crew and watched in amazement as a black soldier unloaded supplies seemingly oblivious to the exploding shells and relentless machine-gun fire around him. "I thought, 'By God, if anybody deserves a medal that man does,'" Ford wrote. It is doubtful that GI got a medal. Compared with other battles, relatively few soldiers who fought on D-Day were recognized for their service. Only four Medals of Honor and 214 Distinguished Service Crosses were awarded for valor on June 6.

Omar Bradley, the celebrated general and commander of the First U.S. Army, would say years after the war that "every man who set foot on Omaha Beach that day was a hero." That was certainly true. Yet there were heroes among the heroes. One of them was a white GI named Carlton William Barrett. The First Division private landed on Omaha Beach under intense fire and plunged into the surf repeatedly to save drowning men, pulling them to safety even as he ignored his own. "He arose as a leader in the stress of the occasion," his citation reads. For his service, Barrett was awarded the Medal of Honor in October 1944. To merit the top award for valor, a soldier must distinguish himself "conspicuously in actual conflict with the enemy." Barrett was not a medic. He was a member of the Eighteenth Infantry Intelligence and Reconnaissance Platoon. It was not his duty to save the dying. Perhaps that is what made the difference. Perhaps the army commanders who considered Waverly Woodson for the Medal of Honor decided that the medic, though wounded, was doing his job on June 6, 1944, on that singular, extraordinary day. Or maybe there was another reason. On this question, the record is silent.

Four decades later, at the urging of black veterans, the army ordered an independent inquiry to determine why no African Americans had received the Medal of Honor in World War II. The investigators concluded that pervasive racism was to blame for the failure to recognize black soldiers. Based on their recommendations, President Bill Clinton awarded the Medal of Honor to seven African Americans on January 13, 1997. Only Vernon Baker, a second lieutenant in the once-vilified Ninety-Second Division, was alive to shake the president's hand. "History has been made whole today," said Clinton, "and our nation is bestowing honor on those who have long deserved it."

Woodson, the 320th's undisputed hero, was not among them, though he had been considered. For the second time in his long life, Waverly Woodson was forgotten.

Epilogue

===

If anything can, it is memory that will save humanity.
—Elie Wiesel, Nobel Peace Prize address, December 11, 1986

While the 320th Barrage Balloon Battalion was in France, back home, the balloons went on tour. Crews from Camp Tyson, Tennessee, traveled around the country raising money for war bonds. They inflated the balloons (with noncombustible helium) in cities across the country and drew enthusiastic crowds. Balloons flew over downtown Milwaukee, where the local papers devoted pages to the finer points of the craft, such as the fact that it takes sixteen cylinders of gas, each holding 191 cubic feet, to inflate one. In Portland, Maine, readers learned that the VLA balloons in Normandy cost six hundred dollars each. "Extra Protection for Our Fighting Men in Europe," blared a headline above a photo of the silvery spheres floating over Omaha Beach.

Before the war was over, the army had begun considering how to improve the balloon defense system. Advances in technology since 1941 had outpaced the balloons. The high-speed V-1 rocket bombs that Germany unleashed on London in the summer of 1944 could snap a balloon cable and escape before the attached bomb did any damage. The debut of the German ME-262—the world's first fighter jet, with a top speed of 540 miles per hour—did nothing to change the course of the war but made it clear what the balloons were up against. At the very least, the balloon cable had to be strengthened and made more flexible.

Yet there was little use for barrage balloons after the war. And because the United States and Britain had manufactured some twenty thousand of them, there were a lot of balloons to dispose of. Surplus U.S. Army balloons were sold for a dollar a yard. Some were bought by companies such as Chevrolet and covered in ads. Millions of yards of balloon cloth were recycled for other uses. Women could buy ruffled summer dresses made from balloon cotton that looked better "with every laundering," raved the *New York Times*. "Light and sheer as silk," the balloon fabric "can be pressed to a glass-like finish." In Britain, the balloons were used to make car covers, raincoats, and tarps for haystacks.

In the conflicts that followed the Second World War, barrage balloons played a limited role. In 1953, balloons were used as a shield during peace talks at the Panmunjom compound between North and South Korea. During the Vietnam War, they flew over Hanoi to protect against low-level bombing raids. In recent years, balloons have gone back to their Napoleonic roots as sky spies. Today's high-tech balloons, called aerostats, come armed with long-range radar, cameras, listening devices, and sensors. Made of highly durable fabrics such as Kevlar, modern balloons can reach altitudes of eighty-five thousand feet and withstand high winds to stay aloft for days or months. They have been sent up to measure pollution and to monitor communications like satellites from the stratosphere. Experiments are under way to use Wi-Fi-equipped balloons to bring the Internet to remote corners of the globe.

In the early 2000s, the U.S. Defense Department sent the bullet-shaped craft, upwards of sixty feet long with three tail fins, to snoop on insurgents in Iraq and Afghanistan. As the American presence in those countries was reduced, many of the aerostats moved to the U.S. border with Mexico to counter drug trafficking. Cameras on the latest models can see in the dark for up to twelve miles. In Singapore, the government sent aloft an observation balloon the size of an Olympic swimming pool in late 2014 to monitor the skies two thousand feet above the island. One reason cited for the need for increased surveillance was the mysterious disappearance of a Malaysia Airlines jet earlier that year.

THE 320TH BARRAGE BALLOON BATTALION served 140 days in France. In late July 1944, two of the battalion's four batteries moved west to the tip of the Cotentin Peninsula to fly a balloon barrage at Cherbourg, the key port city captured by the Allies three weeks after D-Day. The remaining two batteries stayed on the beaches, their balloons flying over Omaha and Utah until early October, when deteriorating weather prevented ships from landing. On October 24, the men of the 320th boarded boats bound for England. "Morale of troops was very high," the unit history says. In fact, the men were ecstatic. They were going home. On November 11, the freighter USAT *Excelsior* left Southampton with the battalion aboard. Fifteen days later, the ship docked in New York.

Any hopes the men may have retained that discrimination in America had eased during their one-year absence were shattered on December 27, when they arrived at Camp Stewart. The Georgia post, dubbed a "hellhole" by one black newspaper, had been the scene of some of the worst racial strife of 1943. The reception accorded the 320th indicated that attitudes had not changed. "The first words we heard was, 'Here comes that nigger group. Got all them medals over there in France. We're gonna make sure that we take care of them while they're down here,'" Waverly Woodson recalled.

Despite that inauspicious start, the men spent four months at Camp Stewart with no major problems reported. In April 1945, they boarded a train headed west. All bets were on a posting in the Pacific. As a further hint, records show their training in Georgia had included courses on tropical diseases and "jungle living." The 320th would be the only barrage balloon battalion to serve in Europe and the Pacific. On May 6, the 320th disembarked on Oahu and settled at Aiea, near Pearl Harbor, not far from the heights where Japanese spy Takeo Yoshikawa had noted the absence of barrage balloons in December 1941. It was on Oahu, one year after D-Day, that the army decided to give the 320th men swimming lessons.

Whatever mission was planned for the battalion, it was not to be. The 320th spent the remaining months of the war in Hawaii. There are no existing records revealing what was in store for the men, but some officers, including their commander, Leon Reed, said after the war that the balloon crews had been slated to participate in a land invasion in Japan. Some men speculated that the battalion was headed to Okinawa, where the Americans had landed in April in what became the largest amphibious operation in the Pacific. Further assaults in Japan were obviated when the Americans dropped atomic bombs on Hiroshima and Nagasaki over two days in August 1945. Japan surrendered shortly after, and the war officially ended on September 2.

WAVERLY WOODSON RETURNED HOME eager to resume his premed studies. During his absence, his parents had left West Philadelphia and bought a three-story brick house on a tree-lined block in Germantown, in the northwest corner of the city. After graduating in 1948 from Lincoln University in Pennsylvania, Waverly applied to Howard University, which had one of the few medical schools that enrolled blacks. To his great disappointment, there were no places for him. He was put on the waiting list, an outcome he attributed to being older, at age twenty-six, than the other prospective students. Determined to pursue a career in medicine, and with few options, he enrolled at Franklin Institute in Philadelphia and finished in 1950 with a degree in medical technology. He remained in the Army Reserve and was called back to active service during the Korean War. He was sent again to Camp Stewart, to work as a specialist in communicable diseases, but as soon as he arrived, he was told there had been a mix-up: the job wasn't open to a Negro. Instead, Waverly was stationed at Walter Reed Army Medical Center in Bethesda, Maryland, where he was director of the morgue and taught a class on anatomy.

While he was there, Waverly went to a USO dance in Forest Glen, Maryland, where he met twenty-one-year-old Joann Katharyne Snowden. Waverly was smitten with pretty Joann, who had brown curls and a heart-shaped face. They were married in August 1952. Their two girls, Elaine and Lorrayne, were born in close succession, and a son, Stephen, followed in 1958. Waverly and Joann built their dream house in 1962, on five acres of land in Clarksburg, Maryland, a well-off town of sedate green pastures and dairy farms about thirty miles northwest of Washington, DC. Clarksburg had a long history of integration, with many skilled black settlers working as farmers and artisans. Four generations of Snowdens had lived in Clarksburg, and together they owned hundreds of acres. The five acres had been a gift to the couple from Joann's great-uncle. Waverly loved the quiet and the open spaces. His family back in Philly teased him that the city boy had gone country.

In 1980, Waverly retired from the National Institutes of Health, where he had worked in medical technology, ending his career as a supervisor in the Clinical Pathology Department. He spent a busy retirement tending to his passions: raising champion roses and tropical fish, building large-scale models of trains and ships, and photographing still lifes with his collection of Nikons. He was a self-taught electronics whiz and built a color TV and a stereo from scratch. There was only one thing in life that Waverly detested: pineapples, after eating too many of them in Hawaii.

When the fiftieth anniversary of D-Day came around, attention returned to the once-shy medic. Newspapers and TV correspondents came to Clarksburg to interview him. Joann heard his war stories for the first time. Waverly and Joann flew to France, courtesy of the French government, where Waverly, at age seventy-two, was one of three American veterans given a palm-size medal commemorating the invasion. "I don't know why they chose me, but it was a wonderful thing," Waverly said. "I was the only black man of the three." Waverly had stopped thinking about the high honors that he had never gotten from his own country. He was proud of the Bronze Star he had received in January 1945, along with a Purple Heart for his injuries on Omaha Beach. Besides, Waverly said, Medals of Honor weren't given to black men. He didn't know about the note that had passed between the War Department and the White House in 1944, mentioning him as a candidate for exactly that award. Woodson told his D-Day story again in 1993, to the independent researchers who were reviewing the case files of dozens of African Americans who had served in World War II, to determine if their service merited the nation's highest decoration. They would conclude that because Woodson's service records were missing, it was impossible to determine whether he should be recommended for the Medal of Honor.

In the last years of his life, Waverly sometimes spoke about the disappearance of black men from the story of D-Day. Joann said her husband was never a bitter man, but it hurt him deeply that only white men were credited with landing on the Normandy beaches on the morning of June 6. Waverly was particularly stung after watching the 1998 film *Saving Private Ryan*, which showed not a single black man on Omaha Beach. When reporters came to visit, Waverly would pull out the scrapbook that his father had put together while he was off at war. It was fat with clippings from the papers about Philadelphia's "No. 1 Invasion Hero."

Waverly Woodson died on August 12, 2005, eight days after his eighty-third birthday. His resting place is at Arlington National Cemetery, where America buries its heroes. Every May, around Memorial Day, Joann visits the plain white marble headstone marking her husband's grave, a large spray of red roses in her arms. She clips the stems and arranges the blooms that Waverly loved so much. Then she drops to her knees and prays.

. . . .

WILSON MONK IMMENSELY ENJOYED his seven months in Hawaii, which included a stint at a camp called Punch Bowl. He adored the sunshine, the swaying palm trees, vast pineapple groves, and the impossibly turquoise sea. He especially loved the soft white sand that reminded him of Atlantic City. Monk would return to Hawaii three more times during his life with Mertina, his war bride. They married on December 6, 1944, during the four-week furlough the 320th men were allowed after they landed in New York. On the inside of Wilson's right forearm was a souvenir from Hawaii: "Mert darling" tattooed inside a pair of entwined hearts.

Wilson never considered staying in the army—four and a half years was long enough. He returned to Atlantic City and studied dental technology, then moved to Washington, DC, and worked for twenty-six years in the dental prosthetics laboratory at Walter Reed Medical Center, where he made dentures and supervised a team of six. In his forties, he was diagnosed with multiple sclerosis, a condition that sometimes seized him without warning and left him paralyzed—and then just as quickly disappeared.

Wilson and Mertina had two children, Wilson Jr. and Mertina. They moved to a ranch-style house in Silver Spring, Maryland, with a steeply sloping driveway at the top of which Wilson parked a succession of Cadillacs. He was a champion fisherman, once landing a twelve-foot, 449-pound marlin off Nags Head, North Carolina, which got him a write-up in the *Washington Post*. With his fishing buddies he started the High Risers, a poker group. Through the years, he enjoyed taking trips with Mertina—to Japan, China, Africa, even Bora Bora. Closer to home, they visited 320th friends such as Sam Small, in New York City, and Bill Ektor, in Chicago. Forrest Redd, in Cleveland—Uncle Redd to the Monk kids—was a regular presence in Silver Spring.

Wilson didn't talk about the years of Jim Crow and the army until the last years of his life. When asked why, he shrugged. *Nobody asked*. That wasn't quite true—Wilson Jr. had asked—but like many men of his generation, Monk had tucked those often-painful memories into a back corner of his mind. Over time, the stories became easier to tell.

One day in July 2013, the phone rang at the Monk house. A caller from the French embassy in Washington told Wilson Jr. that his father had been selected to receive the Legion of Honor, the country's highest award. Wilson Jr. walked into the bedroom where his father lay terminally ill, took his hand, and told him the news. His father cried. Two weeks before his ninety-fourth birthday, on July 21, Wilson Caldwell Monk died quietly at home.

One of Wilson's great regrets was losing touch with Jessie Prior, the kind woman who had welcomed him into her home in Wales and treated him like a second son. I never got the chance to tell Wilson that I tracked down Jessie's grandchildren in Wales. Her granddaughter, Cheryl Morgan, remembered stories about Jessie's dear black GI. Mertina Monk, who had also exchanged letters with Jessie, was happy finally to see a picture of the little Welsh woman with pale eyes who had extended so much love to Wilson. On January 28, 2015, Mertina Monk died at age ninety-four, her daughter Tina by her side. "I love you more than yesterday," Wilson had told Mertina often during their sixty-eight years together.

I asked Wilson during our many talks how he could live without bitterness. I told him I doubted that I could ever forgive being denied a table in a restaurant in my own country because of the color of my skin—the same restaurants that welcomed enemy prisoners of war. "You can't let those things constantly gnaw at you," he told me in his soft voice. Despite the limitations placed on them, Wilson and millions of other African American men of his generation built successful lives, with families and homes of their own. They lived to see their children attend college and become lawyers, professors, and investment bankers. Through the years, Wilson had witnessed important changes that had given him hope and brought him peace. There was *Brown v. Board of Education* outlawing racial segregation in public schools. The following year, the arrest of Rosa Parks in Montgomery, Alabama, marked the beginning of the end of segregated public transportation. Martin Luther King Jr.'s "I Have a Dream" speech in 1963 at the Lincoln Memorial came during the largest demonstration in U.S. history. Amid the strife of the 1960s, America saw the passage of the Civil Rights Act of 1964, and a Nobel Peace Prize for Dr. King. The Voting Rights Act of 1965 eliminated the poll taxes and literacy tests used to keep African Americans from casting ballots and serving on juries.

For Wilson Monk, the pinnacle was living to see Barack Obama elected president in 2008. It was the second-happiest day of his life.

HENRY PARHAM CLEARLY REMEMBERED the voyage home in November 1944 aboard the *Excelsior*, which in some ways was like the trip to Scotland aboard the *Aquitania*. The risk of U-boat attack in the North Atlantic had diminished, thankfully, but a spectacular storm slowed the journey, and terrified the men. Gambling was a frequent distraction during the journey, and once again the 320th's wiry little cardsharp, Rudolph Valentino Frelo, cleaned up. As for Hawaii, Henry was not a fan. He disliked the heat. One time, he said, a sugarcane field caught fire in the sun. Did he consider staying in the army? "No, no, no, no. I never cared for the uniform that much. We were all glad to get out of there." Henry surprised his family in Richmond, Virginia, when he returned home in late November 1945. He resumed his job as a porter at the bus station, and then decided, on a lark, to move to Pittsburgh and use the GI Bill to learn electronics and television repair.

President Roosevelt had signed the Servicemen's Readjustment Act into law on June 22, 1944. Called the GI Bill of Rights, it offered millions of returning soldiers a sweeping package of benefits, from college and trade school tuition with extra money for living expenses, to low-interest loans to buy homes and start businesses. The legislation, which passed both houses of Congress with no opposition, opened up the once-exclusive gates of academia to the working classes. For many black veterans, though, the GI Bill would prove to be a familiar disappointment. There was no provision to ensure equal application, which allowed Jim Crow to block black advancement just as it always had. Banks that refused to lend to Negroes continued that practice, and although many white universities began accepting blacks or expanding slots open to them, there were not enough places for all the African Americans who deserved them. Although the white middle class expanded in leaps and bounds thanks to the law, for blacks the economic and educational gap with whites widened. For those lucky enough to get one, a college education was hardly a guarantee of a decent job. Henry P. Hervey Jr., a Tuskegee Airman, graduated from Northwestern University, but could find jobs in Chicago only as a janitor or mailroom clerk. (Despite those early setbacks, he eventually rose to become a bank president.)

Many black veterans like Henry Parham were intent to learn a practical trade that would allow them a measure of job security. Yet many were conned by sketchy vocational schools that sprang up, mostly across the South, in the months after the legislation was passed. In other cases, veterans were steered away from perceived "white" trades. Henry was told that electronics repair was not open to Negroes, and he was directed instead to a tailoring course. "They can teach me war but they can't teach me to fix a TV? It didn't make no sense to me," Henry said. With no money to do anything else, Henry took the course and learned to sew. Then he got a job in construction. He worked as a heavy equipment operator for thirty-three years, retiring in 1986.

Henry, a bachelor, took all his meals at a friendly place called Ethel's Diner, where he met a freckle-faced waitress named Ethel, who came from Louisiana's Gulf Coast. He pestered Ethel Perry for a date, and three months later she said yes. After an eight-year courtship, Henry asked Ethel to marry him, which she did, on October 13, 1973. They live a peaceful dotage in a small apartment in a sedate part of Pittsburgh. They're not rich, but they get by. Henry could never afford a trip back to France, but at Ethel's urging, he did make it to Hawaii in 2005, for an American Legion convention. Henry liked Hawaii better that time around. To get there, he took a plane and flew in three legs, thinking that might calm his nerves about the prospect of flying over the ocean. Ships were out. The *Excelsior* was the last one he ever set foot on. "The Lord saved me through a war," he explained. "Why should I keep pushing myself?"

Through the years, Henry became active in veterans' affairs. He was a frequent presence in the Pittsburgh media, talking about his D-Day experience. Sometimes the invitations were tiring, but Henry never said no. He never made a dime from D-Day. One time a local TV station invited him to speak and didn't pay his parking bill. The stoic man from Greensville County, Virginia, never complained.

In May 2013, a letter came from the French embassy informing Henry that he had been named a *chevalier*, or knight, of the Légion d'Honneur. Exactly sixty-nine years after the day the French call *le débarquement*, Henry Parham, age ninety-one, stood with nineteen other American veterans at the embassy in Washington, DC, as the French consul general pinned the Legion of Honor medal on his lapel. Olivier Serot Alméras thanked the men for their service to France and told them, "We will always remember."

WHEN THE BLACK CORRESPONDENT Roi Ottley toured Europe late in the war, he asked black soldiers what message they wanted to send to people back home. The answer, he wrote, was usually the same: "Tell them we want to see the end of ole Jim Crow in America and equal treatment for everyone." Black GIs, Ottley wrote, were profoundly concerned about the future of American race relations. Southern white

GIs were also fixated on how Negroes could possibly be "remolded into Jim Crow" again after enjoying such liberties—that is, except for the southerners who had fought alongside black troops in Italy, Belgium, France, and Germany. Those soldiers had shared the bond of combat, and for many of them, that was enough to change their minds. They could envision a better life for black men and women in America.

On their return from Europe, the Tuskegee Airmen expected a measure of respect. But when their ship docked in Boston, there were two lines at the end of the gangway: "Blacks over here, whites over here," said pilot Roscoe Brown. "Many of us had illusions of how things would be," he said. Any illusions Brown still harbored after the war were shattered when he applied for a job at Eastern Air Lines and a clerk threw his application in the trash, telling him, "We don't hire colored." Other airmen had similar problems. They were told the public would never accept black pilots.

Medgar Evers, the future civil rights leader, had served in the Red Ball Express but wasn't allowed to vote back home in Mississippi. His brother James Charles Evers, who served in the Pacific, was in uniform when a bus driver told him, "Nigger, you can't sit there. Get in the back." In Georgia, a black veteran named Macio Snipes was dragged from his house and shot to death in July 1946 after casting the only black ballot in Taylor County. Before the elections, a sign posted on a black church had read, "The First Nigger to Vote Will Never Vote Again." Returning soldiers were subjected to a barrage of violence, and it was one of these crimes that finally grabbed the attention of the White House.

In February 1946, an army sergeant named Isaac Woodard boarded a bus in North Carolina on his way home to Georgia. During the journey south, the bus made a stop and Woodard, who was in uniform, asked to use the restroom. The driver cursed him, and the men exchanged words. The driver stopped the bus again, in a town called Aiken, and told Woodard to get off. Two cops were waiting for him.

The sheriff beat Woodard with his billy club and jammed it in the soldier's eyes. Woodard was permanently blinded. Photographs of the GI, his head swathed in bandages, shocked the nation. Even President Harry S. Truman was touched. "This shit has to stop," he told his staff.

It took two more years for Truman to sign Executive Order 9981, on July 26, 1948, ending racial segregation in the U.S. armed forces. Critics saw the action as the president's attempt to win black votes. Military commanders who thought Truman might lose his 1948 reelection bid ignored the order. Yet there was no going back. "Black veterans identified with the civil rights movement and became part of it," said John Lewis, the Georgia congressman who as a young activist endured police beatings while protesting for voting rights. Black vets held a mirror up to American society and demanded that everyone take a look, said the historian Walter B. Hill Jr. "African Americans clearly decided, 'this is our country, we can't have black men fighting for democracy in Europe and not have it here.'" The army was the last branch of the military to integrate. It wasn't until October 1954 that the last all-black unit was dissolved.

AFTER THE WAR, WILLIAM DABNEY went back home to his grandmother's house outside Roanoke, Virginia, and finished his last year of high school. He took a course in electronics and TV repair but couldn't find a job. Even janitor work eluded him. "They said I was overeducated to push a mop." He learned how to lay flooring and tiles, and found a man who hired him to do that. A few years later, he started his own business, Dabney Floors, Inc. So as not to lose white customers, Bill hid the fact that he was a black man. "It was the only way to get paid," he said. On the job, his customers would tell him things about "Mister Dabney," like how "Mister Dabney must be laid up there in a big leather chair while you guys are doing a massive job here." The real Dabney, ever cheerful, would laugh, just as he did when he told me the story. One time a customer asked one of Bill's workers if he would deliver a check to his boss. The worker pointed to Bill and told the customer, "'There he is right there, under the table laying carpet.'" Bill cracked up laughing as he recounted the story. "The cigar fell out of the guy's mouth."

After the war, Bill's buddy from Camp Tyson, Harry Cecil Curtis Jr., returned home to Roanoke, too. The men would remain best friends all their lives. Cecil built an impressive career as an entrepreneur and was cofounder of one of the largest black funeral homes in Roanoke. He worked well into his eighties. He died in October 2012, at age ninety-one.

Despite his success, Cecil had a rocky time at the start. After the war, he tried unsuccessfully to obtain a loan under the GI Bill. He wanted to open a drive-in restaurant, which he eventually did, finding the money through other means. The same was true for Bill's efforts to secure a home loan with his wife, Beulah, whom he married in 1951. "We went to bank after bank, and they wanted to know how much collateral we had, and we had three pieces of furniture," Beulah said. An important GI Bill benefit was mortgage approval with no down payment. Eventually, a black-owned insurance company gave the Dabneys a loan, and they bought a white Cape-style house in Roanoke, where they raised three sons—Vincent, Michael, and Marlon—and where they still live today.

Dabney Floors was in business for more than forty years. Bill didn't so much retire as slowly drift away. He worked part-time well into his eighties because he enjoyed it. He liked that each day brought with it different designs, varying colors. Over time, he would suffer hearing loss that he attributed to the damage inflicted on his eardrums on D-Day.

In June 2009, six decades after he landed on the shores of Normandy, Bill Dabney returned to France at the invitation of the French government. On the sixty-fifth anniversary of the landings, under a bright blue sky, Bill and other aging veterans received accolades from the world's most important leaders at the American Cemetery overlooking Omaha Beach. President Obama shook his hand. "I read about you, Dabney," the president told him. First Lady Michelle Obama gave him a hug and a planted a kiss on his cheek. Bill, who was eighty-five, joked later that he would never wash that cheek.

One day earlier, Bill had received the Legion of Honor at a ceremony in Paris. It was the finest medal he had ever seen: a five-point white cross adorned with green laurels suspended from a scarlet ribbon. After the ceremony, Bill shook the hand of Steven Spielberg, who directed the film *Saving Private Ryan*, and of Tom Hanks, who starred in it. The men were strangers to Bill, who had never heard of them until that day. Yet, as with every black veteran I met, Bill was well aware that the movie failed to show any African Americans on Omaha Beach.

No matter. Bill Dabney knew he'd been there.

Acknowledgments and Primary Sources

I have a habit of flipping to the acknowledgments before I begin reading a book. I don't know if this is normal behavior or the voyeuristic impulse of a newspaper journalist accustomed to short articles who couldn't imagine how a writer could go on for 350-odd pages. I will attempt to answer that question in this overview of the most important sources that informed this book.

Forgotten began as a seed of an idea in the summer of 2009 and grew into its own thanks to the generous help and support of a great number of people. My friend, journalist and author Robert Kolker, told me that my idea to turn an article I'd written on the 320th Barrage Balloon Battalion into a magazine-length piece wasn't enough. "That's a book," he said. I agreed with him, in theory, but I had no idea how to *know* if there was a book there. My doubts were somewhat eased when literary agent Rachel Sussman told me without a second's hesitation, "I can sell a book about a forgotten unit in World War II." With that, Rachel became my agent, and her confidence, advice, and editing were priceless as I cobbled together, over years of research, a voluminous outline of the book I wanted to write. If it hadn't been for my eagle-eyed editor at Harper, Emily Cunningham, this book would have remained a seventy-page proposal. I thank her for having the confidence in me and in this project, and for her careful editing of the manuscript.

The first step in my research was finding the surviving men who had served in the 320th. To do that, researcher Lori Berdak Miller in St. Louis, Missouri, went looking for army payroll records from 1943 at the National Personnel Records Center. From those hundreds of names, researcher extraordinaire Faigi Rosenthal, my ex-colleague at the *Daily News*, set to work finding the men. Working from the scores of public records she dug up, I hit the phones. In the end, we found a dozen 320th men and the families of many others. To all those men and their loved ones I owe a tremendous debt of thanks for spending so many long and tiring hours speaking with me in person and over the phone over the past five years. It's heartbreaking to me that some of these magnanimous souls died before they could see this book in print.

Bill Dabney first introduced me to the 320th and explained how the balloons worked. His wife, Beulah Dabney; their son, Vincent Dabney; and Bill's best friend, Harry Cecil Curtis Jr., helped flesh out the details of Bill's life. In Silver Spring, Maryland, Wilson Monk spent countless hours at his kitchen table telling me stories, and his wartime letters opened my eyes. It was an honor to know him. The same goes for the incomparable Mertina Monk, whose vivid descriptions of growing up in Atlantic City dazzled me and inspired the idea to begin the book on the Boardwalk in 1941. Her delightful friends Vernon Blackwell and Alvin Washington drew for me an exquisite picture of prewar life in the city by the sea. Two fascinating books proved invaluable: *The Northside: African Americans and the Creation of Atlantic City*, by Nelson Johnson, the author of *Boardwalk Empire*; and Turiya S. A. Raheem's *Growing Up in the Other Atlantic City: Wash's and the Northside*.

When I began my research in late 2009, I had no idea how I was going to structure this book. Ideally, I wanted a single character around whom I could build the core narrative. But it soon became clear that this book would have to feature an ensemble. Among other things, I was limited by the absence of so many men who had died without ever speaking of—much less recording—their wartime experiences. In the case of the late Waverly Woodson, there was precious little information besides the interviews he gave about D-Day. The descriptions of Waverly's actions on Omaha Beach are a combination of those interviews, supplemented with army records and corresponding memories from the 320th men I spoke to. For details about Waverly's early and postwar life, I relied on his widow, the effervescent Joann Woodson. I thank her for all her help, and Waverly's longtime friend, retired army colonel Harry W. Townsend.

It is often a delicate matter to shine a light into the distant past. Henry Parham, a very private man, reluctantly agreed to tell me his stories of his boyhood in Greensville County, Virginia. I thank him for that. His wife, Ethel Parham, became a faithful correspondent. To help round out the picture of life in rural Virginia in the share-cropping era and after, I must credit the wonderful Elizabeth Wells Mason, Robert Wells, and James W. Parham Jr. To learn about the long history of Jim Crow in and out of the U.S. military, I relied on a raft of books and reports. One surprise was Walter White's wide-ranging autobiography, *A Man Called White.* For the best portrait of wartime America, Doris Kearns Goodwin's *No Ordinary Time* was impossible to put down.

There are many fine overviews of African Americans in the military. Two of my favorites were Robert B. Edgerton's *Hidden Heroism: Black Soldiers in America's Wars* and Gail Buckley's *American Patriots: The Story of Blacks in the Military from the Revolution to Desert Storm.* I didn't expect to be so, well, swept away by the fascinating history of hot air and gas balloons. A fun primer is *Falling Upwards: How We Took to the Air* by Richard Holmes.

Before I began this book, I hadn't used a library in years. Oh, what I've missed! The Library of Congress proved an invaluable research tool, and there would have been many holes in this book without the help of three knowledgeable people: Krystal M. Cook-Elliott at the Meherrin Regional Library in Lawrenceville, Virginia; Roy Bonis of the Virginia Commonwealth University Library in Richmond; and Heather Perez at the Atlantic City Free Public Library.

The 320th men who rounded out this cast are a special group, and I am humbled that they trusted me to tell their stories. Arthur Guest, Willie O. Howard, Samuel L. Mattison, Theolus Wells, and Albert Grillette Wood filled in the blanks as best they could—about the unit and a mission they hadn't talked about for nearly seventy years. For me, knowing them was a priceless education. The same goes for George R. Hamilton, Samuel J. Harris, and Floyd H. Siler. Thanks to my old friend Péralte Paul in Atlanta for doing a video interview with veteran James Hardy Sims. I am grateful to family members of men in the battalion who helped me better understand their experiences, notably Gary Wood, Samuel L. Mattison Jr., Sharon Harris, and Brenda and Ina Siler. I was able to include some 320th men in this book's photo gallery thanks to their children and grandchildren, who combed through old boxes in basements and attics and sent me photos of their loved ones, along with army discharge papers and other documents. For this I owe a debt of gratitude to Barbara Corprew, Kaci Easley, Ted Lavizzo, Brian Worthy, Charlotte Chase, Nina Hart, Gerald and Geoff Gordon, and John, Patrick, and Charlotte Reed.

As my research progressed, I held out hope that a wartime-era diary chronicling a 320th man's experiences in detail would surface, but one never did. I was lucky to meet Bill Davison, whose late father, George Davison, wrote an account of his service decades after the war. Bill photographed his father's handwritten notebook and, one by one, e-mailed the one hundred images to me. George's writings on D-Day helped me imagine life in a foxhole on Omaha Beach. Bill Davison's frequent e-mails and insights made me smile as I wrote this book.

I met Bill Davison thanks to Alice Mills, a French scholar of African American history whose extensive research alerted the world that black men fought and died in Normandy. She is the author of the 2014 book, written in English and French, *Soldats Noirs Américains: Black GIs, Normandy 1944.*

Memories can be tricky business, as several historians warned me. You can't build a book around them. The lack of documentation on this unit nearly killed this book at the start. A brief battalion history written during the war provided an overview, but beyond that, there were few records with the sort of details I needed to tell the story of the 320th. With the assistance of archivists at the National Archives in College Park, Maryland, I found enough information over three extended visits to keep this project alive. Richard Boylan taught me how to navigate the Archives' exceptionally complicated system of record searching; Amy Schmidt helped me find evidence that there were small bombs attached to the balloons—a true eureka moment; and Timothy K. Nenninger helped me brainstorm strategies to hunt for records relating to Waverly Woodson's medals. Historian and author Elliott V. Converse was a savior, sending me copies of records his team used in the study of African Americans and the Medal of Honor. His advice and encouragement were much appreciated.

America scatters its World War II records in archives far from the mother ship in College Park. And so it was that I found myself among a steady stream of researchers traveling 150 miles from the nearest major airport to reach the Dwight D. Eisenhower Presidential Library in Abilene, Kansas; and then 160 miles in the opposite direction to the Harry S. Truman Presidential Library in Independence, Missouri. Many thanks to the friendly experts at both libraries, who helped me dig up key documents about black soldiers, barrage balloons, and racial strife. To tell the story of Camp Tyson, journalist Shannon McFarlin in Paris, Tennessee, was kind enough to answer myriad questions and share with me passages from her forthcoming book, *As If They Were Ours: The Story of Camp Tyson, America's Only WWII Barrage Balloon Facility.* The charming Hattye Thomas

Yarbrough, born in 1921, was a fount of information on Paris and Tyson, and a pleasure to talk to.

My search also took me to the British Library and the Imperial War Museum in London, along with the sedate British National Archives in Kew, where I came up short in my hunt for records about the 320th, but found fascinating letters, memos, and other documents relating to African American soldiers. I would thank the staff there, but I had no contact with them. Their efficient record-keeping system is entirely accessible on databases that researchers can navigate themselves. For guidance, I relied on an excellent book, *When Jim Crow Met John Bull*, by Graham Smith. In Wales, the cheery staff at the Gwent Archives helped me find useful and fun details on wartime life, as did the staff at the Pontypool Museum. Meeting Jesse Prior's family was a joy, and I thank David and Pat Prior, Cheryl Morgan, and Jeffrey Prior for their help. Local historian and writer Ken Clark kept me laughing and fielded my endless e-mails; he suggested that I tell the local newspaper what I was up to. Because of the *Free Press* of Monmouth County, many people contacted me to share their childhood memories of the black GIs. The same was true in Oxfordshire, after an article appeared in the *Henley Standard*. Thanks to these appeals, I was able to describe what it was like to live in the towns where the battalion was billeted. In Checkendon, historian Tim Corbishley gave me a tour of the area where the 320th men circulated, including a few of the rusted Nissen huts—still in use—that left the 320th men shivering. Thanks also to Laureen Williamson for sharing her knowledge of local history.

To understand the workings of the great British ocean liners turned troop transports, I got help from Nathaniel Patch at the National Archives in College Park; Siân Wilks at the Cunard Archives in Liverpool; and Mike Holdaway of the website convoyweb.org.uk. I was able to breathe life into the 320th's journey thanks to the men's memories supplemented by Alister Satchell's *Running the Gauntlet: How Three Giant*

Liners Carried a Million Men to War. In New York, researcher Aine Rose Campbell combed maritime records at the National Archives branch there and periodicals at the New York Public Library. I am grateful to my friend Beverly Tabor, who helped me scour hundreds of British and U.S. newspapers for material on black GIs and barrage balloons.

The wartime balloons posed a challenge because there are so few people alive today who know anything about them. One man who knows *everything* about them is Peter Garwood in Wales, who is the proud owner of a Very Low Altitude balloon—type MKVI (British) or M-1 (American) to insiders—and whose late father served in a Royal Air Force balloon squadron during the war. Peter read parts of this manuscript and corrected my mistakes. Another important source was the late James R. Shock's book, *The U.S. Army Barrage Balloon Program*. At the Air Force Historical Research Agency, archivist Archangelo "Archie" DiFante was a valuable resource for alerting me to studies and reports. Is a barrage balloon a blimp? NO. Thanks to Richard Van Treuren of the Naval Airship Association for setting me straight. Several experts helped me understand modern aerostats, particularly Major Gen. John W. Hawley (ret.) of Near Space Systems, Inc.

I spent months trying to piece together when and how the 320th landed on D-Day. Research historian Andrew Woods at the First Division Museum in Wheaton, Illinois, kindly sent me reams of landing tables showing the 320th scattered on many boats. D-Day author and all-around great guy Joseph Balkoski explained the particulars of June 6 with infinite patience. For me, his books on the landings, *Omaha Beach* and *Utah Beach*, were instrumental in reconstructing what happened hour by hour. Of the many D-Day books, articles, and reports I read, Cornelius Ryan's *The Longest Day*, from 1959, remains a great read. I found a 2013 addition to the D-Day panoply to be quite interesting: Steven J. Zaloga's *The Devil's Garden: Rommel's Desperate Defense of Omaha's Beach on D-Day.*

Several army historians pointed me in the right direction and didn't flinch at my often naive questions. William Donnelly at the U.S. Army Center of Military History gave me crucial advice about hunting for records and on army structure, as did his colleague William M. Yarborough. Sanders Marble at the Office of Medical History sent photos and documents about the 320th medics. To research black officers, I got help from Isaac Hampton III, author of *The Black Officer Corps: A History of Black Military Advancement from Integration through Vietnam.*

What did a GI wear, eat, and smoke? For umpteen questions like these, I tapped the incomparable memory and bottomless goodwill of Morley L. Piper, first lieutenant, 115th Regiment, 29th Infantry Division, who landed on Omaha Beach on D-Day morning.

After the research came the finished manuscript, a minefield of potential errors and embarrassment. I was lucky to have a team of pros who kept me on track, reading all or parts of the text: Col. E. Paul Semmens (ret.), Richard A. Clary, David Kaeper, Ted Tabor, and Mary Ann Giordano. Any errors and omissions that remain are entirely my own. Thanks to my editors at the *Daily News* for giving me the opportunity to write about the 320th, among them Martin Dunn, William Goldschlag, and Robert Moore. I'm also grateful to Ed Fay, Ellen Locker, and Robert Shields for their help.

One of those editors, Kirsten Danis, graciously helped me puzzle through problems in the narrative and boosted my confidence. Other dear friends helped as well: Marilyn Kaye and Mary Papenfuss were dedicated readers and critics from the earliest days. Diana Brown McCloy gave me advice about the author's note, and Deirdre DeBruyn Rubio offered many research tips. In Washington, DC, where I spent most of my time, Rita Jupe and Eric Smith kept me fed and watered for weeks on end. I owe them the world. Thomas Regan in College Park, Alison Gendar in Silver Spring, Maryland, and Jennifer Ryan in London also put me up in style. My time in Kansas was brightened by the presence of Phil and Carmen Guries. From Paris to Nice, Timothy Jay Smith and Michael Honegger rescued me multiple times. Cheers to so many other good friends too numerous to list here, who swooped in when I needed it, especially the ladies in Paris. I am very lucky to have you in my life. I thank my family in Lowell, Massachusetts, especially my ninety-three-year-old mother, Rose, for putting up with my sporadic and distracted visits.

Finally, the biggest nod goes to my husband, Phil Serafino, who tolerated countless solo dinners and dog walks during my long absences. He was also the best sounding board, armchair military expert, unflinching critic, and careful editor anyone could hope for. He's also the best partner. Ever.

Notes

ABBREVIATIONS
Archives
AFHRA—Air Force Historical Research Agency, Maxwell Air Force Base
EL—Dwight D. Eisenhower Library, Abilene, KS
MHI—U.S. Army Military History Institute, Carlisle, PA
NARACP—U.S. National Archives and Records Administration, College Park, MD
NARANY—U.S. National Archives and Records Administration, New York, NY
NAUK—National Archives, United Kingdom, Kew, London
NPRC—National Personnel Records Center, National Archives and Records Administration, St. Louis, MO
TL—Harry S Truman Library, Independence, MO

Record Groups
AG—Records of the Adjutant General's Office (US)
CO—Records of the Colonial Office (UK)
ETO—European Theater of Operations (US)
FO—Records of the Foreign Office (UK)
RG—Record Group
SHAEF—Supreme Headquarters Allied Expeditionary Force
WD—War Department, Washington, DC

CHAPTER 1: WAR BREWING
All the personal recollections in this chapter were gleaned from author interviews in person and by telephone between 2010 and 2014 with Wilson and Mertina Monk and their friends and family.

3 Every night was: Nelson Johnson, *The Northside: African Americans and the Creation of Atlantic City* (Medford, NJ: Plexus Publishing, 2010), 158.

5 Even the carousel: Johnson, *The Northside*, 43.

5 Two years later: Ibid.

5 The name Jim Crow came from: Graham Smith, *When Jim Crow Met John Bull: Black American Soldiers in World War II Britain* (New York: St. Martin's Press), 6. The minstrel performer, Thomas D. Rice, took his show on the road and brought it to London in 1836.

6 Although New Jersey had repealed: Slavery would not be permanently repealed in New Jersey until 1946.

6 It is likely, then, that: Johnson, *The Northside*, 6–7. Using 1860 census figures, historian Richlyn Goodard has concluded that slaves were likely used to build early Atlantic City.

6 Each multistory hotel: Turiya S. A. Raheem, *Growing Up in the Other Atlantic City: Wash's and the Northside* (Bloomington, IN: Xlibris, 2009), 14–15.

6 By 1900: Johnson, *The Northside*, 34.

6 About 95 percent: Ibid., xx.

7 They could pay the: Ibid., 10.

7 "Considering the event": Ibid., 11.

7 "the first big step": Isabel Wilkerson, *The Warmth of Other Suns: The Epic Story of America's Great Migration* (New York: Vintage Books, 2010), 11.

8 By four hundred years: The first black slaves arrived along the Carolina coast in 1525, according to Alton Hornsby, Jr., *Chronology of African American History from 1492 to the Present* (Detroit: Gale Group, 2000), xli.

8 There is no simple answer: Johnson, *The Northside*, 40. Johnson writes that racism alone is too simplistic, and attributes the rising animosity to an "emotional brew" of "folk history, religion, sexual taboos, and myths of the old South concocted in the slavery era, together with the fallacious dogma of white supremacy."

8 What had been: Ibid., 40. In 1880, 70 percent of blacks had a white neighbor. By 1915, that figure had fallen to less than 20 percent.

9 To the little girl's: Author interviews with Vernon Hollingsworth Blackwell.

9 A few blocks away: Author interviews with Mertina Madison Monk.

10 The Paradise Club: This is the opinion of musician Chris Columbo in Johnson, *The Northside*, 172.

11 "Every night was": Johnson, *The Northside*, 158.

11 "There were so many whites": Ibid., 172.

11 "Why do you" and "So that your wife": Ibid., 162.

11 "World's Playground": Ibid., 19. Although vice reigned in Atlantic City, censors patrolled to ensure modesty on the beach, even measuring the length of a woman's bathing suit. Up until the 1940s, the law required men to wear tops.

12 Nobody seemed to mind: At least Darrow gave the Northside hot spot Kentucky Avenue its due. Its eighteen-dollar "rent" was almost as much as that for the "white" properties. To see what the Monopoly properties look like today, go to http://www.scoutingny.com/what-the-monopoly-properties-look-like-in-real-life/.

12 "Atlantic City was": Raheem, *Growing Up*, 21.

13 Fathers, mothers, kids: Author interviews with multiple Atlantic City natives.

14 The family moved: Author interviews with Wilson Monk. Despite the hardships, Monk recalled his childhood as an "absolutely" happy time filled with love.

14 At Apex: Apex Board of Trade booklet, 1936, Atlantic City Free Public Library.

15 She was right: *Press of Atlantic City*, March 23, 2012. For more on Sarah Spencer Washington, see www.atlanticcityexperience.org.

15 Madame Washington, as she was known: Advertisement in an Atlantic City Board of Trade booklet, 1936, Atlantic City Free Public Library.

15 hid her identity: Johnson, *The Northside*, 122.

16 Mertina Madison's mother: Raheem, *Growing Up*, 27.

16 One day, the order came: Author interviews with Wilson Monk.

18 "He's a done deal": Author interview with Mertina Madison Monk.

19 The vast majority: Doris Kearns Goodwin, *No Ordinary Time: Franklin and Eleanor Roosevelt—The Home Front in World War II* (New York: Simon and Schuster, 1994), 236.

19 It meant that: Author interviews with Wilson Monk. Prewar base pay for privates was thirty dollars a month, which rose to fifty dollars after June 1942, according to Jonathan Gawne, *Finding Your Father's War: A Practical Guide to Researching and Understanding Service in the World War II US Army* (Philadelphia, PA: Casemate, 2006), 48.

20 Wilson Monk reported: Ulysses Lee, *The Employment of Negro Troops: United States Army in World War II* (reprint; Honolulu, HI: University Press of the Pacific, 1994), 137.

20 Southern officers were: Nat Brandt, *Harlem at War: The Black Experience in WWII* (Syracuse, NY: Syracuse University Press, 1997), 102.

21 "I never knew what": *Yank*, February 23, 1945.

21 "We wanted to know": Author interviews with Wilson Monk.

21 One day in: Author interviews with Wilson Monk. Other examples of discrimination are from multiple sources, including author interviews with dozens of black veterans.

CHAPTER 2: TOO DUMB TO FIGHT

23 The negro . . . is by nature subservient: Memorandum for the chief of staff, Subject: "Employment of Negro Man Power in War," November 10, 1925,

U.S. Army War College, Carlisle, PA, http://www.fdrlibrary.marist.edu/education/resources/pdfs/tusk_doc_a.pdf.

24   As Hitler reveled: Multiple sources, including Joseph Balkoski, *Omaha Beach: D-Day, June 6, 1944* (Mechanicsburg, PA: Stackpole Books, 2004), 1. At the time, only 504,000 Americans were on active duty or in the reserves as compared to 6.8 million Germans. Goodwin, *No Ordinary Time*, 23.

24   War games Goodwin, *No Ordinary Time*, 51.

24   Among them were: Ibid., 47.

24   One high-ranking: Dwight D. Eisenhower, *Crusade in Europe* (New York: Doubleday, 1948), Kindle edition, chap. 1.

24   In London, Ambassador Joseph Kennedy: Goodwin, *No Ordinary Time*, 61.

25   It was a position: Ibid., 64. By December 1940, army and navy commanders were convinced that the United States must enter the war "to save itself and that to save itself it had to save Great Britain," write Stetson Conn, Rose C. Engelman, and Bryon Fairchild, *Guarding the United States and Its Outposts* (Washington, DC: U.S. Army Center of Military History, 1962), online edition, 11.

25   Although the president: Goodwin, *No Ordinary Time*, 147.

25   "If Great Britain goes down": Fireside Chat, December 1, 1940, http://www.presidency.ucsb.edu/ws/?pid=15917.

25   Congress granted: Goodwin, *No Ordinary Time*, 48.

26   Still, it would take: Ibid., 2.

26   Roosevelt's mobilization: Gerald Astor, *The Right to Fight: A History of African Americans in the Military* (Cambridge, MA: Da Capo Press, 1998), 145.

27   The negro is profoundly superstitious: "Employment of Negro Man Power in War."

28   An undated War Department: Astor, *The Right to Fight*, 170.

28   The concept that: Robert B. Edgerton, *Hidden Heroism: Black Soldiers in America's Wars* (Boulder, CO: Westview Press, 2001), 8.

28   A British journalist: Ibid., 9.

28   "As time passed": Ibid., 7.

28   "It is generally": "Employment of Negro Man Power in War."

29   Those findings were reminiscent . . . the author, a doctor: Sanford B. Hunt, MD, "The Negro as Soldier," *Anthropological Review* 7, no. 24 (January 1869): 43. The author noted that cranial measurement can be tricky, as skull thickness can vary; for instance, "the Germans use larger hats than Anglo-Americans of the Northern states."

29   As to why black soldiers were unfit: Memorandum to General Eisenhower from Brig. Gen. R. W. Crawford, GC, John J. McCloy, April 2, 1942, Subject: "The Colored Troop Problem," WD 291.2, RG107, NARACP.

29   The army's reliance . . . It was no surprise: Lee, *The Employment of Negro Troops*, 244–45.

29   The median education: Joseph Schiffman, "The Education of Negro Soldiers in World War II," *The Journal of Negro Education* 18, no. 1 (Winter 1949): 22.

29   The average per capita: "The Colored Troop Problem." The average spent nationwide for a white child was $130.

29   In fact, when: Astor, *The Right to Fight*, 168.

30   Out of 150,000: Schiffman, "The Education of Negro Soldiers in World War II," 23.

30   Eighty percent: Memorandum from Jonathan Daniels to Philleo Nash, Box 27, Papers of Philleo Nash, TL.

30   As a group: Lee, *The Employment of Negro Troops*, 702.

30   War Secretary Henry: Edgerton, *Hidden Heroism*, 134.

30   "Negro-is-too-dumb-to-fight": Multiple sources, including *Pittsburgh Courier*, March 11, 1944.

30   The tests became: Lee, *The Employment of Negro Troops*, 245.

30   The test is not worth: Ibid., 255.

31   A number of black units: Edgerton, *Hidden Heroism*, 16-17.

31   In the War of 1812: War Department Board on Negro Manpower, Subject: Progress Report on the Board Study of the Utilization of Negro Manpower in the Post War Army, October 1945, Box 1, Papers of Alvin C. Gillem Jr., EL.

31   The commander of the First South: Edgerton, *Hidden Heroism*, 27.

32   The men dubbed: War Department Board on Negro Manpower progess report.

32   Their performance was: Edgerton, *Hidden Heroism*, 43.

33   Before the 369th: Peter N. Nelson, *A More Unbending Battle: The Harlem Hellfighters' Struggle for Freedom in WWI and Equality at Home* (New York: Basic Civitas, 2009), Kindle edition, chap. 4.

33   "in the company": Smith, *When Jim Crow Met John Bull*, 11.

33   "Don't spoil the Negroes": Nelson, *A More Unbending Battle*, chap. 6.

33   One of the most famous: Multiple sources, including Edgerton, *Hidden Heroism*, 142. Bullard served with a unit called the Swallows of Death, hence his nickname. He cut a dashing figure in uniform with his pet monkey, Jimmy, perched on his arm. After the war, he worked as a drummer in Paris nightclubs. After France was invaded in 1940, Bullard was wounded in battle. He eventually fled to Harlem, where he was working as an elevator operator in 1960 when French President Charles de Gaulle asked to see him during a visit to New York. Bullard died in poverty the following year, his accomplishments virtually unknown in his home country.

34   "thousand delicate ways": Smith, *When Jim Crow Met John Bull*, 11.

34   "because France gave it": Ibid.

34   But it was in battle: Multiple sources, including Nelson, *A More Unbending Battle*, preface.

34   The regiment earned: Edgerton, *Hidden Heroism*, 85.

34   Their shining moment came: Nelson, *A More Unbending Battle*, chap. 5. Nelson's book contains fascinating details, such as how the French were impressed with how far the 369th men could throw grenades. Many of them had been expert baseball players back home.

34   "Every slash meant something to me": Gilbert King, "Remembering Henry Johnson, the Soldier Called 'Black Death,'" *Smithsonian.com* (October 25, 2011), http://www.smithsonianmag.com/history/remembering-henry-johnson-the-soldier-called-black-death-117386701/?no-ist.

34   The southern writer: Ibid., chap. 5. In his article in *The Saturday Evening Post*, August 24, 1918, Cobb wrote, "If ever proof were needed, which it is not, that the color of a man's skin has nothing to do with his soul, this twain then and there offered it in abundance."

35   "a victim of indifference": Bernard C. Nalty, *Strength for the Fight: A History of Black Americans in the Military* (New York: The Free Press, 1986), 119.

35   Kudos came from: Nelson, *A More Unbending Battle*, 212–13.

35   Theodore Roosevelt . . . would call: Ibid., 233.

35   As bravely as he fought: Ibid., 239.

35   No African American would receive: In 1991, President George H. W. Bush awarded the Medal of Honor posthumously to Cpl. Freddie Stowers of the 371st Infantry Regiment, 93rd Division, for heroism serving under French command during the First World War. In 1997, President Bill Clinton awarded seven black World War II veterans the Medal of Honor.

36   If war came: Nalty, *Strength for the Fight*, 134.

36   Houston had served as: www.naacp.org/pages/naacp-history-charles-hamilton-houston.

37   Those experiences fueled: Ibid.

37   Lynchings had averaged: Walter White, *A Man Called White: The Autobiography of Walter White* (reprint; Athens, GA: Brown Thrasher Book, University of Georgia Press, 1995), 42. See also, Equal Justice Initiative, "Lynching in America: Confronting the Legacy of Racial Terror," 2015, 41, 51–52. The report summary is available at http://www.eji.org/files/EJI%20Lynching%20in%20America%20SUMMARY.pdf.

37   Sociologist Howard W. Odum: C. Vann Woodward, *The Strange Career of Jim Crow* (reprint; New York: Oxford University Press, 2002), 119.

37   No simian-souled: Edgerton, *Hidden Heroism*, 45.

38   Virginius Dabney, a progressive: Woodward, *The Strange Career of Jim Crow*, 120.

38   "If it were a question": Morris J. MacGregor, *Integration of the Armed Forces, 1940–1965* (Washington, DC: U.S. Army Center of Military History, 1981), digital edition, chap. 4.

39   A 1942 army: Alan M. Osur, *Blacks in the Army Air Forces During World War II: The Problems of Race Relations* (Washington, DC: Office of Air Force History, 1986), online edition, 64, http://www.afhso.af.mil/shared/media/document/AFD-100924-008.pdf.

40   Southern conservatives: Edgerton, *Hidden Heroism*, 142.

40   Unlike white squadrons led by experienced airmen: Astor, *The Right to Fight*, 146.

40   Seven decades after: *Breath of Freedom*, directed by Dag Freyer, aired 2014, Smithsonian Channel.

40   I hope for heavens: Astor, *The Right to Fight*, 158.

41   In the 1940s seniority rules: White, *A Man Called White*, 84.

41   All copies were burned, Edgerton, *Hidden Heroism*, 128.

41   "I saw the same thing": Michael Lee Lanning, *The African American Soldier: From Crispus Attucks to Colin Powell* (New York: Citadel Press, 2004), Digital edition, 239.

42   Army policy, stunningly: Nalty, *Strength for the Fight*, 109–12.

42   Col. Vernon A. Caldwell. . . . In a future war: Ibid., 122.

43   They are actually eager: ETO, GC, AJ, RG498, NARACP. The letter, written by an unidentified commander, reveals the complexity of opinions from white officers about black soldiers. While praising his black troops, the commander reverts to paternalistic stereotypes, such as that black troops require excessive praise and respond to flashy outfitting and ribbons. He writes, "You ought to see a big buck with his ribbons. You can imagine what a big shot he is with the women—their weak point."

43   Since its founding: White, *A Man Called White*, 301.

44   To make matters worse: Ibid., 186–87.

44   "Experiments within the army": Astor, *The Right to Fight*, 159.

46   Reporters called him: Goodwin, *No Ordinary Time*, 141.

46   His boss, Secretary Stimson: Gail Buckley, *American Patriots: The Story of Blacks in the Military from the Revolution to Desert Storm* (New York: Random House, 2001), 265.

CHAPTER 3: "THIS IS A WHITE MAN'S COUNTRY"

All details about Henry Parham's life in Greensville County and Richmond, Virginia, were told to the author by Parham in a series of interviews in person and by telephone between 2010 and 2014. Additional details about Parham and his family's early life were gleaned from author interviews by telephone in 2013 and 2014 with Elizabeth Wells Mason and Robert Wells, who are related to Henry Parham, and with James W. Parham Jr., who is not.

47   "The nation cannot expect": Goodwin, *No Ordinary Time*, 328.

48   Although 60 percent of the: Jamie Amanda Martinez, "Slavery during the Civil War," Virginia Foundation for the Humanities, July 2, 2014, Charlottesville, VA, http://encyclopediavirginia.org/Slavery_During_the_Civil_War.

49   Sharecroppers with no shoes: Interview with Jon Hendricks, in *Breath of Freedom*.

49   A British journalist who: Edgerton, *Hidden Heroism*, 122.

49   Records show that twenty-three: *Free African Americans of North Carolina, Virginia, and South Carolina from the Colonial Period to about 1820*, 5th ed., www.freeafricanamericans.com/virginiafreeafter1782.htm.

49   Henry D. Smith was among: Virginia General Assembly, Dr. Martin Luther King Jr. Memorial Commission, http://mlkcommission.dls.virginia.gov/lincoln/african_americans.html#ConstitutionalConvention.

50   Wells was born in: This and other details of his life are from author interviews with Elizabeth Mason Wells.

52   The future Private Parham: Author interview with Henry Parham.

52   Although blacks outnumbered whites: According to the 1930 U.S. Census, Greensville County's population comprised 8,129 blacks and 5,156 whites. The 1940 Census varied slightly, with the same racial proportion.

53   He forged an extraordinary: The story of the Rosenwald schools is told in compelling detail by Stephanie Deutsch in *You Need a Schoolhouse: Booker T. Washington, Julius Rosenwald, and the Building of Schools for the Segregated South* (Evanston, IL: Northwestern University Press), 2011.

53   Virginia was home to: Rosenwald School Plans, Virginia Department of Historic Resources, appendix 1, www.dhr.virginia.gov/registers/Counties/Brunswick/NR_RosenwaldSchoolMPD_part2_text.pdf.

53   Many dropped out: Author interviews with the Parham and Wells families and other Greensville County residents.

54   Black and white children: For an overview of Jim Crow, see Woodward, *The Strange Career of Jim Crow*; Wilkerson, *The Warmth of Other Suns*; and Richard Wormser, *The Rise and Fall of Jim Crow* (New York: St. Martin's Press, 2003).

54   Virginia passed a law segregating streetcars: Woodward, *The Strange Career of Jim Crow*, 33–34.

54   The *Richmond Times*: Ibid., 96.

54   Four decades later, the Swedish: Ibid., 118.

54   It is one of the strange ironies: Ibid., 42–43. Woodward, *The Strange Career of Jim Crow*, writes about the "intimacy of contact between races in the South" in the 1880s that northern visitors often found "distasteful." Such contact was a "heritage of slavery times, or . . . the result of two peoples having lived together intimately for a long time."

55   At the turn of the century: Wilkerson, *The Warmth of Other Suns*, 43.

55   Mississippi governor Adelbert Ames remarked that: Wormser, *The Rise and Fall of Jim Crow*, chap. 1.

55   Historian C. Vann Woodward: Ibid., 51.

55   Such was the mood that: Wilkerson, *The Warmth of Other Suns*, 43.

55   Nearly four thousand African Americans: Equal Justice Initiative, "Lynching in America," 2015, 5.

55   Most of the victims: Arthur Franklin Raper, *The Tragedy of Lynching* (reprint; Mineola, NY: Dover Publications, 2003), 26.

55   Although vigilante violence: W. Fitzhugh Brundage, *Lynching in the New South, Georgia and Virginia, 1880–1930* (Champaign, IL: University of Illinois Press, 1993), 4.

56   Georgia was the lynching: Equal Justice Initiative, "Lynching in America," 16. Also see National Association for the Advancement of Colored People, "Thirty Years of Lynching in the United States, 1889–1918" (1919; reprint 2010).

56   Mobs sometimes terrorized: Multiple sources, including Equal Justice Initiative, "Lynching in America," 14.

56   Greensville County's only recorded: Greensville County Genealogical Society newsletter, June 2008.

56   A grainy photo reprinted: *Southside Virginia Magazine*, February 1992.

56   In any case, the executions: *New York Times*, March 25, 1900.

56   The air was perfumed: Marie Tyler-McGraw, *At the Falls: Richmond, Virginia, and Its People* (Chapel Hill: University of North Carolina Press, 1994), 270.

57   federal government bought most of the 1939 tobacco crop: Ibid., 270.

57   More than 350 million: Ibid., 270.

57   Black passengers had: Walter S. Griggs Jr., *World War II, Richmond, Virginia* (Charleston, NC: History Press, 2013), 80.

57   One observer wrote: Ibid., 81.

58   Maggie Lena Walker: Multiple sources, including http://www.encyclopedia-virginia.org/Maggie_Lena_Walker_1864-1934.

59   One ordinance specified: Jennifer Ritterhouse, *Growing Up Jim Crow* (Chapel Hill, NC: University of North Carolina Press, 2006), 34.

59   If they were forbidden: Woodward, *The Strange Career of Jim Crow*, 100.

60   Civil rights activist Roy Wilkins: *Standing Fast: The Autobiography of Roy Wilkins* (New York: Da Capo Press, 1994), 184.

60   "As he did so": Gordon W. Prange, *At Dawn We Slept: The Untold Story of Pearl Harbor* (New York: Penguin, 1982), 515.

60   Still, this son: Ibid., 514–15.

60   Miller received the Navy Cross: The Navy Cross, awarded for combat and heroism, was created in 1919 as the third-highest award in the U.S. Navy. It was elevated to the second-highest award in August 1942, after the Medal of Honor. See http://www.history.navy.mil/browse-by-topic/heritage/service-medals-and-campaign-credits/navy-cross.html.

61   "This nation has sinned": *The Crisis*, August 1918.

61   "First your Country": Lee, *The Employment of Negro Troops*, 4.

61   The African American poet Langston Hughes: Langston Hughes, *The Collected Poems of Langston Hughes* (New York: Vintage Classics, 1994), 230–31. The poem first appeared in *The Crisis* magazine in June 1941.

62   Their version formed: Buckley, *American Patriots*, 257.

62   In Richmond, people worried: Griggs, *World War II, Richmond, Virginia*, 44–45.

62   Richmonders congratulated: Ibid., 45.

62   Flags began appearing: Ibid., 50.

62   By the end of 1942: Lee, *The Employment of Negro Troops*, 134.

63   A Red Cross field director: *The Nation*, May 29, 1943. Robert Wormser wrote that his experience with the all-black Ninety-Third Division at Fort Huachuca, Arizona, "opened my eyes as never before to the conditions that exist among the Negroes."

63   "This is a white man's": Rawn James Jr., *The Double V: How Wars, Protest, and Harry Truman Desegregated America's Military* (New York: Bloomsbury, 2013), Kindle edition, chap. 10. The first African slaves arrived in Jamestown, Virginia, in August 1619, though slaves traveling with Spanish settlers to North America arrived in 1581, Alton Hornsby Jr., *Chronology of African American History*, 2nd ed. (Detroit, MI: Gale Group, 2000), 5.

CHAPTER 4: SENTINELS OF THE SKY

65   There are no signs: Tokyo to the Honolulu consulate December 2, 1941, Joint Committee on the Investigation of the Pearl Harbor Attack, Congress of the United States, 1st and 2nd Sess., part 5, January 1946, 2409, http://www.ibiblio.org/pha/congress/.

65   After more than a year: Author interviews with Wilson Monk.

65   Sharing his car were forty-five: Author interviews with Wilson Monk, and Unit History, 320th, Operations Reports, CABN-320-0.1, RG407, NARACP.

66   Henry County, Tennessee, was: Multiple sources, including Robert L. Thompson, "Barrage Balloon Development in the United States Air Corps 1923–1942," Army Air Forces Historical Study No. 3, December 1943, AFRA, 38. The other candidate, Danville, Kentucky, was many times more expensive than Henry County's price of fifty dollars per acre.

66   One year before: This and other Tyson descriptions courtesy of Shannon McFarlin from her book *As If They Were Ours: The Story of Camp Tyson, America's Only WWII Barrage Balloon Facility* (Bennington, VT: Merriam Press, 2016).

66   It was easy to get lost: Robert Parkinson, "Camp Tyson," *Tennessee Encyclopedia of History and Culture*, 2014, http://www.tennesseeencyclopedia.net/entry.php?rec=180.

66   The unfortunate, sterile look: Goodwin, *No Ordinary Time*, 218.

67   This is the only barrage balloon training: Brig. Gen. John B. Maynard, 306th Coast Artillery Barrage Balloon Battalion book, 1942, 202-306CA, MHI.

67   In the London area, hundreds of balloons: In 1940, there were 1,400 barrage balloons in all of Britain, and the balloon corps employed 33,000 officers and men, according to Thompson, "Barrage Balloon Development," 100.

67   As a defensive barrier: There were two types of barrages in Britain: Large Mark VII balloons flew at five thousand feet and in winds of up to fifty-five miles per hour and gusts of eighty miles per hour. Smaller Mark VI balloons flew at two thousand feet and in wind speeds of up to forty-five miles per hour. These were usually used in harbor defense or where hydrogen was difficult to obtain. Records of the Barrage Balloon Board, Camp Tyson, RG337, NARACP.

68   The "Japs wouldn't dare": William Weir, *Fatal Victories* (New York: Pegasus Books, 2014), Kindle edition, chap. 13.

69   With 90 percent of its oil: Ibid., chap. 13.

69   The hills overlooking: Multiple sources, particularly Prange, *At Dawn We Slept*, 76.

69   Five days before the attack: Tokyo to the Honolulu consulate, December 2, 1941, Joint Committee on the Investigation of the Pearl Harbor Attack, Congress of the United States, 1st and 2nd Sess., part 5, January 1946, 2406. Though intercepted the same day it was sent, the message was *mailed* to Washington and wouldn't be translated for another twenty-eight days.

69   On December 6: Ibid. This message to Tokyo contained detailed information about the U.S. barrage balloon program worth quoting in full: "On the American Continent in October the army began training barrage balloon troops at Camp Davis, North Carolina. Not only have they ordered four or five hundred balloons, but it is understood that they are considering the use of these balloons in the defense of Hawaii and Panama. In so far as Hawaii is concerned, though investigations have been made in the neighborhood of Pearl Harbor, they have not set up mooring equipment, nor have they selected the troops to man them. Furthermore, there is no indication that any training for the maintenance of balloons is being undertaken. In addition, it is difficult to imagine that they have actually any. However, even though they have actually made preparations, because they must control the air over the water and land runways of the airports in the vicinity of Pearl Harbor, Hickam, Ford, and Ewa, there are limits to the balloon defense of Pearl Harbor. I imagine that in all probability there is considerable opportunity left to take advantage for a surprise attack against these places."

70   As early as 1923: Multiple sources, including James R. Shock, *The U.S. Army Barrage Balloon Program* (Bennington, VT: Merrimam Press, 2006), 5.

70   After the war: Thompson, "Barrage Balloon Development," 4.

70   After bickering: Ibid., 32–36.

70   Some test balloons: Ibid., 14.

70   In one example, German planes: "Barrage Balloons in a Fighter Command," Department of Tactics, Barrage Balloon School, Camp Tyson, TN, October 15, 1942, No. 167043, AFHRA, 14.

70   An army report . . . said as much: Lt. Col. Cheney L. Bertholf to commanding general, Hawaiian Air Force, July 19, 1941, Microfilm Reel No. A7581, AFHRA. Ironically, Bertholf saw the December 7 attack unfolding from a tower at Hickam Field and was one of the first to sound an alarm. In 1944, naval investigators raised the subject of the absent balloons at a hearing. The commander of the Pacific Fleet, Adm. Husband E. Kimmel, told investigators that "the use of barrage balloons would have been a help, because they would have tended to keep the planes so high that they could not have dropped the torpedoes," Navy Court of Inquiry, Joint Committee on the Investigation of the Pearl Harbor Attack, Congress of the United States, 1st Sess., part 32, July 24, 1944, 225, http://www.ibiblio.org/pha/congress/.

70   Back in October 1940: Shock, *The U.S. Army Barrage Balloon Program*, 15.

71   The following February: Henry L. Stimson to Secretary of the Navy, February 7, 1941, Joint Committee on the Investigation of the Pearl Harbor Attack, Congress of the United States, 1st Sess., part 1, November 1945, 280–81, http://www.ibiblio.org/pha/congress/.

71   So what happened: Joint Committee on the Investigation of the Pearl Harbor Attack, Congress of the United States, 1st Sess., part 3, December 1945, 1214, http://www.ibiblio.org/pha/congress/. Supply problems could have been to blame, but at least funding for the balloon program appeared to be sufficient. Some $6.5 million had been released to the program in March 1941, and another $37 million was expected by July, according to Thompson, "Barrage Balloon Development," 31.

71   In the end, the balloons were: Multiple sources, including Lt. Col. Cheney L. Bertholf to commanding general, Hawaiian Air Force, July 19, 1941, Disc A7581, AFHRA. The previously cited July 1941 army report praising the effectiveness of the balloons had nevertheless recommended against their installation in Hawaii, saying they would interfere with air force and naval aviation.

71   Yet, after the worst attack: British balloons and antiaircraft guns were rushed to the Panama Canal and the Pacific Coast, FO371/34115, NAUK.

71   Their mythology spans: Richard Holmes, *Falling Upwards: How We Took to the Air* (London: William Collins, 2013), 11.

72   Paid passenger rides: Ibid., 42–43.

72   The balloons and their launches: Ibid., 44–45.

72   After Benjamin Franklin watched: Tom D. Crouch, *The Eagle Aloft: Two Centuries of the Balloon in America* (Washington, DC: Smithsonian Institution Press, 1983), 37.

72   In one cartoon: Eileen F. Lebow, *A Grandstand Seat: The American Balloon Service in WWI* (reprint; Westport, CT: Praeger, 1998), Kindle edition, chap. 1.

73   The balloon's appearance: John Christopher, *Balloons at War: Gasbags, Flying Bombs and Cold War Secrets* (Gloucestershire, UK: Tempus, 2004), 22.

73   Napoleon took: Holmes, *Falling Upwards*, 34.

73   It didn't take long: Crouch, *The Eagle Aloft*, 57.

73   There were ascents: Lebow, *A Grandstand Seat*, chap. 2.

74   "Our children": Holmes, *Falling Upwards*, 102.

74   The outbreak of the Civil War: Multiple sources, including ibid., 126–27.

74   Other aeronauts were rushing: Christopher, *Balloons at War*, 27.

75   "This was an ominous": Holmes, *Falling Upwards*, 129.

75   Lowe's Military Aeronautics Corps: And thirty-two thousand cubic feet of gas, Holmes, *Falling Upwards*, 127–28.

76   The balloon units: Ben Fanton, "Gas Balloons: View From Above the Civil War Battlefield," *America's Civil War*, June 12, 2006.

76   Lowe used one of the oldest methods: Christopher, *Balloons at War*, 33.

76   Through heat and bitter cold: Holmes, *Falling Upwards*, 140.

78   The *Gazelle*'s demise: Ibid., 148. The *Gazelle* ended her days with Lowe, who cut her into patches, which he handed out as souvenirs. The Lowe family donated one of the patches to the Smithsonian National Air and Space Museum: http://blog.nasm.si.edu/hidden-treasures/the-most-fashionable-balloon-of-the-civil-war/.

78   Lacking the Union's capacity: Fanton, "Gas Balloons."

78   "Even if the observers": Ibid.

79   Georges Clemenceau, the mayor: Stanley J. Pincetl Jr. et al., "A Letter of Clemenceau To His Wife By Balloon," *French Historical Studies* 2, no. 4 (Autumn 1962): 514. Clemenceau wrote his letter in impeccable English to Mary, whom he met while living in the United States.

79   Balloons being balloons: Ibid., 511. Clemenceau's letter was returned to his son in France in 1933.

79   Over the course of the four-month siege: Christopher, *Balloons at War*, 46.

79   They therefore set to work: Ibid., 48. Earlier weaponry was modified to target balloons, but the Krupp gun was apparently the first built expressly to target balloons.

79   Of the sixty-six: Edward R. Westermann, "Fighting for the Heavens from the Ground: German Ground-Based Air Defenses in the Great War, 1914–1918," *The Journal of Military History* 65 (April 2001): 642.

80   In a display of early marketing: Christopher, *Balloons at War*, 59.

80   In one test: Westermann, "Fighting for the Heavens," 642.

80   At the World's Fair: Christopher, *Balloons at War*, 61.

81   He was inspired, Crouch, *The Eagle Aloft*, 283.

81   His company built: Multiple sources, including Westermann, "Fighting for the Heavens," 643.

82   One ship built in 1917: Gordon J. Vaeth, *They Sailed the Skies: U.S. Navy Balloons and the Airship Program* (Annapolis, MD: Naval Institute Press, 2005), 2.

82   The pressurized bags: Ibid., 2.

82   Meanwhile, the first class: Ibid., 3–4.

83   Unmanned propaganda balloons: Christopher, *Balloons at War*, 77.

83   "Hardly a train could move": Ibid., 66.

83   The danger was so extreme: Lebow, *A Grandstand Seat*, chap. 10.

83   One study found: Christopher, *Balloons at War*, 67.

84   It was no surprise when: Lebow, *A Grandstand Seat*, chap. 13.

84   Up in the air: Christopher, *Balloons at War*, 66.

84   The Caquot could tolerate: Ibid., 67.

85   Army balloons hadn't seen: Lebow, *A Grandstand Seat*, chap. 2.

85   Balloon cadets were still: Ibid., chap. 3.

85   It would be another: For this and other balloon figures, see ibid., chap. 15.

85   In the final days of the war: Ibid., chap. 13.

86   Perhaps the highest praise: Ibid.

86   The 1923 Gordon Bennet: Vaeth, *They Sailed the Skies*, 17–18.

86   A navy balloon that left: Ibid., 11.

86   Their last message: Ibid., 13.

86   Yet balloons could still: Ibid., 40.

87   Americans rushed outside: Laura Hillenbrand, *Unbroken* (London: Fourth Estate, 2012), 4.

88   During the Second World War: Vaeth, *They Sailed the Skies*, 115.

88   forty-three ships and more than a thousand lives: Goodwin, *No Ordinary Time*, 317.

88   By the end of the war: Vaeth, *They Sailed the Skies*, 125.

88   The Los Angeles area: Conn, Engelman, and Fairchild, *Guarding the United States and Its Outposts*, 82.

88   There was barely any: Ibid., 88.

89   Although some thirty witnesses: Col. John G. Murphy, "Activities of the Ninth Army AAA," *Antiaircraft Journal* 92, no. 3 (May/June 1949): 5.

89   Even Eleanor Roosevelt: Goodwin, *No Ordinary Time*, 296.

89   Germany . . . eventually abandoned: Conn, Engelman, and Fairchild, *Guarding the United States and Its Outposts*, 111.

89   By early 1941: Henry L. Stimson to Secretary of the Navy, February 7, 1941, Joint Committee on the Investigation of the Pearl Harbor Attack, Congress of the United States, 1st Sess., part 1, November 1945, 280–81, http://www.ibiblio.org/pha/congress/.

89   Only one military police: Shock, *The U.S. Army Barrage Balloon Program*, 43.

90   "We had that trouble all the time": Joint Committee on the Investigation

of the Pearl Harbor Attack, Congress of the United States, 1st Sess., part 3, December 1945, 1215, http://www.ibiblio.org/pha/congress/.

90   These models came: Balloon descriptions are taken from multiple sources, particularly Shock, *The U.S. Army Barrage Balloon Program*; Thompson, "Barrage Balloon Development"; and R. E. Turley Jr., "Barrage Balloons," *Coast Artillery Journal* 85, no. 1 (January/February 1942): 20–24.

90   When the balloon was ready: Thompson, "Barrage Balloon Development," 62. The cable had a breaking capacity of 7,100 pounds.

91   In 1942 a barrage: Turley, "Barrage Balloons," 21.

91   A Coast Artillery Corps colonel: Ibid., 24.

91   Borrowing a page: Thompson, "Barrage Balloon Development," 65.

91   A plan to develop: Ibid., 11.

91   To make matters worse: Ibid., 47–48.

92   The explosion of . . . In the end: Naval Inspector General, May 21, 1943, (Navy) Bureau of Aeronautics, GC, RG72, NARACP.

92   Readers could tuck: Colin Curzon, *The Body in the Barrage Balloon: Or Who Killed the Corpse?* (London: Macmillan, 1942). A *Kirkus* review called it "rompish silliness" and "not for serious fans," though it was unclear if that meant fans of barrage balloons or of the author.

92   The clever Bobo: Margaret McConnell, *Bobo, the Barrage Balloon*, (New York: Lothrop, Lee, and Shepherd Co., 1943).

92   One newspaper columnist of: George S. Schuyler, *Pittsburgh Courier*, November 2, 1943, 13.

92   Each battalion counted: Activation of Barrage Balloon Organizations in 1943, January 17, 1943, Maj. Gen. J. A. Green to Commanding General, Army Ground forces, Records of Barrage Balloon Board, Camp Tyson, RG337, NARACP. See also "Barrage Balloons in a Fighter Command," Department of Tactics, Barrage Balloon School, Camp Tyson, TN, October 15, 1942, No. 167043, AFHRA, 9.

       It is unclear how many men the 320th comprised at this time, though the force sent to France in June and July 1944 would contain 687 men, according to a 320th Operations Report, July 7, 1944, CABN-320-0.3, RG407, NARACP.

92   All the top officers: The highest rank held by black officers was second lieutenant, according to interviews with 320th men and Jim Dingus of the 321st Barrage Balloon Battalion.

93   The name changed later: The Anti-Aircraft Command took over the balloon program in March 1942. According to the official 320th unit history, the 320th was renamed again in July 1943, to reflect its new mission, flying very-low-altitude balloons. The new name was thus the the 320th Anti-Aircraft Barrage Balloon Battalion, VLA.

93   "These sky fighters": Francis Yancey, "Four Battalions at Camp Tyson Learn to Fly the Barrage Balloons," *Afro-American*, September 11, 1943, 13.

93   "These colored battalions": *Pittsburgh Courier,* April 3, 1943, 2.

93   Reveille at 6:25: Schedule of calls at Camp Tyson, AG, Operations Reports, CABN-320.0.1, RG407, NARACP.

93   One of the hardest: Yancey, "I Go Through an Army Infiltration Course," 1.

94   The Richmond porter: Author interview with Henry Parham.

94   "Apparently the theory is that": *Afro-American,* February 27, 1943, 20.

94   "Broke 'em down!": Author interview with Arthur Guest.

94   "We learned how to handle": For this and Hamilton's backstory, author interviews with George Hamilton.

95   To avoid static electricity: A. G. Slonaker, *Recollections of a College Dean: Including a Brief History of the 103rd Barrage Balloon Battery* (Parsons, WV: McClain Printing Company, 1975), 46.

95   The armed-cable system worked in two parts: Multiple sources, including documents and author interviews. See Thompson, "Barrage Balloon Development," 62–63, and "Barrage Balloons in a Fighter Command," 6–8.

96   One of these drogue parachutes: Depending on the type of balloon, bombs could be attached at either end of the cable. Several 320th men said that the bombs on the balloons used in Normandy were attached to the top of the cable. In that case, the top parachute was smaller than the bottom chute, and kept the bomb steady as it descended toward the plane.

96   Investigators at Camp Tyson: "Barrage Balloons in a Fighter Command," 10–11.

96   Yet the Army Corps: Capt. Robert J. Turnbull to Major Beverly, February 15, 1943, Records of the Barrage Balloon Board, Camp Tyson, RG337, NARACP.

96   As far as the Tyson men knew: Author interviews with Henry Parham and other 320th men.

96   "since that's the safest way": Associated Press, January 2, 1943.

98   One balloon that broke loose: Message from Fifth Service Command to War Department, June 9, 1943, RG319, NARACP.

98   One balloon set a speed record: *Yank,* May 7, 1943.

98   Fifty-seven balloons in Seattle: Shock, *The U.S. Army Barrage Balloon Program,* 44.

99   The same month, Canadian: *The Globe and Mail,* June 10, 1942, 2.

99   Balloon men wore rubber gloves: Records of the Barrage Balloon Board, Camp Tyson, RG337, NARACP.

99   "The balloon man's lines": Author interviews with Henry Parham and other 320th men.

99   Elsewhere, the balloons: Joint Committee on the Investigation of the Pearl Harbor Attack, Congress of the United States, Hewitt Inquiry, part 36, 623–24, http://www.ibiblio.org/pha/congress/.

CHAPTER 5: "WE WERE LIKE LITTLE DOGS"

101   "I'd rather see Hitler and Hirohito": White, *A Man Called White*, 225.

101   In April 1943 you could catch: Laurie B. Green, *Battling the Plantation Mentality: Memphis and the Black Freedom Struggle* (Chapel Hill, NC: University of North Carolina Press, 2007), 146. Many African Americans were deeply troubled by the stereotypical characters portrayed in *Cabin in the Sky*.

102   "If you wasn't in uniform": Author interview with Wilson Monk.

102   During the war years 425,000: Antonio Thompson, *Men in German Uniform: POWs in America during World War II* (Knoxville, TN: University of Tennessee Press, 2010), 1.

102   Their privileges, often far: Heino R. Erichsen, *The Reluctant Warrior: Former German POW Finds Peace in Texas* (Fort Worth, TX: Eakin Press, 2001), 59.

102   At Camp Claiborne, Louisiana: Mary Penwick Motley, *The Invisible Soldier: The Experience of the Black Soldier, World War II* (Detroit, MI: Wayne State University Press, 1975), 162.

103   A soldier named Davis: On his first furlough; ibid., 266.

103   "You niggahs can't sleep in heah": Ibid., 326. Spellings reprinted from the original text.

103   In 2008 the army threw out: Associated Press, July 26, 2008.

103   "It really hurt us": Author interview with Wilson Monk.

104   the Southern Governors Conference of 1942: Astor, *The Right to Fight*, 161.

104   "Yes, you are a nigger": Phillip McGuire, ed., *Taps for a Jim Crow Army: Letters from Black Soldiers in WWII* (reprint; Lexington, KY: University Press of Kentucky, 1993), 188.

104   A white woman in Alabama spat: Motley, *The Invisible Soldier*, 247.

104   In one of the army's most outrageous: Patrick S. Washburn, *A Question of Sedition: The Federal Government's Investigation of the Black Press during World War II* (New York: Oxford University Press, 1986), 59.

104   After howls of protest: Buckley, *American Patriots*, 267.

105   The sight of so many black men: Nelson, *A More Unbending Battle*, chap. 3.

105   Their white commander understood: Ibid.

105   During the so-called Red Summer: Nalty, *Strength for the Fight*, 126.

105   Mobs took over cities: Woodward, *The Strange Career of Jim Crow*, 114.

105   In 1919, seventy-seven black men: Edgerton, *Hidden Heroism*, 108.

105   Southern whites sometimes lay in wait: Rawn James Jr., *The Double V: How Wars, Protest, and Harry Truman Desegregated America's Military* (New York: Bloomsbury, 2013), Kindle edition, chap. 9.

106   Mississippi senator James K. Vardaman called for: Nalty, *Strength for the Fight*, 126.

106   The police chief in Sylvester . . . "I fought for you in France": James, *The Double V*, chap. 9.

106 In April 1941 a black soldier was found hanging: Nalty, *Strength for the Fight*, 164.

106 Billie Holiday evoked: Written by Abel Meeropol, "Strange Fruit" sold more than one million records. The double lynching in 1930 that is the subject of the song was captured in gruesome photographs.

107 "Day by day, the Negro": Op-ed by William Hastie for various black newspapers, including the St. Thomas *Daily News*, August 6, 1943.

107 Northern black draftees were: *Afro-American*, May 22, 1943, 14.

107 "We might as well have been": Motley, *The Invisible Soldier*, 43.

107 The post's public relations: *Afro-American*, April 11, 1942, 3.

107 The situation remained unchanged: Ibid., May 22, 1943, 14.

108 The incidents certainly belied: Osur, *Blacks in the Army Air Forces during World War II*, 64.

108 A base for a black Army Air Forces: Letter, October 26, 1945, Lt. Gen. Ira C. Baker to War Department Special Board on Negro Manpower; Progress Report on the Board Study, Tab H, Papers of Alvan C. Gillem Jr., EL.

108 The South was more vigorously engaged: Brandt, *Harlem at War*, 101.

108 Black troops there wrote, McGuire, ed., *Taps for a Jim Crow Army*, 13.

108 Four months later a false rumor that: Multiple sources, including Astor, *The Right to Fight*, 180.

108 It looked like a small Battle of the Bulge: Motley, *The Invisible Soldier*, 57.

108 "It was more or less guerrilla warfare": *Afro-American*, June 19, 1943, 1.

108 An inquiry blamed the revolt: Lee, *The Employment of Negro Troops*, 372.

109 Complaints at the post dubbed: *The People's Voice*, May 22, 1943, 1.

109 "We demand the removal of": Letter, May 3, 1943, Bowman to Roosevelt, Inspector General Correspondence, RG159, NARACP.

109 "These boys should be protected": Letter, May 1, 1943, Timpson to Roosevelt, Inspector General Correspondence, RG159, NARACP.

110 "Most slave owners were good-hearted": Roy Wilkins to Henry L. Stimson, January 25, 1944, RG 159, Inspector General Correspondence, NARACP.

110 Racial strife rocked: Edgerton, *Hidden Heroism*, 136.

111 "Negroes will be considered only as janitors": Goodwin, *No Ordinary Time*, 246.

111 We have not had a Negro working: Ibid., 247.

111 Randolph told the president: Ibid., 251.

111 He was two decades ahead of his time: Brandt, *Harlem at War*, 76.

111 "A tall, courtly black man": Wilkins, *Standing Fast*, 180.

112 By 1943, American production: Goodwin, *No Ordinary Time*, 449.

112 Detroit was turning out: Ibid., 363.

112 An admiring Joseph Stalin called: Ibid., 477.

112 "We can no longer indulge": Fireside Chat, October 12, 1943, http://docs.fdrlibrary.marist.edu/101242.html.

112 An estimated fifty-three thousand jobs opened: Nalty, *Strength for the Fight*, 182.

112 Six million women who went to work: Goodwin, *No Ordinary Time*, 416.

112 Black workers content: White, *A Man Called White*, 227.

112 "It gives one a feeling": Goodwin, *No Ordinary Time*, 444.

113 Thousands seeking jobs in automobile: Ibid., 326–27.

113 "I'd rather see Hitler and Hirohito": White, *A Man Called White*, 225.

113 "Race War in Detroit": *Life*, July 5, 1943, 93–101. The magazine reported that white rioters yelled, "You damn Gestapo" and "Just like Germany" when police tried to curb them.

113 In the end twenty-five blacks and nine whites: *Chicago Defender*, July 10, 1945, 6. The tally was taken from an Urban League report. Also see White, *A Man Called White*, 226–27.

114 The United Automobile Workers union refused: Astor, *The Right to Fight*, 181.

114 "Experiments within the army": Ibid., 159.

114 To those arguments: *Time*, July 10, 1944, 66.

114 Problems at southern bases . . . After rioting in Beaumont: Jonathan Daniels to Philleo Nash, June 24, 1943, Box 27, Papers of Philleo Nash, TL. Such incidents were recounted in a weekly "minorities roundup," compiled by region, by the Office of War Information.

115 It was the most complex: Roi Ottley, *New World A-Coming: Inside Black America* (Boston: Houghton, Mifflin Company, 1943). Ottley, whose birth name was Vincent Lushington Ottley, is all but forgotten today but was a well-known journalist of his day who worked for Harlem's *New York Amsterdam News* and other black newspapers, and for *PM*, a daily newspaper that employed prominent white liberals.

115 Yet in the summer of 1943, Harlem: White, *A Man Called White*, 235.

115 Mirroring the larger: Ottley, *New World A-Coming*, 1.

115 It wasn't unusual to find: Brandt, *Harlem at War*, 36.

115 White-owned department stores . . . defense plants: Multiple sources, including White, *A Man Called White*, 235.

115 The people of Harlem found a uniting force: James Baldwin, *Notes from a Native Son* (reprint; Boston: Beacon Press, 1984), 101.

116 Harlem had needed something: Ibid., 111.

116 Six people were killed: Edgerton, *Hidden Heroism*, 136.

116 The future Harlem congressman: Ibid., 136.

116 We say to Mr. Roosevelt: *Afro-American*, June 26, 1943, 4.

117 His position toward civil rights was: James, *The Double V*, chap. 11.

117 Mrs. Roosevelt's exhaustive travels: Goodwin, *No Ordinary Time*, 162.

117 Her activism sparked: Ibid., 371. The FBI concluded that higher-paying factory jobs were luring away black domestic workers.

117   "It is blood on your hands": Ibid., 446.

118   "We didn't like her one bit": Ibid., 116.

118   The year before the riots: Ibid., 351–53.

118   Between 1908 and 1942: *Afro-American*, July 11, 1942, 1.

118   "I never had a chance": Goodwin, *No Ordinary Time*, 352.

118   "I could hear tears": Ibid., 353.

118   One of those letters: Ibid., 421–22.

119   Some bases didn't allow: Edgerton, *Hidden Heroism*, 141.

119   "Screw this!": Brandt, *Harlem at War*, 108.

119   As long as he worked there: Astor, *The Right to Fight*, 175.

119   The question "Do you think that," Osur, *Blacks in the Army Air Forces*, 186.

120   After the Carlsbad sergeant: Goodwin, *No Ordinary Time*, 423.

120   Lt. Col. Leon J. Reed: Author interview with John Reed.

120   George Davison of Waynesburg . . . Later in the war: George A. Davison
      unpublished memoir, courtesy of Bill Davison.

120   "He didn't talk to you like you were a man": Author interview with Wilson
      Monk. Interestingly, George Davison grew to like Taylor and, after Taylor's
      death, maintained a correspondence with his widow.

121   Others like Hattye Mae: Author interview with Hattye Thomas Yarbrough.

121   She lived with her aunt and uncle: Ibid. Presumably quarters for black offi-
      cers were insufficient, so they lived off base.

121   While there was a handful of black churches: Author interviews with Hattye
      Thomas Yarbrough and 320th men.

121   The white bus had one hundred seats: Letter, January 5, 1943, signed "Just a
      Soldier of Camp Tyson" to Truman K. Gibson Jr., Civilian Aide to the Sec-
      retary of War, GC, RG107, NARACP.

121   On base black troops: Author interview with Hattye Thomas Yarbrough,
      who worked one summer at Service Club No. 3.

121   That scene was too tame: Author interviews with William Dabney and Harry
      Cecil Curtis Jr.

123   One 320th man who decidedly: Author interview with Albert Grillette
      Wood.

124   While not slavery in name: Douglas A. Blackmon, *Slavery by Another Name*
      (New York: Anchor Books, 2009), 4.

124   Each had received: *Associated Negro Press* report reprinted in the *New York
      Amsterdam News*, October 21, 1944.

124   When an earnest white private: Letter, September 27, 1942, Victor Barnouw
      letter to his family, WD 291.2, GC, John J. McCloy, RG107, NARACP. Bar-
      nouw's extraordinary four-page letter is worth quoting further. The anthro-
      pology student told the MPs who arrested him that there was "no scientific
      basis for any theories of racial supremacy." This prompted the question of
      whether Barnouw would let his sister "sleep with a nigger." Barnouw replied,

"Sure I would, if she wanted to," infuriating his questioners. "You must like Mrs. Roosevelt," one of them said. Barnouw agreed that he had "a lot of respect" for the First Lady. "For Christ's sake! For that alone I ought to kick your ass in," a senior MP told him. Barnouw's mother sent his letter to Eleanor Roosevelt, who apparently forwarded it to the War Department. Barnouw went on to finish his PhD and spent his career teaching and researching the Chippewa Indians and other cultures. In his obituary in May 1989, he was remembered by a colleague at the University of Wisconsin for a simple and direct writing style that is evident in his wartime missive.

125 "That is the second murder": Wilson Monk letter to Rosita Monk, June 22, 1941.

125 "The officers got scared": Letter, Wilson Monk to Rosita Monk, August 19, 1941.

125 Southern civilian police also were: Motley, *The Invisible Soldier*, 42. The incident was recounted by Sgt. Eugene Gaillard.

125 There were exceptions: Author interview with Willie Howard.

126 The white cops were looking for: Author interview with Samuel Mattison.

126 At Hastie's urging: Memo, February 14, 1942, AG's Office to commanding general of field forces, ETO, WD 291.2, RG498, NARACP. Army Regulation 600-10 stated, "Superiors are forbidden to injure those under their authority by tyrannical or capricious conduct or by abusive language. While maintaining discipline and the thorough and prompt performance of military duty[,] all officers, in dealing with enlisted men, will bear in mind the absolute necessity of so treating them as to preserve their self-respect. A grave duty rests on all officers and particularly upon organization commanders in this respect."

126 "To address a Negro soldier": Brandt, *Harlem at War*, 116. Hastie and the crusading NAACP lawyer Thurgood Marshall joined in submitting the report.

127 "I was very happy": Author interview with Samuel Mattison.

128 Somehow Mattison beat assault charges: Ibid. There are no existing records about Mattison's court-martial in 1943. Records from 1944 and 1945 list charges filed against Mattison by military police on two occasions though not their dispositions.

128 A report by the Tyson: Report of Death of Pvt. Herman Hankins, July 31, 1943, First Lt. Wm. O. Hudnall, Army Intelligence Project, Camp Tyson, RG319, NARACP.

128 His fellow soldiers challenged: Associated Negro Press, August 14, 1943.

128 Hankins's death was first: Multiple sources, including the *Pittsburgh Courier*, August 14, 1943, 4.

129 Whatever happened the: Ibid.

129 "After Hankins's death": Author interview with Wilson Monk.

129 who was angry about being demoted: Author interviews with Henry Parham and William Dabney.

129 "There is a tense feeling": Letter, June 19, 1943, Fred Hart to Truman K. Gibson Jr., Civilian Aide to the Secretary of War, GC, Camp Tyson, RG107, NARACP.

129 Colonel Reed ordered weapons locked: Letter, July 6, 1943, Fred Hart to Truman K. Gibson Jr., Civilian Aide to the Secretary of War, GC, Camp Tyson, RG107, NARACP. Misspellings are in the original text.

130 Losing respected: Unsigned letter, July 28, 1943, to Truman K. Gibson Jr., Civilian Aide to the Secretary of War, GC, RG107, Camp Tyson, NARACP. Misspellings and underscores are in the original text.

131 On the afternoon of July 7: Report, July 23, 1943, Army Intelligence Project, Camp Tyson, RG319, NARACP.

131 "They pointed to the insignia": Letter, October 5, 1943, Louis R. Lautier to Carl Murphy, Civilian Aide to the Secretary of War, GC, Camp Tyson, RG107, NARACP.

131 In October sixty-four black: *Afro-American*, January 15, 1944, 4.

131 The black press called the: *Chicago Defender*, December 11, 1943, 1.

131 "The colored troops here": Letter, October 20, 1943, Wilson Monk to Rosita Monk.

CHAPTER 6: LAST STOP, U.S.A.

135 "Even in the summer when it is light": *Life*, July 27, 1942, 66.

135 A gauzy fog settled: The voyage of the 320th Battalion was reconstructed through author interviews with 320th veterans, Port of New York documents, 1943 articles in newspaper and magazines, and weather reports. Also of immense help was Alister Satchell's vivid memoir, *Running the Gauntlet: How Three Giant Liners Carried a Million Men to War, 1942–1945* (reprint; London: Chatham Publishing, 2001).

135 These ships would: *A Guide to the New York Port of Embarkation*, 56, New York Public Library, MFY94-345.

136 British prime minister: Satchell, *Running the Gauntlet*, 9.

136 Pier 86 was home to: Troop figures from multiple sources, including ibid., 11.

136 The future president: *New York Times*, June 2, 1945, 4.

136 The sinking of any one of them: Satchell, *Running the Gauntlet*, 11.

137 The *Aquitania* promised: *New York Times*, March 8, 1941, 2.

137 The ship . . . counted: Mark Chirnside, *RMS* Aquitania: *The Ship Beautiful* (Gloucestershire, UK: The History Press, 2009), 10.

137 Fluted columns adorned . . . "faultless as anything": Satchell, *Running the Gauntlet*, 30.

137 Comparisons were drawn: *New York Times*, May 31, 1914, 6.

137 Dinner in the Grande: Satchell, *Running the Gauntlet*, 31–33.

138 Conveniently, there was a bank: Chirnside, *RMS* Aquitania, 36.

138 Speed was the: Ibid., 28.

138 She was a workhorse: Satchell, *Running the Gauntlet*, 21.

138 The 1,625 people aboard: *New York Times*, September 17, 1939, 45. The passengers included 669 Americans.

139 She looked like some huge: Chirnside, *RMS* Aquitania, 31.

139 Their journey had begun: Unit History, 320th Operations Reports, CABN-320-0.1, RG407, NARACP.

139 They arrived two days later: Records of the Historical Record NYPE, Box 7, RG336, NARANY. Troops began arriving at Camp Shanks in April 1943, with as many as eight thousand processed each day.

139 It was, the *New York Times* proclaimed: *New York Times Magazine*, December 24, 1944.

139 At Camp Shanks: Description of equipment from multiple sources, including Port of New York documents and newspaper articles.

140 If they wanted it: Records of the Historical Record NYPE, Box 7, RG336, NARANY. GIs could buy $148 million worth of life insurance and $2 million worth of war bonds.

140 or at least: Multiple sources. For a vivid picture of life during wartime, see Jan Morris, *Manhattan '45* (Baltimore, MD: Johns Hopkins University Press 1986). According to Morris, Manhattan was relatively prosperous, crime-free, and exulting in its place as the center of the New World. A Gallup poll showed 90 percent of New Yorkers considered themselves happy—no doubt a historical one-off.

140 They played football: Davison, unpublished memoir.

140 This voyage of the *Aquitania*: Tenth Fleet convoy and routing files, AT-74, RG38, NARACP; and Satchell, *Running the Gauntlet*, 142.

140 As the roster was called: Author interview with Arthur Guest.

140 "Lady, I want to go home": Ibid.

141 He marveled at the: This and other details about Guest's early life from author interviews with Arthur Guest.

141 Only three stacks were technically: Satchell, *Running the Gauntlet*, 30.

141 Though his mother: Ibid. Prewar base pay for privates was thirty dollars a month, rising to fifty dollars after June 1942, according to Jonathan Gawne, *Finding Your Father's War: A Practical Guide to Researching and Understanding Service in the World War II US Army* (Philadelphia, PA: Casemate, 2006), 48.

142 But the F Deck: Satchell, *Running the Gauntlet*, 17.

142 The two Australian cipher officers: Ibid., 56. Satchell was one of those officers.

142 A woman serving: Chirnside, *RMS* Aquitania, 78.

142 Belowdecks, admission to the mess: Robert Towle, *Troopship Days*, www.roblightbody.com/liners/aquitania/emails.htm.

143   A group of black soldiers: Norman Longmate, *The G.I.'s: The Americans in Britain 1942–1945* (London: Hutchinson and Co., 1975), 49.

143   Troop carriers usually: Multiple sources, including *Guide to the New York Port of Embarkation*, April 1943–March 1944, New York Public Library, 23. Sailing time listed in Tenth Fleet convoy and routing files, AT-74, RG38, NARACP.

143   It was a view that: Satchell, *Running the Gauntlet*, 18.

143   Wilson Monk prayed: Author interview with Wilson Monk, who noted the "irony" of seeing the Statue of Liberty upon leaving Jim Crow America. Monk also prayed he would return to see his sweetheart, Mertina Madison.

144   Before Pearl Harbor, the United States: Conn, Engelman, and Fairchild, *Guarding the United States and Its Outposts*, 97.

144   Finally in September 1941: Goodwin, *No Ordinary Time*, 278.

144   Even so, during the first four: Conn, Engelman, and Fairchild, *Guarding the United States and Its Outposts*, 96.

144   "The broad oceans which have": Fireside Chat, February 23, 1942, http://millercenter.org/president/fdroosevelt/speeches/speech-3326.

144   In port, thick concrete pens: Satchell, *Running the Gauntlet*, 46.

144   The loss of shipping: Andrew Williams, *The Battle of the Atlantic: The Allies' Submarine Fight against Hitler's Grey Wolves of the Sea* (New York: Basic Books, 2003), 106.

145   At her usual twenty-three knots: Multiple sources, including Chirnside, *RMS Aquitania*, 8.

145   With no torpedoes left: Clay Blair, *Hitler's U-Boat War: The Hunters 1939–1942* (London: Cassell and Co., 1996), 547.

145   German propaganda boasted: Harry C. Butcher, *My Three Years with Eisenhower: The Personal Diary of Captain Harry C. Butcher, 1942–1945* (New York: Simon and Schuster, 1946), 149.

145   Even electric razors were banned: Satchell, *Running the Gauntlet*, 138–39.

145   sinking eleven merchant ships: Ibid., 18.

145   One of them, the *Admiral*: Ibid., 49.

146   What a torpedo would do: Blair, *Hitler's U-Boat War*, 447. There was a second explosion aboard the *Lusitania* that contributed to its sinking, perhaps caused not by the munitions aboard, as some believed, but more likely by explosive dust that clouded empty coal bunkers that ignited: Erik Larson, *Dead Wake: The Last Crossing of the Lusitania* (New York: Crown Publishers, 2015), Kindle edition, 319. In any case, the *Aquitania's* manifest does not show munitions aboard.

146   "The British sailors said we could": Davison, unpublished memoir.

146   The *Aquitania's* weapons: Satchell, *Running the Gauntlet*, 75.

146   A GI from Florida: Longmate, *The G.I.'s*, 46.

146   When the carriers began . . . a clock reminded the quartermaster: Satchell, *Running the Gauntlet*, 79.

146 Allied ship production soon: Williams, *The Battle of the Atlantic*, 270.

146 Still at this point in the war: Satchell, *Running the Gauntlet*, 94.

147 "There is wind and fog and horizontal rain": *Life*, July 27, 1942, 65.

147 Before radar was installed: Satchell, *Running the Gauntlet*, 60.

147 In December 1939: Ibid., 38.

147 Before the *Aquitania*'s maiden: *New York Times*, May 17, 1914, 15.

147 Cunard heralded the liner's: Chirnside, *RMS* Aquitania, 14.

147 In addition, Satchell noted: Satchell, *Running the Gauntlet*, 75.

147 Only six of the *Lusitania*'s: Larson, *Dead Wake*, 270. The *Lusitania* had collapsible rafts, some of which were inflated in time to rescue passengers.

148 The convoys that escorted: Ibid., 238.

148 And in any event: Author interview with Wilson Monk.

148 At Camp Shanks, troops had practiced: Multiple sources, including port documents, and *Collier's*, January 20, 1945.

148 More than one man mused: Author interviews with 320th members and other veterans.

148 The skies were mostly clear: Weather reports, November 17, 1943, the National Oceanic and Atmospheric Administration.

148 When troop carriers began . . . Cunard captains had protested: Satchell, *Running the Gauntlet*, 75 and 238.

148 Records show the ship's: Tenth Fleet convoy and routing files, AT-74, RG38, NARACP. Also see Satchell, *Running the Gauntlet*, 142.

149 A ban on gambling was roundly ignored: Author interviews with 320th men.

149 "He was a hell of a gambler": Author interview with Albert Grillette Wood.

149 "I was like the collector": Author interview with William Dabney.

149 Her powerful engines: Chirnside, *RMS* Aquitania, 44 and appendix 1.

149 Even with a speed reduction to 20.5 knots: Tenth Fleet convoy and routing files, AT-74, RG38, NARACP.

149 If he didn't hold his plate: Author interview with Floyd Siler.

149 If needed, the *Aquitania* could: Chirnside, *RMS* Aquitania, 31.

150 One evening an alarm sent: Author interviews with 320th men.

150 After four days at sea: Author interviews with 320th men. Satchell, *Running the Gauntlet*, writes on page 142 that the gale was a force 9.

150 The Harvard-educated preacher: Author interview with Theolus Wells. Background on Albert White: *Afro-American*, September 11, 1943, 1.

150 Pinned in the bottom: Author interview with Wilson Monk.

150 Six German Junkers Ju-88s: Satchell, *Running the Gauntlet*, 142

151 The ship could have used an air escort: Tenth Fleet convoy and routing files, AT-74, RG38, NARACP.

151 The possibility of air cover: Charles M. Sternhell et al., "Antisubmarine Warfare in World War II," Operations Evaluation Group Report No. 51, Navy Department (1946), 48.

151 The *Aquitania*'s captain: Satchell, *Running the Gauntlet*, 136–37.

151 There had been three tense moments: Longmate, *The G.I.'s*, 43.

151 In the first . . . six days later: Satchell, *Running the Gauntlet*, 134–35.

151 One week later, she outran: Ibid.,141.

151 One U-boat captain: Ibid., 91.

151 Twice, she narrowly missed: Ibid., 237.

151 The rolling hills: Ibid., 142, and Tenth Fleet convoy and routing files, AT-74, RG38, NARACP.

152 "It was a beautiful sight": Author interview with Wilson Monk.

152 spanned the northern end: http://www.secretscotland.org.uk/index.php/ Secrets/ClochBoom

152 The pocket-size resort town: Satchell, *Running the Gauntlet*, 96.

152 Mystified Americans quickly learned: Robert Towle, *Troopship Days*, www .roblightbody.com/liners/aquitania/emails.htm.

153 A black soldier could gaze: Except after dark, when blackout curtains were pulled on trains and everywhere else in Britain.

CHAPTER 7: A TASTE OF FREEDOM

155 "The general consensus": George Orwell, "As I Please," *Facing Unpleasant Facts* (New York: Mariner Books, 2009), 167.

155 "My Dear Mrs. Monk": Letter, May 3, 1944, Jessie Prior to Rosita Monk. Reprinted from the original text.

156 He is such a gentleman: Ibid.

156 "One day Hollywood came to town": Author interview with Ken Clark.

157 At first there were no: Although there were white Americans in Wales at this time, people interviewed in the villages around Pontypool recalled that the first Americans they met were black.

157 "The English people show our lads": *Afro-American*, November 14, 1942.

157 "It was a spark of a light": Author interview with Arthur Guest.

158 On low-cloud days a gauzy: Author interview with Ken Clark and other people in the Pontypool area who were children during the war.

158 The bomb reduced a pair: David R. Cullis, *Every Picture Tells a Story: Part 2 Faces and Places, Abersychan, A Social History* (self-published, 2008), 65.

159 "You are coming to Britain": Longmate, *The G.I.'s*, 23. The guide attempted to counter impressions that the British were lacking in courage: "If they need to be," it read, the British "can be plenty tough. The English language didn't spread across the oceans and over the mountains and jungles and swamps of the world because people were panty-waists."

160 Goff and Jessie shared many things: Author interviews with Cheryl Morgan, Jeffrey Prior, and David Prior. In Wales, the Nonconformist movement of the eighteenth century led many believers to break from the Church of

England and join other Protestant denominations. Noddfa Baptist and Trinity Methodist were built in 1846 and 1825, respectively.

160 "Hello, pretty lady": Author interview with Samuel Mattison. Mattison did not remember where the graveyard was situated, but based on his description and the likely location of his billet, Noddfa is probably the place.

161 "This afternoon I made cakes": Letter, May 3, 1944, Jessie Prior to Rosita Monk.

162 Over the next three years . . . strained to meet the needs of some two million Americans: Dwight D. Eisenhower, *Crusade in Europe* (Garden City, NY: Doubleday, 1948), Kindle edition, chap. 4.

162 "It was claimed": Ibid.

162 "We must take care": Ibid., chap. 11.

163 "Colossal sacrifices of the Soviet army": Antony Beevor, *D-Day* (London: Viking, 2009), Kindle edition, 29.

163 FDR ordered his generals to plan: Eisenhower, *Crusade in Europe*, chap. 11.

164 Even so, writes historian: Smith, *When Jim Crow Met John Bull*, 40.

164 British officials at first: Ibid., 38.

164 When it became evident: Ibid., 47.

164 Also opposing the entry: Multiple sources, including Astor, *The Right to Fight*, 163.

164 The War Department mostly ignored: Nalty, *Strength for the Fight*, 167.

164 Young Jamaicans organized: Astor, *The Right to Fight*, 243.

165 "The biggest influx of foreigners": Longmate, *The G.I.'s*, 85.

165 The British government had kept: Ibid., 33.

165 "Morale on the airfield and in the workshops": Ibid., 28.

165 The United States seemed, Ibid., 26.

165 "They ought to win easily": Ibid., 27.

166 a nickname perhaps derived: The origin of GI is unclear. Other sources say it comes from "General Issue" or "galvanized iron," all terms used by the armed forces.

166 Britons were struck . . . "For a while the people" . . . "was certainly something our drab": Longmate, *The G.I.'s*, 91.

166 On the street, the GIs: Author interviews with dozens of Britons and veterans. Although Wrigley's gum was introduced in Britain in 1911, most people didn't have their first stick until the Americans came. Gum came to be the item most identified with the GIs. In the United States, Wrigley took Juicy Fruit and its other brands off the market in order to dedicate its output to the military, according to the company's website.

166 One little girl in Norfolk . . . "They were horrified": Longmate, *The G.I.'s*, 182 and 178.

166 Ten-shilling notes dropped . . . A little seaside church: Ibid., 178.

167   Two telephone installers . . . Chided by their commanders to show proper respect: Ibid., 98 and 113.

167   The only group immune to: *This Is Our War* (Baltimore, MD: The Afro-American Company, 1945), 128. According to the *Afro-American*, the monthly base pay in the British army was $16.40, compared to $50.00 for GIs.

167   Why the U.S. Army stocked: Savvy soldiers also stocked up on stockings before leaving the States. The war correspondent Roi Ottley wrote in July 1944 on his way to Britain, "It seems I am one of the few men aboard [this ship] who didn't bring along a stock of women's stockings, candy, and lipstick for romantic activities in London!" See Roi Ottley, *Ottley's World War II: The Lost Diary of an African American Journalist* (Lawrence, KS: University Press of Kansas, 2011), 43.

167   "You're not going in there" . . . "I am a British subject": Metropolitan Police report, March 1942, FO371/30680, NAUK.

168   "The British Empire is on the whole": Memorandum to War Cabinet, October 9, 1942, FO371/30680, NAUK.

168   Some officials urged: Letter, April 30, 1942, J. J. Paskin to J. W. Ward, FO371/30680, NAUK. In the letter, Paskin wrote, "We are naturally most concerned at this manifestation of colour prejudice in this country, and regard the matter as of such importance that we should be grateful if you would take it up with the United States Embassy with a view to seeing what action can be taken to prevent any repetition of such incidents."

168   Reluctant to upset their: Letter, May 14, 1942, F. E. Evans to J. J. Paskin, FO371/30680, NAUK.

169   Then a cable from London . . . The first African Americans arrived: Smith, 38. Smith describes the cable, dated April 17, 1942, as an "administrative blunder" that was "quickly corrected" by Eisenhower.

169   That didn't stop the British: Smith, *When Jim Crow Met John Bull*, 47.

169   At a meeting of Churchill's War Cabinet . . . "It is rather a scandal": Ibid., 48.

169   In Washington the following month: Telegram, August 12, 1942, R. I. Campbell to Foreign Office, FO954/30A, NAUK. Hopkins emphasized that the subject ought to be kept private, telling the young minister that "it would be a bad thing if this matter were to be treated formally" between the governments.

169   Campbell also met with Marshall: Telegram, August 12, 1942, R. I. Campbell to Foreign Office, FO954/30A, NAUK.

170   "The last war had shown": Message, September 1, 1942, Anthony Eden to Viscount Halifax, FO954/29, NAUK.

170   Eden then took up: Ibid.

170   Churchill's War Cabinet nevertheless: Smith, *When Jim Crow Met John Bull*, 50–51. Eden's view was seconded by James P. Warburg, who was sent

to London to launch the U.S. Office of War Information's propaganda base there. "Actually, it remains to be seen whether the colored troops can take an English winter," he wrote. "I doubt it."

170 Finally Roosevelt put an end: Smith, *When Jim Crow Met John Bull*, 52.

170 British officials agonized over: Ibid., 53.

170 Asked in Parliament if he: Multiple sources, including the *Essex Chronicle*, October 2, 1942, 3.

171 "The white Southerners were making: *Afro-American*, October 24, 1942, 1.

171 A cartoon depicted: Ibid., 4. The parliamentarian was Tom Driberg.

171 Even Capt. Harry C. Butcher: Astor, *The Right to Fight*, 245.

171 "They'd tell all kinds of tales": Author interview with Willie Howard.

171 A black sergeant invited to dinner: Walter White, *A Rising Wind* (Garden City, NY: Doubleday, Doran and Company, 1945), digital edition, chap. 12.

172 He had been told that: Ibid., chap. 6.

172 "Our biggest enemy was": Author interview with Willie Howard.

172 "Discrimination hurt me": Author interview with Albert Grillette Wood.

172 Despite the nation's colonial: Multiple sources, including Ottley, *Ottley's World War II: The Lost Diary of an African American Journalist*, 78.

172 "Any American Negro who comes to Britain": Longmate, *The G.I.'s*, 26.

173 "In 1942," writes: Ibid., 117.

173 "One day, son": Author interview with Ken Rogers. He further explained that using the term "was not offensive as far as we were concerned." Rogers said he grew up with no prejudice and wasn't aware the word was a slur.

173 And Maj. Gen. Arthur A. B. Dowler . . . "Too much freedom": Notes on Relations with Coloured Troops, August 1942, FO371/30680, NAUK. Also see Smith, *When Jim Crow Met John Bull*, 54–57.

174 "It is not the policy": Letter, September 5, 1942, Home Office to Chief Constables, American Coloured Troops, ETO, AG, 291.2, RG498, NARACP.

174 Bracken chided his countrymen: *Sunday Express*, September 20, 1942. The article was circulated with a handwritten note by Nevile Butler of the Foreign Office that read, "I understand that Mr. Bracken wrote this article some time ago and that it was accidental that it came out when it did!" FO371/30680, NAUK.

174 The natural inclination: Memorandum to War Cabinet, October 3, 1942, FO371/30680, NAUK. Also see Smith, *When Jim Crow Met John Bull*, 66-67.

175 Cripps borrowed from Dowler's Notes: This and other points in the memo, Smith, *When Jim Crow Met John Bull*, 75–79.

175 Senior British army officers: War Cabinet minutes, October 16, 1942, FO371/30680, NAUK.

175 Aboard one warship: Smith, *When Jim Crow Met John Bull*, 81.

176 "That's all right": Ibid., 76.

176 In the end, the Cabinet concluded: Ibid.

176   When a vicar's wife: Ibid., 45

176   "Any coloured soldier": Ibid.

177   The *Times* printed a poignant: Letter of October 4, 1942, signed by D. Davie-Distin, excerpted in ETO, AG, 291.2, RG498, NARACP. The black soldier, he wrote, "showed his gratitude by a donation of just twice the amount of his bill in our blind box."

177   "This is a great country" . . . "I have met a great number of friends": Morale Report, September 16, 1942, ETO, AG, 291.2, RG498, NARACP.

177   Eisenhower understood that: Lee, *The Employment of Negro Troops*, 624.

177   Eisenhower assured reporters: Butcher, *My Three Years with Eisenhower*, 20.

178   even though Ike sometimes used: Astor, *The Right to Fight*, 245.

178   "It is absolutely essential": Memorandum, September 5, 1942, Eisenhower to General John C. H. Lee, ETO, AG, 291.2, RG498, NARACP.

178   He also took the progressive step: Butcher, *My Three Years with Eisenhower*, 59.

178   When a New York journalist: White, *A Rising Wind*, chap. 6.

178   If questioned, Lee said: Memorandum, September 28, 1942, Lee to Col. E. G. Plank, ETO, AG, 291.2, RG498, NARACP. To be fair, Lee often championed his black troops albeit in a paternalistic manner. Later in the war, when replacement combat troops were gravely needed, he boldly pushed the idea that black platoons of riflemen be mixed with white infantry units. The army went forward with his plan, and the result was historic: the first integrated combat units.

178   Eisenhower's deputy chief of staff: Letter, September 3, 1942, Brig. Gen. John E. Dahlquist, to F. A. Newsam, ETO, AG, 291.2, RG498, NARACP.

179   A year after Dowler's Notes, an American: Leadership of Colored Troops, July 15, 1943, ETO, AG, 291.2, RG498, NARACP.

179   "Colored soldiers are akin": Ibid.

179   After protests from black: Memorandum, October 7, 1943, Colonel C. R. Landon to General Lee, ETO, AG, 291.2, RG498, NARACP.

179   An army colonel directed that: Memorandum, August 5, 1942, Col. M. M. Montgomery to General Lee, ETO, AG, 291.2, RG 498, NARACP.

179   As for housing and feeding: Butcher, *My Three Years with Eisenhower*, 56.

180   The sailors were pointed to the Negro canteen: Astor, *The Right to Fight*, 278–79, and James Jr., *The Double V*, chap. 19.

180   Although it was widely understood: Multiple sources, including Astor, *The Right to Fight*, 158.

180   The slight was all the more egregious: Multiple sources, including Buckley, *American Patriots*, 268.

180   An order that transportation: White, *A Rising Wind*, chap. 6.

180   "Any system that attempts": Astor, *The Right to Fight*, 246.

180   Upon arrival in Birmingham: Yvonne Latty, *We Were There: Voices of African*

American Veterans, from World War II to the War in Iraq (New York: Amistad, 2005), 33–35. Gladys O. Thomas-Anderson of the 688th Central Postal Directory Battalion was surprised to be cheered by white people. "They thought we were beautiful," she said.

181 Later the women were barred: Smith, *When Jim Crow Met John Bull*, 109–10.

181 The black war correspondent: Ottley, *Ottley's World War II: The Lost Diary of an African American Journalist*, 45. Ottley writes that the Russians and Czechs aboard ship, however, "expressed amazement" at separation of the races.

181 As honestly devoid: George W. Goodman, "The Englishman Meets the Negro," *Common Ground*, August 1944, 6. Goodman was sent to England in 1942 to open a Red Cross Club.

181 "They always had massive": Author interview with Barbara Dennett Holtom.

182 "As I danced" . . . "She couldn't understand it": *Daily Mail*, February 2, 1994.

182 Local artist Peggy Beeton: *Checkendon, Our Village in Wartime*. The undated booklet was believed to have been written in the 1940s. It also features a drawing by Beeton of the Nissen huts where the men were billeted. The history does not mention the battalion number, but it says that prayers were led by the Reverend White, the 320th chaplain.

182 There, in the biggest city: Author interview with Theolus Wells.

182 The "Brown Bomber" was one of the few: The story of Joe Louis is a lesson in the limits of fame in the world of Jim Crow. When war broke out in Europe, Louis was the most popular black man in America, sharing the spotlight with the track star Jesse Owens. Their respective victories transformed these sons of poor Alabama sharecroppers into potent anti-Nazi symbols. Owens's four gold medals at the 1936 Berlin Olympics had laid waste to Hitler's theories of racial supremacy. As Hitler's war machine was building steam, Louis beat the German Max Schmeling in a first-round knockout in 1938. Schmeling had KO'd Louis two years earlier, and their rematch at Yankee Stadium, one of the most popular bouts of all time, assumed an extra layer of patriotism as Americans rallied behind Louis. Even FDR told the boxer it was up to him to prove that America could defeat Germany.

　　There were some whites who donned Nazi-like uniforms and booed Louis, but the majority of white Americans were behind him. Perhaps the largest radio audience of all time tuned in to the match. Louis and Schmeling became good friends later in life, according to Edgerton, *Hidden Heroism*, 127.

183 When the boxer: Smith, *When Jim Crow Met John Bull*, 109.

183 In Abersychan, the men: Author interviews with 320th men and with Ken Clark. Britain interned some ten thousand "enemy civilians" from Axis countries, including the Italian-born Belli, who was imprisoned for a short time on the Isle of Man.

183 In Checkendon, the beech forest: Author interview with John Cox.

183   "They shipped in some of them" . . . "I have seen nice looking white girls" . . .
One lieutenant noted: Morale Report, September 16, 1942, ETO, AG, 291.2,
RG 498, NARACP.

184   The red line for the average white: Multiple sources, including Gunnar
Myrdal's influential 1944 study, *An American Dilemma: The Negro Problem and Modern Democracy*. He writes that the average southern man was
raised to believe it was his overarching duty to protect the virtue of southern
womanhood from the Negro. The same obligation to protect black women
from white men did not exist.

184   "Will never, never permit": *Life*, April 24, 1944, 32.

184   We got really scared: Longmate, *The G.I.'s*, 128.

184   In southeastern Wales, there were: Author interview with Ken Clark.

184   The locals took the side: Nalty, *Strength for the Fight*, 154–55.

184   In other instances: Multiple sources, including the *Cornishman and Cornish
Telegraph*, October 21, 1943, 4.

185   Fifty-six racial clashes: Smith, *When Jim Crow Met John Bull*, 140. The source
is the army inspector general.

185   Some white soldiers kept a list: Longmate, *The G.I.'s*, 128.

185   They grabbed it: Ibid., 129.

185   When reports of racial strife . . . prompting Stimson to urge the president:
Goodwin, *No Ordinary Time*, 383.

185   "Then I wouldn't feel like such": White, *A Rising Wind*, chap. 4.

185   A white soldier from Georgia: Ibid. chap. 2.

186   There were no problems: Ibid.

186   "It looks very different from": Ibid., chap. 4.

186   Little more than half of all British homes . . . a bath was a weekly luxury:
Longmate, *The G.I.'s*, 82.

187   Even Eisenhower acknowledged: Eisenhower, *Crusade in Europe*, chap. 4.

187   The average GI: This and other findings, "An American Looks at American Troops in Britain," No. 40, March 11, 1943, FO371/34116, NAUK. The
Home Intelligence Office hired an American trainee unbeknownst to army
officers to interview and eavesdrop on U.S. soldiers. No black soldiers were
sampled.

187   "Brag, conceit and cocksureness were": Memorandum of Good Relations between the People of Great Britain and the USA, January 1943, FO371/34114,
NAUK.

187   In Checkendon, a white soldier fired two shots: Author interview with Tony
Allum, then the village blacksmith's apprentice, who repaired the weathervane.

187   "They took everyone's gates off": Author interview with Gus Gray.

187   "Overpaid, overfed, oversexed": Longmate, *The G.I.'s*, 106. Longmate writes,
"The American retort that British servicemen were 'underpaid, underfed,
undersexed and under Eisenhower' is usually forgotten."

188 Even the fat from: Longmate, *The G.I.'s*, 39.

188 More than 75 percent: Black Americans in 1945 earned an annual salary of $1,294, compared to $2,491 for white Americans, according to the U.S. Department of Commerce, Current Population Reports Consumer Income, 1945. British salary figures taken from Report of Walter White to Eisenhower, February 11, 1943, WD 291.2, GC, John J. McCloy, RG107, NARACP.

188 The general consensus: Orwell, "As I Please," 167. Orwell received letters attacking him for his attack on the Americans. He addressed his critics on December 17, 1943, 176: "Before the war, anti-American feeling was a middle-class, and perhaps upper-class thing, resulting from imperialist and business jealousy and disguising itself as dislike of the American accent, etc. The working class, so far from being anti-American, were becoming rapidly Americanized in speech by means of the films and jazz songs. Now, in spite of what my correspondents may say, I can hear few good words for the Americans anywhere. This obviously results from the arrival of the American troops."

188 Some pub owners: White, *A Rising Wind*, chap. 1.

188 On one occasion, a black GI: Longmate, *The G.I.'s*, 130.

188 One evening at a dance: Report on Negroes, March 2, 1944, FO317/38609, NAUK.

189 "They were considered inferior": Author interview with Ken Clark.

189 Newspapers covered good deeds: *Derby Evening Telegraph*, October 2, 1942.

189 One case that gripped all of Britain: This and subsequent descriptions of the Henry case from multiple sources, notably Smith *When Jim Crow Met John Bull*, 1–4 and 185–86.

190 Although the prosecutor conceded: London *Tribune*, June 9, 1944.

190 A later study indicated: Smith, *When Jim Crow Met John Bull*, 186.

190 He was saved by the British public: Ibid., 3–4.

190 Yet Ballot was sentenced to life: White, *A Rising Wind*, chap. 2.

191 "Their form of justice": Letter to the editor, *Gloucester Echo*, May 10, 1944, 3.

191 The use of courts-martial: White, *A Rising Wind*, chap. 2.

191 Their sergeant wrote a letter of protest: Ibid. The sergeant also was fined and demoted to private.

191 "WHAT ARE WE GOING": *Sunday Pictorial*, August 19, 1943, 1.

192 "Is it fair, is it just": Letter, June 29, 1943, Walrond to Colonial Secretary Oliver Stanley, CO874/15, NAUK.

192 A lieutenant colonel proposed: Letter, October 22, 1943, B. W. Rowe to J. L. Keith, CO874/15, NAUK. That suggestion was rejected by Brigadier E. H. A. J. O'Donnell in a November 1, 1945, letter to Keith.

192 Few of these cases led: White, *A Rising Wind* , chap. 2.

192 Equity in the empire was not: Multiple sources, including ibid., chap. 3, and Ottley, *Ottley's World War II: The Lost Diary of an African American Journalist*, 78.

192   At a London dinner party with: White, *A Rising Wind* , chap. 3. Early in his
       career, White often passed as a white man when investigating black lynch-
       ings in the South. Later in his life, White caused a scandal in the black com-
       munity when he divorced his wife in 1949 and married Poppy Cannon, a
       white woman, with his own family among those who claimed that White
       had always wanted to be white. Two years earlier, in an article titled, "Why
       I Remain a Negro," White wrote, "I am not white. There is nothing within
       my mind and heart which tempts me to think I am."

193   In a February 1943 cartoon: Longmate, *The G.I.'s*, 78.

193   "It was miserable to sleep": Author interview with Henry Parham.

193   Men at a bomber base in: Longmate, *The G.I.'s*, 76–77.

194   More versatile than the larger . . . and other details: Shock, *The U.S. Army
       Barrage Balloon Program*, 40–41. The balloons were also known as type M-1.

194   Upon arrival in Checkendon . . . The 320th had been set: Unit History,
       320th, WWII Operations Reports, CABN-320-0.1, RG407, NARACP.

195   "These balloons will move": *Chicago Defender*, July 15, 1944, 14.

195   Physical training was stepped up: Unit History, 320th, WWII Operations
       Reports, CABN-320-0.1, RG407, NARACP.

195   The men experimented with: Ibid., and Study 38, Tactical Employment
       of Antiaircraft Artillery Units, General Board Reports, ETO, Entry 427,
       RG407, NARACP.

195   The new fifty-pound winch: Jonathan Gawne, *Spearheading D-Day: American
       Special Units in Normandy* (Paris: Histoire et Collections, 2011), 189.

195   So many senior U.S. officials: Butcher, *My Three Years with Eisenhower*, 548.

195   One loose-lipped general: Multiple sources, including Forrest C. Pogue, *The
       United States Army in World War II, European Theater of Operations: The Su-
       preme Command* (Washington, DC: Office of the Chief of Military History,
       Department of the Army, 1954), 163.

195   When an ill-packed envelope: Ibid., 163.

196   In the strangest twist: Cornelius Ryan, *The Longest Day* (New York: Touch-
       stone, 1959), 48–49.

196   Berlin had learned: Ibid., 50.

196   Conditions were elaborately: Multiple sources, including Stephen E. Am-
       brose, *D-Day: June 6, 1944, the Climactic Battle of World War II* (London:
       Simon and Schuster, 1994), 138–39.

196   In the worst catastrophe: Joseph Balkoski, *Utah Beach: The Amphibious Land-
       ing and Airborne Operations on D-Day, June 6, 1944* (Mechanicsburg, PA:
       Stackpole Books, 2005), 331. The casualty count is unclear, as was often the
       case during World War II. Some accounts say 946 servicemen were killed.
       Intrigue has surrounded Tiger, with some reports alleging that it was friendly
       fire, not German torpedoes, that killed the men. One report, later disproved,
       said ten high-ranking officers with knowledge of D-Day plans went missing

in the disaster, raising fears that they may have been captured and their information revealed to the enemy.

197 They were effectively cut off: Multiple sources, including Eisenhower, chap. 13. Descriptions of camp life come from multiple sources and author interviews with 320th men.

197 One afternoon, white GIs: Author interview with Willie Howard.

198 They were planning a wedding: This and other details from author interviews with Wilson Monk.

CHAPTER 8: THE GREATEST HOUR

201 "If a Nazi bird nestles": *Chicago Defender*, July 15, 1944, 3.

201 In the dark, choppy waters: "It was serene, pretty and green," Waverly Woodson told the *Baltimore Sun* in an article on June 5, 1994. I compiled Woodson's descriptions of D-Day from his many interviews with journalists in 1944, 1994, and in later years. Besides the *Sun*, notable sources include Woodson's own unpublished account of D-Day written in 1994, courtesy of Joann Woodson; the Associated Press, June 8, 1994; the *Daily Mail*, February 2, 1994; and Latty, *We Were There*, 29–31. I used army records to supplement events, including a European Theater of Operations press release describing Woodson's actions, dated August 28, 1944, from Box 27, the Papers of Philleo Nash, TL. Finally, I interviewed many D-Day veterans and historians and consulted dozens of books, articles, and reports to complete the portrait of what Woodson and the other men saw, felt, and smelled on June 6, 1944. As has been my practice in all these pages, there is no extrapolation of *any* detail; all descriptions are taken from these sources.

202 On this early morning: Williamson Murray, *Strategy for Defeat: The Luftwaffe, 1933–1945* (Maxwell Air Force Base, Montgomery, AL: Air University Press, 1983), 280. The figure of twenty-three thousand includes the glider corps.

203 To Ernest Hemingway: Ernest Hemingway, *Hemingway on War* (New York: Scribner's, 2003), 316. Hemingway, who was working as a correspondent for *Collier's*, described how the men in his boat were awed by the battleship *Texas*: "Under the steel helmets they looked like pikemen of the Middle Ages to whose aid in battle had suddenly come some strange and unbelievable monster."

203 "struck your ear like a punch": Ibid., 316.

203 An Associated Press reporter: Balkoski, *Omaha Beach*, 83.

203 Lt. Gen. Omar Bradley: Associated Press, April 7, 1944.

204 He was only one of two: Associated Press, June 8, 1994.

204 Woodson's LCT carried one Sherman tank: Waverly Woodson's unpublished account of D-Day, courtesy of Joann Woodson.

204 Hemingway, who was aboard one: Hemingway, *Hemingway on War*, 317.

205 The rest of the 320th Barrage Balloon Battalion: Battalion Diary, Leon J. Reed to Commanding General, June 20, 1944, 49th AAA Brigade, WWII Operations Reports, CABN-320-0.3, RG407, NARACP.

205 Thousands of barrage balloons: SHAEF, Air Strips and Balloons 452.4, RG331, NARACP.

205 Most of the 621 men: The "residue," or remaining sixty-six men of the 320, arrived in France on July 3, according to a 320th Operations Report, July 7, 1944, CABN-320-0.3, RG 407, NARACP.

205 Once known as Beach 313: Balkoski, *Omaha Beach*, 11.

205 In the seventeen hours of daylight: Ibid., 54. Normandy shares the same latitude with Newfoundland, with long days in summer and short days in winter.

205 War planners expected a bloodbath: At least in public, Gen. Omar Bradley had called those fears "tommyrot" and had told troops, "Some of you won't come back, but it will be very few," according to the Associated Press, April 7, 1944. The previous January, a British soldier who carried out a bold mission to collect soil samples at Omaha Beach told Bradley upon his return that he feared "tremendous casualties" there. "I know, my boy," replied Bradley. "I know." See Beevor, *D-Day*, 9.

205 After that, the assembled forces: Multiple sources, including Ryan, *The Longest Day*, 60.

206 Omaha was the worst: Multiple sources, including Balkoski, *Omaha Beach*, who calls it "an invasion planner's worst nightmare" (p. 11). Ambrose, *D-Day*, offers a good description of the challenge Omaha posed to war planners on pp. 320–21.

206 Despite those challenges . . . The beaches there: Steven Zaloga, *The Devil's Garden: Rommel's Desperate Defense of Omaha's Beach on D-Day* (Mechanicsburg, PA: Stackpole Books, 2013), 50–51.

207 though he was already beefing up a veritable fortress: Ryan, *The Longest Day*, 14.

207 By June 1944 about 80 percent: Zaloga, *The Devil's Garden*, 51.

207 And he wanted to lay as many as: Ibid., 107.

207 By June some 1.7 million: Ibid.

207 In *The Longest Day*: Ryan, *The Longest Day*, 163.

207 Rommel had designed most: Ibid., 28.

208 He considered the Hitler's Wall: Ibid., 27.

208 By mid-July, the Red Army . . . three hundred fifty thousand Germans: Beevor, *D-Day*, 229.

208 There had been other D-Days: D+1 was June 7, and so on. For more on the story behind the name, see www.nationalww2museum.org/assets/pdfs/the-meaning-of-dday-fact.pdf.

208 In one of the most thoroughly choreographed: Gordon A. Harrison, *The European Theater of Operations: Cross-Channel Attack* (reprint; New York: BDD Special Editions, 1993), 274.

209 Rommel had left Normandy: Ryan, *The Longest Day*, 37.

209 "How stupid of me": Ibid., 260.

210 and the nearly two hundred thousand men: Ibid., 60.

210 "Soldiers, sailors and airmen": Beevor, *D-Day*, 78.

210 The 329 bombers assigned . . . Not one of their 13,000 bombs: Ryan, *The Longest Day*, 187.

210 Machine guns spraying twelve hundred bullets: Balkoski, *Omaha Beach*, 121.

211 The tide caused half: Harrison, *The European Theater of Operations*, 317.

211 suffering among the highest casualties: The casualty rate among engineers was 40 percent for the day, though it was much higher for the earliest arrivals, according to ibid., 317.

211 With the tide rising about one foot: Balkoski, *Omaha Beach*, 143.

211 Some of the smaller boats couldn't handle: Multiple sources, including Ambrose, *D-Day*, 325.

211 Some flopped forward: After the disastrous Excercise Tiger in Britain (see chapter 7), Brig. Gen. E. W. Timberlake, commander of the 49th Anti-Aircraft Artillery Brigade, ordered his men to wear their life belts under their armpits, rather than ringing their waists, to keep them upright. He also ordered them to keep their packs light. The 320th was attached to the 49th Brigade for the invasion. See E. W. Timberlake to J. C. Mazzei, May 12, 1944, ETO reports, Intelligence memos, RG407, NARACP.

211 They staggered toward the shingle: For a good description of the shingle of "apple-sized" stones, see Balkoski, *Omaha Beach*, 126–27. Joseph Balkoski described the shingle to me and its relation to a seawall on the western end of the beach in greater detail via e-mail.

212 The skippers of the landing craft . . . "You are not a rescue ship!": Ryan, *The Longest Day*, 195.

212 First, Woodson's craft hit a mine: This and other descriptions of the boat compiled from multiple interviews with Waverly Woodson.

212 Inside it, medic Warren Capers: *Philadelphia Inquirer*, August 24, 1944.

212 "I am dying": Woodson's unpublished account of D-Day.

212 "Close . . . mighty close": *Baltimore Sun*, June 5, 1994.

213 It was 9:00 a.m.: Battalion Diary, Leon J. Reed to Commanding General, June 20, 1944, 49th AAA Brigade, WWII Operations Reports, CABN-320-0.3, RG407, NARACP. Like many details of D-Day, there is conflicting information in army records about the time the medics landed. Lt. Col. Leon J. Reed, the 320th's commanding officer, wrote 9:00 a.m. in the aforementioned record, and later 8:00 a.m. Waverly Woodson wrote in 1994 that the medics were on the beach at 8:00 a.m. Newspaper accounts in 1944 say the medics were at the rear of the first wave, or in the third landing barge of the first wave. The mostly likely time appears to be 9:00 a.m.

213 In the shelter of the shingle: Multiple sources, including *Pittsburgh Courier*,

September 2, 1944, 1. Based on Woodson's description, it is likely he set up his tent roll at the shingle. Another possibility is that he landed near the seawall at the western end of the beach, which is where the Twenty-Ninth Division landed, though many elements landed far east of their assigned targets. Woodson said the medics landed with the Twenty-Ninth.

213 "At that time": Woodson interview, *Daily Mail*, February 2, 1994.

213 Thirty hours after: Multiple sources, including newspaper articles from 1944, and Army European Theater of Operations press release, August 28, 1944, Box 27, Papers of Philleo Nash, TL.

213 Bill Dabney plunged: For this and other descriptions of his landing, author interviews with William Dabney.

213 A barrage balloon about the size: Author interview with William Dabney.

214 Dabney was among the: The *Afro-American* on August 5, 1944, reported the racial breakdown of the officers and noncoms in the battalion: The fifteen senior officers were white, and seventeen junior officers were black. There was a sole black captain, the chaplain Albert M. White.

214 "It didn't take you long to dig a hole": Author interview with William Dabney.

214 This system of handling the balloons: Army records mention the "plum tree" with no elaboration, but Peter Garwood, a British barrage balloon expert, explained the term and the process to me in an interview.

214 "It was like putting a tall billboard": Joe Hagen, "Operation Overlord: 'Time to Earn Our Pay,' *Memories of World War II*," in LandingShip.com, 2002, http://landingship.com/50/hagen4.htm.

214 At least they could take comfort in knowing: Ibid.

214 Beach commanders ordered the first bags ashore: Study 38, Tactical Employment of AAA Units, General Board Reports, ETO, May 1946, RG407, NARACP.

215 During practice exercises: Ibid. For an excellent explanation and map of the German aim points he calls "one of the deadly secrets of D-Day," see Zaloga, *The Devil's Garden*, 75 and 88.

215 Reconnaissance planes had not: Ibid., 89.

215 The 320th men were slated to begin landing: This and other landing details from multiple sources, including the Battalion Diary.

216 "Get the hell off" . . . "If you stay on": Balkoski, *Omaha Beach*, 198.

216 Not until 11:00 a.m. would: Ibid., 237. By 9:00 a.m., some companies had already neutralized several German strongpoints, though the commanders didn't know this.

216 Frustrated they could not eliminate: "Barrage Balloons in a Fighter Command," Department of Tactics, Barrage Balloon School, Camp Tyson, TN, October 15, 1942, No. 167043, 14, AFHRA.

216 George Davison took refuge behind . . . "bodies being blown to bits": These and other details from his unpublished memoir.

216 The brothers would meet by chance: The brothers met on August 28. George
     Davison's papers include a portion of a newspaper clipping on the brothers.
     Other family information provided by George's son, Bill Davison.

217 "Hit the beach!": This and other details of Davison's landing taken from his
     memoir.

217 he plunged into the fifty-six-degree surf: Log of the USS *Butler*, http://www
     .uss-corry-dd463.com/d-day_u-boat_photos/butler_corry_survs_thx.htm.

217 whose soaring exhortations could: Col. E. Paul Semmens, *The Hammer of
     Hell: The Coming of Age of Antiaircraft Artillery in WWII* (Fort Bliss, 1990),
     online edition, chap. 5, http://www.skylighters.org/hammer/.

217 "We'll write our history in the skies": Ibid. The 320th was attached to the
     49th AAA Brigade until August 1, 1944, according to a unit after-action
     report, September 15, 1942, ETO Reports, RG407, NARACP.

218 "Get down" . . . "I saw the glint": Author interview with Harold Baumgarten
     of the 116th Infantry, *Daily News*, June 6, 2009, 12. George Davison did not
     witness this incident, but I used it here because it reflects the frenetic mo-
     ments that he recounts in his memoir.

218 "There was other guys": Davison, unpublished memoir.

218 "They could put a mortar down": Author interview with Morley L. Piper,
     who landed on Omaha Beach with 115th Infantry at 11:00 a.m.

218 "I made a couple of giant steps": Davison, unpublished memoir.

218 By the time they set off for good: Ibid.

218 Davison and his 320th crew: Ibid. Davison praised the men of the "First
     Army," but he was certainly referring to the First Infantry Division, which
     was part of the U.S. First Army and had seen combat in 1942 and 1943.

219 "If I let you live": Ibid.

219 "Those are for the dead": This and other landing details from author inter-
     view with Willie Howard.

219 These well-fortified bunkers: Balkoski, *Utah Beach*, 184.

219 Their preparations had included: Ibid. 31.

220 Balloon crews from Camp Tyson: Exercises of the 302nd Experimental Bar-
     rage Balloon Amphibious VLA Platoon, December 31, 1942, Records of the
     Barrage Balloon Board, Camp Tyson, RG337, NARACP. The exercise took
     place at Carrabelle, Florida.

220 Utah's 589 casualties: Zaloga, *The Devil's Garden*, 12. For Omaha's 4,720,
     see Balkoski, *Omaha Beach*, 352. Casualty figures for D-Day have never been
     confirmed, and an overall count of the dead has never been established. On
     Utah Beach, there were believed to be fewer than 200 casualties, but Zaloga
     cites an updated estimate of 589. Balkoski combines casualties from Utah
     Beach with operations on the Cotentin Peninsula to reach his figure of 3,510
     casualties on p. 331 of his book *Utah Beach*. Many are surprised to learn that
     the deadliest battle, and the largest, in U.S. history was not the Normandy

invasion but the Meuse-Argonne offensive in World War I, which left 26,277 Americans dead and nearly 96,000 wounded.

220   to join the more than 17,000 American airborne troops: W. F. Craven et al., *The Army Air Forces in World War II, Volume 3: Europe Argument to V-E Day, January 1944 to May 1945* (Washington, DC: Office of Air Force History, 1983), 188.

220   *"Do something!"*: E. W. Timberlake to J. C. Mazzei, Intelligence memos, May 12, 1944, ETO reports, RG407, NARACP.

220   So would others: Battery C of the 320th was set to land at 10:30 a.m. on June 6, according to the Neptune landing plan, 49th AAA Brigade, May 15, 1944, Intelligence memos, ETO General Board Reports, RG407, NARACP. Based on interviews with several Battery C men, it appears that they landed roughly on schedule.

220   One crew to a landing craft: 49th AAA Brigade, May 15, 1944, Intelligence memos, ETO General Board Reports, RG407, NARACP.

220   The twenty-five balloons: Battalion Diary.

220   "The beach was covered with dead soldiers": Author interview with Floyd H. Siler.

221   "I thought I would be better off": For this and other recollections, author interviews with Arthur Guest.

221   "When the bombs stopped": Author interview with Theolus Wells.

221   "I'm an American!" the flier yelled: Ibid.

221   On June 7 an American: Beevor, *D-Day*, 119.

221   When the shelling eased: Author interview with Willie Howard.

221   Later in the day, more than a thousand: A total of twelve hundred black troops landed on Utah Beach. Besides the 320th, the other units were the 582nd Engineer Dump Truck Company, the 385th Quartermaster Truck Company, and four companies of the 490th Port Battalion. On Omaha Beach, the assault force included fewer than five hundred black troops out of nearly thirty thousand. Besides the 320th, there was one section of the 3275th Quartermaster Services Company, according to Lee, *The Employment of Negro Troops*, 637–38. Thousands of black troops poured into France in the days and weeks after the invasion, including AAA battalions.

222   It was the water that surprised: For this and other details of the landing, author interviews with Henry Parham.

222   Albert Grillette Wood from Baltimore: Author interview with Gary Wood, son of Albert Grillette Wood. The elder Wood began talking about the water, and a dead mule he saw during the landing, while he was a bit dazed following an MRI scan. "That's how we found out what he did" on D-Day, said Gary Wood.

222   By early afternoon one of the draws: Ambrose, *D-Day*, 477.

222   One 320th battery would set up a command post: Battalion Diary.

223   Corporal Jessie L. Sumlin . . . Sergeant Israel W. Hughes: Ollie Stewart, *Afro-American*, August 5, 1944, 1.

223   Davison heard a voice shouting: For this and other details on the beach, Davison unpublished memoir.

223   Units of the 320th were scattered: Only twelve of fifty-five crews that landed on Omaha Beach had balloons with them, according to the Battalion Diary. There were 6,600 cylinders of hydrogen planned for transport to the beaches, according to SHAEF, Air Strips and Balloons 452.4, RG331, NARACP.

223   All the balloon crews: Battalion Diary and Unit History, 320th, WWII Operations Reports, CABN-320-0.1, RG407, NARACP. The landings were supposed to be completed by the end of the second tide.

223   Colonel Reed would write later: Battalion Diary.

224   The higher altitudes also: Multiple sources, including Thompson, "Barrage Balloon Development, 106. The function of the AAA guns was to unleash a "wall of lead," as one retired army colonel told me, at a fixed point in the sky from which an aircraft could not escape. The guns were most effective aiming at targets at four thousand to twenty thousand feet, according to multiple sources.

224   The balloons on the American beaches: Unit History. The presence of mines forced the balloons to fly closer together than two hundred feet, resulting in some tangled cables and loss of equipment.

224   The *Junkers* Ju-88, the twin-engine plane that would: 49th AAA Brigade Journal, ETO General Board reports, RG407, NARACP.

224   The balloon's nearly invisible cable: The original design called for a ³⁄₁₆-inch, 7-by-19 preformed steel cable with a breaking strength of 5,100 pounds. This was later amended to a ¼-inch, 6-by-1 preformed steel cable with a breaking strength of 7,100 pounds, according to Thompson, "Barrage Balloon Development," 61–62. Preforming refers to the "forming of the individual wires of a strand into a helix so as to enable them to all be 'closed' into a uniform cylinder capable of retaining its shape when cut," according to http://thecableconnection.com/cable-construction.html.

224   Early articles written about the balloons: *Afro-American*, September 11, 1943, 1.

225   When the pin was removed: Existing 320th records do not detail the type of bombs used in Normandy, but they were almost certainly the British-made No. 4 MK IV bomb, which was the type used by U.S. barrage balloon crews in Italy. See Operations Reports, CABY-102-0.3-104.0.1, RG407, NARACP. Also in those same records, a 320th report dated July 24, 1942, "Developments in Barrage Balloon Equipment," says that the British-type bomb was recommended for standardization for the U.S. low-altitude balloons, which were the larger type of balloons used in barrages along the West Coast and elsewhere. As further proof, in March 1944, the adjutant general's

office decided it unnecessary to manufacture bombs in the United States. See Coast Artillery Branch Decimal File, Report No. 770, VLA Balloon Bomb, AG to Headquarters Army Ground Forces, RG337, NARACP.

225   "One of the most important missions": (Norfolk, VA) *New Journal and Guide*, September 9, 1944, A20.

225   "The primary aim": Ibid.

225   "If a Nazi bird nestles": *Chicago Defender*, July 15, 1944, 3.

CHAPTER 9: FORGOTTEN

227   "Every man who set foot": Ambrose, *D-Day*, 434.

227   Approaching the summer solstice: Multiple sources, including Balkoski, *Omaha Beach*, 53.

227   By nightfall more than 57,000: Williamson Murray, *Strategy for Defeat: The Luftwaffe, 1933–1945* (Maxwell Air Force Base: Air University Press, 1983), 280. Like most figures on D-Day, troop numbers are often conflicting.

227   Searchlights and flares lit: Author interview with Willie Howard and other 320th men.

227   One soldier compared it to the Fourth of July: Balkoski, *Omaha Beach*, 335.

228   "This is where": Davison unpublished memoir.

228   "The Americans controlled only the soil": Balkoski, *Omaha Beach*, 333.

228   "Every ship in the English Channel": Ambrose, *D-Day*, 580.

229   Cornelius Ryan writes: *The Longest Day*, 86. Ryan writes on p. 85 that he found varying figures for the number of fighters in France on June 4 but that he believed there were 183, of which 160 were considered serviceable. Of those 160, a squadron of 124 fighters was being moved from the coast that day.

229   As Ryan tells it: Ibid.

229   So, early on the morning of: This and further details of the German fliers' mission on D-Day from ibid., 245–48.

229   In nine days' time: Mike Spick, *Luftwaffe Fighter Aces* (reprint; South Yorkshire, UK: Frontline Books, 2011), 191.

229   Allied planes chased off: Craven et al., *The Army Air Forces in World War II, Volume 3*, 190. This account says twenty-two enemy planes attacked shipping on the night of June 6, inflicting slight damage.

229   As many as 319 planes: German Air Historical Study VII/31, "The Normandy Invasion," No. 00212123, 512.621, AFHRA.

230   Flying fourteen thousand missions: Murray, *Strategy for Defeat*, 280. Murray writes that the Allies lost only 127 aircraft.

230   Enemy troop reinforcements racing: German Air Historical Study VII/31, "The Normandy Invasion," No. 00212123, 512.621, AFHRA.

230   Nearly half of the Luftwaffe's: Matthew Cooper, *The German Air Force, 1933–1945: An Anatomy of Failure* (London: Jane's, 1981), 321–22. Cooper

writes that of the 4,850 aircraft available, 1,710 were on the Eastern Front, 505 were in the Mediterranean, and 2,625 were in the West.

230 By June 1944 the Luftwaffe: Ibid., 321.

230 Many of these machines: Harrison, *The European Theater of Operations*, 266. By February 1944, some thirteen hundred planes were lost or damaged, about half the month's production. This was blamed on mechanical failure or pilot error.

230 In any event, by 1943 the Allies: Cooper, *The German Air Force*, 321.

230 the Luftwaffe lost half its single-engine fighter planes and one-quarter of its pilots: Murray, *Strategy for Defeat* (277), cites German records.

231 most German pilots were: Beevor, *D-Day*, 339–40. A new pilot in 1944 had as little as 50 hours of training compared with 260 hours in 1942, according to Harrison, *The European Theater of Operations*, 265–66.

231 By early 1944 . . . The Germans had failed to develop: Cooper, *The German Air Force*, 323. The new Mustang was the P-51B.

231 Göring's team had bet: Ibid., 327.

231 Fighter pilots would be forced: Beevor, *D-Day*, 340.

231 Lulled . . . by the dismal weather: Harrison, *The European Theater of Operations*, 275, and Cooper, *The German Air Force*, 333. Effective British fighters and AAA defense also deterred the *Luftwaffe* from sending reconnaissance planes to Britain, writes Cooper (*The German Air Force*, 333).

231 Told about these communications: Ryan, *The Longest Day*, 99.

231 commanders did not take them seriously: Harrison, *The European Theater of Operations*, 275.

231 Field Marshal Gerd von Rundstedt still believed: Ryan, *The Longest Day*, 171.

232 The Allies predicted 1,350 enemy: D-Day Orders, May 15, 1944, ETO General Board Reports, RG407, NARACP.

232 "We have had a very easy run" . . . He believed the great air battle: Ken Delve, *D-Day: The Air Battle* (London: Arms and Armour Press, 1994), 121.

232 that the first barrage balloon was flying . . . It served as a sentry: Battalion Diary, June 20, 1944, Lt. Col. Leon J. Reed to Commanding General, 49th AA Brigade, Operations Reports, CABN-320-0.3, RG407, NARACP. With few precise records, it is impossible to reconstruct the 320th's exact movements on and after June 6 in Normandy. But with the help of newspaper accounts from the summer of 1944, and interviews with 320th men, it is possible to paint in broad strokes what likely occurred. George Davison's memoir places Leon Reed on Omaha Beach on the afternoon of June 6, which is an indication that Reed, who was awarded a Bronze Star for his service, was likely the force behind establishing command posts around the E-1 draw and the first balloon aloft near the E-3 draw and assembling as many men as he could to fly the balloons on Omaha, though the balloon crews essentially operated as independent three- or four-man units.

232   The Americans would not capture it until: Balkoski, *Omaha Beach*, 334.

233   The chaos of the Sicily landings: 103rd Barrage Balloon Battery Historical Records, September 5, 1943, WWII Operations Reports, CABY-102-0.3-104.0.1, RG407, NARACP. Also see Slonaker *Recollections and Reflections of a College Dean*, 56.

233   They also learned that it was more: 102nd Barrage Balloon Battery, Report on Balloon Tactics, September 9, 1943, WWII Operations Reports, CABY-102-0.3-104.0.1, RG407, NARACP.

233   The ship-based balloons did not always: Ibid.

233   These batteries differed from the: Shock, *The U.S. Army Barrage Balloon Program*, 69.

233   It is unknown why the army: This is the reason cited by historian Jonathan Gawne on page 187 of *Spearheading D-Day*. I believe Gawne is correct, but that the answer is more complex.

234   Where villages coated in ankle-deep dust: Slonaker, *Recollections and Reflections of a College Dean*, 56. For fleas and other details, see 103rd Barrage Balloon Battery historical records, October 22, 1943, WWII Operations Reports, CABY-103-0.3, RG407, NARACP.

234   The landings on the southern Italian: 102nd Barrage Balloon Battery, Report on Balloon Tactics, September 9, 1943, and Historical Records, October 31, 1943, WWII Operations Reports, CABY-102-0.3-104.0.1, RG407, NARACP.

234   As enemy guns raged, seven men . . . For their efforts: 102nd Barrage Balloon Battery, Historical Records, October 31, 1943, WWII Operations Reports, CABY-102-0.3, RG407, NARACP.

234   The 104th Barrage Balloon Battery was flying: RG407, Historical Record of Organization, 104th Barrage Balloon Battery, September 1, 1943, WWII Operations Reports, CABY-102-0.3-104.0.1, RG407, NARACP.

234   In November, a plane hit a cable near: J. L. Flentie to Commanding General Fifth Army, November 30, 1943, WWII Operations Reports, CABY-102-0.3, RG407, NARACP. The exact number of downed planes credited to the U.S. balloon crews is not recorded. It was often difficult to distinguish whether balloons, often in the clouds, or AAA guns were responsible for downing a plane.

234   In Palermo, the 103rd reported: Slonaker, *Recollections and Reflections of a College Dean*, 59.

234   Army commanders lauded them: Historical Record of Organization, 104th Barrage Balloon Battery, September 1, 1943, WWII Operations Reports, CABY-102-0.3-104.0.1, RG407, NARACP.

235   "barrage balloons are a vital element": *Army and Navy Register*, April 15, 1944, Reprint, Box 282, U.S. Army Reports of the General Board, EL.

235   Throughout the day, shells: Balkoski, *Omaha Beach*, 332, Battery A, Morning Report, June 7, 1944, NPRC, and author interviews with 320th men.

235 The unit would bury 456 men: Ibid., 332. The quartermaster unit was white. In subsequent days, the troops who buried the dead on the Normandy beaches were usually black, according to multiple sources.

235 During the morning of June 7 . . . On Utah Beach: Battalion Diary. Jonathan Gawne writes on page 191 that an American engineer in a foxhole shot down a balloon on June 6, curious to learn what would happen if he fired a tracer into it.

235 They would be replaced with: Unit History, 320th, Operations Reports, CABN-320-0.1, RG407, NARACP.

235 By the evening of June 7 . . . artillery fire would claim: Battalion Diary.

235 three of his men were killed . . . Seventeen others were wounded: Unit History, 320th, Operations Reports, CABN-320-0.1, RG407, NARACP.

235 The Germans rushed three hundred additional: Murray, *Strategy for Defeat*, 281. The Luftwaffe moved two hundred planes to France within thirty-six hours and another hundred by June 10.

235 On June 7, four fighters strafed Utah . . . Nine more fighters: Col. E. Paul Semmens, "D-Day, June 6th, 1944, Antiaircraft Artillery fight their way off the invasion beaches," *Air-Defense Artillery Yearbook* (1994), 29.

236 By the end of the first week, more than a thousand: Richard R. Muller, "Losing Air Superiority: A Case Study from the Second World War," *Air and Space Power Journal* 17, no. 4 (Winter 2003): 61.

236 Soon, nearly six hundred: Murray, *Strategy for Defeat*, 281. The losses occurred between June 6 and 19.

236 "Every night Jerry visits": First Sgt. James Hugo Madison, (Norfolk, VA) *New Journal and Guide*, July 22, 1944, 2.

236 In Normandy, they raised their balloons: Multiple sources, including newspaper accounts from 1944 and author interviews with 320th men.

236 The raiders that menaced: 49th AAA Brigade Journal, ETO General Board reports, RG407, NARACP. In "The German Air Force" Cooper writes (pp. 335–36) that Luftflotte 3, the German air fleet in Normandy, flew up to three hundred fifty sorties by day and fifty by night in June. In July, there were up to four hundred missions by day and eighty by night.

236 Most of them were "single plane": D-Day Orders, May 15, 1944, 49th AAA Brigade, ETO General Board Reports, RG407, NARACP.

236 The exception was an attack: Historical Record for July, 49th AAA Brigade, ETO General Board Reports, RG407, NARACP.

236 Damage was likely minor: This is according to after-action reports viewed by this author at the National Archives, College Park, MD. In addition, Beevor, *D-Day* (p. 319), writes about a daring Luftwaffe raid on July 18 against British tanks outside Caen, in Normandy.

237 Still, the men on the beach: Author interview with Theolus Wells and other 320th men.

237 First came the flares: Author interview with Willie Howard.

237 From his foxhole: Author interview with Theolus Wells.

237 Their rifles at the ready: (Norfolk, VA) *New Journal and Guide*, July 22, 1944, 2.

237 The men didn't know that: Ambrose, *D-Day*, 47.

237 as many as 143 balloons: Daily balloon tallies recorded between June 6 and July 4, 1944, 320th Operations Report, July 7, 1944, CABN-320-0.3, RG407, NARACP. Unit records show that the number of balloons flying in June steadily increased, with a high of 143 on June 26, of which 9 were lost. The highest daily balloon loss was reported on June 19, when 47 of 113 balloons were either shot down or lost in another way.

237 The Ju-88 was one of two or three planes: Memorandum, July 10, 1945, Col. C. G. Patterson, First U.S. Army Office of the Antiaircraft Artillery Command, Box 14, SHAEF General Staff, EL. The Battalion Diary dated June 20 says two planes were claimed, both by balloons manned by Battery B. The Unit History says, "a large number of probables, or assists, were credited to the battalion during the early days."

237 On three occasions: Ibid. These incidents, attributed to Battery A, were called "inertia links to fire," occurring when an explosive charge inside the link detonated, thus cutting the cable from the balloon.

237 This could happen if a plane struck the cable and escaped: Author interview with Peter Garwood, a British barrage balloon expert.

237 The bags were often flying under cloud cover and at night: Ibid.

238 Battalion records show that only one: Unit History, 320th, Operations Reports, CABN-320-0.1, RG407, NARACP; and Memorandum, July 10, 1945, Col. C. G. Patterson, First U.S. Army Office of the Antiaircraft Artillery Command, Box 14, SHAEF General Staff, EL. James Hugo Madison wrote that only one plane got below the barrage during the first night. See (Norfolk, VA) *New Journal and Guide*, July 22, 1944, 2.

238 The balloons "confounded skeptics": Allan Morrison, *Stars and Stripes*, July 5, 1944. Morrison was one of the rare African American war correspondents working for a publication with a mostly white readership.

238 "It seems the whole front": Richardson Reports, August 9, 1944, Box 50, Walter Bedell Smith WWII documents, EL.

238 Richardson, who was the first editor of *Yank*: Elizabeth Richardson, "A Soldier's Story," August 10, 1995, *Charlotte Observer*, 1E.

238 Wrote a series of private reports: It appears the reports were private because there is no record of the dispatches being published.

238 flagged the balloon-related dispatch: Richardson Reports, August 9, 1944, Box 50, Walter Bedell Smith WWII documents, EL. Richardson betrays his low opinion for African Americans by lacing his report with patronizing comments such as "Riding past you can see the broad grins of the Negro boys and hear them laughing, and see the children gesticulating. You can see

both of them talking a mile a minute—God knows how and what about—but they understand each other somehow through that divine gift given to children and the simple people of this world." Yet Richardson correctly noted that the "main problem with colored troops is getting word back home of their status and work." The mainstream white press seldom covered the heroics of black soldiers. Unfortunately, Richardson concludes, "If they were more articulate, they would perform this function themselves in letters."

238   Eisenhower landed on Omaha: Butcher, *My Three Years with Eisenhower*, 578.

238   by African Americans who manned the Red Ball Express: About three-quarters of troops in the Red Ball Express, which operated from August 25 to November 1944, were African American, according to Lee, *The Employment of Negro Troops*, 633.

239   They were praised for: First U.S. Army Office of the Quartermaster, July 14, 1944, Box 14, SHAEF General Staff 1943-45, EL.

239   "Despite the losses sustained": Unit History. Black newspapers praised the crew of Battery B that downed the plane.

239   They threw a net over the balloon: This and other details of balloon duties from multiple sources, including author interviews with William Dabney, Henry Parham, and other 320th men.

239   A balloon man who wasn't wearing: (Norfolk, VA) *New Journal and Guide*, July 22, 1944, 2.

239   most of the balloons were guarding: Unit records, and author interviews with 320th men. In the early days of the invasion, the battalion borrowed hydrogen cylinders from RAF balloon squadrons stationed on the British beaches. Portable generators later arrived and allowed them to make their own gas, according to *Afro-American* articles on August 5 and September 16, 1944.

239   The men moved from foxholes: Author interviews with 320th men and newspaper articles in the summer of 1944.

239   George Davison joined a patrol: Davison unpublished memoir. A Signal Corps photo at NARACP dated June 10, 1944, shows a group of black soldiers that includes Davison, who identifies himself in a note he wrote on a copy of the photo that is in his personal papers. The Signal Corps caption reads, "A platoon of Negro troops surround a house as they prepare to eliminate a German sniper holding up an advance on Omaha Beach near Vierville-sur-Mer.

240   He also ferried messages: Ibid.

240   Sam Mattison was told to bury: Author interview with Sam Mattison.

240   He enjoyed the show: Author interview with Bill Dabmey.

240   Contact with the French was limited: Multiple sources, including author interviews with 320th men and Normandy residents.

240   "Things over here are pretty hot": Letter, July 13, 1944, Wilson Monk to Rosita Monk.

240   He was among sixty-six battalion reserve troops: The remaining sixty-five enlisted men and one officer of the 320th had stayed behind in England, according to a 320th Operations Report of July 7, 1944, CABN-320-0.3, RG407, NARACP.

240   In a letter the following week: Letter, July 18, 1944, Wilson Monk to Rosita Monk.

240   He found a German gas mask: Author interview with Wilson Monk.

241   By the end of July: Murray, *Strategy for Defeat*, 274.

241   "We were fighting": Beevor, *D-Day*, 319.

241   By August, the skies over Normandy: 49th AA Brigade, After-Action Report, September 15, 1944, ETO General Board Reports, RG407, NARACP.

241   By September, the once-mighty: Cooper, *The German Air Force*, 337.

241   The Reich would urge: Murray, *Strategy for Defeat*, 278.

241   Fighting his own exhaustion: This and other details from multiple sources, including army records, various newspaper articles from 1944, and interviews with Woodson.

241   Later that afternoon he collapsed . . . worked for thirty hours: Multiple sources, including newspaper articles from 1944, and an Army European Theatre of Operations press release, August 28, 1944, Box 27, Papers of Philleo Nash, TL. The press release says Woodson treated more than 200 men.

241   They described the medic: Randy Dixon, *Pittsburgh Courier*, September 2, 1944, 1.

241   Back home, the local paper: Ibid.

242   The unsigned note addressed to: Jonathan Daniels was the administrative assistant to President Roosevelt and a frequent correspondent of Nash's. The note is in Box 27, Philleo Nash's Papers, in a folder of his correspondence with Daniels, at TL.

242   "Here is a Negro from Philadelphia": Ibid.

242   The Bronze Star, created in February: Box 14, SHAEF General Staff, Awards and Decorations in the ETO, EL; Elliott V. Converse et al., *The Exclusion of Black Soldiers from the Medal of Honor in WWII* (Jefferson, NC: McFarland and Company, 1997), 79. Not all historians agree with that conclusion; some believe there were ample Bronze Stars awarded for heroism, or valor. A ribbon emblazoned with a V was added to the Bronze Star when awarded for valor. The next-highest award for heroism is the Silver Star.

242   The records trail ends: The note is undated but included the army press release of August 28, 1944. In an article published in the *New Journal and Guide* on December 15, 1944, page 1, the *American Negro Press* reported that Woodson had been recommended for a Distinguished Service Medal but that Col. Leon Reed had held it up until it was too late, and so instead Woodson received the Bronze Star. This is probably untrue. Unit records say Woodson and the four other medics were recommended for unspecified awards

in August 1944. The *ANP* dispatch also says that "to add insult to injury," Woodson was never officially presented with the Bronze Star. That part was true. Up to that point, Woodson was still awaiting his decoration.

242 Of the 433 Medals of Honor: The figure includes Medals of Honor awarded in all branches of the military.

242 More than one million African Americans: Statistics on black service in World War II are inconsistent, ranging from 900,000 to 1.2 million. Selective Service figures show that 1,056,841 blacks were inducted into the armed forces as of December 1, 1945. See "Selective Service and Victory: The 4th Report of the Director of Selective Service" (Washington, DC: Government Printing Office, 1948).

242 Nine black soldiers received: Converse, *The Exclusion of Black Soldiers from the Medal of Honor in WWII*, 13.

243 In 1942, it was elevated: See http://www.history.navy.mil/browse-by-topic/ heritage/service-medals-and-campaign-credits/navy-cross.html

243 the mortally wounded captain: Prange, *At Dawn We Slept*, 514.

243 "You can't make a first-class": Ottley, *Roi Ottley's World War II*, 43.

243 "You don't know what you're in for": Interview with Paul L. Bates, *The Invisible Soldiers: Unheard Voices*, directed by William H. Smith, ComTel Productions, Inc., 2000.

243 "I don't care what color you are": Lee, *The Employment of Negro Troops*, 661.

243 They spent the war treated as "pariahs": Interview with Lee Archer, *The Invisible Soldiers: Unheard Voices*, directed by William H. Smith, ComTel Productions, Inc., 2000.

244 "At all times every man realizes: Quoted in David P. Colley, *Blood for Dignity: The Story of the First Integrated Combat Unit in the U.S. Army* (New York: St. Martin's Press, 2003), 24.

244 "We had no idea that: Interview with George Barnett, *The Invisible Soldiers: Unheard Voices*, directed by William H. Smith, ComTel Productions, Inc., 2000.

244 Most of America wouldn't: J. Todd Moye, *Freedom Flyers: The Tuskegee Airmen of World War II* (New York: Oxford University Press, 2010), 172. The 1995 film, produced by HBO, was called *The Tuskegee Airmen*.

244 The division commander, Maj. Gen. Edward M. Almond: Edgerton, *Hidden Heroism*, 151.

244 Years after the war, a white colonel: Joseph Galloway, "Debt of Honor," *U.S. News & World Report* online, May 5, 1996. Retired lieutenant general William McCarthy was interviewed about Almond shortly before seven black soldiers, including two from the Ninety-Second Division, were awarded the Medal of Honor.

245 "We ate together, slept together, fought together": Obituary, Matt Schudel, *Washington Post*, February 26, 2012.

245   "I have never seen any soldiers: Edgerton, *Hidden Heroism*, 153.

245   Two New York veterans received: Shaila K. Dewan, "2 Black Soldiers Get Bronze Stars," *New York Times*, June 2, 2000.

245   The 614th became the first: Astor, *The Right to Fight*, 281.

245   Five black members: Converse et al., *The Exclusion of Black Soldiers from the Medal of Honor in WWII*, 79.

246   The role played by black troops: Rudi Williams, "Black WWII Vet Recalls Terrible Time Building 'Ledo Road,'" American Forces Press Service, July 7, 2004, at http://www.defense.gov/news/newsarticle.aspx?id=25745.

246   The only black paratrooper outfit: Buckley, *American Patriots*, 279–80.

246   When they were off duty in: Astor, *The Right to Fight*, 302. The original spelling of the 555th nickname was Triple Nickles, from the old English. The American spelling has commonly been adopted in recent years, and is used here.

246   "I thought, 'By God": Christopher Paul Moore, *Fighting for America: Black Soldiers—The Unsung Heroes of World War II* (New York: Ballantine, 2006), 179–80.

246   Only four Medals of Honor: The army awarded 3 Medals of Honor and 153 Distinguished Service Crosses for service on Omaha Beach on June 6, 1944. On Utah Beach there was 1 Medal of Honor given and 61 Distinguished Service Crosses, according to Balkoski, *Omaha Beach*, 353–55, and Balkoski, *Utah Beach*, 332–33.

246   "Every man who set foot": Ambrose, *D-Day*, 434.

247   "He arose as a leader": See Carlton W. Barrett citation at http://www.history.army.mil/moh/mohb.html.

247   To merit the top award for valor: Box 14, SHAEF General Staff, Awards and Decorations in the ETO, EL.

247   Perhaps the army commanders who: There were cases of medics who received awards for doing their job under fire. In one example, two black medics from the 452nd Anti-Aircraft Artillery Automatic Weapons Battalion won the Silver Star for their service in France on September 17, 1944. Converse et al., *The Exclusion of Black Soldiers from the Medal of Honor in WWII*, 79.

247   The investigators concluded: The investigators found no explicit written records to prove that African Americans suffered discrimination, but concluded that the failure to award the medal to any black soldiers "lay in the racial climate and practice within the army in World War II." Converse et al., *The Exclusion of Black Soldiers from the Medal of Honor in WWII*, 10–11.

247   Only Vernon Baker: John R. Fox, a first lieutenant in the Ninety-Second Division killed in battle in Italy, was also awarded the Medal of Honor. For more information about the seven recipients, see http://www.history.army.mil/moh/mohb.html.

247   "History has been made whole": *New York Times*, January 14, 1997.

247   Woodson the 320th's undisputed: Converse et al., *The Exclusion of Black Soldiers from the Medal of Honor in WWII*, 80.

EPILOGUE

249   "If anything can, it is memory": Elie Wiesel, "Hope, Despair, and Memory," Nobel Lecture, December 11, 1986, http://www.nobelprize.org/nobel_prizes/peace/laureates/1986/wiesel-lecture.html.

249   Balloons flew over downtown: *Milwaukee Sentinel*, June 10, 1944, and *Milwaukee Journal*, June 25, 1944.

249   In Portland, Maine, readers learned: *Portland Sunday Telegram and Sunday Press Herald*, July 2, 1944.

249   The high-speed V-1 rocket bombs: "Improvements of the VLA Barrage Balloon Lethal Device and Flying Assembly," April 13, 1945, Records of the Barrage Balloon Board, RG337, NARACP.

250   At the very least, the balloon cable: Ibid.

250   And because the United States and Britain: James R. Shock, *U.S. Army Airships 1908–1942* (Edgewater, FL: Atlantis Productions, 2002), 45.

250   Surplus U.S. Army balloons: *Hartford Courant*, July 20, 1945.

250   Women could buy: *New York Times*, October 16, 1943.

250   In Britain, the balloons: Author interview with Peter Garwood.

250   During the Vietnam War: Shock, *U.S. Army Airships*, 47.

250   Made of highly durable fabrics: Multiple sources, and author interviews with aerostat experts.

250   Experiments are under way: Will Oremus, "Not as Loony as It Sounds," *Slate*, December 2, 2014.

250   the U.S. Defense Department sent: Multiple sources, and author interviews with aerostat experts. Also see Christopher Leake, "2,000 Ft Up, the New 'Barrage Balloon' Spying on the Taliban, *Mail Online*, September 25, 2010.

250   Cameras on the latest models can see: Thomas Black, "The Latest Border Control: Iraq War Blimps," *Bloomberg*, February 10, 2015.

250   In Singapore, the government sent: Kyunghee Park, "Eye-in-the-Sky Blimp Boosts Singapore's Spying Ability," *Bloomberg*, November 3, 2014.

251   "Morale of troops was very high": Unit History, 320th, WWII Operations Reports, CABN-320-0.1, RG407, NARACP.

251   "The first words we heard was": Interview with Waverly Woodson, *The Invisible Soldiers: Unheard Voices*, directed by William H. Smith, 2000, PBS.

252   After graduating in 1948 from Lincoln: Multiple interviews with Waverly Woodson and author interviews with Joann Woodson.

254   "I don't know why they" and "I was the only black man": Woodson interview; and Latty, *We Were There*, 31.

254   They would conclude that: The investigators wrote that they did not recommend Woodson for a higher award because they could not find records

related to his case. "Thus, it has not been possible to determine from the official record what award was originally recommended or whether higher echelons considered elevating the award." Woodson's award file has not been found, they wrote, and his individual personnel records were destroyed, along with many others, in a fire in 1973 at the National Personnel Records Center in St. Louis, Missouri. See Converse et al., *The Exclusion of Black Soldiers from the Medal of Honor in WWII*, 80.

I examined records at two army archives and was unable to find any trace of higher decorations for Woodson. In an e-mail to me, Elliott V. Converse, a member of the study group, said that the Philleo Nash note was not sufficient evidence. Converse explained the decision not to recommend Woodson for the Medal of Honor:

> The Army asked the study group to find evidence that black soldiers had been recommended for the Medal of Honor or that any recommendation had been disapproved. We found no official record showing that a black soldier had been recommended for a Medal of Honor. But, given the prevailing climate of racial prejudice in a segregated Army (especially clear evidence of prejudice by white officers commanding black units), the impact of that policy and those attitudes on black units (a limited opportunity for blacks to serve in combat), and the difficulty of distinguishing between heroic acts recognized with a Medal of Honor or a Distinguished Service Cross, we recommended that the Army review the cases of the nine black soldiers awarded a Distinguished Service Cross for possible upgrade to the Medal of Honor. Additionally, we recommended that the case of one soldier (Ruben Rivers) who was awarded a Silver Star also be reviewed. In Rivers' case, we had first-person evidence (but not an official, written record) that he had been recommended for a Medal of Honor. Rivers' company commander insisted that he had filed a recommendation for the Medal of Honor. The evidence in Waverly Woodson's case was not strong enough—entirely hearsay—to make that recommendation.

255 Wilson Monk immensely enjoyed: Author interview with Wilson Monk.

256 A caller from the French embassy: Author interview with Wilson Monk Jr. His father died before he could receive the Legion of Honor, which is not awarded posthumously.

257 It was the second-happiest day: The first, of course, was marrying Mertina.

257 Gambling was a frequent: Author interview with Henry Parham.

258 Banks that refused to lend to Negroes: Multiple sources, including Louis Lee Woods II, "Almost 'No Negro Veteran . . . Could Get a Loan': African Americans, The GI Bill, and the NAACP Campaign against Residential Segregation, 1917–1960," *The Journal of African American History* 98, no. 3, Symposium: "St. Claire Drake: The Making of a Scholar-Activist" (Summer

2013), 393. In December 1944, the NAACP established its own division to examine veterans' claims that they were unable to obtain mortgages and other benefits available to white servicemen.

258   Although the white middle class: Ira Katznelson and Suzanne Mettler, "On Race and Policy History: A Dialogue about the G.I. Bill," *Perspectives on Politics* 6, no. 3 (September 2008): 523. Katznelson and Mettler differ on the overall impact of the GI Bill. Mettler believes the legislation benefited African Americans, while Katznelson disagrees.

258   Henry Hervey, a former Tuskegee Airman: Ibid., 529.

258   Despite those setbacks: Obituary, *Chicago Tribune*, April 7, 2003.

258   But many were conned by: Katznelson and Mettler, "On Race and Policy History," 522.

259   Olivier Serot Alméras: "Remembering D-Day: U.S. Veterans Honored at Embassy," June 7, 2013, France in the United States, Embassy of France in Washington, DC, http://ambafrance-us.org/spip.php?article4617.

259   "Tell them we want to see the end of": Ottley, *Roi Ottley's World War II*, 172.

260   "Blacks over here, whites over here": Interview with Roscoe Brown, in *The Invisible Soldiers: Unheard Voices*, directed by William H. Smith, ComTel Productions, 2000.

260   "Many of us had illusions" . . . "We don't hired colored": Astor, *The Right to Fight*, 305.

260   "Nigger, you can't sit there": Interview with James Charles Evers, *Breath of Freedom*, directed by Dag Freyer, Smithsonian Channel, 2014.

260   In Georgia, a black veteran: Buckley, *American Patriots*, 337.

260   During the journey south: Multiple sources.

261   "This shit has to stop": Truman K. Gibson et al., *Knocking Down Barriers: My Fight for Black America* (Evanston, IL: Northwestern University Press, 2005), 226.

261   Critics saw the action as . . . The army was the last branch of the military to integrate: Isaac Hampton, *The Black Officer Corps: A History of Black Military Advancement from Integration through Vietnam* (New York: Routledge, 2013), Kindle edition, chap. 2.

261   "Black veterans identified with the civil rights movement": Interview with John Lewis, in *Breath of Freedom*, directed by Dag Freyer, Smithsonian Channel, 2014.

261   "African Americans clearly decided": Interview with Walter B. Hill Jr. in *The Invisible Soldiers: Unheard Voices*, directed by William H. Smith, ComTel Productions, 2000.

261   "They said I was overeducated to push": For this and other details, author interviews with William Dabney.

262   "After the war, he tried": Author interview with Harry Cecil Curtis Jr.

262   "We went to bank after bank": Author interview with Beulah Dabney.

263   One day earlier, Bill: Linda Hervieux, "All-Black Battalion That Landed in Normandy, France, on D-Day to Be Honored," *Daily News*, June 5, 2009.

Bibliography

BOOKS

Ambrose, Stephen E. *D-Day: June 6, 1944, The Climactic Battle of World War II.* London: Simon and Schuster, 1994.

Astor, Gerald. *The Right to Fight: A History of African Americans in the Military.* Cambridge, MA: Da Capo Press, 1998.

Atkinson, Rick. *The Day of Battle: The War in Sicily and Italy 1943–1944.* London: Abacus, 2013.

Baldwin, James. *Notes from a Native Son.* Reprint. Boston: Beacon Press, 1984.

Balkoski, Joseph. *Omaha Beach: D-Day, June 6, 1944.* Mechanicsburg, PA: Stackpole Books, 2004.

———. *Utah Beach: The Amphibious Landing and Airborne Operations on D-Day, June 6, 1944.* Mechanicsburg, PA: Stackpole Books, 2005.

Beevor, Antony. *D-Day.* London: Viking, 2009. Kindle edition.

———. *The Second World War.* New York: Little, Brown and Company, 2012. Kindle edition.

Blackmon, Douglas A. *Slavery by Another Name.* New York: Anchor Books, 2009.

Blair, Clay. *Hitler's U-Boat War: The Hunters 1939–1942.* London: Cassell and Co., 1996.

Bond, Beverly G., and Janaan Sherman. *Beale Street.* Charleston, SC: Arcadia Publishing, 2006.

Brandt, Nat. *Harlem at War: The Black Experience in WWII.* Syracuse, NY: Syracuse University Press, 1997.

Brundage, W. Fitzhugh. *Lynching in the New South: Georgia and Virginia, 1880–1930.* Champaign: University of Illinois Press, 1993.

Buckley, Gail. *American Patriots: The Story of Blacks in the Military from the Revolution to Desert Storm.* New York: Random House, 2001.

Butcher, Harry C. *My Three Years with Eisenhower: The Personal Diary of Captain Harry C. Butcher 1942–1945*. New York: Simon and Schuster, 1946.

Chirnside, Mark. *RMS* Aquitania*: The Ship Beautiful*. Gloucestershire, UK: The History Press, 2009.

Christopher, John. *Balloons at War: Gasbags, Flying Bombs and Cold War Secrets*. Gloucestershire, UK: Tempus, 2004.

Colley, David P. *Blood for Dignity: The Story of the First Integrated Combat Unit in the U.S. Army*. New York: St. Martin's Press, 2003.

Conn, Stetson, Rose C. Engelman, and Bryon Fairchild. *Guarding the United States and Its Outposts*. Washington, DC: U.S. Army Center of Military History, 1962. Online edition.

Converse, Elliott V. III, Daniel K. Gibran, John A. Cash, Robert K. Griffith Jr., and Richard H. Kohn. *The Exclusion of Black Soldiers from the Medal of Honor in WWII*. Jefferson, NC: McFarland and Company, 1997.

Cooper, Matthew. *The German Air Force, 1933–1945: An Anatomy of Failure*. London: Jane's, 1981.

Craven, W. F., and J. L. Cate, eds. *The Army Air Forces in World War II, Volume 3: Europe Argument to V-E Day, January 1944 to May 1945*. Washington, DC: Office of Air Force History, 1983.

Crouch, Tom D. *The Eagle Aloft: Two Centuries of the Balloon in America*. Washington, DC: Smithsonian Institution Press, 1983.

Cullis, David R. *Every Picture Tells a Story, Part 2: Faces and Places, Abersychan, A Social History*. Self-published, 2008.

Delve, Ken. *D-Day: The Air Battle*. London: Arms and Armour Press, 1994.

Deutsch, Stephanie. *You Need a Schoolhouse: Booker T. Washington, Julius Rosenwald, and the Building of Schools for the Segregated South*. Evanston, IL: Northwestern University Press, 2011.

Edgerton, Robert B. *Hidden Heroism: Black Soldiers in America's Wars*. Boulder, CO: Westview Press, 2001.

Eisenhower, Dwight D. *Crusade in Europe*. Garden City, NY: Doubleday, 1948. Kindle edition.

Erichsen, Heino R., and Jean Nelson-Erichsen. *The Reluctant Warrior: Former German POW Finds Peace in Texas*. Fort Worth, TX: Eakin Press, 2001.

Gawne, Jonathan. *Finding Your Father's War: A Practical Guide to Researching and Understanding Service in the World War II US Army*. Philadelphia, PA: Casemate, 2006.

———. *Spearheading D-Day: American Special Units in Normandy*. Paris: Histoire et Collections, 2011.

Gibson, Truman K. Jr., and Steve Huntley. *Knocking Down Barriers, My Fight for Black America*. Evanston, IL: Northwestern University Press, 2005.

Goodwin, Doris Kearns. *No Ordinary Time: Franklin and Eleanor Roosevelt—The Home Front in World War II*. New York: Simon and Schuster, 1994.

Green, Laura B. *Battling the Plantation Mentality: Memphis and the Black Freedom Struggle.* Chapel Hill: University of North Carolina Press, 2007.

Griggs, Walter S. Jr. *World War II: Richmond, Virginia.* Charleston, SC: The History Press, 2013.

Hampton, Isaac II. *The Black Officer Corps: A History of Black Military Advancement from Integration through Vietnam.* New York: Routledge, 2013. Kindle edition.

Harrison, Gordon A. *The European Theater of Operations: Cross-Channel Attack.* Reprint. New York: BDD Special Editions, 1993.

Hemingway, Ernest. *Hemingway on War.* New York: Scribner, 2003.

Hillenbrand, Laura. *Unbroken.* London: Fourth Estate, 2012.

Holmes, Richard. *Falling Upwards: How We Took to the Air.* London: William Collins, 2013.

Hornsby, Alton Jr. *Chronology of African American History from 1492 to the Present.* 2nd ed. Detroit, MI: Gale Group, 2000.

Hughes, Langston. *The Collected Poems of Langston Hughes.* New York: Vintage Classics, 1994.

James, Rawn Jr. *The Double V: How Wars, Protest, and Harry Truman Desegregated America's Military.* New York: Bloomsbury, 2013. Kindle edition.

Johnson, Nelson. *The Northside: African Americans and the Creation of Atlantic City.* Medford, NJ: Plexus Publishing, 2010.

Kaplan, Alice. *The Interpreter.* New York: Free Press, 2005.

Lanning, Michael Lee. *The African American Soldier: From Crispus Attucks to Colin Powell.* New York: Citadel Press: 2004. Digital edition.

Larson, Erik. *Dead Wake: The Last Crossing of the Lusitania.* New York: Crown Publishers, 2015. Kindle edition.

Latty, Yvonne. *We Were There: Voices of African American Veterans, from World War II to the War in Iraq.* New York: Amistad, 2004.

Lebow Eileen F. *A Grandstand Seat: The American Balloon Service in WWI.* Reprint. Westport, CT: Praeger, 1998. Kindle edition.

Lee, Ulysses. *The Employment of Negro Troops. United States Army in World War II.* Reprint. Honolulu, HI: University Press of the Pacific, 1994.

Longmate, Norman. *The G.I.'s: The Americans in Britain 1942–1945.* London: Hutchinson and Co., 1975.

MacGregor, Morris J. Jr. *Integration of the Armed Forces, 1940–1965.* Washington, DC: U.S. Army Center of Military History, 1981. Digital edition.

McFarlin, Shannon. *As If They Were Ours: The Story of Camp Tyson: America's Only Barrage Training Facility.* Bennington, VT: Merriam Press, 2016.

McGuire, Phillip, ed. *Taps for a Jim Crow Army: Letters from Black Soldiers in WWII.* Reprint. Lexington: University Press of Kentucky, 1993.

Mills, Alice. *Soldats Noirs, Américains Normandie 1944: Black GIs Normandy 1944.* Cabourg, France: Editions Cahiers du Temps, 2014.

Moore, Christopher Paul. *Fighting for America: Black Soldiers—The Unsung Heroes of World War II*. New York: Ballantine, 2006.

Morris, Jan. *Manhattan '45*. Baltimore, MD: Johns Hopkins University Press, 1986.

Motley, Mary Penwick. *The Invisible Soldier: The Experience of the Black Soldier, World War II*. Detroit: Wayne State University Press, 1975.

Moye, Todd J. *Freedom Flyers: The Tuskegee Airmen of World War II*. New York: Oxford University Press, 2010.

Nalty, Bernard C. *Strength for the Fight: A History of Black Americans in the Military*. New York: The Free Press, 1986.

Nelson, Peter N. *A More Unbending Battle: The Harlem Hellfighters' Struggle for Freedom in WWI and Equality at Home*. New York: Basic Civitas, 2009. Kindle edition.

Nwachuku, Levi A., and Martin L. Kilson. *Pride of Lions: A History of Lincoln University, 1945–2007*. Lincoln University, PA: Lincoln University Press, 2011.

Orwell, George. *Facing Unpleasant Facts: Narrative Essays*. New York: Mariner Books, 2009.

Osur, Alan M. *Blacks in the Army Air Forces During World War II: The Problems of Race Relations*. Washington, DC: Office of Air Force History, 1986. Online edition at http://www.afhso.af.mil/shared/media/document/AFD-100924-008.pdf.

Ottley, Roi. *Roi Ottley's World War II: The Lost Diary of an African American Journalist*. Lawrence: University Press of Kansas, 2011.

———. *New World A-Coming: Inside Black America*. Boston, MA: Houghton, Mifflin Company, 1943.

Patton, Gerald W. *War and Race: The Black Officer in the American Military, 1915–1941*. Westport, CT: Greenwood Press, 1981.

Pershing, John J. *My Experiences in the World War*. Vol. 2. New York: Frederick A. Stokes Company, 1931.

Pogue, Forrest C. *The United States Army in World War II: European Theater of Operations: The Supreme Command*. Washington, DC: Office of the Chief of Military History, Department of the Army, 1954.

Prange, Gordon W. *At Dawn We Slept: The Untold Story of Pearl Harbor*. New York: Penguin, 1982.

Raheem, Turiya S. A. *Growing Up in the Other Atlantic City: Wash's and the Northside*. Bloomington, IN: Xlibris, 2009.

Raper, Arthur Franklin. *The Tragedy of Lynching*. Reprint. Mineola, NY: Dover Publications, 2003.

Ritterhouse, Jennifer. *Growing Up Jim Crow*. Chapel Hill: University of North Carolina Press, 2006.

Roberts, Mary Louise. *What Soldiers Do: Sex and the American GI in World War II France*. Chicago: University of Chicago Press, 2013.

Ryan, Cornelius. *The Longest Day*. New York: Touchstone, 1959.

Satchell, Alister. *Running the Gauntlet: How Three Giant Liners Carried a Million Men to War, 1942–1945.* Reprint. London: Chatham Publishing, 2001.

Scannell, Vernon. *Argument of Kings: An Autobiography.* London: Robson Books, 1987.

Semmens, Col. E. Paul. *The Hammer of Hell: The Coming of Age of Antiaircraft Artillery in WWII. ADA Magazine* reprint. Fort Bliss, 1990. Online edition at http://www.skylighters.org/hammer/.

Shock, James R. *U.S. Army Airships, 1908–1942.* Edgewater, FL: Atlantis Productions, 2002.

———. *The U.S. Army Barrage Balloon Program.* Bennington, VT: Meriam Press, 2006.

Slonaker, A. G. *Recollections and Reflections of a College Dean, Including a Brief History of the 103rd Barrage Balloon Battery.* Parsons, WV: McClain Printing Company, 1975.

Smith, Graham. *When Jim Crow Met John Bull: Black American Soldiers in World War II Britain.* New York: St. Martin's Press, 1987.

Spick, Mike. *Luftwaffe Fighter Aces.* Reprint. South Yorkshire, UK: Frontline Books, 2011.

This Is Our War: Selected Stories of Six War Correspondents Sent Overseas. Baltimore, MD: The Afro-American Company, 1945.

Thompson, Antonio. *Men in German Uniform: POWs in America during World War II.* Knoxville: University of Tennessee Press, 2010.

Tyler-McGraw, Marie. *At the Falls: Richmond, Virginia, and Its People.* Chapel Hill: University of North Carolina Press, 2004.

U.S. Army Historical Section Staff. *Omaha Beachhead: June 6–June 11, 1944.* Reprint. Washington, DC: U.S. Army Center of Military History, 2002. Digital edition.

Vaeth, Gordon J. *They Sailed the Skies: U.S. Navy Balloons and the Airship Program.* Annapolis, MD: Naval Institute Press, 2005.

Wallin, Homner N. *Pearl Harbor: Why, How—Fleet Salvage and Final Appraisal.* Washington, DC: Naval History Division, 1968.

Washburn, Patrick S. *A Question of Sedition: The Federal Government's Investigation of the Black Press during World War II.* New York: Oxford University Press, 1986.

Weir, William. *Fatal Victories.* New York: Pegasus Books, 1993.

Werner, Herbert A. *Iron Coffins: A U-Boat Commander's War, 1939–1945.* London: Cassel, 1969.

White, Walter. *A Man Called White: The Autobiography of Walter White.* Reprint. Athens: Brown Thrasher Book/University of Georgia Press, 1995.

———. *A Rising Wind.* Garden City, NY: Doubleday, Doran and Company, 1945. Digital edition.

Wilkins, Roy. *Standing Fast: The Autobiography of Roy Wilkins.* New York: Da Capo Press, 1994.

Wilkerson, Isabel. *The Warmth of Other Suns: The Epic Story of America's Great Migration.* New York: Vintage Books, 2010.

Williams, Andrew. *The Battle of the Atlantic: The Allies' Submarine Fight against Hitler's Grey Wolves of the Sea.* New York: Basic Books, 2003.

Williams, Juan. *Eyes on the Prize: America's Civil Rights Years, 1954–1965.* Reprint. New York: Penguin, 2013.

Woodward, C. Vann. *The Strange Career of Jim Crow.* Reprint. New York: Oxford University Press, 2002.

Wormser, Richard. *The Rise and Fall of Jim Crow.* New York: St. Martin's Press, 2014. Kindle edition.

Zaloga, Steven. *The Devil's Garden: Rommel's Desperate Defense of Omaha Beach on D-Day.* Mechanicsburg, PA: Stackpole Books, 2013.

JOURNALS AND REPORTS

Air Force Historical Research Agency. "The Normandy Invasion." German Air Historical Study VII/31, no. 00212123, 512.621.

Air Force Historical Research Agency. "Barrage Balloons in a Fighter Command." Barrage Balloon School, Camp Tyson, TN, October 15, 1942, no. 167043.

Army War College. "Employment of Negro Manpower in War." Nov, 10, 1925, http://www.fdrlibrary.marist.edu/education/resources/pdfs/tusk_doc_a.pdf.

Equal Justice Initiative. "Lynching in America: Confronting the Legacy of Racial Terror," 2015, 1–88. http://www.eji.org/lynchinginamerica.

Fanton, Ben. "Gas Balloons: View from above the Civil War Battlefield. *America's Civil War,* June 12, 2006. http://www.historynet.com/gas-balloons-view-from-above-the-civil-war-battlefield.htm.

Hallion, Richard P. "D-Day 1944: Air Power over the Normandy Beaches and Beyond." *Air Force History and Museums Program* (1994): 1–46. http://www.afhso.af.mil/shared/media/document/AFD-100924-019.pdf.

Haydon, F. Stansbury. "First Attempts at Military Aeronautics in the United States." *Journal of the American Military History Foundation* 2, no. 3 (Autumn 1938): 131–38.

Hillson, Franklin J. "Barrage Balloons for Low-Level Air Defense." *Airpower Journal* (Summer 1989): 1–12.

Hunt, Sanford B., MD. "The Negro as Soldier." *Anthropological Review* 7, no. 24 (Jan. 1869): 40–54.

Katznelson, Ira, and Suzanne Mettler. "On Race and Policy History: A Dialogue about the G.I. Bill," *Perspectives on Politics* 6, no. 3 (September 2008): 519–37.

King, Gilbert. "Remembering Henry Johnson, the Soldier Called 'Black Death.'" *Smithsonian.com* (October 25, 2011). http://www.smithsonianmag.com/history/remembering-henry-johnson-the-soldier-called-black-death-117386701/?no-ist.

Martinez, Jamie Amanda. "Slavery during the Civil War." Virginia Foundation for the Humanities, July 2, 2014. http://encyclopediavirginia.org/Slavery_During_the_Civil_War.

Muller, Richard R. "Losing Air Superiority: A Case Study from the Second World War." *Air and Space Power Journal* 17, no. 4 (Winter 2003): 55–66. http://www.airpower.maxwell.af.mil/airchronicles/apj/apj03/win03/win03.pdf.

Murray, Williamson. *Strategy for Defeat: The Luftwaffe,1933–1945.* Maxwell Air Force Base: Air University Press, 1983.

Murphy, Col. John G. "Activities of the Ninth Army AAA," *Antiaircraft Journal* 92, no. 3 (May–June 1949): 2–14.

National Association for the Advancement of Colored People. "Thirty Years of Lynching in the United States, 1889–1918." Reprint, 2010. http://msa.maryland.gov/megafile/msa/speccol/sc5300/sc5339/000070/000000/000056/restricted/html/naacp-0001.html.

Parkinson, Robert. "Camp Tyson." *Tennessee Encyclopedia of History and Culture.* Online version 2.0, updated Jan. 1, 2010. http://www.tennesseeencyclopedia.net/entry.php?rec=180.

Parkinson, Russell J. "United States Signal Corps Balloons, 1871–1902." *Military Affairs* 24, no. 4 (Winter, 1960–61): 189–202.

Peck, James, L. H. "Defense against Air Attack." *Science Digest,* June 1940, 8.

Picinich, R. G. Jr., "Sky Sentries on Guard." *Scientific American* 169, no. 1 (July 1943): 6–8.

Pincetl, Stanley J., and Clemenceau G. "A Letter of Clemenceau to His Wife by Balloon." *French Historical Studies* 2, no. 4 (Autumn 1962): 511–14.

Reid, Lota Spence. "A Story of Development in Education in Greensville County, Virginia, 1781–1980." *Greensville County High School* (1981).

Schiffman, Joseph. "The Education of Negro Soldiers in World War II." *The Journal of Negro Education* 18, no. 1 (Winter 1949): 22–28.

Semmens, Col. E. Paul. "D-Day, June 6th, 1944, Antiaircraft Artillery Fight Their Way off the Invasion Beaches." *Air-Defense Artillery Yearbook* (1994): 22–29.

Sternhell, Charles M., and Alan M. Thorndike. "Antisubmarine Warfare in World War II." Operations Evaluation Group Report No. 51, Navy Department, 1946, 1–183.

Thompson, Robert L. "Barrage Balloon Development in the United States Air Corps 1923–1942." Army Air Forces Historical Study No. 3, Air Force Historical Research Agency, December 1943, 1–160. http://www.afhra.af.mil/shared/media/document/AFD-090602-024.pdf.

Turley, R. E. Jr. "Barrage Balloons." *Coast Artillery Journal* 85, no. 1 (January–February 1942): 20–24.

Westermann, Edward R. "Fighting for the Heavens from the Ground: German Ground-Based Air Defenses in the Great War, 1914–1918." *The Journal of Military History* 65, no. 3 (April 2001): 641–49.

Woods, Louis Lee II. "Almost 'No Negro Veteran . . . Could Get a Loan': African Americans, The GI Bill, and the NAACP Campaign against Residential Segregation, 1917–1960." *The Journal of African American History* 98, no. 3, Symposium: "St. Claire Drake: The Making of a Scholar-Activist" (Summer 2013): 393–417.

VIDEO AND FILM

Breath of Freedom. Directed by Dag Freyer. Smithsonian Channel, 2014.

A Distant Shore: African Americans of D-Day. Directed by Douglas Cohen. History Channel, A&E Television Networks, 2007.

The Invisible Soldiers: Unheard Voices. Directed by William H. Smith. ComTel Productions, Inc., 2000.

The Negro Soldier. Directed by Stuart Heisler. Black History, A Retrospective. Mill Creek Entertainment, 1944.

Permissions

Grateful acknowledgment is made for the permission to reprint the following:

Index

About the Author

Linda Hervieux is a journalist and photographer whose work has appeared in the *New York Times* and the New York *Daily News*, among other publications. A native of Lowell, Massachusetts, she lives in Paris, France, with her husband. This is her first book.